CHRONICLES OF
THE AMERICAN DANCE

CHRONICLES OF
THE AMERICAN DANCE

FROM THE SHAKERS TO MARTHA GRAHAM

EDITED BY PAUL MAGRIEL

A DA CAPO PAPERBACK

Library of Congress Cataloging in Publication Data

Magriel, Paul David, 1906-   ed.
    Chronicles of the American dance.

    Includes bibliographical references.
    1. Dancing—United States—History—Addresses,
essays, lectures. I. Title.
GV1623.M33   1978b   793.3'1973   78-9067
ISBN 0-306-80082-9

ISBN: 0-306-80082-9

First Paperback Edition 1978

This Da Capo Press paperback edition of *Chronicles of
the American Dance* is an unabridged republication of
the first edition published in New York in 1948.

Copyright 1948 by Dance Index

Published by Da Capo Press, Inc.
A Subsidiary of Plenum Publishing Corporation
227 West 17th Street
New York, New York 10011

THE DANCE has had a long history on the American continent. Before the New World was "discovered," there was dancing in the Mexico of Montezuma and the pueblos of the Southwest. Countless centuries before the Spanish invader brought the horse to the Great Plains, the unmounted, pedestrian tribes danced for the hunt, for war, and for medicine. When Virginia and Florida were explored in the sixteenth century, French and English adventurers sketched the ceremonials they witnessed and left descriptions that have come down to us today.

The empire-building nations brought their national customs into this widening cultural stream. To Peter Stuyvesant's New Amsterdam, the Dutch settlers took their colorful *Kermesse* with its traditional festivities and figures. Even in austere New England, people danced. When time permitted and circumstance was fitting, grave Puritans observed the ritual by the book. The "plaine and easy rules" of John Playford's *English Dancing Master* were approved by the elders who taught country dances that were not "mixt."

From diverse sources—ceremonial, social, and theatrical—evolved the salient aspects of the American dance. Little has been written on religion and the dance, although there is much to draw upon in early documents. Important among these was Increase Mather's *An Arrow Against Profane and Promiscuous Dancing, drawne out of the Quiver of the Scriptures*. Published in 1688 by "the Ministers of Christ at Boston in New England," it was the first of a series of tracts to be issued in unbroken number for more than two hundred years, and often read from the New England pulpit in the form of sermons. Mather's *Arrow* condemned only dancing that aroused the passions. The sentiments voiced are easily traced to the theocrat, John Cotton, who wrote in 1625:

Dancing (yea though mixt) I would not simply condemn. For I see two sorts . . . in the Old Testament . . . the one religious . . . the other civil. Only lascivious dancing to wanton ditties and in amorous gestures and wanton dalliances, especially after great feasts, I would bear witness against.

The religious tracts are something less than rewarding to the dance historian. They cast less light upon the dance than upon official Puritan morality.

Therefore the opening essay in this book, *The Dance in Shaker Ritual*, has particular importance for its treatment of the subject in its essentially religious and hence ceremonial character. The curious Shaker sect has almost disappeared in this country. E. D. Andrews makes a pioneering contribution to the history of our national cultural backgrounds and affords, as well, an interesting parallel to the many studies of the arts and crafts produced by this extraordinary community.

v

The essays which follow *The Dance in Shaker Ritual* carry the thread of continuity through those artists who created the basis of our theatrical dance from contemporary sources, the major personalities who extended the horizons of dance expression beyond their own times.

The first professional artist-dancer of whom there is record was John Durang. Born in Lancaster, Pennsylvania, in 1768, he made his stage debut at the Old South Street Theatre in Philadelphia. The milieu in which he lived, performed, and raised a family of dancers is presented in full review by Lillian Moore.

Marian Winter's piece on Juba, the almost legendary minstrel, next traces the origins of our first native contribution to theater history. Miss Winter's *American Minstrelsy* treats this indigenous theater form from the time of George Washington Dixon and Daddy "Jim Crow" Rice to the heyday of the Christy Minstrels and the beginnings of American vaudeville. Much interesting and valuable material included here suggests a full length study of this fascinating aspect of our American theater.

The first of the super spectacles which had a direct bearing on theatrical dancing in this country was the production of *The Black Crook*. Presented in 1866 at Niblo's Garden with a stage entirely reconstructed for the extravaganza, it ran 475 consecutive nights, a record for its time, and earned over a half million dollars. It was produced season after season with imported ballerinas, many of whom stayed on to teach, and see their pupils dance in the numerous revivals of the same spectacle. As late as 1929, a version of *The Black Crook* was offered in Hoboken, New Jersey. American spectacles are discussed by a critic uniquely qualified for this subject. George Freedley is theater curator of the New York Public Library, and actually has at his command the vast material from which a production of *The Black Crook* could be mounted today.

The last of the essays devoted to historical backgrounds of the dance is Rosetta O'Neill's on the Dodworth family. By the middle of the nineteenth century, social dancing was *de rigeur* for well-bred young ladies and gentlemen. Of the numerous academies that catered to this vogue, the most noted was Allen Dodworth's, in New York. Dodworth was the senior member of a clan of teachers under whom one could study not only the graces proper to the ballroom but also the codes of a young and new society that was growing conscious of its manners. Dodworth published a *vade-mecum* on deportment as well as how-to-dance books of a kind not unfamiliar today. The story of the Dodworths and their era is nostalgically told by Miss O'Neill, dean of New York's teachers of the social dance and spiritual custodian of the tradition founded by the people of whom she lovingly writes.

Next treated in our chronicle is the appearance in this country of the classic modes. With the exception of the minstrels, almost all theatrical dancers were Europeans. There soon arrived on the scene three artists, all native-born Americans, and all highly accomplished in the universally accepted idiom of the ballet.

Making her debut in *The Maid of Cashmere*, the first of these was Mary Ann Lee, born in Philadelphia in 1824. Her rival, Augusta Maywood, also made her initial appearance in the same ballet, which seems to have been the standard initiation work. Both of these artists competed on equal terms with their European contemporaries and won wide acclaim as ballerinas. Naturally linked with Mary Ann Lee and Augusta Maywood is the name of George Washington Smith, our first native-born male interpreter of the classic dance.

The importance of these three artists is revealed in the essays by Lillian Moore and Marian Winter. Their patient research in old documents, newspapers, and letters has resulted in the emergence of George Smith,

Mary Lee, and Augusta Maywood as distinguished pioneers in the art of the ballet, thus adding a new chapter to the history of dancing here and abroad.

It was not, however, until the beginning of the present century that American dancers were to have a revolutionary effect on this art form. Most important of the innovators was Isadora Duncan. Her life has been the subject of dozens of books—not least among them her *Autobiography*—which have described her career and defined her influence on the aesthetic of the dance. Of the many things written on Isadora, William Bolitho's essay from *Twelve Against the Gods* is one of the most brilliant and deserving of a place in these pages.

Loie Fuller was another American visionary who, like Isadora Duncan, enjoyed her greatest successes abroad. She was fascinated by the theory of light; and her unique contributions to the dance are herein related by Clare de Morinni. Maud Allan's concerts in the New York of the mauve decade are nostalgically remembered by Carl Van Vechten, and the perennial Denishawns are the subject of a brief historical résumé by Baird Hastings. Martha Graham, whose experiments have engendered a whole new catechism of the dance, is presented in a final essay by Robert Horan.

This collection of essays does not constitute a history of the dance in America, nor is it intended to do so. It is the editor's hope that the compilation will sketch the outlines of this vast subject interestingly, and serve the cause of scholarship by organizing materials for more comprehensive use.

P. M.

ACKNOWLEDGMENTS

FOR THE USE of the material which is included in the major portion of this book I am indebted to the magazine *Dance Index* and a number of its contributors who have given me their generous consent for republication of their original articles. Mr. E. D. Andrews for *The Dance in Shaker Ritual*; Baird Hastings for *The Denishawn Era*; George Freedley for *The Black Crook and the White Fawn*; Clare de Morinni for *Loie Fuller*; Rosetta O'Neill for *The Dodworth Family and Ballroom Dancing in New York*; Robert Horan for *The Recent Theater of Martha Graham*; Marian Hannah Winter for *Augusta Maywood* and *Juba and American Minstrelsy*; Lillian Moore for *John Durang—The First American Dancer*, *Mary Ann Lee—First American Giselle* and *George Washington Smith*; Carl Van Vechten and *The New York Times* for permission to reprint the reviews of Maud Allan which appeared in the *Times*, January 21 and 30, 1910. Isadora Duncan is reprinted from *Twelve Against the Gods* by William Bolitho copyright, 1929, by Simon and Schuster, Inc., which I wish to acknowledge with thanks.

To all the above I am deeply grateful for providing a rich variety of factual and critical information on the American Dance which may well serve as a basis for a full history of this subject. I also wish to thank the Department of Theatre Arts, Museum of Modern Art; the New York Public Library; the Harvard Theatre Collection; and Mr. George Chaffee for providing the major portion of the pictorial material used in this book. I am indebted to Mr. Carlus Dyer for providing the design for the jacket of the book. For the drudgery of proofreading and aiding in many ways to help the book on its way to the press, I am most grateful to my coworkers on *Dance Index* and in Ballet Society: Marne Eames, Grace Mullins, and Sylvia Wallach.

Maurice Serle Kaplan has been most helpful in discussing with me problems relating to the typographical layout of this book as well as other Ballet Society publications and to him I wish to express my gratitude. Finally to Lincoln Kirstein, founder of the Ballet Society and godfather of the Ballet Society publications, for his advice, aid, and encouragement, my most grateful thanks.

CONTENTS

HISTORICAL ASPECTS

Morning Meetings. Woodcut by an unknown artist. From David
R. Lamson, *Two Years' Experience among the Shakers*, 1848.

THE DANCE

IN SHAKER RITUAL

BY E. D. ANDREWS

DURING THE FIRST YEARS of the Revolutionary War rumors were frequent, in the country around Albany, New York, of a small band of English colonists, five men and four women, who practiced a strange kind of religion in the swampland country of Niskeyuna, a few miles northwest of the town. During the day, it was said, these people were busy clearing and tilling the land, building cabins, and working at the forge and loom; but the evenings, far into the night, were spent in rapturous singing and dancing. One of the number, the story went, professed to be a second Christ whose mission was to redeem the world.

These reports were first verified by two young men, disillusioned subjects of a New Light revival in New Lebanon, N. Y., who, journeying westward in the spring of 1780, stopped one night at the cabin in the wilderness. Hospitably received by the leader of the colony, "Mother" Ann Lee, a native of Manchester, England, the travelers learned that these poor but industrious folk were called Shakers, or Shaking Quakers: that she, the prophetess Ann, believed that the Christ spirit had made its second appearance in and through her, ushering in the awaited millennium; that the Shakers, having confessed their wrongs, repudiated marriage and forsaken all "carnal" practices, held themselves to be without sin; that they proposed to found in America a religious order separated from the world; and that they welcomed into this communion all who were sick of futile creeds, formal worship, and the evils of a corrupt society. After witnessing the ecstatic "exercises" of the "foreigners," the visitors, deeply affected, returned to New Lebanon convinced that the promises of the revival, about which they had despaired, were about to be fulfilled.

New England, under the influences of Jonathan Edwards' preaching and the Great Awakening, was fertile ground for programs of salvation. It was the exalted worship of the "convulsioners," however, more than any other aspect of the Shaker faith, that aroused the curiosity of the world. This was so strangely rhapsodic, so hypnotic in its effect, that the people who flocked to Niskeyuna in ever greater numbers could ascribe it only to transcendental causes and accept it as evidence that the kingdom of God was truly at hand. The earliest account of a meeting (by one Valentine Rathbun, in 1780) portrayed, indeed, a remarkable scene:

Everyone acts for himself, and almost everyone different from the other; one will stand with his arms extended, acting over odd postures, which they call signs; another will be dancing, and sometimes hopping on one leg about the floor; another will fall to turning around, so swift, that if it be a woman, her clothes will be so filled with the wind, as though they were kept out by a hoop; another will be prostrate on the floor . . . some trembling extremely; others acting as though all their nerves were convulsed; others swinging their arms, with all vigor, as though they were turning a wheel, etc. . . . . They have several such experiences in a day, especially on the Sabbath. [1] *

The United Society of Believers in Christ's Second Appearance was to be found in Bolton and Manchester as early as 1747. James and Jane Wardley were the first English Shakers, or as they were first called "Shaking Quakers." Their beliefs derived from certain Huguenot sects, notably the Camisards, whose ideas descended in an almost unbroken line since the period of the Albigensian heresy. There was an ancient heretical tradition for dancing as part of the adoration of God. The heterodox Gnostics of the second Christian century conducted the rites of the *Agape* or love feast, with dances. Ritual dancing was supposedly permitted in English churches until 1604. Late into the seventeenth century dancing had a part in some Parisian churches and there are further fragmentary survivals, notably in Los Seises, the dancing youths of the Cathedral of Seville.

In England, the early Shakers had danced the same way: "singing, shouting, or walking the floor, under the influence of spiritual signs, shoving each other about—or swiftly passing and repassing each other, like clouds agitated by a mighty wind." At the rites of the Eucharist primitive Christians had also "gesticulated with their hands, danced with their feet, flung their bodies about." The worship of many spiritual sects was similar: the early Quakers and Baptists, the French Prophets,

the Merry Dancers of New England, the Kentucky Revivalists, the Girlingites or Shakers of the New Forest, the Shaker Indians of Puget Sound, the Tremolanti recently expelled from Rome. As with other orders, the Shaker exercises were largely involuntary, charged with emotionalism and characterized by divine "gifts."

The period 1780-87 was one of spiritual ferment and proselytism. Ann Lee died in 1784, after spreading her mystic doctrine and establishing ecclessiae in various parts of New England and New York. Her successor, Father James Whittaker, died in 1786, soon after he had built the first Shaker meetinghouse at New Lebanon. Then, a year later, Joseph Meacham, a New Light preacher from Enfield, Connecticut, who had been a leader of the Lebanon revival, started to gather the Believers together into socio-industrial religious communities conceived in monastic terms and consolidated by a covenantal agreement.

With the organization of the society in "church order," the manner of worship underwent a distinct change. Energies formerly dissipated in incessant travel, disputes with authorities, and exhaustive meetings were concentrated on the practical tasks of building communes. A certain reaction from the initial ardors was aided by the desire to placate the world by whom the Shakers had been persecuted, but with whom, if they were to survive as an economic order, they knew they must come to terms. In the eleven communities organized by 1792 [2] the meetinghouses, the first structures erected, were provided with spacious halls for an expanded ritual, with seats along the walls for the "world's people," who were prospective converts to the faith. Furthermore, as a believer in order and utility in all things, Father Joseph was opposed to *immoderate* worship, holding such excess to be wasteful of power, purposeless, and prejudicial to the gospel. It was probably for the latter reason that he introduced, in 1788, the first distinct dance, "the square-order shuffle,"

* Superior numbers in the text of articles refer to *Notes and Bibliographical Data* beginning on page 263.

patterned according to legend on Meacham's own vision of angels dancing around the throne of God.

Reflecting the Puritan tradition to which it was heir, the square-order was a solemn exercise, a forward-and-backward movement of ranks, the brethren and sisters in separate groups shuffling toward and away from each other, three paces each way, with a double step or "tip-tap" at the turn. This primitive dance, accompanied by a rhythmic but tuneless chant, was an impressive though doubtlessly grotesque performance:

The crowd begin to slowly shove, each person one foot at a time, and to face as soldiers do when training; but every time they turn, they bow, or rather crouch in a very extraordinary and particular manner, bending the body to an almost horizontal posture, the back a little curved, the knees bowing forward, the hands sprawling forward and downward, and the posterior part of each projecting so as to nearly approach the face of the next one.[3]

In a variant of the square-order introduced in 1788, a livelier measure called "the square step," the assembly advanced four times, three steps at a time, with "tip-taps" at the intervals, "receding backwards" the same way.

The advent of worded songs, and subsequently of a trained chorus, also had a marked effect on the manner of worship. The Schismatics or Christians of Ohio and Kentucky (Methodists and Baptists), the nucleuses out of whom the Western Shaker communities were formed early in the nineteenth century, had sung revival songs and spirituals in their backwoods meetings, and had been exercised in dancing and other spontaneous or automatic gifts. Recognizing the value of a more animated ritual as a means to conversion, the Eastern leaders about 1807 began to encourage the adoption and composition of lively songs and dances expressive of the spiritual upsurge which began to sweep over the whole society. The initiative was taken by Lucy Wright (1760-1821), Joseph Meacham's successor as head of the order, whose inspiration was again a vision, but now, one of angels *joyfully* dancing. Mother Lucy rearranged the ranks according to age and position, stepped up the square-order tempo to what was known as "the skipping manner," introduced marches (and later ring dances), and in general freed the ritual of its old restrictions. The early posturing of arms and hands, likened to that of "kangaroos" or "dancing dogs," also evolved into more graceful gestures: in one form, by extending the forearms with the hands turned upward as if to receive spiritual blessings, in another, by waving the hands inward as if gathering or dispensing spiritual grace. The "back" manner of worship, the "promiscuous" exercises of the first Shakers, was not discouraged, however. At the height of a meeting, someone (usually a sister) might suddenly step from the ranks and begin to whirl, bow, tremble, or run about clapping the hands and shouting; another would follow, and soon the assembly would be turned into a confused mass of sound and movement. Often the presiding elder, after the hymns and exhortations and prescribed rehearsed dances of the regular service, would deliberately begin such exercises with the words, "Let us labor," bringing them to a close only when the worshipers were completely exhausted.

Various types of dancing developed in the different localities. Young tells us that at Harvard, Massachusetts, the "hollow step" was done to a shuffling step, "the two ranks facing each other, on the north and south, advance up towards each other, turn, and return . . . the east and west ranks advance and recede."

By the Civil War, a freshness of movement disappeared with the decreasing power of their mysticism. Lassitude and backsliding set in. No longer was there the "autointoxication of rapturous movement, that self-forgetful union with the not-self which the mystic ever seeks" described by Havelock Ellis. Once the decline started, it was cumulative. The members could

Shakers near Lebanon. A square-order dance. Hand-colored lithograph. Published by A. Imbert, ca. 1825. Later this print was pirated by Currier.

no longer sublimate their desires and take their minds off "carnal sin," and they did not possess the determination of Mother Ann, who having four of her children die in infancy and being deserted by her husband, had found that this was God's penalty for sexual intercourse. (Incidentally, God became a double Deity when the principle of absolute equality for women was recognized by the Shakers at the end of the eighteenth century.)

With the organization of singing classes, the adoption of letter musical notation, and the appearance of unharmonized manuscript hymnals in the early 1820's a renewed interest in song and its co-ordination with dancing became evident. They rarely had any singing except in unison. Variants of circular dances, standing dances, and shuffles were introduced,

as well as elaborations of the marches and square orders. In the round dances the participants would march or skip around a stationary chorus, sometimes facing in and bowing or shuffling at the "set" part of the tune; or else form a "continuous ring," in the shape of the letter *C*, moving in single or double files in such a manner as to bring everyone face to face. This was one type of the so-called "union dance." In another, after the brethren and sisters had formed two parallel lines confronting each other, those at the end alternately moved up the rows, to the tune of a union song, grasping the hand of every fellow member. In still another, the sexes shuffled forward and backward in a series of parallel lines, weaving, as it were, a fabric of union and love. Reminiscent of the Virginia

The Dance, square order. By Benson Lossing. From *Harper's New Monthly Magazine*, 1857.

reel was a fourth exercise, known in a lively version as "the checks," in which groups of brethren and sisters, arranged in a hollow square facing inward, "labored" up to the opposing group and back.

Shaker music and songs were at first improvisory or "inspired," then learned by rote, but later tunes were borrowed from the English hymnody, or Irish, Scotch, French, Bohemian folk sources, and even popular songs and dances of the day. It is yet to be proved that the floor pattern of the Shaker ritual dances borrowed from the elaborate contredances or quadrilles of the twenties and thirties. When music instruction was introduced the Shakers developed their own composers. A group of singers and dancers appeared in a Shaker program on the stage of the Ameri-

can Museum in New York for seven weeks in the forties, and "Fi, Hi, Hi The Black Shakers," a song in the blackface idiom, was performed by the Fellows Ethiopian Troupe of Minstrels in the 1850's.

Dancing as a deliberate and purposive art, it will be noted, was a gradual development. The "odd postures" and random bizarre exercises of the first meetings were involuntary acts, "acceptable gifts of God," many of which, indeed, entered into the traditional ritualism. But as time went on, and in part, perhaps, because the Shakers danced before an audience, there dawned a consciousness of purpose, and with it a tendency to rationalize and justify, as well as to elaborate the gifts. Thus, according to the apologists, the early gifts, being "mortifying" in character, taught humility and aided in purifying the soul. When a Believer trembled, he was "shaking off doubts" or "keeping down the life of the flesh." Later, spokesmen for the sect, in reply to widespread criticism of the dance as a means of worship, had recourse to scriptural precedent, to the examples set by Miriam the Prophetess, by Jephthah's daughter, by the daughters of Shiloh, and by David and all Israel when they danced before the Lord.[4] Every created faculty, they contended, the hands and feet, the tongue, the whole body, should "express outwardly and assist the inward reverence of the soul."

Pantomime, as a means of enriching outward expression, played an increasingly characteristic role as the attitude toward the dance grew more objective. Gestures such as bowing, stamping, whirling, acting out "signs" (pantomimic gestures, pretending to play orchestral instruments, etc.), originally involuntary, were incorporated into the structure of worship, assuming, to a lesser or greater degree, symbolic meaning. They were known, even from the beginning, by the scriptural term "gifts." One had the gift of shaking, turning like a wheel, singing in unknown tongues, healing, prophesying or "seeing" spirits. Such gifts were often expanded or combined into complex rituals affecting the regular dance movements and devotionalism as a whole. It is impossible, in fact, to isolate the dance per se from the sacraments and ritualistic play, which, in the mountain meetings of the 1840's, reached their most dramatic and fantastic manifestations. The record is an involved one which we will only briefly survey.

Individual "gifts," such as bowing and whirling, might be either unwilled or intentional, in the latter case to induce, perhaps, a state of humility or a sense of "freedom from bondage." Others, such as "chasing the Devil," developed into distinct communal rites. This "warring gift," for instance, was originally the accompaniment of a certain "exercise-song" where, at a given passage, the dancers stamped

on an imaginary serpent or devil, plucked the mark of the devil (sometimes called "Great I"—pride—or "Old Ugly") from their foreheads, or made signs as if they were mowing down evil spirits or sweeping them from the room. Later, the gift was elaborated. A "backslider" would be surrounded by the faithful, who, pointing their fingers at the afflicted one, would shout "woe, woe," "damn his devil," or attempt in other ways to exorcise the corrupting spirit.[5] Again, during meeting, a sentinel having warned the worshipers that the devil had entered the room, they would drive the intruder off or fire spiritual guns at him. Here, as in much of the pantomime attendant on the great Shaker revival which opened in 1837, a strong element of play was manifest.

During this phenomenal period, lasting over ten years, protracted rituals were common. In one, the "cleansing gift," preceded by prayer, fasting, and confession, a group of singers and mediums ("instruments") marched through the dwellings and shops, sweeping and cleaning with spiritual brooms, after which they returned to the place of worship "to scour and scrub, from its floor, the stains of sin." In another, known as "The Midnight Cry," the members arose at midnight and marched through the halls behind instruments bearing lamps, singing of the Lord of Hosts, who, with a lamp in His hand, had come to search out sin.

To the Shaker ministry, in 1842, came word that meetings should be held semiannually, in the spring and fall, on the highest elevation in each community. On the evening before the event, colorful spiritual garments were distributed to all. The next day, thus attired, the singing procession marched to the mountaintop, where daylong ceremonies were joyfully held around a sacred "fountain." The rites were manifold. The instruments were ordained and anointed. Incense was burned in spiritual censers. Imaginary sponges, dipped in water from the central fountain, were used in cleansing each other's bodies, which were dried afterward with spiritual towels. In one part of the program, the brethren and sisters paced rhythmically over the clearing, sowing spiritual seed and watering it from vessels of spiritual water. Then, following the example of an instrument or leader, they would enact some gifts of mortification, "acting the fool," singing silly songs, or indulging in various grotesqueries. Presents and rewards were frequently exchanged: chains of comforts, balls of love, robes of purity, baskets of flowers, fans of truth, bowls of wine, gospel trumpets, singing birds, precious stones, leaves from the tree of life, and so on—with appropriate gestures by the giver and recipient. After many songs, dances, and revelations by the "instruments," the mountain meetings closed with a love feast, a sumptuous repast of the rarest and most delicious foods and wines. Though all was make-believe, those who partook of the sacraments left the feast grounds refreshed in body and soul.

"Mother Ann's Second Appearing," as this period (ca. 1845) was called, was productive of many "eccentric" dances and songs. The most curious, perhaps, arose from the belief that the spirits of the departed of many nations, such as Lafayette, Mahomet, and Napoleon, and of various Indian tribes in particular, perhaps the adjacent Iroquois or Algonquin, returned to the Shaker meetings to learn the way of God.[6] Here their presence actually transformed behavior. If the visitors were Indian spirits, the subjects "possessed" would sing versions of native songs or dance in Indian fashion. The reception of Negro spirits would be similarly heralded by songs in the appropriate dialect, of a Scotch company by Scotch songs or a highland fling, of a group of Eskimos by pantomime in imitation of northlanders driving dog sleds over the snow. And so on. The adoption of Indians and Negroes did not lessen the vigor of the dance. The gifts attendant on such visitations were of course spontaneous, belonging to the same category as the early "promiscuous" dances or

the exercises following the drinking of spiritual wine. Hundreds of Indian and "Negro" songs, "drinking" songs, "vision" and "gift" songs were composed for the occasion.

The feast days on the mountains, the Christmas services in the family dwellings, and those Sabbath-day meetings which were closed to the world in the early 1840's were, in fact, extravaganzas and planned for audiences. A profound sense of destiny, however, vitalized the order during the revival years, resulting in a heightened consciousness of the holiness of worship. The "holy laws,"[7] hitherto an oral or secret code, were now written down for the "protection" of all, requiring Believers, among other injunctions,

to retire to their rooms in silence for the space of half an hour, and labor for a sense of the gospel, before attending meeting . . .

to sit erect in straight ranks in retiring time and . . . attend to the reading of the hymn or anthem that is to be sung in meeting . . .

by the order of God, not to present themselves to worship Him, when under the condemnation of sin unconfessed. But . . . to present themselves to worship with clean hands and pure heart and justified conscience . . .

to go into meeting in the fear of God, walking upon the toes, and two abreast . . . keeping step together.

Maintenance of order and union was expressly charged:

When brethren and sisters place themselves in a body in meeting . . . the ranks should be strait, not only to the right and left, but also forward and back. Forward ranks should always be as long as any of the rest, and by no means should there be variance in the ranks; it has a tendency to excite disunion.

So regular were the ranks and so perfect was the discipline that the marches—except for the "powerful enchantment" and the "bounding, elastic step, quite different from

The Shakers in Niskeyuna. Religious exercises. Wheel-within-a-wheel dance.
Possibly drawn by Joseph Becker. From *Leslie's Popular Monthly*, 1885.

that of the soldier of the world"—suggested to many the movement of troops.

Variants of the square and ring dances were common during the "Great Revival": lively lines, finished crosses, the square and compass, the moving square, the double square, the changeable dance, mother's star, the diamond, and others—performed to special songs and involving, as did most Shaker exercises, much repetition of movement. All the dances assumed a new significance. The devotees felt that they were indeed marching heavenward, that the circle was the perfect emblem of their union. The "wheel-within-a-wheel," three or more concentric circles turning in alternate directions around a central chorus, became a figure of the all-inclusiveness of their gospel: the outer ring the ultimate circle of truth, the Shaker dispensation; the singers, the harmony

and perfection of God that were at the heart of life. In another exercise, "The Narrow Path," a single file of dancers, with heads bowed, placed one foot before the other as they trod the narrow way to salvation. The earnestness and sincerity of worship, with its graceful movements, the noble symbolism in the gesturing of the hands, and its recognition "of the symbolical nature of all outward life," impressed many an observer sensitive to the implications of liturgy.

By the middle of the century the dance had reached its fullest development. What it was like then, and how different from the noisy "heavy dancing" of Rathbun's day, may best be seen in an eyewitness account of a typical meeting. The author was the artist Benson Lossing.[8] Reference is to the square-order and two ring dances:

10

Promiscuous Dance. An evening meeting by lamplight. A glimpse of the "back-manner" of dancing. Wood engraving by A. Boyd Houghton (1836-1875). From the *London Graphic*, 1870.

The worshipers all turned their backs to the audience, except those of the two wall rows, and commenced a backward and forward march, or dance, in a regular springing step, keeping time to the music of their voices, while their hands hung closely to their sides. The wall rows alone kept time with their hands moving up and down, the palms turned upward. The singing appeared like a simple refrain and a chorus of too-ral-loo, too-ral-loo, while all the movements with hand, foot, and limb were extremely graceful. . . .

The worshipers . . . formed themselves in serried ranks as before. Then, with graceful motions, they gradually changed their position into circular form, all the while moving with springing step, in unison with a lively tune. In the center stood twenty-four singers in a circle, twelve men

and twelve women; and around them, in two concentric circles, marched and countermarched the remainder of the worshipers, the men three and the women two abreast. A brief pause and they commenced another lively tune and march, all keeping time with their hands moving up and down, and occasionally clapping them three or four times in concert. The women were now three and the men two abreast. . . . The music was unlike anything I had ever heard; beautiful, impressive, and deeply solemn. . . .

The worshipers now formed four circles, with the singers as the central one, and held each other by the hand, the men and women separately. These circles symbolized the four great Dispensations. . . . In this hymn they sang of Union, as exhibited by their linked hands; and

11

Shakers at Meeting. The final procession. A march. Wood engraving by Houghton. From the *London Graphic*, 1870. This English illustrator of *The Arabian Nights* found his only sympathetic subject in America in the Shakers.

when it had ceased they all lifted up their hands, and gave a subdued shout—the shout of victory—the final victory of Christ in all the earth, and the triumphs of the Shaker, or Millennial Church. . . .

Their movements in the dance or march, whether natural or studied, are all graceful and appropriate; and as I gazed upon that congregation of four or five hundred worshipers marching and countermarching in perfect time, I felt certain that, were it seen upon a stage as a theatrical exhibition, the involuntary exclamation of even the hypercritical would be, "How beautiful!"

An analogy may be drawn between the worship of the Shakers and their handicraft. In the beginning workmanship was somewhat crude, consisting of experimental attempts to achieve forms satisfying to the communal mind and conscience. Eventually a specific type of furniture and architecture emerged, pure in line, rightly proportioned, suited in every way to the needs of the order. But though Shaker design was the acme of simplicity, and free of all "superfluity" and dross, it was yet possible to create endless combinations and variations of the elements of which it was composed. So in the dance. The steps were made more graceful, postures were refined, and the original linear and circular movements developed into finished, precise maneuvers. The wheeling of ranks had the same polished but simplified perfection as the turning on the posts of a table or chair. The dualism of Shaker life and doctrine was reflected not only in its artisanship, in the way many houses and much furniture of the "joint inheritance" were constructed, but in its ritual, in the symmetrical disposition of the sexes and the balanced performance of separate corps. In both cases, motivation was deeply religious.

The element of inner conflict, the inevitable attribute of a religious culture, also influenced the ritual. The life of the Believers was a war between flesh and spirit, a struggle to suppress or sublimate desires and normal instincts. The code of separation alienated them from kith and kin. The principle of celibacy parted the sexes. Social and worldly intercourse were carefully controlled. Humility, plainness in dress and speech, consecrated labor, doctrinal meditation, the submergence of self for the common good—all were cardinal virtues. And though the worshipers could find spiritual recreation and release in the songs and dances, though the urge to break through the prescribed "manners" and frolic, embrace, and dance alone was often irresistible, even these tendencies were affected by ingrained habits of order and obedience. The effect of such opposition of forces was to imbue the exercises of worship with a quality of tension, unpredictability, and meanings partly veiled. The dance was a virginal expression, but not without dynamic physical character.

For what it both revealed and suggested the ritual thus symbolized the peculiar genius of the order: its belief in the actuality of good and evil, its primitive credulity, its awareness of spiritual presences, its sublime motives, its persistent search for perfection. Until they were abandoned early in the present century, the songs and dances were the signs of this seeking, of the struggle to realize, in a world of reality, an ideal communion.

NOTES ON SETTING AND COSTUME

Setting. The assembly room in the meetinghouse was a large rectangular hall, unfurnished except for the benches built along one wall, the tiers of seats or platform for the "world's people" on the opposite side, and the movable backless forms used at the beginning of the service. In the daytime the light from many windows illuminated the white plastered walls, along which rows of greenish-blue pegboards extended in colorful relief. The moldings along the top of the walls, the paneled doors and window casings, and the plain dado were painted this same rich hue, forming a striking background for the deep reds or yellows of the benches. Floor markings guided the votaries in the execution of intricate dances. Candle sconces or oil lamps, shedding at night a flickering, eerie light, hung from the ceiling or were placed at intervals along the walls. In the winter the room was heated by long wood-burning "box" stoves, one at each end of the hall. The absence of all but necessary furnishings, the pure colors and the airy spaciousness and serenity of this interior marked it as a holy place, the inner court of the Shaker temple.

Costume. For about twenty years after the Shaker Church was organized, the Sabbath "uniform" of the brethren consisted of a blue, fulled cloth coat, with a cape lying flat to the shoulders, cut straight in front and extending to the knees; a blue jacket; a blue or white stock buckled behind; black or blue "lasting" breeches strapped, buckled, or buttoned over long stockings just below the knee; and calfskin shoes with straps and brass shoe buckles. Blue sleeve strings were worn in the dance, when the coats were usually taken off. For them blue was the most "heavenly" of colors.

Light-colored striped short "gowns," with sleeves extending just below the elbow, were worn in summer, during the same period, by the sisterhood. Over the gown was a checked apron of homespun linen, bound in white, with white tapestrings tied in front. Under the gown was a black (later a blue) worsted petticoat. The fine lawn or linen caps, secured to the fillet by a pin, could be tied with tapestrings under the chin. The "shoulder handkerchiefs," which were always a characteristic feature of the sisters' dress, were at first (for Sabbath wear) black silk, and later white lawn, home-woven, neatly spread and pinned over the shoulders. The shoes were of cloth, with wooden heels. In winter the sisters wore to meeting long gowns, of butternut-colored worsted. These were fitted snugly to the back and hips, with plaited cuffs fitted to the bend of the arm, and boxplaits behind. The aprons were blue or white checked, the kerchiefs blue cotton with white borders.

Early in the last century the style changed. Summer gowns for sisters under forty or fifty were white cotton, short waisted and plaited behind (and later at the sides), with aprons of the same cloth attached in front. (The older sisters used a striped material.) For a brief period the kerchiefs were drab, soon replaced by hand-woven silk dyed in lovely soft colors.

Shoes were of blue prunella. Linen or cotton pocket handkerchiefs, or "napkins"—blue and white, copperas and white, or white with blue borders—were folded over the arm in the exercise of worship, and placed neatly on the lap during the intervals between dances.

Developments in Shaker cloth manufacture and dyeing also affected the brethren's clothes. For a while the trousers were of a gray mixture in winter, and blue-and-white checked linen or cotton in summer. Later the trousers were nutgall dyed, and the coats and jackets colored drab. Hooks replaced buttons, white silk neckcloths substituted for stocks, and strings for buckles on the shoes. About 1830 "the feelings had become so set for blue" that both summer and winter jackets, for Sabbath wear, were changed from drab to fine blue fulled cloth, and later to light blue, fine-wale worsteds.

JOHN DURANG

THE FIRST AMERICAN DANCER

BY LILLIAN MOORE

JOHN DURANG was the first native American to win widespread recognition as a dancer. It would be foolish to try to claim that he was a great artist, or that he made any distinctive individual contribution to the art of the dance. Evidently he had a certain amount of skill, a great deal of charm, and that indefinable something called "box-office appeal," or his popularity would never have been able to survive the fierce competition to which it was subjected. When his lack of training and education, and the inauspicious circumstances of his childhood are considered, it is amazing that he was able to hold his own among the well-schooled foreign artists who flooded the American stage in the latter part of the eighteenth century.

Durang must have been passionately fond of the theater. He was active in almost every one of its branches. Although known chiefly as a dancer, at various times he was also an actor, a mime, a choreographer, a property man, a singer, a tightrope performer and acrobat, a designer and scene painter, a puppeteer, a circus clown, an author, and even a theatrical manager.

John Durang was the son of Jacob Durang, who was born in Strasbourg, Alsace-Lorraine. The latter served as a surgeon in the French army, under Louis XV, from 1755 to 1767. He married Mary Arten of Vizeburg, and they came to the United States in November, 1767, settling in York, Lancaster County, Pennsylvania. During the Revolutionary War Jacob Durang served in the York County Militia. He died in South Carolina, about 1804. Jacob was the father of seven children, of whom the eldest was John.

Little is known concerning John Durang's childhood. He was born in York (not in Lancaster, the place given by most theatrical histories) on January 6, 1768. Evidently the Durang family spoke French or German at home, for John's sister Caroline was seriously hampered in her ambitions as an actress by her inability to speak English. John himself had difficulties with the language, as we learn from a letter of his son Charles, which is now in the Harvard Theatre Collection. Writing in 1862 to Thompson Westcott, who was then engaged in the preparation of an extra-illustrated copy of Durang's *History of the Philadelphia Stage*,[1] Charles says:

That interior of Rickett's Circus is bound up in a MS. book of my Father's so that it can't be taken out without tearing it apart. I'll send you the book—but I must promise it is kind of an old

15

family secret affair—not for every eye. That is, there is nothing wrong or immoral in it that any man may be ashamed of. My father there indulges in some whims that may excite the risibilities of the indifferent peruser. It is written in half French-German and English. He never received an English education—save that he got in being engaged as a dancer and pantomimist about the Old American Company and other English companies, where he endeavored to gain a knowledge of our language to make himself useful in the drama. Therefore his orthography is very queer and incorrect.

In about 1778 or 1779 (just after the terrible winter of Valley Forge, which is not very far from York) the Durang family moved to Philadelphia, where Jacob acquired property on Second Street. It is difficult to imagine how John Durang was able to obtain any kind of training for the theater. Miss Ann Barzel's extensive researches into early dance teachers in America have revealed very few instructors in Philadelphia at that period. In 1774, before the Durangs came to the city, a certain Signor Tioli taught in Philadelphia, assisted by a Mr. Godwin. There was also a dancer named Pietro Sodi, who claimed to have been ballet master of the Italian Opera in London, who paused briefly in Philadelphia in June of the same year, was beneficiary at a concert, where he danced a rigadoon, a minuet, and an *allemande* with "Miss Sodi," and then went on to greener fields in Charleston, South Carolina. The next teacher found in Philadelphia was a dancer and pantomimist named Roussel or Russel, who taught there in 1785, the year after John Durang's debut on the stage. Durang may possibly have had some training from him.

There was good reason for this scarcity of dance instruction. In October, 1774, the first Continental Congress passed a resolution which strongly recommended the closing of all public places of amusement. Not only theaters, but even public balls and dances were frowned upon. The British actors who had been giving performances in New York, Philadelphia, Baltimore, and Annapolis before the Revolution hastened back to their homeland at the outbreak of hostilities. When the war was finally over, the first actor to come back to the newly christened United States was Lewis Hallam, who arrived in Philadelphia in 1784.

Hallam had been the leading actor in the Colonies for fifteen years before the Revolution, and his father had been a distinguished actor and manager before him. In spite of his fame, Hallam found that it was absolutely impossible to obtain a license for the production of regular plays. The government was still strongly opposed to the theater. Nevertheless, Hallam obtained the old Southwark Theatre, gathered together a small company, and proceeded to give entertainments which he disguised as "lectures." The members of this first troupe were Mr. and Mrs. Allen, British actors, Miss Caroline Durang, a singer, and John Durang, who was engaged to dance. The first "lecture" took place on December 7, 1784. It consisted of excerpts from Shakespeare, "A Monody to the memory of the Chiefs who had fallen in the cause of American Liberty, accompanied with vocal incantations, etc.," and a "Rondelay Celebrating the Independence of America, with Music, Scenery and other Decorations." At the next performance, on December 14, John Durang probably had his first real opportunity, for the program listed a "Peasant's Dance." These "lectures" continued intermittently throughout the winter. The shadow of the war still hovered over the country. Everywhere there were suffering and anarchy. The British players were actually persecuted, partly because of their nationality, partly because their profession was felt to be too frivolous for such distressful times. In the effort to curry favor, every theater advertisement ended with the words *Vivat Respublica*, and patriotic spectacles were prominently featured.

During this first season John Durang was

DURANG'S HORNPIPE

NEW YORK, Published at O. TORP'S Music Magazine, 465 Broadway.

Original music for John Durang's *Hornpipe*.

Interior of the John Street Theatre. The J. Clarence Davies Collection,
Museum of the City of New York.

just seventeen years old. So far as we have been able to discover, he was without training. He made himself generally useful about the theater, and probably helped to make the simple properties and settings, for he was clever at such things. A handsome young Frenchman, Charles Busselott, who had been an officer in the Guards of Louis XVI, joined the troupe at about this time. He was an expert swordsman and a clever mechanician. Assisted by Durang, he staged several effective shadow plays, one called *Les Grandes Ombres Chinoises*, and a later sequel, *Les Petites Ombres Italiennes*. Durang, meanwhile, danced between recitations, scenes, or spectacles. He danced, in fact, whenever he could get the stage. One of his contributions was a comedy number called *La Fricassée*. His favorite, then and throughout his career, was

the hornpipe. His son, Charles Durang, admits that much of John's early success was due to his nationality. He was the only American-born member of the company, and, "being a native citizen, was always received with applause," as Charles says.

In the summer of 1785 the little company, now somewhat enlarged under the joint management of Hallam and Allen, decided to try its luck in New York. No sooner had they left Philadelphia than the Pennsylvania Legislature began a heated debate on the subject of the theater. A bill for the suppression of vice and immorality was then before the House, and a clause absolutely forbidding all theatrical performances had been suggested. During the debates Robert Morris spoke in favor of the theater, while General Anthony Wayne even advanced the modern idea that it could

The old South Street Theatre.

The old South Street Theatre, Philadelphia. From a drawing by Edwin Forrest Durang, grandson of John Durang. University of Pennsylvania Library.

be made an effective instrument of government propaganda! The objectionable clause was finally rejected, but a little later, on September 25, 1786, a law was actually passed forbidding all theatrical performances in Philadelphia.

In New York the players met with a reception that was definitely hostile. During the occupation of the city by the British, the John Street Theatre had been used for amateur plays presented by the officers of the enemy garrison, and consequently had acquired a bad name with the loyal New Yorkers. Nevertheless, the actors braved public opinion and opened on August 11, 1785, with another "lecture," consisting of the usual Shakespearean excerpts and a patriotic "Monody," while Durang danced a hornpipe and an "Alamande." It is to be feared that his execution

of the last dance was then as awkward as his spelling of it. On August 20, the company came forward more boldly, announcing a lecture with "a variety of entertaining *Characters*, a *caricature* introduction," and, inevitably, a hornpipe. The bill concluded with a full-length pantomime, *"The Genii of the Rock*, with *Music, Scenery, Machinery* and *Decorations* incidental to the performance." On August 26 we meet, for the first time, the name of Bentley, who had "selected and composed" new music for *The Cave of Enchantment, or The Stockwell Wonder.*

John Bentley was a young English harpsichordist who, in 1783, had founded the "City Concerts," given every two weeks by the finest musicians of Philadelphia. He joined Hallam's company in the spring of 1785, and came with it to New York. He played the harpsichord in the pit, or led the orchestra if there was one, composed incidental music when it was needed, and acted "bit" parts on nights when pure drama was presented.

The Old American Company, as it was now called, frankly announced, for September 1, its first harlequinade, *The Touchstone, or Harlequin Traveler*. This was patterned after Dibdin's pantomime, but Bentley composed new music for the American première. This production utilized the full strength of the little company, which numbered eight people: Hallam was Harlequin, Durang was Scaramouche, Miss Durang was Columbine, Allen was Pierrot, and other stock roles of the Italian-English pantomime were played by Mr. Moore, Mr. Lake, and Mrs. Allen, with Bentley, of course, at the harpsichord.

The harlequinade had been a favorite form of entertainment in England since 1717, when the celebrated mime and manager John Rich began his long series of successful comedy pantomimes. The standard characters, Harlequin, Columbine, Pierrot, Scaramouche, etc., were drawn from the old Italian comedy, and appeared again and again in different situations. A modern parallel is found in the Disney cartoons, where we meet the familiar favorites, Mickey and Minnie Mouse, in all sorts of varied settings and situations. Lewis Hallam was an expert Harlequin. Charles Durang, writing in 1854, says of him:

As a pantomimist, Hallam was *au fait*. He displayed much activity and grace as a ground harlequin. The modes of then executing that agile parti-colored cavalier's movements are now entirely obsolete and unpracticed by the modern representatives of his antics. The style of the *mime* has changed as well as that of the actor . . . and of the ballet dancer. . . .

Later in his career, John Durang often assumed the hero's role of Harlequin. To give an idea of the scope and variety of this particular type of pantomime, here are a few of the harlequinades in which John Durang appeared:

The Birth of Harlequin, Harlequin Neptune, The Sorcerer's Apprentice, or Harlequin Woodcutter, Harlequin Pastry Cook, Harlequin Balloonist, Harlequin Everywhere, The Death and Renovation of Harlequin, Harlequin Mariner, Harlequin in Philadelphia, Harlequin's Revenge. Some of these pieces were adaptions of pantomimes which had been successfully presented in England, while others, like *Harlequin in Philadelphia*, obviously were newly invented for special occasions. Sometimes Harlequin would be introduced in a plot built around a topic of current interest.

The first New York season of the Old American Company met with considerable opposition. Several letters were written to the papers, protesting against the opening of the theater while the city was still in ruins, and there was need for the greatest industry and economy. A letter signed "Old Citizen," which appeared in the New York *Packet* for September 17, 1785, said that if the theater was opened "let it not be with Harlequin farces, by a set who, one or two excepted, are *British strangers*. . . ." Hallam and Allen, endeavoring to placate the press and the authorities, offered a gift of $100 to the Alms House of New York City, but the Commissioners refused it on moral grounds, saying that the playhouse had been opened "without license or permission of the civil authorities." Fifty years later Fanny Elssler was to meet with similar opposition in Boston, where her gift of $1,000 was almost refused on the ground that she was "a foreign opera dancer."

John Durang, the native citizen, was of course the only one to benefit by the storm. He continued to dance the hornpipe almost nightly, to enthusiastic and patriotic applause.

Undaunted by criticism, Hallam announced for September 20 something closely resembling a real ballet:

A superb Pantomimical Fete, in which the powers of *Music*, *Machinery*, and *Painting* are combined to cause the most pleasing effects. The *Fete* consists of the most favorite scenes, selected from the Pantomimes already exhibited, so connected as to form a regular Plot in DUMB SHEW. In which will be introduced, the Scene of the Vaux-Hall, with the song of Ted Blarney, and a comic dance called *La Fricassée*. The whole to conclude with the celebrated Skeleton Scene.

Durang's next contribution was "a grotesque Necromantic Dance," introduced into the pantomime *The Witches, or Harlequin in the Moon*, on September 22.

The season continued until November 3, with a different production almost every night. In the plays, Durang sustained insignificant roles: one of four sailors in *Thomas and Sally*, a servant in *The Taming of the Shrew*, and so forth. On October 14, a certain M. Bellair made his debut in a "French dance." Could this stranger have been an exponent of the classic ballet? At any rate, he was not a success, for he appeared no more, and Durang's hornpipe was not contested again that year.

Charles Durang tells us how, during that very first season in New York, his father made the acquaintance of a German dwarf named Hoffmaster. This little fellow, only three feet tall, was a talented musician and a prominent and popular figure in New York's artistic circles. He composed for the American dancer a melody which became famous as *Durang's Hornpipe*. This tune has survived in an edition published nearly half a century later, in 1834, by Otto Torp of New York. Thanks to Charles Durang, we have not only the music, but a step-by-step description of his father's dance. He published it about 1855, in one of his numerous little pocket guides to social and theatrical dancing.[2] The fancy title, *Pas de Matelot*, is at first misleading, and we suspect that this is something Charles Durang copied from the numerous French ballet dancers with whom he was associated later in his career, but the second line, "A Sailor Hornpipe—*Old*

Style" is a dead giveaway. Surely this is John Durang's original hornpipe! Charles had a strong love of the past, revealed in the many nostalgic little phrases which have crept into his writings, and naturally he would have wished to preserve his father's most famous dance.

PAS DE MATELOT

A Sailor Hornpipe—Old Style

1. Glissade round (first part of tune).
2. Double shuffle down, do.
3. Heel and toe back, finish with back shuffle.
4. Cut the buckle down, finish the shuffle.
5. Side shuffle right and left, finishing with beats.
6. Pigeon wing going round.
7. Heel and toe haul in back.
8. Steady toes down.
9. Changes back, finish with back shuffle and beats.
10. Wave step down.
11. Heel and toe shuffle obliquely back.
12. Whirligig, with beats down.
13. Sissone and entrechats back.
14. Running forward on the heels.
15. Double Scotch step, with a heel Brand in Plase. (sic)
16. Single Scotch step back.
17. Parried toes round, or feet *in* and *out*.
18. The Cooper shuffle right and left back.
19. Grasshopper step down.
20. *Terré-à-terré* (sic) or beating on toes back.
21. Jockey crotch down.
22. Traverse round, with hornpipe glissade.

Bow and finish.

Each step takes up one strain of the tune. There are a variety of other shuffles, but the above are the principal, with their original names.

A good dancer with imagination could easily reconstruct much of John Durang's hornpipe from this simple description, for many of these phrases are still familiar or recognizable: the *double shuffle*, the *pigeon wing*, and the *heel and toe haul*, for example.

The hornpipe is, of course, an acknowledged ancestor of the modern tap dance. The directness of the descent is quite evident here, and one unfamiliar step, the *Whirligig, with beats down*, is vividly suggestive of a certain swift tapping turn, executed with arms extended and a renversé movement of the head and shoulders, which was presumably invented by Miss Eleanor Powell. Unfortunately the names of many of Durang's steps are meaningless today. We are at a loss to explain the *Double Scotch step* (it sounds a bit intemperate!), *Parried toes round*, the *Cooper shuffle* or the provocative *Grasshopper step*. Could the *Double Scotch step* be an early American relative of the Russian peasant steps executed in a deep *plié?*

After their first season in New York, John Durang and his sister withdrew from the Old American Company and returned to Philadelphia, where they embarked on an interesting little venture of their own. Joining forces with Charles Busselott, they evaded the strict anti-theater laws by presenting a series of puppet plays in a third-story room of the house in Second Street. John Durang made the puppets, Busselott prepared the scenic effects, and the dialogue and songs were delivered by Mr. and Mrs. Allen, and Caroline Durang. The first Philadelphia performance of George Washington's favorite ballet opera, *The Poor Soldier*, was made through the medium of these puppets. The improvised theater was crowded every night, at 50 cents a ticket. It was impossible, of course, for John Durang to resist for long the temptation to break into the hornpipe; soon it appeared on the bills, along with the *Fricassée* and other old favorites. At about this time Caroline Durang married Charles Busselott, and retired from the stage.

By June, 1788, the Old American Company dared to appear again at the Southwark Theatre in Philadelphia. The one new production in the repertoire was a patriotic one, *The Fourth of July, or the Sailor's Festival*, which must have offered a neat opportunity for Durang. There was still active opposition to the theater, and a petition signed by the Quakers was presented to the Philadelphia Assembly on July 18, protesting against those "schools of seduction" and "resorts of the licentious," the playhouses. A week later the company decided that discretion was the better part of valor, and moved on to finish the summer in Baltimore. They opened again in Philadelphia in January, 1789. The poor players must have breathed a sigh of relief when the anti-theater law of 1786 was finally repealed on March 2, 1789, and they could announce their performances legally, *By Authority*. Mr. Hallam celebrated the occasion by presenting, in the fifth act of *The Roman Father*, "AN OVATION for Publius's Victory over the Curatii"; Mr. Durang celebrated by dancing— a hornpipe!

On March 20, the company presented Robert Brinsley Sheridan's pantomime of *Robinson Crusoe, or Harlequin Friday*. This popular piece had been in the repertoire for two years, but this was John Durang's first appearance as Friday. As Lincoln Kirstein has pointed out, this "blackface clown in coffee-colored fleshings" was a direct ancestor of the Negro impersonators who, typified by "Jim Crow" Rice, were so popular during the nineteenth century.[3]

For the next seven years Durang remained with the Old American Company almost continuously, alternating between the John Street Theatre, New York, and the Southwark, Philadelphia, with occasional brief excursions to Baltimore, Harrisburg, Hartford, Lancaster, Newport, and other towns.

During the season of George Washington's inauguration as first President of the United States, the company was in New York, which was then the capital. Washington attended the theater frequently, and must have seen John Durang dance many times. Later the capital was transferred to Philadelphia, and Washington continued his attendance at the

CHARLES DURANG.
Actor, Author and Manager.
From an original drawing in the collection of Mr. Thomas J. McKee.

Southwark Theatre. Charles Durang describes one of these festive occasions, as his father had related it to him:

Washington's reception at the theater was always exceedingly formal and ceremonious. A soldier was generally posted at each stage-door, four soldiers were placed in the gallery; a military guard attended. Mr. Wignell, in a full dress of black, with his hair elaborately powdered in the fashion of the day and holding two wax candles in silver candlesticks, was accustomed to receive the President at the box-door and conduct Washington and his party to their seats.

The old Southwark (or South Street) Theatre deserves more than passing mention, since it was the scene of so many of the triumphs of John Durang and, later, of his entire family. Its appearance has been preserved for us in a water-color drawing made by Edwin F. Durang, the son of Charles and grandson of John Durang. The Southwark Theatre was opened on November 21, 1766. It had two tiers of boxes, and a gallery on the same level with the upper boxes. The corridors were extremely narrow, and papered; the outside was painted red. The stage was large and well equipped; it was, in fact, the best part of the house. The lighting was provided by oil lamps without glasses. In May, 1821, it was almost entirely destroyed by fire, with all its valuable stock of scenery, costumes, and music. Another building, raised on the old foundations with parts of the original walls, was used as a grain distillery until it was finally torn down in 1912.

In Philadelphia, on November 7, 1790, Durang introduced a new variation of an old favorite, when it was announced that he would dance "a Hornpipe on 13 eggs, Blindfolded, without breaking one." A few days later, on November 11, he made his first appearance as the hero of an extremely popular "Pantomimic Dance," *The Wapping Landlady*, which was also known as *The Sailor's Landlady, Jack in Distress,* and *Poor Jack.* This concoction was to be given over and over again, in every city in the country, before the close of the century. It was a particular favorite, naturally, with John Durang.

About 1787, Durang had married a dancer named Mary McEwen. She made her debut at the Southwark Theatre on March 11, 1789, as Mrs. Gazette in *The True-born Irishman.* Probably she was already a mother, for her eldest son made his debut two years later. Her career was frequently interrupted, for she had at least seven children, but she continued to appear intermittently, as a dancer and actress of small roles, until her death in 1812, at the age of 43.

On July 7, 1791, at the Southwark Theatre, a "Master Durang" made his first appearance as Harlequin Pigmy in *The Birth of Harlequin.* His father was Harlequin, his mother Columbine. The identity of this particular youngster is somewhat confused. Miss Barzel calls him "Frederick," a name which does not occur in the later annals of the Durang clan. Possibly the little fellow died in childhood. He was certainly not Charles, Ferdinand, or Augustus, the three best-known Durangs, for they were not born until 1794, 1796, and 1800, respectively.

John Durang had been on the stage for seven years before he came into close contact with well-trained European dancers of established reputation. Later he was to appear under the four best choreographers of eighteenth-century America: Alexander Placide, M. Francisquy, James Byrne, and William Francis. Until 1792, however, he had gone blithely along, apparently content with his hornpipes and *Fricassées.* Now he met with real competition, and, alas, was forced to bow before it.

Since the end of the war and the repeal of the anti-theater laws, foreign artists had been gradually drifting back to the United States. In 1790 a M. Duport, who claimed to be a pupil of the great Gardel, appeared at a concert in Philadelphia. He later opened a school in New York. A M. Du Moulin, with a small company of French dancers, appeared in Philadelphia in 1791-92, while Durang was in New York. A few years later Durang and Du Moulin were to be members of the same company. In 1790, while Durang was in Philadelphia, a M. and Mme. St. Aivre danced minuets, gavottes, and allemandes at the John Street Theatre in New York.

On January 25, 1792, Alexander Placide and his wife made their New York debuts in the "Dancing Ballot" (sic) *The Bird Catcher.* Placide danced the title role, Mme. Placide was Rosetta, and poor Durang was relegated to the ensemble of Hunters. The ballet featured a Minuet de la Cour and a gavotte, danced by the new stars. The Placides were trained in the classic ballet, acrobatics, tumbling, and dancing on the tightrope. They had been appearing for a year in Charleston, South Carolina, with their own company. On the day of their debut, Hallam and Henry (the managers of the Old American Company) announced that they had sent to Charleston for the rest of the Placide troupe, and were confident that "the united exertions in agility and pantomime of these much-applauded strangers . . . will prove acceptable." M. Placide also danced the hornpipe, but on a rope, suspended high in the air! In New York he produced two more "Dancing Ballets": *The Return of the Labourers,* which included a "Sabotière Dance," and *The Two Philosophers, or the Merry Girl,* which won enduring popularity, and was later revived in Philadelphia at the special request of President Washington. During the engagement of the Placides, Durang modestly retired to insignificant roles, and even his famous hornpipe was conspicuously absent from the bills. On only one occasion did he play Harlequin to the Columbine of Mme. Placide: on April 27, 1792, when *The Birth of Harlequin* was produced, with the little Master Durang probably cast again in his role of Pigmy.

The Placides remained with the Old American Company during the summer season in Philadelphia, where they produced four new pantomimes, *The Old Soldier, The Enchanted Nosegay, Columbine Invisible,* and *Harlequin Balloonist,* and repeated the successful "Dancing Ballets," which were probably closer to our present-day conception of a ballet than anything which had been seen in the United States up to that time.

After this Philadelphia engagement the Placides continued south to their old post at Charleston, where Alexander eventually became manager of the theater and a person of considerable importance.

During his brief association with the accomplished Placides, Durang had not been wasting his time. He, too, was learning to dance on the tightrope and slack wire, an accomplishment which he did not perfect for two more years, but which was to serve him well in his later circus days.

This glimpse of French artistry had made New York audiences dissatisfied with raw native talent, and in the New York *Journal* for February 13, 1793, a disgruntled "Amateur" complained that "We cannot conclude without . . . expressing our doubts, whether the managers suppose we can be amused by the agility of Mr. Durang, or whether we should be diverted with him as the character of a clumsy stage dancer!" [4]

In 1794, Durang participated in an event of great interest in musical history: the première of *Tammany,* one of the first operas written in America, with an American subject. The artistic merits of this much-discussed work are somewhat doubtful, as it seems to have been the center of a violent political storm. The Republicans praised it extravagantly, while the Federalists condemned it just as strongly. William Dunlap called it "a mélange of bombast . . . seasoned high with spices hot from Paris, and swelling with rodomontade for the sonorous voice of Hodgkinson," and although he admitted that it was "received with unbounded applause," he laid this to the fact that the audience consisted of "the poorer class of mechanics and clerks."

The libretto of *Tammany* was written by Mrs. Anne Julia Hatton, a sister of the great actress Mrs. Siddons. She had interested the Tammany Society in her opera, and it was produced partly under its auspices. The story concerned the struggle between the Indian hero, Tammany, and the Spanish adventurers, led by Columbus. The libretto has not survived and its details are obscure.

The music was composed by James Hewitt, a fine violinist who had been for two years the leader of the orchestra of the John Street Theatre. Born in England in 1770, he was only twenty-four years old when he wrote *Tammany.* Later he became a music publisher, and his imprints are now collectors'

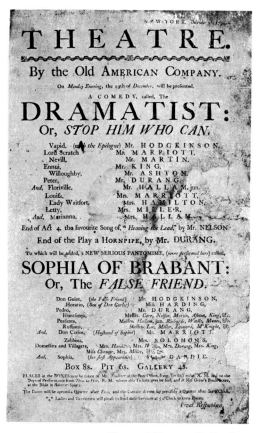

Harvard Theatre Collection.

items. Unfortunately he received little credit for his creative work, and the first-night audience, dissatisfied with the new music of *Tammany*, demanded a popular tune instead. When Hewitt refused to comply with their wishes he was violently hissed!

The scenery was painted by Charles Ciceri. This name will be extremely familiar to students of the romantic ballet, for Pierre Luc Charles Ciceri designed the original settings for Taglioni's *La Sylphide*, *Nathalie*, and *La Fille du Danube*, as well as for the first production of *Giselle*. It would be interesting to trace the exact relationship between the two Ciceris. Pierre, born at St. Cloud in 1782,

may have been Charles's nephew or cousin.

The life of Charles Ciceri reads like an adventure story. He was born in Milan, spent his youth with an uncle in France, ran away several times, and finally served for five years as a mercenary soldier in Santo Domingo. There he occupied his spare time in painting scenery for the local theater. He returned to Europe and worked briefly in the theaters of Paris, Bordeaux, and London. On his way back to Santo Domingo he was shipwrecked on the Bahamas, and eventually found his way to the United States. Engaged as scene painter for the New Theatre in Philadelphia, which was supposed to open in 1793, he was driven from the city by a terrible epidemic of yellow fever which broke out that summer. He came to New York and obtained a position at the John Street Theatre. Dunlap says of him: "His architectural scenery was always good. He was long a most valuable auxiliary to the *corps dramatique*. . . ." His scenes for *Tammany* were "gaudy and unnatural, but had a brilliancy of coloring, reds and yellows being very abundant." Charles Durang also had a good word to say for Ciceri, calling him "a very ingenious artist, in various ways." Ciceri remained in the United States until 1798, when he returned to France.

John Durang's part in *Tammany* consisted of an Indian Dance, in which he shared the honors with a Mr. Miller (probably a rope dancer and gymnast who had been appearing at Vauxhall). It is interesting that the first opera-ballet given in this country should have been an American Indian dance!

The first performance of *Tammany, or the Indian Chief* took place on March 3, 1794. It was given four times that season in New York (quite a record, in those days when most productions were given only once or twice) and later revived. The *New York Daily Advertiser* (an anti-Federalist paper, it must be admitted) said on March 6, 1794: "The language of the piece is sublimely beautiful, nervous, and pathetic; its sentiments such as must be approved by every wise and virtuous person. . . . The whole of it is replete with beauty, and discovers a genius of the first order; and the managers have got it up in a manner which proves that they were sensible of its worth, and the advantage they would reap from it."

Another letter, signed "A Calm Observer," said in the *Daily Advertiser* of March 7: "There was a great deal of liberty and equality in it—Tammany received much applause for his noble and independent spirit. . . . The Prologue and Epilogue were brim full of the present popular notions of liberty, and of course went down with great éclat. To be serious, however, *Tammany* has some merit, and was tolerably supported by most of the performers, and with good music and scenery." There seems to be no mention of the Indian dances in any of these contemporary letters, but another correspondent in the same paper praises the whole scenic production: "Much credit is due to Messrs. Hallam and Henry for the pains they have taken in decorations, scenery, etc., and I doubt not A Citizen will hear whenever *Tammany* is performed, the warm, the juvenile exclamation, Oh! What a beautiful sight!" [5]

Durang took advantage of the popular preoccupation with *Tammany*, and at his benefit performance on June 11 presented a new pantomime ballet called *The Huntress, or Tammany's Frolics.* Durang may have staged this composition. If so, it was one of his first attempts at choreography. At the same performance he surprised his old friends by dancing for the first time on the slack wire. A year earlier, Durang had collaborated with Bissett in the preparation of a comic pantomime, *The Grateful Lion, or the Lilliputian's Power,* which was given at the John Street Theatre at their benefit performance on June 7, 1793. Perhaps the Lilliputian was Master Frederick (?) Durang.

Soon after *Tammany* was produced in New York, an event of the greatest importance in the history of the ballet in America took place in Philadelphia. This was the première of the ballet pantomime *La Forêt Noire,* which was the first *serious* ballet to be given in this country. Of almost equal importance was the American debut, on the same evening, of the exquisite Madame Gardie, the first ballerina to win renown here as both dancer and mime. Contemporary accounts agree unanimously that she was an artist of exceptional ability and charm. Her influence on John Durang was a profound and lasting one. The pathetic story of her brief life is one of the real tragedies of the theater.

Madame Gardie was born in Santo Domingo, and when a very young girl made her debut at the theater in Cape François. There she contracted a union with a man named Maurison, by whom she had a son. They separated, and he went to France. In the meantime a dissipated young French nobleman, named Gardie, arrived in Santo Domingo. He fell in love with the beautiful dancer, married her, and took her back to France. His aristocratic family refused to receive her, and she proudly returned to her profession. One evening a Parisian audience demanded that she sing the *Marseillaise,* and she refused (whether from Royalist sympathies, or just a dancer's typical inability to sing, is not known!). A furious mob drove her from the theater, and she had to leave the country. Her husband accompanied her to Santo Domingo. There they were forced to flee once more because of the terrible race riots which had broken out. They finally found their way to Philadelphia, where Wignell and Reinagle engaged Madame Gardie for a series of appearances at their New Theatre on Chestnut Street. Her husband found occasional employment as a music copyist, but his inability to support his wife preyed on his mind, and he became more and more despondent and melancholy. Madame Gardie appeared with several companies (including, notably, the Old American) with extraordinary success, but salaries were small, and, in

1798, she found herself without an engagement. The situation of the little family became desperate. Gardie finally agreed to return alone to his family in France (she refused to go to them) while she made arrangements to take her little son, then about seven years old, to Santo Domingo. On the eve of his departure, Gardie, unable to bear the thought of separation from his beautiful wife, crept into the room where she slept with the boy, stabbed her to death, and then killed himself. The tragedy took place early in August, 1798, in a third-story room of a house at the corner of Broad and Pearl Streets, in New York City. In the same house George Washington had bade farewell to his officers at the close of the American Revolution.

In 1794, however, Madame Gardie was young and lovely and full of hopeful ambition. The New Chestnut Street Theatre was the best-equipped playhouse in America, with a fine orchestra of twenty musicians, and a ballet company under the direction of William Francis, who was later to be closely associated with John Durang. *La Forêt Noire*, the vehicle chosen for her debut, was prepared with the greatest care. It was based on a French pantomime, in which Madame Gardie had probably appeared during her stay in Paris. New music was composed for the occasion by Alexander Reinagle, the distinguished conductor of the Philadelphia "City Concerts," and director of the orchestra at the Chestnut Street Theatre. This fine musician, born in England of Austrian parents, was an intimate friend of Carl Philipp Emanuel Bach. He had traveled widely and acquired some European reputation before he came to the United States in 1786. The examples of his music which have survived are very much in the style of Bach.

It has been impossible to discover exactly who was responsible for the original choreography of *La Forêt Noire*. It may have been the French dancer Quesnet (Quesnay, or Quenet) who made his debut at the Chestnut a month later, and joined the Old American Company with Madame Gardie in the following autumn. William Francis, staff ballet master, probably assisted. Madame Gardie herself may have had a good deal to do with the staging. A libretto of *La Forêt Noire*, published in Boston when it was presented there in 1795, has survived, and a copy is to be found in the library of the University of Pennsylvania. The authorship of this delightful little booklet is attributed in the University catalogue to Madame Gardie, although her name occurs only as Lucille, the heroine, in the listing of all the members of the Boston cast. The twelve-page libretto is written so vividly that one can almost see the charming old-fashioned pantomime. A bit of action by a comedy character, Lucille's despised suitor, reminds one of the similar character in Dauberval's *La Fille Mal Gardée*: "The Abbé falls over a chair and table and pulls them on him, after a while rises, sees the letter, goes to the portrait (of Lauridan, to whom Lucille is secretly married) sees who it is, weeps ridiculously, takes a light and examines the portrait, and at last concluding that it is not so handsome as himself, goes out admiring his person." In another scene a thrilling bit of melodrama is described:

She traverses the stage, shewing much fatigue; sees a grotto, is desirous of entering for repose; as she is going in, a Robber comes out and seizes her by the Arm; she struggles, escapes, and flies to the opposite side; a second Robber stops her . . . she struggles, her strength fails, and she falls fainting into their arms. They whistle; the Captain enters with the child and all the Robbers. The child knows his mother, and wishes to go to her; the Captain stops him, makes one of the men hold him, and taking Lucille from the Robber, strives to recover her. She recovers by degrees, and screams at seeing herself in the arms of the Captain; throws herself on her knees. He lifts her up, and tells her that if she will embrace him, she shall have her child. She repulses him with contempt. He persists. She perceives a poignard in his girdle, feigns consent, approaches him, snatches the poignard, retires and then advances rapidly to strike him. The Robbers who hold the child, draw their sabres upon him; she seeing it, shrieks and drops the poignard. The Captain looks at her laughing—she seeing that she can obtain nothing by these means, falls on her knees and demands her child, with softness. The Captain appears to speak to the Robbers. Lucille, thinking that she is unseen, endeavors to escape with her child. The Robbers perceive the flight, follow and bring them back. . . .

The advertisements of the first production of *La Forêt Noire* note: "Books, descriptive of the Pantomime, to be had at the Theatre." Perhaps a copy of this original Philadelphia edition has survived, too. It must surely be one of the first ballet librettos published in this country.

La Forêt Noire was a tremendous success, and was given six times during that season. It remained in the repertoire for many years. Its popularity was due largely to the lovely Madame Gardie, of whom Charles Durang writes:

Madame Gardie created quite a sensation with her pantomimic acting. Her face, figure and action were truly beautiful and enchanting, and the town were in exstacies (sic) with her and with this species of performances. Madame Gardie's character inspired as much respect in her private life as her short professional career had excited the admiration of the public. With splendid talents, she combined all the vivacious fascinations of her gay and polite nation. Perhaps she never had her equal in these accomplishments on our stage. This we have had from one who performed with her in the pantomimes, and who personally esteemed her. . . .

This was, of course, his father, John Durang, who met Madame Gardie in the following autumn when she joined the Old American Company during its Philadelphia season. M. Quesnet came with her, and for a time Durang again retired to small roles. Several elaborate new ballets were produced at the old Southwark Theatre that year. *The Danaïdes*, with choreography by Quesnet, was

presented on October 8, and repeated twice within a week. This ballet was probably adapted from Salieri's opera, given at the Paris Opéra in 1784. Ciceri designed the scenery, and the music was composed by Victor Pelissier, a French horn player who, like Madame Gardie, had fled from the race riots in Santo Domingo. He was a member of the orchestra at the John Street Theatre, New York, and later went to the Chestnut. Before the turn of the century he had composed incidental music for eighteen plays, farces, harlequinades, and ballets.

On November 1, another ballet-pantomime, *Sophia of Brabant, or the False Friend*, was presented. The music was again by Pelissier. Charles Durang says that this pantomime had enjoyed a run of one hundred nights in London. In his "History of the American Theatre" William Dunlap, completely ignoring *La Forêt Noire*, claims that *Sophia of Brabant* was the first serious ballet given in this country. He was probably confused by the fact that in New York City it did precede *La Forêt Noire*.

The Philadelphia season of 1794 closed on December 4, the very day that Charles Durang was born, and the company proceeded at once to New York, where they opened on the 15th. *Sophia of Brabant* was presented on December 29. Madame Gardie completely captivated New York. Her beauty, grace, and charm were extravagantly praised by the press and the public. "The appearance and manner of this lady," wrote one New York critic, "are prepossessing beyond any example on our stage."

During this season *Tammany* was revived, as well as *The Wapping Landlady* (masquerading under the new title of *Poor Jack*). Here Durang had the leading role and a good chance to dance the hornpipe again. *La Forêt Noire* had its New York première on March 20, 1795, and was another triumph for Madame Gardie.

That summer the company went to Hartford, where the ballets presented were *La*

Forêt Noire, Sophia of Brabant, and a revival of Placide's *The Bird Catcher.*

On October 21, 1795, the Old American Company began its first engagement in Boston. In the plays John Durang had very small parts, but in almost every ballet he danced opposite Madame Gardie. Among those produced were *La Forêt Noire, The Sailor's Landlady, The Bird Catcher,* and William Francis's "Scots Pastoral Dance," *The Caledonian Frolic.* Francis was not a member of the company, and it is possible that Madame Gardie may have supervised the staging of his ballet. She had been at the Chestnut Street Theatre when he produced it there in the previous year. In addition to the ballets and plays, Durang appeared in such *divertissements* as a grotesque "Dwarf Dance," a classic *allemande* danced with Madame Gardie, and the inevitable hornpipe. During this Boston season Joseph Jefferson, grandfather of the actor of *Rip Van Winkle* fame, made his American debut at the age of 22. He and John Durang formed a friendship which lasted for the rest of their lives.

Returning to New York, the Old American Company opened at the John Street Theatre on February 10, 1796. In this same month a choreographer of great talent and originality arrived in New York. M. Francisquy had been for nearly two years a member of Placide's troupe in Charleston, South Carolina. In that city he was often billed as "Francisque," a name which, if we are not mistaken, occurs in the roster of the Paris Opéra Ballet in the latter half of the eighteenth century. Probably discouraged by the consistent mispronunciation of the Colonials, the dancer changed the spelling to Francisquy. Gathering together a small group of French dancers, in the autumn of 1795, Francisquy proceeded by easy stages, pausing to give performances in Richmond and other cities, to New York. The little company, which included M. and Mme. Val and M. Dubois, was engaged to give special performances with the Old American Company

beginning on March 3. Madame Gardie joined them to dance leading roles, and John Durang, somewhat overshadowed by the French stars, began with small ones.

Francisquy's first production was *Pygmalion,* announced as "a lyric scene of the celebrated J. J. Rousseau, with musical interludes by the same author." M. Val was Pygmalion, Madame Gardie was Galathea. On the same program were two new comic pantomimes, arranged by Francisquy: *The Milkmaid, or the Death of the Bear,* and *The Cooper, or the Guardian in love with his Pupil.* In the latter, John Durang played the part of a miller.

Soon the little ballet troupe became an integral part of the Old American Company. Now began the period which, so far as the ballet was concerned, was the most brilliant the young United States had ever seen. During the next four months the inventive Francisquy staged a seemingly endless procession of ballets and pantomimes. On March 26 he offered *The Whims of Galathea,* a sequel to the successful *Pygmalion.* There was new scenery painted by young Joseph Jefferson, and new music, probably composed by James Hewitt. Francisquy took the role of Damon, Jefferson was Dorilas, Durang was Alexis, Mrs. Durang was Philida, and Madame Gardie played Galathea. A few days later *La Forêt Noire* was revived, followed on April 13 by a new ballet-pantomime called *The Milliners.* This may have been based on a burletta by T. Harpley, acted at Liverpool at 1790. Leading roles were sustained by Francisquy and Madame Gardie, while Durang joined Jefferson, Prigmore, and Hallam, Jr., as one of four officers.

On April 18 Benjamin Carr's opera *The Archers,* with a libretto by William Dunlap based on the legend of William Tell, was given for the first time. Dunlap says that Carr's music was "pleasing and well got up," but he gives no details about the incidental dances. Madame Gardie and Madame Val were cast as "Maidens of Uri," so we may safely assume that they preceded Marie Taglioni by thirty-three years in dancing the Swiss Tyrolienne, which the great ballerina introduced in Rossini's *William Tell* at the Paris Opéra in 1829. Durang, Des Moulins, and several other dancers were in the cast; so the incidental ballets must have been rather elaborate.

Another Francisquy ballet, *Rural Waggish Tricks, or the Enraged Musicians,* was given at Madame Val's benefit performance on April 21. A special feature was a new "Country Dance," *Yankee Doodle!* Durang, Dubois, Francisquy, Mrs. Durang, Madame Val, and Madame Gardie all had prominent roles. On May 3, for the benefit of his lovely *première danseuse,* the indefatigable Francisquy presented a "Grand Historic and Military Pantomime, *The American Heroine,*" with Madame Gardie in the title role. Indian dances were a feature of this spectacle, in which Durang and most of the other male dancers were cast as savages. On May 18 there was still another new ballet, *The Old Man Grown Young,* with the choreographer in the title role, Durang as Colas, Madame Gardie as Laurette, and Master Stockwell as Cupid. The final pantomimic production of this prolific season was *The Independence of America, or the Ever Memorable 4th of July, 1776.* It began with an allegorical prologue, included a pastoral dance, and ended with the Declaration of Independence. Madame Gardie must have made a lovely figure as America. Evidently she had overcome her repugnance to patriotic demonstrations, for she appeared in many of them in this country. Durang took a small part, the First Citizen, Francisquy had the character role of an Old Woman, Mr. Tyler, as the General, was made up to resemble George Washington, and other characters were Britannia, the Goddess of Liberty, and the President.

For the rest of his career, whenever he had a chance at production, John Durang was to draw on these ballets and spectacular pantomimes of Francisquy's. The French choreographer seems to have taken a genuine interest in the American dancer, and in the *divertissements* given between the acts on play nights, they frequently appeared together. On March 30, for example, they danced a Spanish fandango with Mmes. Val and Gardie. This must have been one of the earliest presentations of the Spanish dance in this country.

At the close of this brilliant season the ballet contingent of the Old American Company went alone to Newport, Rhode Island, while the actors began a summer season at Hartford. The principal dancers were Francisquy, Val, Dubois, Durang, and Madame Gardie, and the repertoire included such established favorites as *Robinson Crusoe, Harlequin's Ramble, The Wapping Landlady,* and *The Bird Catcher,* with Francisquy's new ballets, *The Cooper* and *The Milliners,* as added attractions. In spite of all this, the Newport season was a disastrous failure. Sonneck says that "From a pitiful appeal to the public it would appear that John Durang and his associates barely escaped starvation." [6] As the result of this unfortunate excursion, the fine ballet of the Old American Company was completely broken up. Poor Madame Gardie was evidently left without employment—she did not dance again in New York until shortly before her death—and John Durang returned to Philadelphia to join the circus troupe at Ricketts' Amphitheatre.

John B. Ricketts, a Scotchman, had arrived in Philadelphia in 1792 and opened a circus and riding school. His establishment was just across the street from the new Chestnut Street Theatre, under the management of Wignell and Reinagle. Ricketts soon began to compete with the larger theater in the production of pantomimes and farces. Wignell, furious at what he considered an invasion of his territory, announced for December 25, 1795, an entertainment of leaping, balancing, and acrobatics, called *T' Other Side of the Gutter.* Nevertheless Ricketts persevered in his new policy, and in the autumn of 1796 engaged John Durang to direct the pantomimes.

Durang's first production, given with the circus on October 19, 1796, was a comic ballet called *The Country Frolic, or the Merry Haymakers.* Mrs. Durang participated, but the rest of his cast, composed of regular circus performers, was probably none too expert in the art of pantomime. At any rate, the ballet was given only once. Other new productions of the season, probably directed by Durang, included the pantomimes *Mirth's Medley* and *The Valiant Soldier,* and the comic ballet *The Two Huntsmen.*

Ricketts, however, was in search of an outstanding novelty. Early in November he engaged James Byrne, former ballet master at Sadler's Wells and Covent Garden in London, to produce a "Grand Serious Pantomime" called *The Death of Captain Cook.* Byrne and his wife had just arrived from England, and were awaiting their debut at the Chestnut, across the street. *The Death of Captain Cook,* given on November 7, had a sensational success and was given five successive times. Durang had two roles, Perrea, and a Priest. From a program in the collection of the Museum of the City of New York, we learn that this production (brought to New York in the following year) had

original music and accompaniments by
Mons. Rochefort

NEW SCENERY, DRESSES & DECORATIONS

Descriptive of the Manners and Customs of the Natives of Owyhee in the Pacific Ocean. With the characteristic dances and processions, and the Marriage Ceremonies (peculiar to that country) of

PERREA and EMAI

To Conclude with the Assassination of
Captain Cook.

On December 3, Byrne produced his greatest London success, *Oscar and Malvina,* at Ricketts' Amphitheatre. The cast is not known, but Durang, as Ricketts' leading dancer, probably had the role of Oscar. This ballet was frequently revived by other companies, but its first production was somewhat shadowed by the disastrous debut of the Byrnes at the Chestnut Street Theatre, four days later. For the occasion, Byrne had produced *Dermot and Kathleen,* a ballet adapted from the opera *The Poor Soldier.* The Philadelphia audience thought that Mrs. Byrne's costume was inadequate, and hissed her off the stage. At the next performance she wore pantalettes down to the ankle, but it was too late. She was never successful in this country. Byrne remained in the United States until 1800, producing many ballets, but his path did not again cross that of John Durang.

After the Byrne disaster, Ricketts turned from ballet production for a time. One new pantomime, *The Magic Feast,* was given January 14, 1797. This may have been the same as *The Magic Tree, or Neptune's Favor,* which Durang staged for Ricketts three months later in New York. On February 7, for his benefit performance, Durang presented Francisquy's popular *Independence of America.* A week later another choreographer, M. Spinacuta, trespassed on Durang's territory, producing the pantomime of *The Magic Fight, or The Little Cripple Devil.* Spinacuta was a rope dancer and acrobat, who had been associated with Placide for many seasons.

In the spring Ricketts' company went to New York, where they appeared in a magnificent new amphitheater on Greenwich Street. Here Durang produced several new ballets: *The Peasant of the Alps, The Country Wake, or the Frolicsome Crew* (with a hornpipe by Durang, Ricketts, and Franklin), and *The Magic Tree,* mentioned above. He also revived Francisquy's *The Milliners* and Byrne's *Oscar and Malvina.* In the circus performances, Durang regularly appeared as the clown.

On June 8, 1797, Durang presented a pantomimic ballet called *The Harvest Home, or*

Rustic Merriment. The title suggests a similarity to William Francis's *Rural Merriment,* given at the Chestnut Street Theatre two years earlier. Another pantomime, *The Humours of Bartholomew Fair,* was produced for Mrs. Durang's benefit on July 3. An advertisement of this performance, now in the Harvard Theatre Collection, shows that the Durangs lived at No. 18 Thames Street.

On July 18 John Durang presented a really original pantomime, with a good lusty title: *The Western Exhibition, or The Whiskey Boys' Liberty Pole.* It is too bad that no description of this intriguing production has survived. Soon after, Ricketts' Circus embarked on a tour which took them all the way to Canada. In August they were appearing in Albany, where Durang was advertised as "Clown to the Horsemanship," and announced with Ricketts in an exhibition of "Still Vaulting, or a Trial of skill, over a single Horse." This Albany program also included *The Taylor's Disaster, or Johnny Gilpin's Journey to Brentford,* by Mr. Durang. This may have been a pantomime, but more probably it was just a comic song. He sang more often, and danced less, in his later years.

Durang remained with Ricketts' Circus until its Philadelphia headquarters was destroyed by fire on December 17, 1799. He participated in several interesting productions during these years. In 1798 he and Spinacuta painted the scenery for a pantomime called *The Battle of Trenton.* They introduced a realistic snowstorm, with the snow falling on the American Army marching by night to the British camp. This novel effect was much admired. On January 23, 1799, Durang made his debut as an author, with the sketch *The Death of Miss McCrea,* which he had written in conjunction with John B. Rowson.

On February 17, 1799, Durang produced another pantomime with a marvelous title, *The Battle of the Kegs.* This was billed as "The memorable Historical Representation.

With all the Scenery of the Delaware, Front Street, wharves, flat-men, corders, carters, citizens, &c." This was certainly a far cry from the fanciful British harlequinades. Durang seems to have been a real pioneer in the introduction of spectacles based on American themes.

On the night of the burning of Ricketts' Circus, Durang had been announced to play *Don Juan* in the popular pantomime based on Gluck's opera. The playbill announced that "The last scene represented the infernal regions, with a view of the mouth of hell, Don Juan being reduced by his wickedness to the dreadful necessity of leaping headlong into the gaping gulf in a shower of fire amongst the furies, who receive him on the points of their burning spears, and hurl him into the bottomless pit."

At that time there was a strong theatrical superstition that it was bad luck to play *Don Juan,* and although the fire began before the start of the pantomime, the audience blamed it on the wicked Don.

The destruction of his theater ruined Ricketts, and Durang was thrown on his own resources. That summer, 1800, he joined forces with John B. Rowson and presented a two months' season at the old Southwark Theatre. This was his first venture as an impresario. The entertainment was named *The Thespian Panorama,* which irritated a group of amateur actors who called themselves *The Thespian Society.* They complained in the newspapers, Durang and Rowson replied, and the resultant publicity probably did the little venture much more good than harm. The programs consisted of short comedies, pantomimes, tightrope dancing, and, we suspect, a good many hornpipes.

Soon after, Durang became a member of the stock company of the Chestnut Street Theatre. There he remained until the end of his career. His family was growing rapidly (he already had three sons, even if little Frederick was dead) and he wished to make a permanent home for them. Each year the company played a brief autumn season in Baltimore, but the winter was spent comfortably in Philadelphia. The Durang family lived at 216 Cedar Street, which was then on the edge of town. Durang and his wife acted small roles in the plays, and continued to appear in the pantomimes and ballets, which were under the direction of William Francis.

Francis was a real character. His real name was Francis Mentges, and he was a Dutchman. He had made his first appearance in Philadelphia in 1772, when he was announced as "from the theater in Amsterdam." Under his own name, he served as a colonel in the Revolutionary Army, and when General Washington came to the Constitutional Convention in Philadelphia in 1787, Francis was one of those who met him and escorted him into the city. Going to England that same year, he resumed his profession as a dancer, appearing in Manchester, Dublin, and Liverpool. When Wignell went to England in 1793 to find people for the new Chestnut Street Theatre, he engaged Francis and his wife at the joint salary of $40 a week—an extremely good figure for those days, when actors often received only $5 a week, and dancers less. Francis was a talented choreographer, specializing in rustic and comic ballets. Several of his productions have already been mentioned. In his later years he was a well-known comedian.

Francis taught dancing in Philadelphia for many years. His classes featured the French cotillion, the minuet, and the English country dance. "On his ball nights," writes Charles Durang, "the pupils and visitors were delighted to see Mr. Francis standing at the head of the ballroom, as master of ceremonies, ushering all to places with his airy and amusing suavity. In dress, he was neatness personified. Fashionably cut small clothes, white silk stockings, neatly made shining pumps, set off a well-made leg. His head was carefully dressed and powdered, and his face wreathed with smiles. . . ."

John Durang soon became Francis's associate in teaching, and also in staging the ballets at the Chestnut Street Theatre. Gradually the young members of the Durang family were taken into the company. In those days, according to Charles Durang, "the ballet corps was not composed of supernumeraries—they were not resorted to, even to fill up a procession. . . . The very minor business, and the ballet performances, were executed, principally, by the sons and daughters of the performers, who had received a suitable education in all of these requirements. . . . The children, thus employed, were taught dancing and music, and the accomplishments necessary to a theatrical education, and which would make them, afterwards, acceptable in society. The theater was then a school; they were, of course, placed out of the theater, under masters, to learn other branches of education. . . ."

Charles and Ferdinand Durang made their debuts together, in 1803, at the ages of nine and seven respectively, in a "pigmy pantomime" arranged by Francis, and titled *Harlequin Prisoner, or the Genii of the Rocks*. It may be recalled that the first pantomime in which John Durang appeared in New York, in 1785, was called *The Genii of the Rock*. Possibly this was an arrangement of the same harlequinade. Ferdinand was Pantaloon, and Charles was Harlequin, "with original attitudes and a leap."

Augustus Durang, born in Philadelphia in 1800, made his New York debut at the Park Theatre, as Tom Thumb, when he was just six years old. At the first Philadelphia performance of James Byrne's London pantomime, *Cinderella* (restaged by William Francis at the Chestnut in January, 1806), Charles, Ferdinand, and Augustus were all Cupids. As a child Augustus specialized in comic songs, but as soon as he was old enough he gave up the stage to become a sailor. He was lost at sea soon after.

John Durang had at least three daughters,

Charlotte, born in Philadelphia in 1803, Julia Catherine, born in Baltimore in 1805, and a mysterious "Miss K. Durang," who may have died in childhood. Some early playbills list all three little girls, so we know that the "K" did not stand for a variation of Catherine or Charlotte. There was also a "Miss M. Durang" who danced a double hornpipe with John at the Chestnut Street Theatre on May 22, 1816. This was probably the daughter Mary Anne, mentioned in John Durang's will.

All these children were trained as dancers, and began appearing in public quite regularly when they were little more than babies. By the time Julia and Charlotte made their New York debuts, at the ages of sixteen and eighteen respectively, they were real veterans. They first appeared at the Park Theatre on January 7, 1821, as Red Riding Hood and Lubin in the ballet *Little Red Riding Hood*.

In the summer of 1807 John Durang's former employer, Lewis Hallam, gave him the use of the old Southwark Theatre rent free. The season opened on July 22, with a performance of Francisquy's *Independence of America*, which now included a hornpipe by Ferdinand Durang and a song, "Giles Scroggins' Ghost," by seven-year-old Augustus. During the summer John Durang revived Placide's *The Two Philosophers*, Francis's *Caledonian Frolic*, Byrne's *The Death of Captain Cook*, and his own *Peasant of the Alps*. On July 30 he presented "a curious Pantomimical Dance, called the *Lilliputian Frolic*," in which the little Durangs must have been delightful. A Scotch ballet called *Auld Robin Grey* included a highland fling, a strathspey, a *pas seul* and a garland dance.

During this season many plays were presented, and John Durang, who had so often played tiny parts, at last had a chance at the leading roles. The climax of his career as an actor came on August 3, when he played Petruchio in *The Taming of the Shrew*. Ten days later Lewis Hallam and his wife joined the company as guest stars, appearing inter-mittently until the season closed in October. These were Hallam's last appearances on the stage. He died in the following year.

Charles Durang tells us that on his benefit night, that summer of 1807, John Durang "flew from the gallery to the stage, bringing in \$350." Unfortunately he does not reveal just how this feat was accomplished. Perhaps he walked a tightrope. At any rate, it was worth while, for the usual nightly returns were about \$75.

Almost every summer, John Durang would take his family and a few assisting artists on a brief tour of the neighboring towns. They often appeared in Lancaster, Harrisburg, and York, and in 1809 went as far afield as lower Canada. Their varied programs consisted of bits of plays, farces, pantomimes, and ballets. It was during one of these tours that Mrs. John Durang died, in Harrisburg, on September 12, 1812.

During the War of 1812, John Durang and two of his sons, Charles and Ferdinand, served in the Pennsylvania Militia. Charles was one of the little garrison of the six-gun battery at North Point, Baltimore, during the battle which inspired Francis Scott Key to write "The Star-Spangled Banner." It was Ferdinand Durang who first fitted the words of our national anthem to its present tune, an old English drinking song called "Anacreon in Heaven." He was also the first to sing it in public, at the Holiday Street Theatre, Baltimore, while Charles led the chorus.

John Durang retired from the stage in 1819. During his last years he appeared much more often as an actor than as a dancer. Nevertheless, on April 12, 1819, just before he retired, he played the role of Guzman in a "Spanish Ballet" called *Love Among the Roses*.

For the last three years of his life, Durang was confined to his house by asthma. His daughters Julia and Charlotte supported him, for by that time they were popular dancers. John Durang died in 1822. Charlotte did not survive him for many years. She danced at the Park Theatre, New York, until 1824, and then returned to Philadelphia to die of tuberculosis at the age of twenty-one.

Julia Durang won a modest success as an actress. About 1824 she married Francis R. Godey, brother of the editor of *Godey's Lady's Book*. He must have been connected with the theater in a technical capacity. Although there is no mention of him as a performer, he and his wife were engaged at the Lafayette Theatre, New York, for the season of 1825, at a joint salary of $25—about $7 a week! Charles Durang says of his sister: "She was of a very petite figure, with a lively, pleasing, joyous countenance, that imparted a merry vivaciousness to her dramatic impersonations. . . . It was, however, upon her talent as a dancer that she rested her pretensions rather than upon her skill as an actress. . . . As a ballet performer Miss Durang was popular for many seasons, as a neat, modest and pleasing artist. . . ." After the death of Godey in 1836, Julia married James J. Wallace. She died in Philadelphia in February, 1849.

Ferdinand Durang had a brief but colorful career as an actor. He had been dancing and playing small roles for years, and was more or less taken for granted at the Chestnut Street Theatre when, in 1816, he had a quarrel with the managers, Warren and Wood, over a fine which he felt had been unjustly imposed. An English equestrian named West had recently opened a circus at the near-by Olympic Theatre, and was preparing an elaborate spectacle called *Timour the Tartar*. Ferdinand Durang walked out of the Chestnut, applied for the leading role in *Timour*, got it, and had a sensational success. In this part he had to perform all sorts of acrobatic equestrian feats, for which his dance training had prepared him well. "Ramparts were scaled by the horses, breaches were dashed into, and a great variety of new business was introduced," Durang records. "The horses were taught to imitate the agonies of death and they did so in a manner which was astonishing." The "Eques-

trian Melodrama" played for twenty-seven nights, between November 28, 1816, and January 4, 1817, and the receipts reached over $800 a night.

In 1824, Ferdinand Durang went to New York, where he appeared as an actor at the Chatham and Bowery Theatres. He died there in 1831. His daughter, Rosalie (who used the name of *Durand*), carried the theatrical tradition of the family into the third generation. She made her debut in the title role of Balfe's *Bohemian Girl* at the Broadway Theatre, New York, in 1855. Her career was a short one, and she died in 1866.

Charles Durang had the most varied and interesting life of all John's children. He was a member of Alexander Placide's company in Richmond, Virginia, when on December 26, 1811, the theater was burned to the ground, with terrible loss of life. He escaped unhurt, and made his New York debut two months later, on February 17, 1812, at the Park Theatre, in a pantomime called *The Genii* (the same *Genii of the Rock*, perhaps), with a hornpipe between the acts. He was only seventeen.

He married a young English dancer and actress, Mary White, who had made her debut at the Chestnut Street Theatre on September 18, 1811. He danced with her at Vauxhall Garden, Philadelphia, in the summer of 1819. Later she made a debut as an actress at the Anthony Street Theatre, New York.

Charles Durang was a member of the fine ballet company at the Bowery Theatre, New York, in 1827. The ballet master was M. Labasse, and other soloists were M. and Mme. Achille, and Mme. Hutin, pioneers in introducing the "French style of dancing" (which probably meant dancing on the pointes and supported adagio, hitherto unknown in this country). The star was thirteen-year-old Mlle. Celeste, who later enjoyed such a brilliant career as a ballerina, mime, actress, and manager.

At various times Charles Durang was an actor, ballet master, stage manager, author,

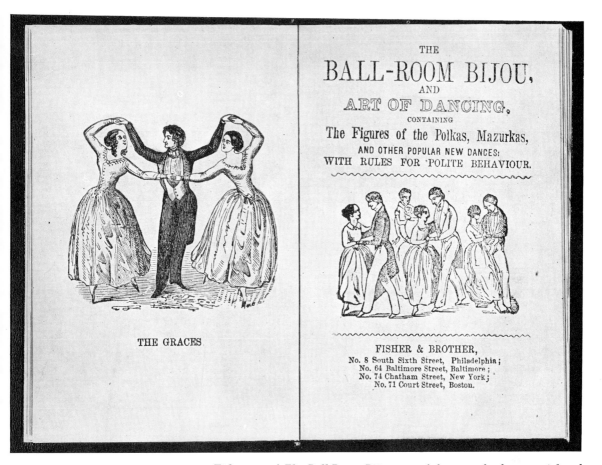

THE
BALL-ROOM BIJOU,
AND
ART OF DANCING,
CONTAINING
The Figures of the Polkas, Mazurkas,
AND OTHER POPULAR NEW DANCES:
WITH RULES FOR POLITE BEHAVIOUR.

THE GRACES

FISHER & BROTHER,
No. 8 South Sixth Street, Philadelphia;
No. 64 Baltimore Street, Baltimore;
No. 74 Chatham Street, New York;
No. 71 Court Street, Boston.

Title page of *The Ball-Room Bijou*, one of the many books on social and theatrical dancing, written by Charles Durang, ca. 1855.

and critic. For many years he was prompter at the Chestnut Street Theatre. After his retirement from the stage, he taught dancing in Philadelphia, assisted by his daughter Caroline. Charles Durang had ten children, of whom the most talented was Edwin Forrest Durang, a well-known architect, who designed theaters at Harrisburg, Reading, and York. F. Ferdinand Durang, Jr., the grandson of Edwin F. Durang and the great-great-grandson of John Durang, served in Ireland with the armed forces of the United States during the Second World War.

Charles Durang published several guides to dancing, which show that he was thoroughly familiar with the fundamentals of the classic ballet and the writings of Noverre and Blasis, as well as with the social dances of the eighteenth and nineteenth centuries. He saw the full pageant of the theatrical dance as it changed from the simple English style popular in his childhood, through the exquisite art of Fanny Elssler, who danced in Philadelphia in the forties, to the dry, technical acrobatics of the Italian ballerinas who held the stage after the production of *The Black Crook* in 1866. Charles Durang died in Philadelphia on February 15, 1870, at the age of seventy-six.

Cakewalk. Original American water color, 1890. The Museum of Modern Art.

JUBA AND

AMERICAN MINSTRELSY

BY MARIAN HANNAH WINTER

THE HISTORY of Negro dance and its music in North America is fundamentally so integrated with our entire music and dance history that it may seem curious here to isolate or limit its boundless divergencies. However, no sequential survey has been made in any general history to date, and episodic treatments can give no concept of the Afro-American contribution in continuity or importance. Hazards are always involved when social and economic problems inexorably impinge on any phase of Negro cultural history, and objectivity becomes an elusive lodestar.

This is in part the saga of William Henry Lane, known as Master Juba. This most influential single performer of nineteenth-century American dance was a prodigy of our entire theater history. Almost legendary among his contemporary colleagues, Master Juba dwindled into oblivion. Negro historians, intent on apotheosizing Ira Aldridge, the African Roscius, ignored him. Yet this is equivalent to writing a twentieth-century theatrical history of the Negro, mentioning only Paul Robeson and omitting Bill Robinson, the great Bojangles. It is more outrageous in that Robinson has embellished an already established form, whereas Juba was actually an initiator and determinant of the form itself. The reper-

toire of any current tap dancer contains elements which were established theatrically by him. Herein is the cornerstone of his memorial.

Negroes were first brought to America in the sixteenth century. They came principally from the Gold Coast, Ivory Coast, Congo, Angola, Benin, Gambia, Senegal, Nigeria, Dahomey, and Togoland. Conditioned physiologically and psychologically to elaborate, legalistic tribal ritual and the extrovert, centrifugal community ring-shout, then to the restricted disorder of slave-ship holds, plantation huts, and enforced dissolution of their cultural traditions, with only the slightest elements of western European tradition to draw upon, they evolved art forms which became indigenous manifestations of American culture.

That Negro music making survived is miraculous when we consider the Slave Laws of 1740, which remained among the basic regulatory laws for Negroes during the subsequent century and a quarter. These were promulgated after the Stono Insurrection of 1739, in South Carolina. A group of slaves attempted an escape to Florida, got hold of some rum en route, stopped to celebrate with a song-and-dance bout, and were captured in

39

a bloody charge. They had marched "with colors flying and drums beating." The laws of 1740 stringently prohibited any Negro from "beating drums, blowing horns or the like which might on occasion be used to arouse slaves to insurrectionary activity." Since most states patterned their slave laws after those of South Carolina and Virginia, the effect of these prohibitions would have discouraged any people inherently less musical.

Substitutions for the forbidden drum were accomplished with facility—bone clappers in the manner of castanets, jawbones, scrap iron such as blacksmiths' rasps, hand clapping, and foot beats. Virtuosity of footwork, with heel beats and toe beats, became a simulacrum of the drum. In modern tap dancing the "conversation" tapped out by two performers is a survival of African telegraphy by drums. Since African dance had already developed rhythms stamped or beaten out by dancers as counterpoint to antiphonal musical accompaniment, and solo dances set against the communal ring-shout, the formal source material surmounted any restrictions. The slave created the *bonja*, too, made from a hollow gourd without resonance board, slack strung, which developed into the banjo of minstrelsy and jazz.

The juba dance (simplified from *giouba*) was an African step dance which somewhat resembled a jig with elaborate variations, and occurs wherever the Negro settled, whether in the West Indies or South Carolina. One variation—crossing and uncrossing the hands against kneecaps which fanned back and forth—was incorporated in the Charleston of the nineteen twenties. Juba and Jube are recurrent slave names particularly associated with dancers and musicians. Juba also occurs as the name of a supernatural being in some American Negro folklore, and became the popular name for an expansive weed, the *Juba's-bush* or *Juba's-brush*.

The Negro dancer on the American stage was originally an exotic, much the same as

blackamoors in a Rameau ballet opera. Blackface "Negroes" appeared in eighteenth-century Captain Cook pantomimes and Sheridan's *Robinson Crusoe* (New York, 1785). In 1791 a Negro troupe of comedians and entertainers, under the direction of one Louis Tabary, gave performances in New Orleans. A typical playbill announcement offers *Paul and Virginia*, with music by Mazzinghi and Reeve, and accompaniments by James Hewitt, featuring a "NEGRO DANCE by Monsieur Labottiere and Mrs. Darby" (New York, 1805). By 1810 the singing and dancing "Negro Boy" was established with the traditional clown as a dance-hall and circus character. These blackface impersonators simply performed jigs and clogs of Irish or English origin to popular songs with topical allusions to Negroes in the lyrics.

Blackface minstrel songs, to the accompaniment of a genuine Negro instrument, the banjo, abetted by tambourine and bone clappers, were popular by 1820, but genuine Negro performers continued to appear only in sporadic interludes. The African Company gave a New York version of the London burletta *Tom and Jerry* in 1821, but the comic dance by the characters *African Sal* and *Dusty Bob* had long been performed in blackface.

"Daddy" Rice, the famous, original "Jim Crow," was a blackface performer who first definitely used a Negro work song. Picked up from a livery-stable porter, this monotonously cheerful refrain—"spin about and turn about and jump Jim Crow"—with accompanying jig and shuffle, focused attention on the Negro as theatrical source material in 1829. Traditional Anglo-American fiddle breakdowns, such as *Turkey in the Straw*, and popular ballads as well, were absorbed into the minstrel amalgam. The minstrel show, as a unit of songs, dances, and jokes, crystallized in the eighteen forties. Although the stock "Negro" was already formed, there was some slight effort initially to approximate Negro music.

Composer-performer Dan Emmett, for example, made a particular effort to keep Negro elements in his work, especially in the "walkaround" finales for which he was noted. These were usually in two parts—the first containing melodies embellished with rhythmic phrases, ejaculations, and verbal interjections (in the best Negro tradition), followed by a chorus and dance based on an old-fashioned fiddle tune. These early works are in distinctly

"Daddy" Rice as Jim Crow. English copperplate engraving after original American lithograph. Ca. 1830.

ZIP COON

American lithograph.

Time to Tarry," "Billy Patterson," "High, Low, Jack," "Chaw Roast Beef," "Turkey in de Straw," "Loozyanna Low Grounds" (not lowlands, as it is generally sung), "K.Y. Ky. or Whose Foot Am Dat Aburnin'?" which was produced in 1860, and "High Daddy" in 1863.

Unquestionably the Negro qualities of minstrel music dwindled, and even the adapted Negro techniques of performance which had been taken over grew vague and sloppy, save in rare instances. Yet because of the vast influence of one Negro performer, the minstrel-show dance retained more integrity as a Negro art form than any other theatrical derivative of Negro culture.

Juba, born William Henry Lane, circa 1825 or later, seems to have sprung full-panoplied from the brow of Terpsichore. Probably a free-born Negro and, from the first records of his appearance at about fifteen, unencumbered by family, he was generally adopted by the entire fraternity of white minstrel players, who unreservedly recognized his genius. He had supposedly learned much of his art from "Uncle" Jim Lowe, a Negro jig and reel dancer of exceptional skill, whose performances were confined to saloons, dance halls, and similar locales outside the regular theaters. By 1845 it was flatly stated by members of the profession that Juba was "beyond question the very greatest of all dancers. He was possessed not only of wonderful and unique execution, but also of unsurpassed grace and endurance." A *New York Herald* feature writer has left us a description of his early extratheatrical performances.

At the time when he performed at Pete Williams', in Orange Street, New York, those who passed through the long hallway and entered the dance hall, after paying their shilling to the darky doorkeeper, whose "box office" was a plain soap box, or a wooden one of that description, saw this phenomenon, "Juba," imitate all the dancers of the day and their special steps. Then Bob Ellingham, the interlocutor and master of ceremonies, would say, "Now, Master Juba, show

different vein from Foster and the later sentimental ballad repertoire. An anonymous scribe for the *New York Herald*, writing at the late date of 1895, was exceptional in realizing this difference.

One great essential to the proper presentation of Negro character, song-and-dance acts was fitting music of a catchy, swinging, Ethiopian nature. While "Dan" Emmett never figured or posed as a dancer, he is responsible for some of the very best "walk-arounds" ever written. Most of these, if not all, were composed for Bryant's Minstrels in the year 1859. Among the most notable and popular ones may be mentioned "I Ain't Got your own jig." Whereupon he would go through all his own steps and specialties, with never a resemblance in any of them to those he had just imitated.

The best in the profession danced there, as well as Juba. A most amusing feature of the entertainment was the comic "walk-around," given in true darky style, with the lean, the fat, the tall, the short, the hunchbacked, and the wooden-legged, all mixed in and hard at it. It was from a one-legged performer there, whose second leg was a wooden one, that Dave Reed learned his celebrated "stiff" leg steps.

(This reminds one of Peg-leg Bates, whose handicap turned him into an amazing virtuoso performer among our current dancers.) Negro

art forms always reached the public in the popular dance halls, even when the legitimate theaters were closed to them.

Juba's fame was already so legendary that by 1845 he achieved the unprecedented distinction of touring with four white minstrels and received *top billing!* I am quoting their 1845 handbill, from the Harvard Theatre Collection, in full, since it gives an idea of the musical mainstays. Juba, incidentally, was a first-rate singer and tambourine virtuoso.

Great Attraction! Master Juba! The Greatest Dancer in the World! and the Ethiopian Minstrels! Respectfully announce to the Citizens of this place that they will have the pleasure of

Juba at Vauxhall Gardens.
Ca. 1849.

American colored wood engraving. 1860-1875.

appearing before them During the Day Under a Pavilion. The Company is composed of Four Skilful Members, and from the immense success which has attended them wherever they have appeared, they are confident in promising their auditors the most irresistible, ludicrous, as well as scientific Entertainment that they have ever listened to.

Master Juba   Mr. J. T. Brown

The Champion Tambourineur
Mr. T. Fluter   Mr. A. L. Thayer
The Unrivalled Banjo Player

Program—Part I

Song Life by de Galley Fire   Brown and chorus
 "   Town of Tuscalore   Fluter
 "   Who dat knocking at de door
                              Thayer

Part II

Statue Dance   by Juba

Part III

Song I must go to Richmond   Thayer and chorus
 "   Old Gal come to de garden gate
                              Brown and chorus
 "   Juliana Johnson   Juba and chorus
 "   Forty-five miles   Thayer and chorus

Part IV

Solo on the Tambourine   by J. T. Brown

Who will go through his imitative powers on the Tambourine, particularly where the locomotive runs off the track and bursts the Boiler, also the rattling of Cannon in the distance, his Reveillie beating the Troops to quarters, his imitations of a celebrated French Drummer, executing single and double drags in perfect time—his Grist Mill grindings showing the power of steam, (of course) and the rattling of a Cotton mill and machinery. Language cannot convey any idea of his brilliant rapidity of execution on his Tambourine.

Part V

Song	Early in de morning	Thayer
"	Farewell Ladies	Juba
"	Lynchburg Town	Brown

Part VI

Solo on the Banjo   by T. Fluter

The entertainment to conclude with the Imitation Dance, by Mast. Juba,

in which he will give correct Imitation Dances of all the principal Ethiopian Dancers in the United States. After which he will give an imitation of himself—and then you will see the vast difference between those that have heretofore attempted dancing and this WONDERFUL YOUNG MAN. Names of the Persons Imitated: 1. Mr. Richard Pelham. New York. 2. Mr. Francis Brower. New York. 3. Mr. John Daniels. Buffalo. 4. Mr. John Smith. Albany. 5. Mr. James Sanford. Philadelphia. 6. Mr. Frank Diamond. Troy. 7. Master John Diamond. New York.

The program is an interesting dictionary of the foremost "Ethiopian" dancers at that period. Of these, Pelham, Brower, and most particularly Master John Diamond, were most important. The latter, somewhat Juba's senior, was his only serious rival, and considered second only to Juba.

Master Diamond (1823-1857) achieved prominence about 1839. He was billed as a performer of the Negro Camptown Hornpipe, Ole Virginny Breakdown, Smoke House Dance

The Great CanCan Dance. Johnson and Powes, San Francisco minstrels. 1878.

and Five Mile Out of Town Dance, in "all of which he will come in those Unheard of, Outlandish and Inimitable Licks, what is Death to all de Long Island Darkies, and which secures to him the title of King of Diamonds."

(In jazz repertoire today there are at least three *Smokehouse* variations and the *Camptown* is well represented. Those "Inimitable Licks" survived as the "hot licks" of swing. There is a definite continuity of terminology.)

Life in Philadelphia. Color engraving by Charles Hunt. London, ca. 1827.

Negro Minstrels. 1860-1875.

Diamond's style was considered a wonder. "Small of stature, he executed in an extremely neat and slow fashion." An incurable dipsomaniac, his dancing was held to be "considerably better than his temper and disposition." Since the "Master's" respective merits were continually debated, a series of "Challenge Dances" was initiated to award the indisputable palm. They danced their first match at John Tryon's Amphitheatre in 1844.

These challenge matches demanded the same attention for an artistic matter that our ancestors lavished on their sporting events. There were at least three judges, for time, style, and execution. On occasion an audience had the decisive voice in determining the victor. "The time judge sat on the stage in the first right entrance, the style judge sat in or near the orchestra pit, and the judge of execution sat *under* the stage. There, with pad and pencil, the execution judge checked the missing taps, defective rolls and heel work, the lagging in the breaks. At the conclusion of the contest the judges compared notes and awarded the prize on points." (Douglas Gilbert, *Lost Chords*. N. Y., Doubleday, 1942.)

When Juba next toured with the Georgia Champion Minstrels in the New England states, he was entitled to this billing: "The Wonder of the World Juba, Acknowledged to be the Greatest Dancer in the World. Having danced with John Diamond at the Chatham Theatre for $500, and at the Bowery Theatre for the same amount, and established himself as the King of All Dancers. No conception can be formed of the variety of beautiful and intricate steps exhibited by him with ease. You must see to believe." (The word "beautiful" was almost never used to describe minstrel dancing.)

In the summer of 1848 Juba arrived in London, to augment an already famous black-face minstrel troupe—Pell's Ethiopian Serenaders. His press releases had the spirited description from Charles Dickens' *American Notes* (1842), which purportedly represented Juba. For lack of further documentation there is a slight uncertainty here, although the dancer was everywhere billed as "Boz's Juba," and it was flatly stated by such respectable journals as the *Illustrated London News* that he was the youth Dickens had celebrated. Since Boz was an extremely vocal person he would probably have protested any infringement on, or misrepresentation of, his work. Thus his record of a Negro dance hall in New York's Five Points district must be included in the Juba saga, at least in part.

The corpulent black fiddler, and his friend who plays the tambourine, stamp upon the boarding of the small raised orchestra in which they sit, and play a lively measure. Five or six couples come upon the floor, marshaled by a lively young Negro, who is the wit of the assembly, and the greatest dancer known. He never leaves off making queer faces, and is the delight of all the rest, who grin from ear to ear incessantly. Among the dancers are two young mulatto girls, with large, black, drooping eyes, and headgear after the fashion of the hostess, who are as shy, or feign to be, as though they had never danced before, and so look down before the visitors, that their partners can see nothing but the long fringed lashes.

But the dance commences. Every gentleman sets as long as he likes to the opposite lady, and the opposite lady to his, and all are so long about it that the sport begins to languish, when suddenly the lively hero dashes in to the rescue. Instantly the fiddler grins, and goes at it tooth and nail; there is new energy in the tambourine; new laughter in the dancers; new smiles in the landlady; new confidence in the landlord; new brightness in the very candles. Single shuffle, double shuffle, cut and cross-cut; snapping his fingers, rolling his eyes, turning in his knees, presenting the backs of his legs in front, spin-ning about on his toes and heels like nothing but the man's fingers on the tambourine; dancing with two left legs, two right legs, two wooden legs, two wire legs, two spring legs—all sorts of legs and no legs—what is this to him? And in what walk of life, or dance of life, does man ever get such stimulating applause as thunders about him, when, having danced his partner off her feet, and himself too, he finishes by leaping gloriously on the bar counter and calling for something to drink, with the chuckle of a million of counterfeit Jim Crows, in one inimitable sound!

The British were completely transported by their American visitor, and wrote of him with an enthusiasm and affection usually reserved for pantomime clown Grimaldi and ballerina Fanny Elssler. Among the effusions one finds an occasional astute evaluation—an unusual occurrence in either the gushing or pompous "harkback" schools of criticism then prevalent in England and the United States. Regrettably Juba did not appear in France, for Gautier was supremely the critic of that period who could have done a masterly analysis and description of his style.

London rank, fashion, and people all frequented Vauxhall Gardens at one time or another. Instantly Juba appeared there, the London journals rightly predicted that he would attract many thousands to the gardens during the season. An anonymous critic wrote:

There never was such a Juba as the ebony-tinted gentleman who is now drawing all the world and its neighbours to Vauxhall; there never was such a laugh as the laugh of Juba—there is in it the concentrated laugh of fifty comic pantomimes; it has no relation to the chuckle, and, least of all to the famous horse laugh; not a bit of it—it is a laugh distinct, a laugh apart, a laugh by itself—clear, ringing, echoing, resonant, harmonious, full of rejoicing and mighty mirth, and fervent fun; you may hear it like the continuous humming sound of nature, permeating everywhere; it enters your heart and you laugh sympathetically—it creeps into your

ear, and clings to it, and all the subsequent sounds seemed to be endued with the cachinnatory quality. . . . "Well, though the laugh of Juba be wondrous, what may be said of Juba's dancing?"

The critic answers himself by saying that there was never such a combination of "mobility of muscles, such flexibility of joints, such boundings, such slidings, such gyrations, such toes and heelings, such backwardings and forwardings, such posturings, such firmness of foot, such elasticity of tendon, such mutation of movement, such vigor, such variety, such natural grace, such powers of endurance, such potency of pastern."

A sardonic side light, in relation to the later intensive propaganda to prove that plantation slavery was the beneficent patron of Negro genius, is this critic's recollection of dancing at "Major Bosh Sanderson's, who owned two thousand niggers at the junction of the Wabash and Congaree rivers, in South Car'lina," whose "choreographic manifestations were but poor shufflings compared to the pedal inspirations of Juba"; our good observer seems to have been surprised. Then there is the concluding accolade—"We hear that Juba has been commanded to Buckingham Palace."

The *Illustrated London News* (May 8, 1848) which offered a woodcut of Juba, noted in the text that

. . . the Nigger Dance is a reality. The "Virginny Breakdown," or the "Alabama Kick-up," the "Tennessee Double-shuffle," or the "Louisiana Toe-and-Heel," we know to exist. If they did not, how could Juba enter into their wonderful complications so naturally? How could he tie his legs into such knots, and fling them about so recklessly, or make his feet twinkle until you lose sight of them altogether in his energy? The great Boz immortalized him; and he deserved the glory thus conferred. If our readers doubt this, let them go the very next Monday or other evening that arrives, and see him at Vauxhall Gardens.

Another anonymous clipping of that same season is prophetically headed *Juba the American Dancer.*

Last night a select party was invited to Vauxhall Gardens to witness a private exhibition of the dancing capabilities of Juba, the celebrated American dancer. He is one of a party of six Americans, whom Mr. Wardell, the spirited proprietor of the gardens, has brought to this country. Their performances, vocal and instrumental, were last night of a character which cannot fail to prove a great attraction, but the dancing of Juba exceeded anything ever witnessed in Europe. The style as well as the execution is unlike anything ever seen in this country. The manner in which he beats time with his feet, and the extraordinary command he possesses over them, can only be believed by those who have been present at his exhibition. Scarcely less singular is the rapidity with which he sings one of his favorite songs. The American Juba has for some years drawn immense audiences whenever he has appeared. He is quite young, being only in his seventeenth year. Mr. Dickens, in his *American Notes*, gives a graphic description of this extraordinary youth, who, we doubt not, before many weeks have elapsed, will have the honor of displaying his dancing attainments in Buckingham Palace.

The *Theatrical Times* critic in August, 1848, gave one supremely important reason for Juba's greatness. "The performances of this young man are far above the common performances of the mountebanks who give imitations of American and Negro character; there is an *ideality* in what he does that makes his efforts at once *grotesque and poetical, without losing sight of the reality of representation.*" (Italics mine.)

In Liverpool Pell's Serenaders continued their triumphal progress, with Juba performing tirelessly. Again, one of the critics notes in passing one of the great characteristics of American tap dancing, even today, that the dancer is equivalent to a musical instrument. He compares Juba's steps to Pell on the bones

Pell's Ethiopian Serenaders. Ca. 1848.

Trick Clog Dance. 1860-1875.

and Briggs on the banjo; ". . . this youth is the delight and astonishment of all who witness his extraordinary dancing; to our mind he dances demisemi, semi, and quavers, as well as the slower steps."

Working an almost superhuman schedule, thoroughly enjoying his work, and reacting normally to the excitement of his triumphs, Juba burned up his energies and health. In America a pious commentator and theater historian, Allston Brown, smugly noted that "Success proved too much for him. He married too late (and a white woman besides) and died early and miserably." Rice is considerably more restrained, noting only that he was considered the greatest dancer in his line and that he died in 1852, in London.

From the age of fourteen Juba seems to have danced for his supper; at that time the standard culinary recompense "on the house" where he danced was a dish of fried eels and ale, which was scarcely a balanced diet. That Juba worked both night and day, consistently, from 1839 to 1850, is record. Small wonder if years of irregular food, irregular sleep, and regular strenuous physical exertion finally produced a breakdown, which had nothing at all to do with "success proving too much for him." His greatest white contemporary—John Diamond—had a somewhat similar background, was an acute dipsomaniac and melancholic, and also died prematurely—in Philadelphia.

The influence of Master Juba and other

minstrel dancers who followed him to England was extensive. There was a curious transference of his characteristics to English clowns. The "Gay Negro Boy" had made his initial entree in American circuses, and was adopted by the British in that same medium. The minstrel dance changed the clowns' entree, adding splits, jumps, and cabrioles, as well as blackface make-up, to form a new type. Between 1860 and 1865 this character was taken over to France by touring British circuses, and later became a fixture in French and Belgian *cirques et carrousels*. The vogue for Lautrec's famous Negro clown Footit was part of this trend. English clowns, such as the Majiltons and Hanlon-Lees, returned to whiteface, but kept certain characteristics of blackface performers—the manic gaiety, he-who-gets-slapped apprehensions, and dance acrobatics—evolving thereby a slightly macabre, almost surrealist personage.

The blackface clown persisted in European circuses and fairs; his grotesque mask emerges in the paintings of Ensor, and his influence just touched a new generation of painters and composers considerably before 1900. It supplanted another exotic impetus of the nineteenth century, Orientalism, which had prevailed in such diverse works as Moore's *Lalla Rookh*, Delacroix's *Arabs* and Whistler's *Japonaiserie*. Coincident with the rise of Western imperialism in Africa came the influence of Afro-American jazz and Gold Coast sculptures. Orientalisms of the 1900 Paris Exposition eventually ceded to Stravinsky's *Ragtime* and Milhaud's experiments with *le jazz hot*.

In America it was Juba's influence primarily which kept the minstrel-show dance, in contrast to the body of minstrel-show music, in touch with the integrity of Negro source material. There was almost a "school after Juba." Certain of these white performers maintained his tradition with such integrity, and were such worthy artists, that a brief notice of them is necessary to our history.

Richard M. Carroll (1831-1899?) made his first public appearance at the age of fifteen as "Master Marks"; he was an understudy to the bibulous John Diamond. A contemporary writes:

Carroll took pattern to a great extent from Juba, and after him, may safely be said to be one of the very first "all-around" dancers this country has ever seen.

Dave Reed (1830-1906) was another blackface performer who went directly to the Negro for his source material. He took a fancy to a fairly indifferent music-hall ballad, *Sally, Come Up*, which did not go too well. He then decided to work in some additions which he had learned from the Negroes when he used to dance on the steamboat *Banjo* on the Mississippi, a "certain comical and characteristic movement of the hands, by placing his elbows near his hips and extending the rest of his arms at right angles to his body, with the palms of his hands down," in addition to some new footwork. The dance caught on like wildfire.

The *Herald* correspondent also gives an interesting version of the origin of the famous *Shoo-Fly* song and dance.

Shoo-Fly is said to have come originally from the Isthmus of Panama, where the Negroes sang "Shoo-Fly" and "Don't Bodder Me" antiphonally while at their work. A Negro from there, Helon Johnson, took it first to California and taught the song to Billy Birch. Dick Carroll and others also had versions of it which they performed.

The entire dance repertoire finally became synthesized in the so-called "essence" dances, made famous by Billy Newcomb. The music for these drew upon folk fiddle tunes, enhanced by the Negro's rhythmic gift and development of the offbeat which is the syncopation of jazz. Southern mountain songs— *Cotton Eyed Joe*, *Cripple Creek*, *Sourwood Mountain* (based on the yodel song), and popular traditional jigs and hornpipes—*Tur-*

key in the Straw, Old Zip Coon, Arkansas Traveler, Durang's Hornpipe, and Fisher's Hornpipe were incorporated. In turn many square dances of the South and Southwest used or adapted minstrel songs—Old Dan Tucker, Buffalo Girls, Jim Along Josey and Hop Light Loo recur most frequently, and Botkin notes that the danse aux chansons of American play-party games had "songs often sung by the nondancing part of the party to mark the rhythms—much, it might be added, after the fashion of patting out the rhythm in Negro dances." (American Play-party Song, cf. Hudson.)

Dance Scene from Uncle Tom's Cabin. Niblo's Garden. New York, 1876.

Against this musical mélange was set minstrelsy's most famous dance—*Essence of Old Virginny*—performed initially in the make-up of a decrepit and tatterdemalion darky, but soon turned into a flashy young dude number. Based firmly on Negro source material, this theatrical showpiece was made famous by several excellent blackface performers. W. W. Newcomb is credited as its originator; his style was called "quintessence" and was done in rather fast time. In contradistinction Dan Bryant, its most famous exponent, who made important technical advances in the development of clog dancing, performed his famous *Essence* very slowly. George F. Moore originated the noiseless, soft-shoe *Essence* about 1875, and the last, whirlaway performance was that of Eddie Girard.

At this point, after looking at the blackface masks, it is necessary to evaluate the Negro position. By the eighteen seventies there was a relentless, and impalpable, pressure to stereotype the stage Negro completely. Although groups such as the Fisk Jubilee Singers toured America and Europe, they reached only a small minority of the general audience. Increasingly the Negro was forced into his caricature. Lack of education had caused the Negro to retain, through word-of-mouth retelling, innumerable superstitions which had been commonplaces among the white settlers in the seventeenth and eighteenth centuries; therefore superstition and fear were "Negro peculiarities," and an adjunct of Negro "make-up" was the "shock" or "fright" wig, listed in the old theatrical catalogues, which could be made to rise and stand on end. Ignorance, vanity, and childlike display of emotions constituted other characteristics which writers of that period continually referred to as "peculiar to the Negro." This last stricture is particularly interesting in view of an analysis by Herskovits (in *Freudian Mechanisms in Negro Psychology*) of the African "insult" song and dance, which are used as "socially institutionalized release." According

to West African ritual, repressing emotions such as anger and hate is considered a primary cause of insanity; hypocrisy is a cause of illness, and the person who practices it gradually sickens. Thus there was a traditionally rather sound and healthy basis for emotional display, which was caricatured out of all proportion into a component of the cliché.

The Negro performer found that unless he fitted himself into the mold cast for him as typical, he could get no work. This represents one facet of a vast attempt at justification of the slave system long propounded—the cliché that plantation life for the Negro had been a joyous lark, that happy, lazy Negroes spent their days dancing, singing, and indulging in childish pranks, with occasional spells of cotton picking, and that the Negroes were wistfully lonely to be back at said plantations, which they were convinced constituted the happy land of Dixie. A Negro who had left the plantation or local mill was selected as a butt of ridicule—in the character of the "dandy nigger"—who squandered his earnings on flashy clothes and scorned his own people. Particular emphasis was always placed on class distinctions among the Negroes themselves, which were the basis for countless skits and dialogues.

There were songs such as P. S. Gilmore's *Freedom on the Old Plantation*, and program descriptions such as *Plantation Pastimes*, *Plantation Revels*, and *Plantation Frolics*, "to show Negro life in the South before the war, introducing solos, duets, choruses, moonlight pastimes, cotton-field frolics, and terminating the scene with the exciting Virginia Reel . . . a most realistic sketch." (1884.) That same year the Frohmans, now proprietors of Callender's and Haverly's companies, took a troupe to London with a now inevitable *Alabama Pickaninnies in Plantation Pastimes*. A book of words to this company's songs was published in London for their tour; it was a

Right: McIntyre and Heath. Ca. 1915.

Left: Courtright and Gilbert, "Big and Little." Ca. 1875.

Ken Mason wearing a "fright" wig. Ca. 1875.

complete recapitulation of all current minstrel ditties, with no glimmer of original material.

Another curiosity was the extremely successful attempt to reintroduce the Negro as an exotic, attempted about 1883 by the Callender-Kersands company. The dancers' drill, a nineteenth-century theatrical fashion, which had its inception in classic ballet, was popularized in France, and taken over by England and America for all types of extravaganza. There were drills of Tartars, Amazons, Naiads, Turks, Brigands, Airy Sprites, and Skeletons. The Zouaves, with their colorful red-and-blue costumes and dark complexions, were a "natural" for the Negro dancers.

One Sergeant Simms, "formerly an officer in the 6th Mass. Regiment," organized this "Grand Military Pageant Presenting an Army of Clog Dancers in an entirely New Kaleidoscope Phase; conceived and arranged by Wm. Welch." Holcomb, the famous clog dancer; Anderson and Kersands, the famous "Bones" and "Tambo" team; and Banks the comedian are among the top-notch Negro performers listed as *The Dancing Zouaves*. The program descriptive outline offers: "A. Dress Parade of African Zouaves. B. Grand Drill. C. Lightning Bayonet Exercise. D. Sergt. Simms and Musket. Clog Tournament terminating with the following Battlefield Pictures: 1. Awaiting the Attack. 2. Skirmishing. 3. The Defence. 4. The Rally by Fours. 5. The Charge. 6. The Dying Zouave." There is no clue to the music, but one can imagine the "Military Potpourri" which was pieced together. Sergeant Simms was still prospering more than a decade later, for he played New York with his "original novelty by his twelve little Indian boys from the Bahamas. Life on the Tented Field." This was a new version of his old Zouave drill, and the program states that "this novelty was especially engaged for the World's Fair, and brought from the Bahamas in charge of Sergeant Simms." With or without the Sergeant, the Callender Zouaves became an established feature, and similar drills were incorporated

in Callender's blackface minstrel companies as well.

Occasionally a Negro artist would even gain some celebrity outside the minstrel field. Such a notable figure was Horace (or Howard) Weston. He was born a free Yankee Negro in Derby, Connecticut, in 1825. His father was Jube Weston, teacher of music and dancing. It would be interesting to know more of the history of a Negro music and dancing master in a small New England community such as this. In 1855, Horace, who continued his father's métier of music and dancing teacher, took up the banjo, which had become a great popular instrument. His professional career was interrupted by service in the Civil War. He resumed it by appearing in blackface minstrel companies and subsequently went to England with the Georgia Colored Minstrels in 1867. On his return to America he worked for Barnum, then played at Baur's Saloon, Robinson's Hall, and continued teaching. For three seasons, from 1876 to 1878, he played on the showboat *Plymouth Rock* for Jarrett and Palmer; late in 1878 he went to England with their *Uncle Tom* company and scored an enormous hit. He then made what at any time, by any artist, would have been considered an exceptional tour—Berlin, Breslau, Vienna, Hamburg, then a tour of France, and back to America for coast-to-coast appearances. He also toured with the two important Negro minstrel shows, Haverly's and Callender's. His obituary in the *New York Clipper* for June 7, 1890, presents him as one of the most esteemed performers of his period.

Kersands, Weston, the Hunn brothers, and some few others were actually the only Negroes *on the stage* who had steady employment; even they were more or less compelled to comply with the stereotypes. Their musical repertoire consisted increasingly of the sentimental ballad budget and music-hall jigs typical of all minstrel shows; the Negro element remained primarily in the rhythmic

treatment of this material, the "intangibles of performance," and a phenomenal virtuosity in "trick" dances. William Allen's *Pedestal Clog* was danced on a surface fifteen inches square and four feet high; stunt dancing on a peck measure or a square of glass one inch thick was commonplace. Generally, Negro dancers and musicians had a better chance for artistic integrity in the music halls.

Negro iconography is scant in contrast to the vast body of "blackface" material. The pictures have a vitality which inspires and confounds. Possibly it is because those people who achieved the professional stature to warrant such records knew that theirs was an almost unique achievement, a tribute grudgingly accorded by that hostile world, wherein a Negro minstrel company's manager was described in the publicity as "white, *of course.*" (Italics mine.)

Even as the Negro performer was at the threshold of his first great "period" theatrically, which might be generally characterized as the Williams and Walker era, concerted efforts were made to place every difficulty athwart his path. With historical persistence anti-minority action was used as a mask for unrelated grievances. Thus a clipping from the *Sun*, July 22, 1894, under the title "Some Negro Actors," offers the following documentary evidence:

At a rehearsal during the last week of *1492* before it closed for its summer vacation, Herman Perlet, the musical director, threw down his baton and refused to direct the orchestra for a Negro boy whom Manager Rice had engaged to do a dancing specialty.

Mr. Perlet did not draw the color line exactly, but when the darky walked down to the footlights and said, "Say, cull, you'll have to play dat faster if you wants dis coon to dance," the indignity of "being called down by a nigger" was too much for the leader's pride. He left the director's chair and turned in his notice to Mr. Rice. The manager tried to persuade him to reconsider, but the leader was obdurate and insisted on his resig-

Top: Negro Minstrel. Ca. 1890.
Bottom: Horace Weston. Ca. 1855.

nation being accepted at the end of the week. Rice himself got into the leader's chair and conducted the remainder of the rehearsal after a fashion. . . .

The action of Musical Director Perlet in refusing to direct for the Negro dancer cannot be regarded entirely as a case of prejudice on his part, because it has been ascertained that he and Rice had been at loggerheads for a long time, owing to the fact Rice would never give him credit on the program for having written nearly all of the musical numbers for *1492*. But in objecting to the Negro dancer he showed that he had hit upon a pretext that would win him popular approval. And it did in the theatrical profession.

It is a familiar pattern. The next item, too, has many facsimiles.

Last week a mulatto man was singing on a roof garden in this city, billed as "Koo-i-baba, the Hindoo baritone." He did not sing well from a legitimate vocal standpoint, nor did he sing badly. He would have been regarded by an unprejudiced manager as having a good chorus voice. Yet the manager of the roof garden assured the reporter that it would never have done to bill him under the name of Johnson or Jackson. There was such a prejudice, he said, against "niggers" that unless he could be advertised as a Hindoo or some other dusky foreigner it would bust up his show. A notable fact was that the colored man was the only person on the program who made any serious vocal efforts.

It was a rather sad commentary upon the artistic standard of the roof garden entertainments that the only refined singing permitted was that of the Negro, and whereas the manager was willing to employ his talents, he was unwilling to give him credit for being what he really was—an Afro-American.

What then can be the fate of the aspiring Negro singer, reciter, or actor in the face of such prejudice among people who began fighting thirty-three years ago to set him free and put him upon an equality with the whites of the South? The theatrical manager can with honesty maintain an indifference in regard to the social status of the colored man, because all the manager has

to deal with is sure-thing cards, and he knows from former experience that the unadulterated Negro performer drives patrons away from his house. He refuses him upon no other grounds.

It is curious that this last paragraph was written just at the point when the public was shortly to applaud all-Negro shows. It may be that there was the usual fear of sharing the theatrical circuit with additional companies, on the part of the white performers, and so it was expedient to dispense with minority competition, which was unorganized and inarticulate, on the ground that the public didn't want it anyway. Yet a certain public demand must have prompted some venturesome manager to follow in the wake of Callender and Haverly with a Negro company recruited as follows, in a further report by the *Sun* reporter:

That there is no lack of Negro talent was recently demonstrated by a well-known minstrel manager, who intends this season to take out a company composed of half Negro and half white minstrels. He advertised in the dramatic weeklies for forty colored persons who could either sing, dance, play the banjo and bones, or tell a funny story. They were to call on Twenty-second Street near Broadway at 10 A.M.

At the hour named Twenty-second Street was jammed with colored persons waiting to display their various talents to the manager. It was estimated that at least 2,000 had congregated, for many left before the 1,012 first comers had registered their names and addresses with the manager.

Several hotels and barbershops thought that their employees had all gone on strike when they rushed out at 10 o'clock to register their names and addresses with the minstrel manager.

But this manager is shrewd enough to know that he cannot get fifty white men to work with thirty colored men on the stage, so he is to have practically two entirely separate shows. The first show will consist of the real Negroes in "minstrelsy as it was," and the second show upon the same stage the same evening, will have the burnt-cork whites in "minstrelsy as it is." Each show will have its own stage manager, and every effort will be made to keep the colored and white actors separate in hotels and traveling, to avoid trouble that has hitherto attended every attempt to work them together.

In the last minstrel troupe of real darkies which went over the country the end men insisted on corking up as black as possible over their naturally dark skin, because, as they said, the public had gotten used to seeing the Negro minstrel as he is depicted by the whites and when the genuine article came along the public was a little disappointed to find that he was not so black as he was painted.

It was for the same reason that a similar ludicrous event happened at Saratoga several seasons ago. The guests of one of the fashionable hotels had all purchased tickets one evening and were assembled in the large dining rooms awaiting with curiosity a performance to be given by the Negro waiters. When the folding doors were opened they beheld a semicircle of persons of a uniform blackened visage. The Negroes had all corked up in imitation of their white imitators.

Our anonymous reporter, who certainly had an exceptionally sincere and intelligent interest in the whole problem, went to interview T. Thomas Fortune, Negro editor of the Afro-American organ *New York Age*, who told him hopefully:

I believe that within fifteen years the leading comedians, dancers, and musicians of the day will include many Afro-Americans. The colored man is a natural-born humorist, musician, and dancer, and when the prejudice against him which is now moderating shall have been entirely or nearly wiped out, you will find him occupying prominent places upon the amusement stage. The pickaninny band in *Old Kentucky*, composed entirely of colored boys, made a hit. Sam T. Jack's creoles have raised the standard one notch higher than the minstrel show.

Mr. Fortune's hopes for Negro employment within the next number of years were to a certain degree fulfilled. But the larger issue of the racial stereotype was far from resolved. Since the opportunity for literal, literary pres-entation was not afforded, nor any representation of Negro humor save the "unconscious" humor of an outsider having difficulty with an alien tongue (and how many thousands of blackface dialogue "sermons" there were!), it was only in the field of music and dance that the Negro might really leave an impress. An interesting note on the way in which the restrictions of the stereotype finally helped kill off the minstrel show itself was sounded in an interview by Lew Dockstader in 1902, when he told a *Sun* reporter that the Negro had so advanced that the dialects and material for the old-fashioned take-offs were already lacking, and so the "Negro character" was being invalidated, bringing to a close one phase of Negro contribution to the American stage. The clichés and stereotypes persisted, of course, to this day, even among Negro performers. Yet during the latter days of the minstrel shows and the transition period of the nineties, when Negro dance and music in the theater seemed to be losing their identity, the real Negro art kept alive and re-entered through another channel—the social dance—as well as through a medium which we might call a type of highly specialized social entertainment.

We have seen that the Negro as entertainer and musician was long welcome in saloons and dance halls, even when the theaters were difficult for him to attain. This was equally true of bawdyhouses. And in such milieus, where there was no interest in imposing extraneous artistic standards, the Negro musician was empowered to create and perfect his own art. In dance halls and barrooms of New Orleans, St. Louis, Chicago, and the Barbary Coast small Negro orchestras, now with a full complement of instruments, further developed that music which was to sweep the world. Syncopated offbeats, which had been known to Western musicians for centuries, became a particular earmark associated almost exclusively with Afro-American music. The sense of timing and rhythmic "breaks" were equally a part of the dance. A great exhibition dance, the cakewalk, was also developed, with such superb theatrical potentialities that it served as a Negro re-entry permit to the stage. In the declining days of minstrelsy it was incorporated in finale "walk-arounds," an authentic American note at a period when imported operetta and extravaganza were eclipsing most of our indigenous theatrical forms.

Although handled with the bad taste of a supercolossal raree show, *Black America*, presented in 1894 by Buffalo Bill's impresario, Nate Salsbury, was a first effort to make some presentation of the Negro as a person. Salsbury, a kindly man, who had offered such

exotics as Pawnee Indians to the public, felt warranted in presenting the Negro in what was considered his native habitat—a plantation village. Large acreage, such as Ambrose Park in Brooklyn or the Huntington Avenue grounds in Boston, were made the site of a "Negro village," in which cabins and general living quarters were set up, with preacher and meetinghouse, mules, washtubs and hay wagons included, so that visitors might have occasion to see "the unconscious humor of darkies" (publicity release). Salsbury had gathered a choir of five hundred untrained voices, belonging, as a Boston newspaper touchingly explained, "to black men, women,

Home-Town Jazz Band. Ca. 1910.

61

and children, who themselves are devoid of culture." According to the *Illustrated American:* "They were recruited among the farm and mill hands of Georgia, Alabama, and Florida, with a view to securing perfect Negro types, rather than theatrical or musical talent. They arrived in New York ten days previous to the opening of the show, when a Negro minstrel stage manager took them in hand, and, building upon a foundation of inborn imitative aptitude, taught each what he or she was expected to do."

The spectacle itself had a brief introduction of "African tribal episodes and war dance," followed by interludes of song and dance, including a grand cakewalk contest. In every review it is immediately apparent that no audience was able to resist the beauty of Negro music. Again and again there is the same amazement at the beauty and technical ability of these untrained singers. Perhaps this admiration wrested from general audiences, in contrast to the select concert public of the Fisk Jubilee Singers, made this venture something of a triumph in spite of all the tawdry antics which were attendant upon it.

As the survey of Negro minstrelsy closes it might be well to recapitulate the outstanding companies, which were managed invariably by white impresarios. Charles Callender's troupe, later combined with Haverly's, was variously known as Callender's Georgia Minstrels, Callender's Consolidated Colored Minstrels, Callender's Consolidated Colored Spectacular Minstrels, and Callender's Monster Minstrel Festival; Haverly's Mastodon Genuine Colored Minstrels, Hicks and Sawyer's Consolidated Colored Minstrels, Lew Johnson's Georgia Minstrels, the Great Nonpareil Colored Troupe, Sprague's Original Minstrels, and Yarber's Colored Minstrels were among the more active companies. Billy Kersands was the only Negro who at any time seems to have conducted an extensive tour with his own company, although usually he was starred by Callender or Haverly. Among the notable Negro artists were Kersands and his son, an amazing dancer billed as the Infant Kersands, Billy Banks, the Hunn Brothers, the Hyers Sisters, Joseph Holcomb, the pedestal clog dancer, Billy Wilson, William Goss, and many other fine performers, the fraction who represented their people.

In 1897 a brilliant period for Negro entertainment, lasting something more than a brief decade, was inaugurated. It produced musical comedies or extravaganzas which assembled the talents of Will Marion Cook, Ernest Hogan, Will Vedry, Paul Laurence Dunbar, Aida Walker, Jesse Shipp, Bob Cole, and many others. The bright particular stars were the famous team of Williams and Walker.

The titles of many of these shows—*Senegambian Carnival, A Trip to Coontown, The Sons of Ham, In Dahomey, The Smart Set, In Bandanna Land, Abyssinia, Shoofly Regiment, Rufus Rastus*—have a close relationship to the minstrel-show stereotype, and the comedians wore the burnt cork and enormous painted mouth which were *de rigeur* for Negro comics. But the music and dances were unfettered by past conventions, and the raw elements of twentieth-century popular music acquired a style which would supersede the schottisches, waltzes, and cotillions of the nineteenth.

The transition did not come at the turn of the century, but with the First World War. It was a Negro composer, Ford Dabney, working with Vernon and Irene Castle, who set a general pattern both for social dance and theatrical forms. In its purest form hot music is essentially for listening. The great soloists of jazz, the improvisations of the jam session, demanded as much concentrated attention as any other piece of chamber music. Dabney, as accompanist, composer, and collaborator with the Castles, was initiator and popularizer of a new dance music.

Ford Dabney came to New York in 1900 with James Reese Europe, the noted band leader, to appear at the Ziegfeld Roof. From

1904 to 1907 he was official pianist to the President of Haiti. He knew at first hand the unusual rhythms of the tambours, and of heel beats against smooth earth. He listened to and remembered African ceremonial melodies, many of which the Haitians had preserved unchanged. On his return to New York he became one of that talented group of Negro musicians known as the Clef Club. In 1913 he met the Castles and worked with them until Vernon's untimely death. He was the alchemist who fused the divers jazz elements into a popular style.

Master Juba had imposed the Negro tradition on tap dancing. Ford Dabney, with his musical *Rang Tang*, consolidated Negro traditions theatrically as he had done socially. Negro music and dance, which had a virtuosity supported by native vitality, making them difficult to adapt, were finally integrated in the complete panorama of American music and dance.

Marie Bonfanti and partner in *The Black Crook*. 1866.

THE BLACK CROOK AND

THE WHITE FAWN

BY GEORGE FREEDLEY

NEW YORK was a large and sprawling metropolis in the year of 1866. A severe civil war had been fought, hundreds of thousands of lives had been lost through death, dislocation, or economic waste. A whole section of the country had been bled white, but New York was filled with the rich and poor to whom the war had meant too little. Money was flowing freely—the debacle was yet ahead. It is at times such as these that the full outpouring of the musical-dancing branch of the theater comes to its highest point in terms of lavishness and splendor. The public is delighted to pay the high prices such vast assemblages of talent, tons of gorgeous scenery, cartloads of sequined costumes, dozens of divas, and hundreds of coryphees require.

The most elaborate of all nineteenth-century musicals in America, and certainly the most enduring from the point of run (forty years in various forms with added "embellishments" which that age required) is *The Black Crook*. Thanks to the enormous publicity it received eighty years ago and the handsome Hoboken revival nineteen years ago, this is *one* musical of which even untutored audiences have heard.

Its history was a curious one and it owed its enormous success largely to accident and coincidence. Jarrett and Palmer, well-known theatrical managers, had imported from Europe a great deal of scenery which would perform tricks to dazzle the audience as well as a certain number of well-known artistes for a production of *La Biche au Bois*. The contracts had been signed and the scenery commissioned during the season of 1865-66 with the intention of launching it at the Academy of Music on East Fourteenth Street, then the center of the Rialto. On the night of May 21, however, immediately following the performance of the opera *La Juive*, a fire broke out which very nearly trapped some of the theater's employees who were still in the building. By one-thirty A.M. the entire interior of this handsome and popular opera house was destroyed. It was too late for Jarrett and Palmer to cancel their production, but they had no playhouse in which to house it and it would take months to reconstruct their burned-out theater. It was then that the idea of selling the scenery and the contracts of the dancers to William Wheatley, proprietor of the famous Niblo's Garden, occurred to them.

Wheatley had in his possession a completely ridiculous melodrama by Charles M. Barras, known as *The Black Crook*. "Surely," he thought, "if I use this as a framework for the ballet-pantomime for which I have the scenery, I'll have a piece that will certainly arouse curiosity." So he set to work to remodel the backstage space at Niblo's. This was a tremendous task which was extremely expensive. *The New York Times* for September 3, 1866, stated:

NIBLO'S GARDEN—MR. WHEATLEY announces that he has deferred the reopening of his theater until the 10th inst. The wonderful changes behind the footlights render this a necessity. Such a stage as he has built was never seen before in this country. Every board slides on grooves and can be taken up, pushed down or slid out at will. The entire stage may be taken away; traps can be introduced at any part at any time, and the great depth of the cellar below renders the sinking of entire scenes a matter of simple machinery. Very much has been written about the new piece by BARRAS, which Mr. WHEATLEY will produce next Monday, but generally in proportion to their positiveness has been the erroneousness of their statements. *The Black Crook* is not a piece whose success in Paris has been the talk of the *salons*, nor is it a piece whose previous production anywhere justified Mr. WHEATLEY in anticipating a long run and great profit here. It is simply an entirely new and original play written by Mr. BARRAS, of whom Mr. WHEATLEY has purchased the right to produce it. In it he will introduce certain startling transformations and elegant scenes with brilliant effects, purchased by the Messrs. JARRETT AND PALMER across the water; also the ballet troupe whose *première danseuse* is bewitchingly beautiful and exceedingly graceful. In consequence of the immensity of labor required for the perfection of the transformation and the incantation scenes, the opening night has been adjourned from this until next Monday evening. The final scene in the third act, representing a coral grotto, introduces a new feature in scenic painting, the designs being raised and embossed on the canvas. This scene introduces the Costa ballet troupe. C. H. MORTON, E. B. HOLMES, G. C. BONIFACE, ROSE MORTON (a London importation), Mr. BLAISDELL, MARY WELLS, G. ATKINS (from London), and ANNIE KEMP (late of London) are in the cast of the new piece. To give

our readers some idea of what it will cost to bring out this piece we will enumerate a few items: Digging cellar and alteration in stage, $5,000; labor of fifty men $6,400; machinery, properties, scenery, dresses, etc., purchased in London, $3,000; transportation, amounting to 110 tons, $500; properties, wardrobes, etc., purchased here, $1,000; scenery and salaries of artists, $3,000. Besides this, there is the advance money to artists brought from Europe, transportation and salaries since they landed here, amounting to over $7,000, making a total outlay of over $25,000 before the piece is performed. The confidence evinced by Mr. WHEATLEY in this attraction would seem to guarantee to the public an entertainment as absolute as it certainly will be novel.

Was it any wonder that New York was excited? It was rumored that the chorus girls and dancers were to be nearly nude. Such ladies as were willing to risk something of their reputation to view this edifying spectacle wore long veils to conceal their identity. That the naked faces of their escorts gave some clue as to who they were doesn't seem to have occurred to them when they assembled on the hot night of September 12 at Niblo's.

The bill announcing the opening had this to say about the ballet:

THE BLACK CROOK

the sole right of which production has been purchased by Mr. Wheatley, for New York and its vicinity. Mr. Wheatley is likewise happy in having entered into arrangements with Messrs. Jarrett & Palmer for the introduction of their

GREAT PARISIENNE BALLET TROUPE under the direction of the famed Maître de Ballet, SIGNOR DAVID COSTA (from the Grand Opera, Paris).

PREMIER DANSEURS ASSOLUTE

MLLE. MARIE BONFANTI, from the Grand Opera, Paris and Covent Garden Theatre, London.

MLLE. RITA SANGALLI, from the Grand Opera, Berlin, and Her Majesty's Theatre, London.

Their first appearance in America

FIRST PREMIER AND SOLOIST

MLLE. BETTY REGAL, from the Grand Opera, Paris.

Her first appearance in America.

SECOND PREMIERS AND SOLOISTS

Mlle. Louise Mazzeri, Mlle. Giovanna Mazzeri,
 " Giuseppi, " Amele Zuccoli,
 " Lusardi, " Eugenie Zuccoli,
 " Marie Duclos, " Helene Duclos,
  from Berlin, Milan, Paris, and London.

CORYPHEES

Mlle. E. Regal, Mlle. Gabrielle,
 " Amande, " Irban,
 " Nathalie, " Marie,
 " Doche, " Helene,
 " Lacroix, " Delval,

 " Portois, " Bertha,
 " Chereri, " L. Portois,
 " Artois, " Centbertrand
 " Elise, " H. Delval,
 " Duval, " Paulina,

  from Paris, London, and Berlin.

Their first appearances in America

and

FIFTY AUXILIARY LADIES

selected from the principal theatres of London, and America.

What makes *The Black Crook* of interest to us, of course, is this celebrated ballet under the direction of David Costa.

The description of the opening night which appeared in the celebrated *Tribune* of New

The Black Crook. Lithograph. 1865.

Sheet music cover of *The Black Crook* waltzes. The central figure is Marie Bonfanti.

York has frequently been quoted and must be familiar to some through Odell's great *Annals of the New York Stage,* but for the purposes of this collection of contemporary accounts, it will bear repeating once more:

Monday, September 17, 1866: THE BLACK CROOK AT NIBLO'S GARDEN. Niblo's Garden opened in a literal blaze of glory on Wednesday evening. The audience assembled on that occasion was so large that it filled the house in every part, overflowed into the lobbies and in the shape of frequent and large detachments, extended to the street and pervaded the neighborhood. Great enthusiasm prevailed before the curtain and great excitement behind it. A livelier scene than was thus presented could not well be imagined. *The Black Crook* was played by easy stages from 7¾ o'clock until 1¼. Most of the auditors remained until the gorgeous end. Hopes were entertained at one time that the performance would last until the merry breakfast bell should "Wake the snorting (sic) citizens." But these proved fallacious. By dint of great effort on the part of Mr. Wheatley and the mechanics, *The Black Crook* was at length played through; and a patient multitude, dazed and delighted, went to brief dreams of fairyland. It takes time to digest so much radiance, and we have not, therefore, been in haste to describe this extraordinary drama. Having swallowed the rainbows, however, it is now our very pleasant duty to say that they are very good to take. The scenery is magnificent; the ballet is beautiful; the drama is—rubbish. There is always a bitter drop in the sweetest cup, a fly in the richest ointment. Mr. Barras' drama is the bitter drop and the superfluous fly in this instance. Several very fine names are applied to *The Black Crook* in the bill of the play. It is called "grand," "romantic," "magical," "spectacular," and "original." To approach such a production in any other than a spirit of reverential awe, is, perhaps, to fail in proper respect for genius. Mr. Barras is understood to have devoted several of the ripest years of his scholastic life to this stupendous drama. Awe is a spirit that cannot be summoned as easily as Zamiel. Besides, we have read Lord Byron's *Manfred* and Goethe's *Faust,* and Hoffman's stories, and even Mr. Reynold's *Romance of Secret Tribunals.* Then, too, we have seen so many spectacles, in which the fairies war on the demons, and conquer for love's sake and in the holy name of virtue! Mr. Barras, an old reader and an old actor, has picked up a great many literary and theatrical properties, in his time, and they have been more or less useful to him, we dare say; but we must remember that the fields of literature are open to all gleaners, and hence that plenty of people will infallibly recognize Mr. Barras' properties. To call *The Black Crook* "original" is merely to trifle with intelligence. Herein, for example, we encounter our venerable and decrepit friend, the Alchymist, who wants to live forever, and is perfectly willing to give not only his own soul to the Devil, but also every other soul he can possibly send to Avernus. Here, too, is the humble youth, torn from his peasant maid and shut up in the "lowest Cell," ha! ha! by the Baron, cruel and bold. And then the Fiend's minister The Alchymist, surnamed "The Black Crook," is on hand to release him and send him on the road to avarice, vengeance, and perdition. Here are the old manorial or baronial servitors, the red-nosed steward and the high-capped dame; and along with them comes the arch and piquant little village maid, who sings a song, and smiles, and shows her pretty ankles to the sheepish swains. There are the fairies, too, and demons; and in the upshot, of course, the former conquers the latter, and the parted lovers are joined in happiness, and the Baron bold is run through his bold bosy, and the Fiend is cheated of his prey, and the Black Crook is removed through a dreadful hole in the earth, to a region of great heat and many dragons. And that Mr. Barras calls an original drama! For the construction of it, we can only say that the literary materials, stage business, etc., appear to have been put into an intellectual bag and vigorously shaken up together. And there we leave the high dramatic theme. There was, in fact, no pretense of a drama in this instance; or, if there was, almost any old spectacle would have been preferable to *The Black Crook.* All that was needed was a medium for the presentation of several gorgeous scenes, and a large number of female legs; and it was only necessary that the medium should not be tedious. And this brings us to the real merits

Poster for traveling companies of *The Black Crook.*

of the entertainment that is now nightly offered at Niblo's Garden, and, we presume, will be nightly offered there for many weeks to come. Some of the most perfect and admirable pieces of scenery that have ever been exhibited upon the stage are employed in the exhibition of this piece. The best one, we think, from an artistic point of view, is that which closes the second act. A vast grotto is herein presented, extending into an almost measureless perspective. Stalactites descend from the arched roof. A tranquil and lovely lake reflects the golden glories that span it like a vast sky. In every direction one sees the bright sheen or the dull richness of massy gold. Beautiful fairies, too, are herein assembled—the sprites of the ballet, who make the scene luxuriant with their beauty. There is not so much stormy power

in this scene as there is in Mr. R. Smith's *Der Freischutz* combination of horrors, which closes the first act; but it is a successful work in a higher region of art. Both these scenes will bear study. They are not common efforts. They evince rare poetic sensibility and even imagination. Everybody ought to see them. The last scene in the play, however, will dazzle and impress to an even greater degree, by its lavish richness and barbaric splendor. All that gold, silver, and gems and lights and women's beauty can contribute to fascinate the eye and charm the senses is gathered up in this gorgeous spectacle. Its luster grows as we gaze, and deepens and widens, till the effect is almost painful. One by one, curtains of mist ascend and drift away. Silver couches, on which the fairies loll in negligent grace, ascend and descend amid a silver whirl. From the clouds droop gilded chariots and the white forms of angels. It is a very beautiful pageant. The brothers Drew of London devised this scene and they certainly merit great praise. Among the lesser scenes, two bits of painting are especially remarkable; one is "A Wild Pass in the Hartz Mountains," painted by Mr. D. A. Strong; the other is Mr. Hayes's "Valley at the Foot of the Hartz Mountain." But all the scenes are excellent; and though we cannot say that anything has been done for the dramatic art, by the production of *The Black Crook*, we heartily testify

that Scenic Art has never, within our knowledge, been so amply and splendidly exemplified. In respect to the Ballet, it is the most complete troupe of the kind that has been seen in this country. To discriminate between the dancers would be as difficult as to distinguish one rose from another amid a wilderness of roses. But if either be more fascinating than another, it is Mlle. Rigl. The greater share of applause on Wednesday, fell to the lot of Mlle. Sangalli. Marie Bonfanti, too, was welcomed with cordial enthusiasm. We have not space to descant upon the beauties that were so liberally revealed on the occasion—nor is there

Poster for a revival of
The Black Crook.

need. The town will take care to see for itself what treasures of grace Messrs. Jarrett & Palmer have lured from the opera houses of Europe. Mr. Costa, however, is to be especially congratulated on his directorship of the Ballet. There was little acting in the spectacle to detain the critical pen. Mr. Burnett and Miss Wells mainly contributed what there was. Miss Milly Cavendish, one of the new players, made a very pleasing impression, and is unquestionably destined to achieve a high position among the "chamber-maids" of the local stage. *The Black Crook* will be condensed as its runs proceed and thus will pass off more rapidly and pleasantly. The theatre wears a very bright and cheerful aspect and Mr. Wheatley com-(sic) his fall season "with earnest of success."

This and the other accounts of the famous first night which lasted all but indefinitely must rouse memories from those who used to see the "openings" of Florenz Ziegfeld's *Fol-*

"THE WHITE FAWN."

Entered according to Act of Congress, in the year 1868, by J. GURNEY & SON, in the Clerk's Office of the District Court of the United States, for the Southern District of New York.

J. Gurney & Son 707 Broadway N.Y.

Josephine Invernezzi.

lies out of town when he dress-rehearsed into the small hours of morning in front of an audience on the long-suffering road. Those who journeyed to the Hoboken revival of *The Black Crook* [1] in 1929 and lived to tell the tale will horrify you with its one-thirty A.M. curtain if you barely mention it. Christopher Morley, Cleon Throckmorton, and Harry Wagstaff Gribble made every effort to reproduce the great musical spectacle of the sixties and succeeded even beyond their fondest dreams in this respect at least. Persons present at the original opening were invited back, perhaps to repeat their previous experiment, and to drink Hoboken's beer in the darkest days of prohibition. Veils were no longer necessary for the ladies but few of them felt up to the trip across the Hudson.

Four days earlier than the *Tribune*, *The New York Times*, which still prides itself on

Cherabelli.

"THE WHITE FAWN."

Entered according to Act of Congress, in the year 1868, by J. GURNEY & SON, in the Clerk's Office of the District Court of the United States, for the Southern District of New York.

J. Gurney & Son   707 Broadway N.Y.

Electrotype cut of *The White Fawn*—The Enchanted Lake Scene.

its promptness in reporting (now through the good offices of the celebrated Sam Zolotow who frequently refers to himself as Tecumseh), carried a glowing account of the fabulous opening.

NIBLO'S GARDEN—Mr. WHEATLEY opened his beautiful theatre last night after a prolonged recess, during which the house has been cleaned, redecorated, regilded, and put in apple-pie order. A new stage, of the most modern and approved construction, has been made at great expense, and a vast amount of new scenery procured. The house was densely packed with a critical and appreciative audience, additional interest being imparted to the opening with the announcement of a new and original spectacular drama entitled *The Black Crook*.

The Black Crook is a story of sorcery, demonism, and wickedness generally, in which one Hertzog (Mr. MORTON), a deformed and illnatured, but very learned, man, grows desperate in spirit, makes a compact with Zamiel or Satan, by which he agrees to win over to perdition one soul for each year of life to be granted to him, the account to be settled on the last day of the year, before the clock strikes midnight. The lover-hero, Rodolphe, is enamored of Amina; he is a poor painter—she a rural beauty. Count Wolfenstein sees her, and by force of feudal power takes her for himself, locking her lover in a dungeon. The Black Crook in search of a soul for his next New Year, visits Rodolphe, tells him of a cave of gold in the forest, also that his love Amina is noble, and induces him to go in search of the treasure. On the way Rodolphe sees a dove pursued by a serpent, kills the reptile and saves the bird, who proves to be the Fairy Queen Stalacta. She exposes Hertzog's trick, and assists Rodolphe. The reader will now readily see that the Count is slain, Amina rescued and married to Rodolphe, and the Black Crook (Hertzog) himself very justly sent to the Devil, instead of sending the gay young lover.

The house was fairly packed with a mass of humanity, exceeding the crush at any time, even in that house of crushes. The first act is trashy, but affords ample scope for fine spectacular display, and introduces the English and French Ballet troupes, who were received with enthusiasm. Mlle. BONFANTI, the *première danseuse* (sic), is as light as a feather, and exceedingly graceful. She, with Mlle. SANGALLI and Mlle. RIGL, was encored twice during the *Pas de Fleurs*. The *Pas de Sabot* is also a charming arrangement, in which Mlle. ROSI DELVAL received the well-merited applause of the house. Miss MILLY CAVENDISH (Carline) was encored in her song of "The Naughty Men." The act closed with a grand incantation scene laid in a wild glen, whose weird and unholy look was quite apropos to the devilish business there enacted. The curtain went down on the second act at 10:45 o'clock. The features of this act were the dances held in the gorgeous grotto of Stalacta. Mlle. SANGALLI and the full ballet appeared in the *Pas de Naiad*, after which came the ballet success of the night, the witching *Pas de Demons*, in which the demons, who wear no clothes to speak of, so gracefully and prettily disported as to draw forth thunders of applause. No similar exhibition has been made on an American stage that we remember, certainly none where such a combination of youth, grace, beauty, and *elan* was found. The curtain was rung up three times at the close of this act, in compliance with peremptory demands of the house. The late hour not far from morning at which *The Black Crook* closed, prevents a further notice of its merits. Mr. WHEATLEY, who has made an actual outlay of not far from $50,000 in preparation of the piece, is to be congratulated upon its success. It will be repeated every night, and is well worth seeing, as it is decidedly the event of this spectacular age.

In those days managers frequently added to their entertainment so as to attract repeaters

as well as new audiences. Today producers frequently trim their shows to provide a lower operating cost but very rarely expand or add new attractions. Now many people act on the assumption that the original notices are the only ones that count. There is a certain justification for this, of course, perhaps because more people pay attention to what the critics say than they used to do. It is naturally flattering to the reviewers, but it dumps on their shoulders a terrific financial responsibility which a mere shrug does not remove. Too often one hears it said that the monetary loss of the producer, the deprivation of jobs to actors and technical personnel is of no concern to the newspaperman termed critic by his publisher. Legally and literally this is true, but for that reason alone if for no other, he must be deaf and blind to the first-night chit-chat which has a tendency toward damning a show in favor of a wisecrack—bon mots are not made in this age. Or perhaps we don't recognize them.

At any rate Mr. Wheatley did embellish *The Black Crook* as the *New York Daily Tribune* recorded in its issue of May 28, 1867:

NEW YORK DAILY TRIBUNE
May 28, 1867

NIBLO'S GARDEN—*The Black Crook* Renewed.

Those who are familiar with the life of Dr. Johnson know why the good old gentleman refused to continue his visits to the green room of his friend David Garrick's theater. He was frank enough to state the precise reason. If men, nowadays, were as squeamish as the old scholar was, the ballet at Niblo's Garden would attract but small audiences. Tastes differ, however, and so Niblo's Garden is crowded nightly. Last evening it was packed in every part. *The Black Crook* was presented on this occasion, with a new setting, and a very alluring spectacle it was. New dancers appeared, nearly all the costumes were new, and one new scene of singular brilliancy was introduced, that, namely, of the ballroom. It is composed of three vistas, the central one being an arch. The roof is wrought in imitation of fretted gold. On the right are four statue-pillars, and the same on the left. The arch is supported by six four-fold pillars, made of crystal spokes, and encircled with jeweled bands of gold. Statues supporting sconces surrounded each pillar. A central chandelier dispenses light from above. The scene is full of splendor. Of the dances that are danced hereon we can only speak at risk of exhausting our stock of adjectives. Mr. Richard Marston and Mr. Froude, the scenic artist and the machinist, were called out and suitably applauded for this fine work of scenic art. Some delay was made in the course of the fourth act, which the stage manager, Mr. Vincent, explained by a mirthful truism to the effect that the ladies of the ballet "were not dressed," but the patience of the audience was finally rewarded by a gorgeous spectacle. The masquerade scene contained many novelties, of a fanciful and comic character. A balloon and man was one. The final "transformation scene" has been revamped and made even more effective than before. Of the play—*The Black Crook*, that is—little remains; but that little is amply sufficient. Mr. Burnett and Miss Mary Wells are still in the cast, and still remind us that the art of acting has not wholly departed from Niblo's Garden. We cannot here speak on the new dancers, for lack of time and space—and perhaps that is as well. The old favorites, Bonfanti, Sangelli, and Regal, still wear their laurels, notwithstanding the *corps de ballet* has been strongly reinforced. Mr. Dodworth contributed last evening largely to the enjoyment of the audience by his appropriate and pleasing music. The performance terminated at a late hour, but the spectators remained, patient and apparently delighted, till the fall of the final curtain.

Five months later *The New York Times* for October 22 was speaking of further additions which pleased them enormously:

Some cheerful additions were made to *The Black Crook* last evening. This spectacle which, like the Summer rose, is refreshed by every dew that touches it, while the dew itself, though it glistens but a moment and disappears, is never missed, receives new scenes and new people, and absorbs them or casts them off for others without a fluctuation in attractiveness or popularity. Mlle. BILLON, who danced for the first time in the ballet of the ballroom last night, is inexpressibly airy. Her bounds are marvelous, and have a grace which is beyond the mere gymnastic merit which secured her the applause of the crowd. She is the most formidable rival Mlle. BONFANTI has yet had, and is one of the easiest dancers now in this City, which is so well supplied with terpsichorean marvels. M. VAN HAMME, who dances with Mlle. BILLON, resembles a gentleman whom the Ravels introduced here, and name, face, and style agreeing, we take him to be the same. His peculiarity is revolution. Mexico alone can equal M. VAN HAMME in the number and variety of his revolutions. The most entertaining novelty introduced in the spectacle last evening, however, was the baby ballet—a march of intricate military evolutions performed by over a hundred youngsters, varying in height from 35 to 45 inches. These military marches are growing to be great bores, and only the precocity of performers makes the present one interesting—but interesting it certainly is. The infant RAVEL who leads the army and dances the *Pas de Militaire*, is a wonder for his inches, and the completeness of the entire performance must add greatly to the attractiveness of *The Black Crook*. After this "Ballet" nothing ought to surprise us, and if next year Mssrs. PALMER & WHEATLEY would chance to announce that 150 babies of six months old, after undergoing some peculiar process of forcing, are to appear in an original piece composed expressly for them by a brother or sister baby, and that a baby is to take Mr. MOLLENHAUER's baton, and the whole entertainment is to be produced under the special direction of an infant stage manager, there will be nothing left to do but to believe the advertisement and rush to see the prodigies. Although a first night, there were few "hitches" last evening, and the children were perfect.

The same day the *Tribune* in the midst of its admiration of "the bewildering forest of female legs" was able to review the piece in this fashion:

NEW FEATURES IN THE BLACK CROOK: Just as it is necessary once in a while for the clergyman to preach about faith and works, so it is necessary once in a while for the journalist to write about *The Black Crook*. The famous spectacle has become an established feature in the world of local amusement. Borne on the sturdy and handsome legs of the dancers it has traveled a long ways, and we do not doubt that it will travel a good deal further yet. It is now in its second year. It has been seen by millions of persons. Children cry for it. Countrymen coming to town clamor for it, and will not be comforted unless they see it. The rural visitor, in fact, divides his time between Niblo's Garden and Trinity Church, and he certainly sees a good deal at both places. In respect to the manifold charms of *The Black Crook* we have, fortunately, no occasion to be prolix. To enumerate them all would be to fill this sheet with spangles. Its new beauties, howbeit, merit particular mention. We saw the great pageant last night and thus are enabled to describe it. The piece in general passed off very smoothly. There was, indeed, as there always is, a little too much Ballet in the second act; and there was a painfully long "wait" between acts second and third. This was all that marred the pleasure of the occasion—and this as far as the wait is concerned is not likely to occur again. As to the dancing—people in general can scarcely see too much of it. Marie Bonfanti's admirers, in particular, never seem to tire of watching and applauding her amazingly agile and delightfully graceful capers. She was as cordially applauded last night, and as lavishly showered with bouquets, as at the first when her triumph was fresh. And, certainly, there is something wonderfully vital in her style of dancing. She is all alive and she is uncommonly fruitful of beautiful poses and winning ways. The beautiful picture that ends the second act—and certainly, it is very brilliant—was likewise most heartily applauded. We are glad to notice, also, that Mr. Atkin's fun did not miss its reward. This young actor has a thankless part,—as who has not, for that matter, who acts in *The Black Crook?*—and he makes the most of it by earnest endeavor and by skillful by-play. It was pleasant, also, to see that so good an actress as Miss Mary Wells was recognized and applauded amid the sunrise sky

of gorgeous scenery and the bewildering forest of female legs. But we linger in coming to Hecuba, and that is a fault. Hecuba is in the third act. Mlle. Billon, M. Van Hamme, La Petite Ravel, La Guarde Impériale—this act introduces them all. Mlle. Billon made a hit at once. She is a blonde, is pretty, is beautifully formed, and is one of the most agile and elastic human beings whom we have ever seen. Not being learned in the technicalities of dancing we cannot speak critically concerning the lady's accomplishments but she charmed everybody by a certain indefinable dash abandonment, a kind of "brandy-punchy" volatility, as Dr. Holmes might say, which learning and wit would fail to realize. Her Hungarian dance was the gem of her performance, and it struck us that there was much more mind in it than there is in dance in general. The M. Van Hamme proves to be an old acquaintance. He has been seen here before, and much admired. It is he who turns three times in the air—a manifestly difficult achievement before alighting—and he did so last night amid the enthusiastic plaudits of the vast multitude. The Imperial Guard was a great success. The little fellows have been splendidly trained and their evolutions, at once skillful and amusing, won cordial applause, and stimulated the audience to exceeding merriment. La Petit Ravel is, for a four-year-old, a wonderful child. His performance was "encored," and deserved the compliment. The creature could scarcely manage to carry off his gun and the bouquets that were thrown to him. In the last act of the spectacle, great amount of mirth was made by the mechanical donkey—and need we say—the great transformation scene, which is as splendid as ever, was rapturously applauded. In one word, *The Black Crook* has lost none of its beauty, but has gained new ones, and so its new lease on popularity is assured. Mr. Wheatley, the manager, who has but lately returned from Paris was in the audience last night. This evening the performance of *The Black Crook* will be attended, among others, by the Boston Fusillers, in full uniform, and Gilmore's Band. There will be a Matinee on Saturday, at one o'clock.

The Black Crook finally closed in January, 1868. Niblo's stayed empty only one week during which the producers readied the stage

for their own imitation of their success, *The White Fawn.* This play by James Mortimer, fared little better as a play than its predecessor, but the ballet again was a great hit. About the dancers the review said:

NEW YORK TIMES

JANUARY 20, 1868

THE WHITE FAWN AT NIBLO'S

* * *

The best scene, because the most beautiful in color and the most poetic in sentiment, is Sachetti's *Enchanted Lake,* one of the purest and most graceful dances that have ever been seen on the local stage. The comic element in the piece is supplied by a procession of fishes—which evinces great skill on the part of the costumers— and by a pantomime exhibition by the Hemming Brothers and Amy Bennett from London. The pantomime troupe, however, has as yet, given no evidence of particular cleverness. Better performers of this class have been seen at the Circus, at Barnum's, and in the Bowery. The clown is not to be mentioned in the same day with Mr. Fox. Of the "Transformation Scene" we must, of course, reserve description—as the "Bright Realms of the Dragon-Fly" have not yet been burst upon the public gaze. As to the Ballet, it appears to be a very good one, the legs are very numerous, and some of them are beautiful, and most of the young ladies are scant of apparel—a lack, however, which does not seem to occasion poignant regret, either in their own gentle bosoms or in the more rugged breasts of their manly admirers. Bonfanti, Sohike, and Billon are the reigning stars. Most of the other lovely innocents remain nameless, but blaze in groups of sixteen, divided according to nationality. Thus the connoisseurs of dancing and of feminine beauty may delight his mighty mind by subtle discrimination betwixt the German, the English, the Italian, the Spanish, and the American. France, we believe, is sternly ruled out of the miscellaneous Ballet, in order to make its descriptive epithet of "Parisian" more distinctly appropriate. We have no art to reckon the several outbursts of joy wherewith the various efforts of the dancing girls have been greeted by an appreciative public. Enough to say that the dance went on till it seemed as though it would never stop and that joy was unconfined. The Ballet is the main thing; and, as already intimated, the spectacle of an enlightened populace worshipping at this gentle shrine is the most edifying thing in the world, and calculated greatly to exalt one's ideals of the perfectibility of human nature. Once and once only, in the course of the representation the White Fawn, borne in on a shutter, distracted public regard for a brief moment from the mazy dance. A slight clue to the plot was seen in this incident. A princess is changed into a white fawn, by day, becomes a woman again by night. Good and evil fairies contend over the fate of this damsel and, of course, the good fairies triumph in the long run—or, rather, in the long dance—and all is made right in the Realms of the Dragon-Fly. No spectator is likely, though, to make any strenuous endeavor to follow out the plot of *The White Fawn.* It is but a pretext for the dancers, who are all in all, and whose reign is likely to be long in the land (and broad too) while grass grows and rivers run and beauty maintains its magic spell o'er hearts—and pockets.

Portrait of Allen Dodworth. 1847. Montage by Joseph Cornell.

THE DODWORTH FAMILY

AND BALLROOM DANCING

IN NEW YORK

BY ROSETTA O'NEILL

AMONG THE TREASURED MEMORIES of thousands of old New Yorkers are the happy days at Dodworth's—the famous "Dancing Academy" which was such a vital factor in the social development of the city. It was born about a hundred years ago on the crest of a social revolution, the cultural awakening of the country, and passed away on another great social revolution, the Jazz Age.

But for all its importance, it has been singularly slighted in the histories and reference books. When it is mentioned at all in these works it is generally in an oblique way as chronicling the musical activities of the Dodworth family or as housing its literary soirees. The dancing activities of the family are passed over perfunctorily. Even Allen Dodworth, the chief dancing member of the family, has been celebrated principally as a founder and first treasurer of the New York Philharmonic Society and one of its first violinists, though his courageous and far-seeing attitude toward the dance as a social force might well be considered as of more moment.

His book called *Dancing*, published by Harpers in 1885, is a standard work, and besides making delightful reading today is still regarded by many specialists as the best and broadest book on social dancing to have been published in America. He had been teaching fifty years when it was written, and it can accordingly be taken as the substantial and considered summing up of the things he had fought for and believed in. Perhaps the full title of the book gives a tidy epitome of what these things were and of why Allen Dodworth is a figure of importance in the history of dancing hereabouts. It is called *Dancing and Its Relation to Education and Social Life, with a New Method of Instruction, Including a Complete Guide to the Cotillion (German) with 250 Figures.* None of this involved wording is irrelevant or unimportant. He battled with the world on the issue of dancing as a medium of education and cultivated behavior, including health, morals, and manners. He demanded good teaching, consisting of fundamentals and not merely of coaching in the transitory fads of the ballroom, and he strongly advocated the setting up of a standard of practice. If these things still seem to be wanting in accomplishment today, what must their advocacy have meant in 1835 when Dodworth first began to champion them!

It is true that he was not the only reformer in the dance field even in his own time; others had written books on both the current dances and the subject of good manners before he did. Most of them followed largely the same pattern: first, a chapter on the history of dancing with much space devoted to a defense of the practice; second, many pages on manners in general besides the toilette and the etiquette of the ballroom; third, a description of the dances of the day. This last department Dodworth was quick to discount as in part copied from English books, and in part merely incorrect. The hints on personal behavior, however, are not a little amusing, as when the gentleman is instructed not to dance without removing his hat, not to make passes at his partner, and not to spit on the floor. Mrs. John Farrar's *The Young Lady's Friend* (Boston, 1838) contains a stern reprimand on the current affectation of society girls for "jiggling."

"Some girls," she wrote, "have a trick of jiggling their bodies (I am obliged to coin a word to describe it); they shake all over, as if they were hung on spiral wires, like geese in a Dutch toy shop; than which, nothing can be more ungraceful, or unmeaning. It robs a lady of all dignity, and makes her appear trifling and insignificant. Some do it only on entering a room, others do it every time they are introduced to anybody, and whenever they begin to talk to anyone. It must have originated in embarrassment, and a desire to do something without knowing exactly what; and being adopted by some popular belle, it became, at one time, a fashion in New York, and spread thence to other cities."

These books go back to the beginning of the nineteenth century. Elias Howe's *Ball-Room Hand-Book* containing instructions on asking a lady to dance, etc., *Modern Dancing* by L. de Garmo Brookes, and *Dance of Society* by Wm. B. De Garmo were perhaps the best of the latter-day ones. All the magazines, especially *Godey's Lady's Book,* carried articles on dancing, etiquette, and music as regular features. But Dodworth's book was the first real textbook, based on a system of teaching, containing details of method, diagrams, and musical phrases with movements clearly marked. It would be hard to deny, also, that its point of view is more solid and more aware of the world than anything that preceded it.

It was clearly a grand gesture for him to write it, for he had little respect for the average dancing teacher, and had consistently refused to give lessons even to those of his own pupils who thought they would like to teach. His standards for the dancing master were too high to admit every applicant who might happen along. Only a few trusted friends in other cities, such as Mrs. Carrie Spink of Providence, were allowed to use his system of teaching and were taught the new dances as he introduced them to his classes. The system itself was strongly opposed in the field at large, and apparently he protected it from attack by keeping it in safe hands.

Before we can fully understand why such an attitude as his was of more than passing importance and why his successful institutionalizing of it constituted a valuable contribution to American culture, it is necessary to review a bit of social history which touches on the position of the dance.

Dancing had played an important part in the social life of the colonies; even in New England, in spite of opinion to the contrary, people had danced gaily and often, however the elders may have fulminated against it. But after the Revolution, great changes took place in the public mind. Dancing, along with other simple diversions, began to fall under the ban, not alone, as is frequently maintained, because of the religious bias of Puritanism, but to a far greater extent because of the rising worship of commercialism.

"In the rapid development of the continent

Cover to the sheet music of the "Gift Polka." 1852.

which continued through nearly the whole of the nineteenth century," says Watson's Annals, after having put the usual onus upon the Puritans, "devotion to business had been the test of manhood. The sports and amusements which were once followed by all ages and classes had been uniformly considered as degrading and immoral and not allowable to even people of wealth and leisure who respected the opinion of the community."

Dancing, to be sure, did not disappear from the scene, but it headed the list of pastimes that were frowned upon. The contradances and quadrilles (or cotillions as they were incorrectly called) were tolerated, and as time went on, a few brave or bold souls danced the gallopade (which one critic called "the frantic hurley-burley") and the wicked waltz, "the devil's greatest invention."

With the introduction of the polka (about 1840), however, all barriers were broken down and round dancing became the rage. Coming as it did upon a field not too well prepared by way of background, it was mostly a hilarious hop-skip-slide and was not accompanied by the social graces of European society. This was a young republic and there had been little time to learn good manners or fine motion; and besides, even then, were we not being original? In that greatest of dance crazes which got itself known as The Polka Mania, New Yorkers, rich and poor, regardless of public opinion or how little they knew of dancing, joined in and danced and danced and danced.

Those who opposed dancing—and they were still many—took this opportunity to voice their strenuous disapproval, and now with

The Dodworth Family: Thomas J., Charles, Harvey, Allen, and Thomas J. Dodworth, Senior. Ca. 1840.

some fairly sound support under their arguments. Books and sermons denounced dancing with renewed vigor, and even the newspapers contributed in a rather large way to the campaign. The "intellectual" objections are well illustrated in the following quotation from Wilkinson's *Dance of Modern Society:* "SOCIAL AMUSEMENTS—It would be hard to deny it the name by which, with a MEPHISTOPHELIAN sort of pleasantry suspiciously its own, the dance has succeeded in getting itself currently called. But beyond a chance sermon or so each year I am not aware that anything in the form of a book has yet treated exclusively of a subject which, what with the talk that it occasions and the talk that it supersedes, displaces more conversation in so-called society than perhaps any other topic of human interest in the world."

Visitors from abroad criticized us most unkindly for our "barbaric customs" and especially the bad manners of our children. Mrs. Trollope said we had no manners at all, and while our young women were beautiful and had pretty feet, they did not know how to walk and were at a great disadvantage when dancing. Americans were very much hurt by this abuse, and quantities of writing on manners, morals, etiquette, and dancing began to appear not only as importations from abroad, but also as home products from Boston and Philadelphia.

Allen Dodworth's abandonment of his other activities in order to enter the list formally as champion of the dance can perhaps be considered as the full flowering of this twofold movement to put an end to vicious criticism and to remove its justification.

His own version of the history of the situation is perhaps lacking in the general perspective which is possible today, but it is eloquent, authoritative, and specific. In the introduction to his famous book, he gives a clear picture of the "French invasion" which followed the Revolution and which introduced, besides pianos and French pastries, an army of French dancing teachers.

"The first revolution," he wrote, "drove from France many persons of high rank, who took refuge in the larger cities of Europe and America, where their accomplishments could be made available in gaining a livelihood. Among the nobility, at that time, dancing was considered an important element in forming the carriage and manners of a lady or gentleman; consequently, great attention was given to the subject, and all were thoroughly educated in the art. In their days of adversity many had recourse to the teaching of this accomplishment. The stately manners, refined motions, and graceful dancing of these noblemen were reflected in their pupils, having great influence in forming their social manners. They were followed by another class, purposely educated as teachers of social dancing, who, having been under the instruction and influence of their predecessors, continued all their excellent methods. It must be observed that the teachings of both classes had a close relation to the training of those who were to move in private life; not so with a third class, who, having been educated for the ballet, were removed from these influences. They were at one time very popular as teachers, because of a general failure to apprehend the difference between ballet and social dancing, which is as wide as that between operatic and social singing, or the pantomime and conversational motions. The exercise required for these artists (for many were truly such) to gain the strength, endurance, and largeness of motion necessary in their department of dancing, in many cases, produced an excess of action unsuited to private life; they were consequently conspicuous at all times for exuberance of motion and manner, which was burlesqued in the well-known grotesque dancing master of the stage. To them is due the acceptance of the saying, 'He moves and has the manners of a dancing master.'"

This point, which is extremely well taken,

was one of the motivations for his undertaking to become a crusading dancing master. The advent of the round dance was another; and in this connection it is well to remember that the polka was not alone to blame, for he was teaching a good five years before that frisky item was introduced into European society.

The second barrel of his argument he fires at this phase of the local development:

"With the introduction of the waltz, galop, polka, and other round dances, a complete revolution in round dancing took place. These were so easily learned that education in motion was deemed unnecessary; simply to make

Extremely vulgar. Illustration from *Dancing*, by Allen Dodworth.

the motions required was quite sufficient, manner becoming entirely secondary. Many learned from one to the other, frequently transmitting their own mistakes. And as it is true that many of our choice plants and flowers, when left without continued cultivation, return to their simple forms—so it is with human beings; the grotesque is the original form of pleasure given by motion; and so to the grotesque we naturally return, unless sustained by education. The diminishing importance of the dancing lesson, as part of physical and moral education, was followed by a more serious loss to the world; for it

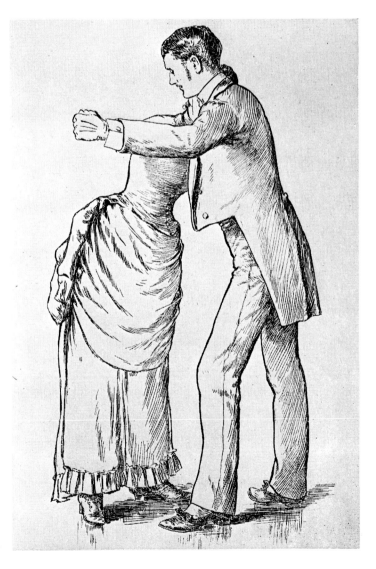

The lady's head too close, the extended arms and bad attitude of hand objectionable.

lowered the position of those who made the teaching of the art a vocation. In consequence, many who were fitted for it by nature, education, and social experience, were deterred from assuming its duties; and as the older teachers passed away, their places were taken by those who were neither by training nor education prepared for so responsible a position. Not having had the advantages of the teaching and association of the older ones, they were not aware of the proper nature of their duties; but they were able to waltz expertly, and the teaching of waltzes and a few other dances was all they believed to be

The proper way.

required from them; they were, therefore, simply dance teachers, not teachers of motion and manner, which is the definition of dancing master as the term was formerly understood. Conscious of their want of knowledge in regard to propriety of motion, they were ever ready to adopt the eccentricities introduced by the inexperienced young people in society, instead of giving direction to their judgment and taste."

His third and final score is made against the deteriorations which came in the wake of the polka:

"About the year 1840 the polka was taken

The extended arms, and the lady's hand grasping the gentleman's arm, are not in good taste.

from the peasants of Germany and adopted by the fashionable society of Paris. From Paris it was disseminated all over the civilised world, with consequences little anticipated at the time; for the introduction of this dance had a serious effect in lowering the respect formerly given to good motions and manners, for the following reasons:

"In Paris the rage to learn this dance became so general that Cellarius was compelled to employ many ballet girls to assist in teaching. This method became so very popular that other places were established, where this was offered as the chief attraction, not only in Paris, but in all the large cities of Europe. Subsequently places were opened in New York, multiplying rapidly in many of our large cities. The managers of these places were not masters of motion, but simply dance teachers, and had very questionable taste in their methods. The young women willing to be employed were naturally those to whom the small amount paid was of importance; they, therefore, exercised little, if any, improving influence upon those who practiced with them. But, being able to dance expertly, and always deeming it part of their duty to be as agreeable as possible to those who came to learn, they made the method very attractive at one time to our young men—the freedom of manners and absence of all attempts to practice the amenities of social life being to some natures enjoyable. Small rooms were generally used, so that the crowding and squeezing of the parlor were repeated, with surroundings not conducive to delicacy, to say the least. Many young men became very expert by this practice, but in gaining skill they lost the modesty and innocence that should accompany the pleasure.

"The bad influence, unfortunately, followed them to the drawing rooms of their friends; being expert, they were desirable partners, but the methods practiced in learning were communicated to their sisters and lady friends;

there was, in consequence, a deterioration in the general tone of motion and manner."

A more vivid and concise history of a major development in American social dancing probably does not exist in print.

Dodworth had ample opportunity to observe the things he was talking about, for since childhood he had been a member of his family's band and orchestra, quite the most fashionable orchestra of the day, which had given him entree into most of the ballrooms and private parties of the city. His taste and background made it impossible for him to stand by idly and see degeneration taking place in an art which he held in high regard.

Just where the dancing strain enters into his background is not clear, for he was the first of his family in this country to make a profession of it. A possible clue has been offered by Dorothy Lawton, the librarian of the New York Public Library's music branch, who reports that her mother was taught dancing in Sheffield, England, by a famous teacher named Dodworth, and it was from Sheffield that Allen Dodworth and his family came to America.

The family seems to have been primarily musical, and played a considerable part in New York's musical life in the days when that life was just beginning. Thomas Dodworth brought his four sons, Allen, Thomas, Charles, and Harvey, from their birthplace in Sheffield to New York in 1825, when Allen was eight years old.

Soon after the family landed in this country, they became members of a group known as the Independent Band which played at Castle Garden, and Mr. Dodworth obliged his boys to learn to play all the instruments in the band, as well as other instruments which were strictly orchestral. At eight Allen played the piccolo, by the time he was fifteen he was an expert trombonist, and at twenty-five he was in the first-violin section of the Philharmonic orchestra. His favorite instrument was the cornet, for which he invented a new key, and in his later years his favorite joy was to sit in his garden and play for the children of the neighborhood.

He had just reached the expert trombonist stage when the family, under his father's direction, founded the National Brass Band, which was a historic organization. It was the first band of its kind in the country, for the musical situation in 1832 was still most informally organized, and groups of musicians were inclined to come together quite casually and only for special occasions. Dodworth's Band, as it was popularly known practically from the beginning, was formal and efficient. Its first parade was at the head of a regiment called the Governor's Guard, with the musicians uniformed in buff and blue.

Long after Allen had concentrated on other matters, the band continued to function with unique distinction until the retirement in 1890 of Harvey Dodworth who had succeeded his father in its leadership fifty years before. It was the regimental band for a number of regiments over the years; it played at the inaugurations of Presidents Van Buren, Harrison, Polk, Tyler, Buchanan, Lincoln, Grant, Garfield, and Cleveland; it was a feature of college commencements and civic festivals all over the country, and played at the opening of the Erie Railroad, the completion of the Atlantic Cable, the famous tour of the Japanese mission, the Yorktown Centennial and the visit of Edward VII as Prince of Wales.

Harvey as leader made many changes in the form of the band. It was he who introduced reed instruments, the saxophone, the bass clarinet, and the BB-flat contrabass tuba to the military band, and invented the string rotary valve instruments. His was the first band to play Wagner and the classics. It was he who introduced the idea of giving band concerts in the park, the first one having been at City Hall Park. On the success of the experiment, an annual series was instituted in Central Park

and continued there for twenty-four years under his leadership.

Allen, even after dancing became his major concern, never lost his active interest in music. In the early days he had composed and arranged much of the music for the band, and for the orchestral form it assumed when, for concerts and balls, it replaced some of the heavy brasses with strings and woodwinds. He was a successful teacher of the violin, and played the instrument not only in the Philharmonic orchestra but for his own dancing classes, after the manner of the old ballet masters. His compositions were many, and sometimes quite casual, as for instance when in his later years he autographed the album of a friend in musical terms. When the Philharmonic celebrated its centennial in 1942, an old composition of his entitled "Maude's Gavotte" was played in an arrangement for strings by way of sentimental tribute. The manuscript in piano form had been found by his grandniece, Mrs. Seth M. Milliken, among old papers in her attic. Apparently he confined himself largely to writing dance music in which he could maintain the standard he desired for his own purposes. Many of these compositions, like the gavotte just mentioned, were occasional pieces and personal tributes. The "Cally Polka" was in honor of his wife who roundly deserved all the tribute he could pay her.

Cally Raymond Dodworth was his second wife, and the cousin of his first wife, the beautiful Miss Crow who had died shortly after the birth of her second son. To Cally was due a large part of the success of the dancing school, for she was clever and ambitious and from the beginning took over the management of the academy, relieving her artist husband of all the administrative details and business cares. This was rather extraordinary in a day when woman's place was definitely in the home. But the combination of an artist with vision and a wife with practical instincts for protecting

Cover to the sheet music of "The Cally Polka." 1846.

that vision made possible the establishment of a social institution which created a style and system without precedent in America and one which has never been surpassed.

In the thirties dancing schools and classes were still not popular. As our national relations with England had become more friendly, many parents, conscious of the importance of the arts and social graces, had swung back to the English style of fashionable life. But their children were taught at home by English governesses with visiting teachers, chiefly French, for languages, music, and dancing. There was a great need, however, for something broader and more attuned to the less sheltered life and atmosphere of America.

Within the outlook, far less great than our own, of the society of Dodworth's time, Dodworth sensed the underlying social values of the method of public teaching as opposed to private. If his statement of the case needs to be separated from its Victorian frame, it is nevertheless persuasive.

"With children," he wrote in one place, "the effort to move gracefully produces a desire also to be graceful in manner, and this is one of the best influences of the dancing school. The frequently recurring circumstances of their social intercourse impress their minds practically with the value and beauty of politeness."

And in another place he has more extensive things to say about educational methods: "All teachers of experience agree in the opinion that for beginners and young children what are called 'private classes' are generally failures in regard to the higher objects that are to be gained. The pupils may be taught to dance, but the influences which usually surround them obstruct the reception of the idea that the study of graceful motion is of importance; they are therefore more ready to imitate the mistakes of their friends than to profit by the instruction of their teacher; their familiarity also prevents the enforcement of that formality which is the beginning of courteous manners.

"It has been many times proved that, in the case of those unfortunate young people who have been neglected until growth is nearly or quite completed, the embarrassment felt in the presence of strangers is much less than that experienced when friends alone are present; one of the reasons is, that in public classes all engaged at the same time are at the same stage of progress."

And again: "Many examples in high places show that our system of education is weak in the formation of moral character. There is a vacant place in the system which must sooner or later be filled. We have schools, academies, colleges, and universities, where morality is incidental to brain stimulation; institutions where morality is secondary to theology. We want schools or places where the practice of moral conduct, especially in all the little incidents of young life, is made the primary and dominant duty of the time and place.

"Our ordinary education rests too much upon the theory that the multiplication table teaches the Golden Rule. Children are talked at about right doing, but have we not too much telling and not enough practicing? . . . Rules are given; so they are in arithmetic, but what use are rules without practice? And here is the vacant place which should be occupied by the dancing school for children; the rules talked about at other times should here be fully put into practice, until morality in little things becomes habitual. When this habit is established in connection with the lesser duties of life, we need have but little fear for the greater."

"The dancing school," he said, "is not a place of amusement"; and dancing itself was for him not a mere pastime but a subject which included rhythm, harmony, beautiful motion, fine human relationships, and matters to do with men's souls. Allen Dodworth had a great spiritual quality as a human being, and this, according to the testimony of many people who knew him, was his greatest asset, which gave him the intelligence to sense the

First opening of the Metropolitan Museum of Art. "A private residence that had been altered for Allen Dodworth Dancing Academy was leased December 1, 1871, for $9,000 annually, the lease to expire May 1, 1874."

needs of the situation and the courage to do something about it. Not many dancing teachers have been so markedly men with missions.

Certainly, however, Dodworth was not mere sweetness and light. He had evolved a thorough technical system and demanded of his pupils the strictest adherence to it. There is no evidence that he had ever heard of the great Renaissance dancing masters such as Guglielmo Ebreo or Cornazano (indeed, it is scarcely possible that he could have, as they have been rescued from oblivion since his time), but his exposition of theory is strikingly similar to theirs in many respects. Much

of it is patently dated, and much was opposed in its own day, but all of it is vivid and consistent.

In introducing his method he begins with a description of the five positions, which "since dancing became an art . . . have been the basis of all motion." Immediately after the description of the first position, with heels together and feet at right angles, he adds a section on "attitude": "The upper part of the body should be slightly inclined forward, the hips backward—the forward inclination just enough to cause a tendency in the heels to rise from the floor; the head erect, legs straight,

94

arms hanging at sides, elbows very slightly turned outward, so that the arms will present curved lines to the front.

"This necessary inclination forward was at one time exaggerated into what was known as 'the Grecian Bend'; the phrase had reference to the fact that in all Grecian statuary, where gracefulness is intended, this beautiful curved line is always present. This should be termed the normal attitude, which should be maintained at all times."

It would be difficult to convey in an equal number of words so clear a picture of a period as this description of the then current concept of good posture. On it can be built with a minimum of effort a whole manual of social gesture and costume, and even a hint or two of the psyche of the times.

When he had finished with the five positions, he presents "The Dodworth Method" as follows: "I present this as the most thorough method yet devised for conveying ideas of motion by language; my own practice, with that of others, having abundantly tested its usefulness. As I am not aware that the method was used previous to its adoption by me, I feel justified in naming it the *Dodworth Method*. If it could be adopted by teachers generally, their pupils from different parts of the country would be able to unite without difficulty in any dance. As my long career as a teacher draws near to an end, I offer this to the art I have so long endeavored to elevate, and to those who teach it, as my last, and I truly believe my most valuable, contribution."

He then proceeds to describe the "six radical motions" which are the key to his method. These are the change, the slide, the step, the leap, the hop, and the halt. "Every dance now used," he states, "is composed of two or more of these radical motions. Knowing these, therefore, enables a learner to comprehend any description by this method without difficulty. Many persons will have difficulty in believing that the waltz and polka, as now danced, are composed of precisely the same

three motions, but the fact is easily demonstrated."

In his descriptions of the various dances, he employs a line or two of music with the several radical motions printed vertically above the notes to which they are executed. For anyone knowing these basic elements, the reading of such a script becomes immediately simple and practical. Because of the importance of the six radical motions, it is perhaps worth while to quote here at least the essentials of his descriptions.

The change can be done sideways, forward, backward, alternately forward and backward with their foot in front.

"*Sideways*—Stand with left in second position. Strike the left heel against the right, immediately extending right to second position, thus changing from one foot to the other. At the moment of changing the feet a slight spring is made. Repeat same, back again from right to left foot."

The other variations are obvious from this.

The slide may be done to the side, or forward or backward either with the same foot or alternate feet.

"*Side Slides*—Stand with left in second position. Slide left, ten inches farther to the side; at the same time transfer the weight of the body to the left foot, leaving right in second position; in the same manner, slide right, leaving left in second position."

The leap "is the most difficult motion of all, so much so, that it has been named the 'Pons Asinorum' of dancing; but, as it occurs in nearly every round dance, the manner of its execution has a decisive effect upon the appearance of a dancer. One may leap with all the flexibility, lightness, and energy of an antelope; another with the stiffness, heaviness, and angularity of a cart horse."

"*Side Leaps*—Stand with left in second position. Bend the right knee and leap to the left ten inches; same to the right."

Forward and backward leaps are similar.

As for the hop: "Spring from and alight

upon the same foot; the position of the other has no connection with the motion, as it may be extended to the side, front, or rear, or the heels may be kept close together while leaping."

"The halt consists simply in stopping in first position."

In the chapter devoted to "General Directions Applicable to All Round Dances" we find an analysis of the elements of dancing which is curiously parallel to that of the Renaissance masters, with due allowance, of course, for the differences of the dances themselves and of the times.

"Taking the waltz as a type of all other round dances," writes Dodworth, "we observe that it consists of six elements:

Attitude,	Flexibility,
Grouping,	Accent,
Precision,	Expertness.

"1. *Attitude* in each dancer should be such as to show familiarity with the requirements of good taste.

"2. *Grouping* of the two must accord with the dictates of modesty and propriety.

"3. *Precision* should exhibit perfect knowledge of the motions belonging to the dance.

"4. *Flexibility* is an important part in gracefulness.

"5. *Accent* must be at all times correct.

"6. *Expertness* is that familiarity with every possible turn and angle which enables dancers to avoid collision."

His directions to dancers are only in volume more important than his directions to musicians.

"We have those," he writes, "who make dance music a specialty, using all their knowledge and technical skill with the enthusiastic feeling which ever governs a true votary of art; when at the piano, or with other instruments in hand, their notes are never tinged with the color of a banknote; they play to give pleasure, and are true artists, not mechanics in music. These are engaged and respected, the others, hired and—"

"In good playing of dance music there are six elements: 1. Speed (technically, *tempo*); 2. Regularity (no *ritardandos* or *accelerandos*); 3. Distinct phrasing; 4. Exact accent (appropriate to each dance); 5. Musical expression; 6. Vim (enthusiasm, energy, excitability, something of the kind, almost inexpressible in language, but vividly felt when present in a pianist)."

Again, not since the Renaissance had ballroom masters concerned themselves so meticulously with music, but Dodworth in apologizing for his apparent presumption in offering his opinions on musical matters reminds his readers that his "early education in that art" gave him "warrant for doing so."

The textbook, published near the close of his professional career, is the fullest and most orderly statement of his principles, but all through the years of his activity he issued from time to time tiny booklets entitled for the most part "Assistant for A. Dodworth's Pupils." These minute publications, only 2⅜ inches by 3⅜ inches in size, contained much valuable advice about manners, toilette, and actual dancing. They were issued at irregular intervals between 1850 and 1879, and from the various addresses of the academy as it moved steadily uptown with the trend of fashionable New York over the years. There were eight booklets in all, and so far as is known the only complete set is the one which was recently presented to the present writer by Mrs. T. George Dodworth, widow of Allen Dodworth's nephew who carried on the school activities after his uncle's retirement, and published a revision of the textbook itself, bringing it up to date in 1905. In these writings we have a complete and perhaps the only accurate record of fashionable dancing in New York for three-quarters of a century beginning, roughly, about 1830. Besides this historical interest, however, they contain a simple and workable exposition of a theory, a practical method of notating ballroom dances which makes possible a universal application of the theory, and an impressive social philosophy of dancing in its relation to the other arts and to the gentle life.

The first Dodworth academy, about 1842, was at 448 Broome Street, then a fashionable part of the city. In addition, a little later a branch was opened at 137 Montague Street, Brooklyn. It seems likely that the family lived at this address at that time. For many years a Brooklyn branch was maintained under the direction of Allen's son, Frank.

The second Manhattan location was at 806 Broadway, next to Grace Church. By this time the Dodworths were well established, and when in the late fifties they decided that it was time to move once more, a fine building was put up for them at Fifth Avenue and Twenty-sixth Street. They were well aware of the social pattern of the city; even in those days (or perhaps especially in those days) it was important to dance in the same quadrilles with the boys and girls of the old families. Though they were convinced that the training, which was incidental to the mere learning to dance, was the source of the real benefits received from their system, they also knew that a good address, elegant furnishings, and fashionable clothes were absolute necessities to their success. The Dodworth ladies were always exquisitely dressed and were, indeed, famous for their wardrobes which generally came from Paris. With their new building, then, they spared neither time nor money to make it one of the most beautiful dancing academies in the world. Many years later when they moved out of it, it was taken over by Delmonico's, who profited greatly from the social prestige they inherited from the school.

This prestige had been assiduously built up over the years. Every summer the Dodworths went abroad, met all the great teachers, studied with and visited them at their schools. They "did" all the fashionable European watering places to see and to be seen, to get the very latest and best in new music, new dances, new styles, in order to keep their pupils up to the minute in all that had to do with social life.

The next academy at 681 Fifth Avenue, on the upper edge of the fashionable district, was if possible even larger and more elegant than its predecessor. Here Dodworth put down the most unusual floor in the city—a parquet inlaid with black walnut squares and lines, designed to ensure the right angle of the pupils' feet which was so important in the method. This building, also, was taken over for a short time by a distinguished tenant. Here was the first temporary headquarters of the Metropolitan Museum of Art.

However, the full extent of the lease was not fulfilled, and after a brief period at another Fifth Avenue address farther downtown, the academy resumed its occupancy at 681 and remained there until 1885. Meanwhile Mrs. Dodworth had died, and Dodworth, now a frail old man, urgently needed help. It was to his nephew, T. George Dodworth, that he turned for an assistant. George had been trained by his uncle and had for years taught the out-of-town classes, and things now passed largely into his hands for direction.

In 1885 Mr. and Mrs. George Dodworth bought the property at 12 East Forty-ninth Street and transformed it into another characteristically elegant Dodworth headquarters. There were extensive alterations in the building; the lower floor was turned into a ballroom with reception rooms and office, all furnished by Sloane's. The dressing rooms were in the basement, and the upper floors were the family's living quarters. Here, in one of the most beautiful rooms in the city, was carried on the Dodworth tradition, now in the hands of the second generation. Allen Dodworth, according to his obituary, retired in 1887 and went to live with his son, Allen, in Pasadena. Mrs. George Dodworth, however, corrected this statement. "Uncle Allen never really retired," she said, "he just dropped in the ballroom, I think." His death occurred on February 12, 1896.

For the later history of the academy, and for many facts and much informal information about the early history as well, we are indebted to Mrs. T. George Dodworth, who very graciously received the writer when she came from California to New York one summer to visit her daughter, Mrs. Milliken. With a wonderful sense of humor and a delightful willingness to help with the preparation of this record of the Dodworth family and its work, she cleared up much that was foggy in the generally accepted data. For example, in response to the remark that Dodworth was not only an artist but a fine businessman, she smiled and said, "Oh, no; that is not correct. Uncle Allen was a great artist and a wonderful man, but neither he nor my George had any business sense, and could not be bothered with the business side of the school. All they thought about was teaching—whether they gave good lessons, the progress of their pupils, etc. No, Cally Dodworth was the wonderful business sense, and when I had to take on her responsibility I felt that I could not do it. Such a big job! I was young and inexperienced, but somehow I learned the management of the house, arranging classes, checking attendance, and so forth. Do you know that after the first day I never had to ask a child his name?"

The classes began in the early fall. Parents were notified of the date and hour at which their children were expected. New pupils were required to present three letters of introduction, and Mrs. Dodworth reserved the right to decline pupils. This she was forced to do many times because the classes were full. She was supposed to have no more than seventy-five "babies," three to five years old, in the two-thirty to four o'clock class, which met twice a week. The older children supposedly met in classes of 150 for a two-hour lesson, but Mrs. Dodworth was obliged continually to let the attendance run over this number. The Saturday morning class was for out-of-town pupils, and was always crowded to overflowing. Everything was strictly in accord with the precedent "Uncle Allen" had established, and the only changes that were made were the introduction of new dances from time to time.

New social times had come into being, times in which social climbers were many and active. The gilded age of the gay nineties with its great wealth and extravagance ushered in a complete change in the dancing-school picture. Socially ambitious mothers, mindful of McAllister's Family Circle Dancing Class and its picked list, realized that the dancing class could be made an important rung on the ladder to smart, sophisticated circles, and they set about accordingly to form small ultrafashionable classes, managed by imposing boards of patronesses, and taught by charming young women from impoverished aristocratic families who had been persuaded to teach because of their connections. Most of them had been Dodworth pupils, but had no training as teachers.

Professional dancers, also, who knew little and cared less for the tradition of the dance as a social manifestation, were engaged to teach small private classes in smart hotels and in the drawing rooms of the wealthy. Mothers, torn between the new with its utter disregard for the grand old style which they had known at Dodworth's and the clamoring of their children to join So-and-So's class at Mrs. So-and-So's house in order to be on the lists for the parties and assemblies, compromised by both joining the new fashion and also continuing at Dodworth's.

The new era produced other fundamental changes, also, among them a new national rhythm. Dancing naturally reflected the great speed and alteration in social standards. The measured elegance and the strict discipline of the Dodworth school were not in tune with this tempo, and neither were the old dances and their music. The dashing two-step was now the swanky dance; the music consisted of the popular ballads, the ragtime and "coon songs" of the day. The Court Quadrille, the Minuet de la Cour, the Pavane, the Polonaise, the Lancers, which were still required by Dodworth's, were too slow, too difficult, and frankly out of date. The German, which had once consisted of well-thought-out figures and good dancing, degenerated into a vulgar display of wealth.

Influences outside the ballroom also entered into the picture. New Yorkers were all stirred by Isadora Duncan's "barefoot" dancing; aesthetic, interpretive, fancy, and stage dancing of all sorts began to intrude and national and folk dances came very much into the picture.

The dance craze of 1911 brought with it the Texas Tommy, bunny hug, turkey trot, one-step, camel walk, etc., all of which George Dodworth and all the old teachers violently opposed. These dances, many of them from the slums and dives, brought with them certain teachers from the same sources.

The Dodworths continued to go abroad. They brought back with them the tango of conservative French society, and though they had large classes of society women, that was not what the young people wanted. Still they persisted; they taught the Lulu Fado, the Pericon, the Brazilian Polka, the Balancello, and the Furlana, which the Pope had endorsed, in the effort to restrain the wildness of the dance revolt. In this effort other teachers and artists joined. John Murray Anderson and his partner tried to bring back the gavotte and minuet; Pavlova and Ivan Clustine introduced three ballroom dances—the Pavlovana, the Gavotte Renaissance, and the Czarina Waltz.

Things were in a chaotic state, and conscientious teachers were frantic for some sort of system. In the spring of 1914, Flora Voorhis, who was teaching at the Hotel McAlpin, approached Mr. Dodworth with the idea of standardizing the dance. A meeting was called of all the legitimate teachers in and around New York, and from that meeting grew the New York Society of Teachers of Dancing with George Dodworth as its first president. This was a radical step for him, for none of the Dodworths had ever joined any of the teachers' societies.

Sad and discouraged, Mr. and Mrs. Dodworth struggled on. Cutting in, bad manners, and vulgar dancing were apparently here to stay, and they could do nothing about it. What was particularly distressing was that former pupils, who were always welcomed as a matter of traditional practice, came in and attempted to do these so-called "collegiate" dances in their ballroom. The "flapper" had no feeling for the fitness of things.

In the spring of 1920 the Dodworths finally gave in. Business was moving uptown into their neighborhood and they had had several good offers for their property; so with little hope left for stemming the tide against them, they sold the house and embarked for California. The last dance to be composed by T. George Dodworth was the "Victory Polka" in celebration of the Allies' victory in 1918. It was presented to the New York Society of Teachers of Dancing in February, 1919. In February of the following year, Mr. Dodworth addressed the society on the subject of ballroom deportment, completing the Dodworth cycle on a characteristic note.

In considering the theory of the Dodworth attitude, it is well to guard against a possible tendency to read into it a sense of snobbery. This is an essential injustice. It must be remembered that the Dodworths were not "society" people, but artist-teachers; their academy became famous and fashionable only through its merits.

Allen Dodworth's ideal was quite clearly one of gentle living, good manners, and culture, and he preached it in a period when the American nation as a whole had grave need of it if it was not to become a country of boors and money seekers. Under his tutelage young ladies and gentlemen were trained not only to dance, but to take their places in a society which was still being formed and which needed constant reinforcement and careful authoritative leadership. It is true that young women came from all parts of the country to be trained for presentation at court, and that there was the most careful selection of pupils who were admitted to any of the large classes. Certainly wealth was never a card of admission. Mrs. Dodworth was the sole judge of who should be admitted and who rejected, and her standards were perhaps intuitive rather than rigidly defined.

There could be no more fitting note on which to close the record than a quotation from his textbook along these lines:

"Would it not be . . . in accordance with sound wisdom for the elder ones to provide those whose nature it is to dance with places and opportunities for the exercise of this pleasure, amid proper circumstances, and not compel them to seek it where they are too frequently surrounded by temptations destructive alike to health and morality?

"The writer's own experience, for more than fifty years, abundantly justifies him in saying that profound impressions may be made upon children during the happy moments of their dancing lessons. This being so,

why should we not take advantage of the fact as a means for their moral elevation? In our public schools a daily lesson in dancing might be given as a recreation, the right of attendance upon which could be made a reward of good conduct. . . .

"The two sexes being brought together, all the courtesies of social intercourse could be insisted upon, making politeness and consideration for others habitual. The lessons would afford ever recurring occasions when children might be made to feel, from immediate practice, how necessary and useful this is; and that in thus treating others, at all times and in all things, with kindness and courtesy, they truly fulfill the precepts of the Golden Rule.

"Surely the daily practice of these social virtues would have a softening effect, and produce a better result than sending the children into the yard or playroom for recreation, as it is called, which usually means to romp and practice rudeness, the strong abusing the weak, and all taking daily lessons in tyranny, imposition and turbulence; the outcome of which is too often lawlessness in later life. The sight of two or three hundred children enjoying themselves, under the influence of their better feelings, and giving expression to their happiness in orderly motion, possibly to their own songs of joy, could not be otherwise than acceptable to a kind father, either on earth or in heaven."

THE CLASSIC DANCERS

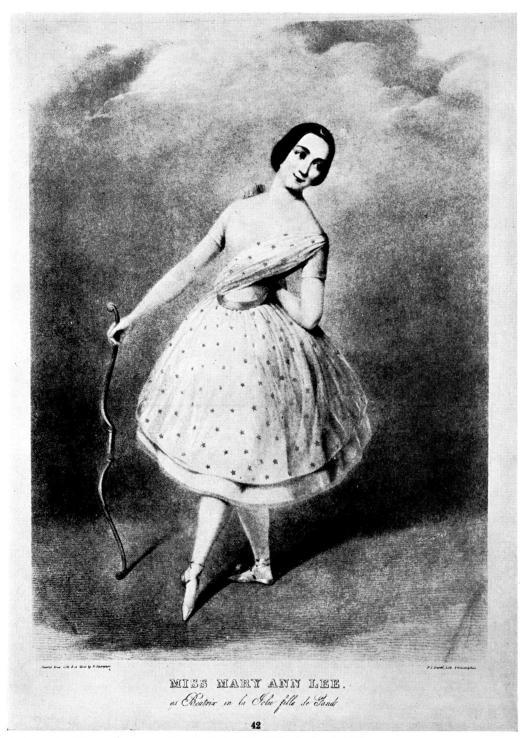

Lithograph of Mary Ann Lee as Beatrix in *La Jolie Fille de Gand.* 1845.

MARY ANN LEE

FIRST AMERICAN GISELLE

BY LILLIAN MOORE

MARY ANN LEE was the first American dancer to attain nation-wide fame as an exponent of the classic ballet. Her career was an amazing triumph over the most crushing of obstacles, extreme poverty. Her father had been a minor actor and circus performer. Although he never attained the slightest degree of success or renown, he must have had an appealing personality, which his charming daughter seems to have inherited. He is mentioned in mildly affectionate terms in several theatrical autobiographies of the period. Charles Durang, in his *History of the Philadelphia Stage,* mentions Lee's engagement at the Olympic Circus in that city in 1822, shortly before the birth of Mary Ann: "Charles Lee was a very useful little member of the corps, filling up important niches in stage and ring performances. Charley was a general favorite—a reward due to his very obliging and honest good nature. He was the father of Mary Ann Lee, who, for many years, was our city's favorite— a graceful and agile danseuse. The winning arch smile that wreathed her features, while reclining into attitudes at the end of every strain, ever won applause, and harmonized with the excellence of her very neat *pas.*"

The actor Joseph Cowell also records his friendship with Charles Lee. Mentioning the fact that some critics declared Mary Ann Lee to be the equal of Fanny Elssler, he continues: "I am no judge of dancing, and I never saw Elssler; but I hope it's the fact; for her father was a worthy creature, and a great favorite of mine, and I have known her to be a very good little girl ever since she was dancing in her mother's arms, and I am old-fashioned enough to have a strong prejudice in favor of old acquaintances. . . ."

Mary Ann's father died when she was a child, and upon her small shoulders fell the task of supporting the widowed mother. Sheer necessity forced her to develop an extraordinary versatility as a dancer and actress: she appeared in everything from Shakespeare to burlesque, danced everything from *La Sylphide* to the Sailor's Hornpipe, and on occasion she even sang!

Born in Philadelphia, about 1823, she appeared as a child actress in most of the theaters of that city. At the age of eleven, she played Francie in *Guy Mannering*, Eustache in *The Hunchback of Notre Dame*, and a page in *Romeo and Juliet.* She made her official debut as a dancer at the Chestnut Street Theatre on December 30, 1837, as Fatima in *The Maid of Cashmere*, an English version of Auber's opera-ballet *Le Dieu et la Bayadère.*

Among the dancers of the *corps de ballet* was listed a Mrs. Lee. Could this have been Mary Ann's mother?

On this occasion the principal role, Zoloe, was danced by Augusta Maywood, stepdaughter of the manager of the theater. Augusta was twelve, Mary Ann but slightly older. In the monograph on Miss Maywood which appears in this book, Marian Hannah Winter has mentioned this double debut and the rivalry which subsequently developed between the two child stars. The incident had little importance in the career of Miss Maywood, who soon left provincial Philadelphia for triumphs in New York and Paris, Italy and Austria. To Mary Ann Lee, however, this joint debut with Maywood was an event of major significance. Augusta was technically the superior of the two, and the desire to equal her in every way seems to have provided Mary Ann Lee with the incentive to study continually with the best teachers to be found in this country, and eventually to follow her former rival to the ballet school of the Paris Opéra.

Both Maywood and Lee had received their first training in Philadelphia under a Frenchman, P. H. Hazard, who had at one time been a member of the *corps de ballet* of the Paris Opéra. He staged the dances for their debut performance. The two young dancers appeared together in a famous *pas de deux,* the Trial Dance, which created such excitement among the members of the audience that descriptions of their behavior equal the wildest demonstrations of present-day balletomanes. The *Philadelphia Saturday Courier,* after one performance, said: "As the opera proceeded bouquets and wreaths were literally showered upon the stage by the admirers of both Augusta and Miss Lee. We never saw so much enthusiasm as was exhibited; peals followed the bestowal of each present, and it kept poor 'Brahma' all the time walking from side to side of the stage gathering up the trophies, until he entirely forgot the bestowal of the stage wreath which in his character he should

have awarded to Fatima. . . . We counted twenty wreaths thrown while Augusta was dancing, besides sundry bouquets, etc.—in one garland glittered a splendid diamond ring. Miss Lee also had her fair share of the honors."

As nearly as it is possible to judge from contemporary accounts, Augusta Maywood must have been at that time much the more brilliant dancer of the two. But Mary Ann, even then, had a winning personality and a way with an audience. Whatever the respective merits of the two little ballerinas, their rivalry added to the excitement of their engagement, and *The Maid of Cashmere* played to crowded houses for more than three weeks.

On January 5 the manager, Robert Campbell Maywood, announced a performance for the benefit of his stepdaughter. The audience demanded that Mary Ann also be granted a benefit. This request was loudly repeated every evening until Maywood, to placate the ticket holders, was forced to announce that Miss Lee would be given a benefit on January 12. This he did most reluctantly, complaining that since he had paid for Mary Ann's dancing lessons, he deserved the profit he was reaping from her talent.

The benefit duly took place, and *la petite Augusta* as she was called, graciously volunteered her services. Mary Ann danced her usual role of Fatima, and also appeared as "Little Pickle" in the afterpiece, a farce called *The Spoiled Child.* The house was jammed, and the little dancers reaped another rich harvest of flowers and gifts, while Mary Ann collected a most welcome profit.

Next day the *Philadelphia Saturday Courier* carried *two* complete criticisms of the performance, one pro-Maywood, one pro-Lee. "Miss Lee is a clever little girl enough in her place," wrote the first reporter condescendingly, "and we are glad the excitement caused a crowded house, but no one in their senses pretends seriously to compare her forced and trembling performances to the

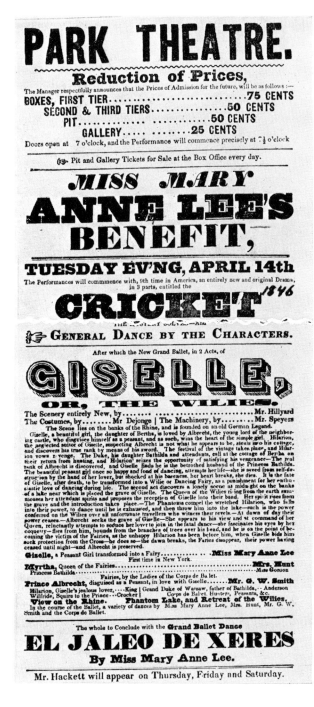

Program of Mary Ann Lee's appearance in *Giselle*. New York, 1846.

finished, graceful, flexible, and confident figures of the astonishing Augusta." The other critic, however, wrote: "We are heartily glad it was a triumphant overflow, a deserving tribute to merit, and a handsome offering to an orphan daughter. Miss Lee deserves all praise for her improvement. Her poetry of motion is of the style of Madame Augusta, the celebrated dancer brought out from France, at the Park, New York." [1]

In February, *la petite Augusta* was whisked off to New York for a successful debut at the Park Theatre. Mary Ann, who had also been offered an engagement there, chose to remain in Philadelphia with her mother. Within a week she was dancing Fatima again, this time in support of the French ballerina Madame LeComte, who was appearing as guest star at the Chestnut Street Theatre. Later in the same year LeComte was to bring Marius Petipa and his father to the United States for a brief and not too happy visit.

In March little Augusta returned from New York, bringing copies of the charming lithographic portrait which had just been published there. Mary Ann Lee's supporters promptly retaliated by arranging for her portrait as Fatima to be published in Philadelphia, and announcement of its publication appeared in the *Public Ledger* on March 22.

Meanwhile Mr. Maywood had staged a new ballet for his stepdaughter. This was *The Dew Drop*, or *La Sylphide*. It seems to have been a cross between the famous Taglioni ballet *La Sylphide* and an opera called *The Mountain Sylph*, which was popular in the United States during the 1830's. At any rate, although it may not have been the authentic *Sylphide*, it must have been based upon it. New and very effective scenery was painted for the occasion by Russell Smith, staff artist of the rival theater on Walnut Street. Augusta Maywood danced the title role, and Mary Ann Lee was Flora. The first performance took place on March 17, 1838. The ballet was amazingly successful, and houses were crowded in spite

of stormy, disagreeable weather. *La Sylphide* ran until early April.

In the spring the entire Maywood family departed for Europe. Augusta never returned to the United States. At this time, however, Mary Ann Lee must have determined that someday she, too, would study under the great European masters of the ballet.

For the present she remained in Philadelphia, and consoled herself with some June performances of *La Bayadère* and *La Sylphide*, this time in support of a young dancer from New York, Miss Harriet Wells. In *Sylphide*, Mary Ann's role was enriched by the addition of a Scotch *pas seul*, and Mrs. Lee also appeared on the program, as Jessamine. Mary Ann continued to dance and act at the Chestnut Street Theatre until summer, when she ventured as far afield as Baltimore. There she appeared for the first time in the title role of *La Sylphide*. Her success may be judged from the following effusion, which was the tribute of an anonymous admirer:

La Sylphide [2]

Ne'er did the Grecian chisel trace
A Sylph, a Naiad, or a Grace
Of finer form or lovelier face;
And seldom was a wreath amid
Such locks of golden beauty hid;
Nor ever beamed of heavenly hue,
Eyes of more sweet and radiant blue;
Each changeful movement of her breast,
Her varying features still confest;
Whether joy danced in her bright eye,
Or woe and Pity claimed a sigh,
Or Filial Love was glowing there,
Or meek devotion poured a prayer,
And while upon her speech there hung
Accents more sweet than wind harps tongue,
These silver sounds, so soft, so clear,
The listener held his breath to hear.

I.H., M.D.

In the autumn Mary Ann transferred her allegiance to the Walnut Street Theatre. Since the occasion of her benefit performance, Mary

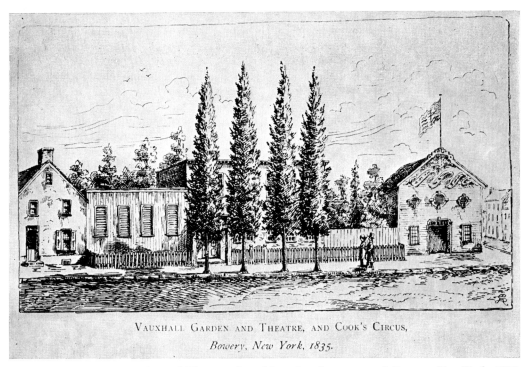

VAUXHALL GARDEN AND THEATRE, AND COOK'S CIRCUS,
Bowery, New York, 1835.

Vauxhall Garden and Theatre where Mary Ann Lee appeared. Bowery, New York, 1835.

Ann's relations with Mr. Maywood had been somewhat strained. On the other hand, Francis Courtney Wemyss, manager of the Walnut, was a great admirer of hers. He did much to further her career, and later paid tribute to her talents in his book, *The Life of an Actor and Manager*. On September 13, 1838, he produced for her a new ballet called *The Lily Queen*, in which Mary Ann had the imposing title of "Queen Lily of the Silver Stream." There seems to be no record of the composer, although "new music and scenery" were advertised; but the story and choreography were by J. H. Amherst, an obscure but versatile young man who appears to have been a dancer, writer, circus performer, and horse trainer. Unfortunately the success of his ballet was short lived, and a few days later Mary Ann was appearing, more humbly, in "a new Tambourine Dance."

Throughout the winter season Miss Lee remained a member of the company at the Walnut Street Theatre. She acted everything from "Little Pickle" to the role of Albert in *William Tell*, in support of the great tragedian Edwin Forrest. On the slightest provocation, however, she would execute "A new Fancy Dance," or a *grand pas seul*. She continued her lessons with Hazard, and in the spring came her reward. On April 27, 1839, she was permitted to essay for the first time the leading role, Zoloe, in *La Bayadère*. This time she had an outstanding success, which led to an engagement at the Bowery Theatre in New York.

Mary Ann Lee made her New York debut on June 12, 1839, in *La Bayadère*, a ballet which seems to have been associated with almost every important event in her career. A few days later a new ballet called *The*

107

Sisters was produced for her. It seems to have been one of those very rare things, an original American ballet, not based on any of the latest successes of the Paris Opéra or Drury Lane. Yet the directors of the Bowery were so modest about it that they neglected to mention in the advertisements the names of the composer, ballet master, or designer! All we know is the cast: Mr. Addis was Henry, Mr. Rice was Cormac, Miss Lee was Fanny, one of the sisters, and Julia Turnbull was the other sister, Laura. The new ballet ran for only a week.

This engagement at the Bowery marked Mary Ann Lee's first professional association with a dancer whose career to a certain extent paralleled hers, and who was certainly her most formidable American rival. Born in New York in 1822, Julia Turnbull had been on the stage since she was six, and had been dancing and playing children's roles at the Park Theatre ever since 1834. Although she had appeared in innumerable brief *divertissements, The Sisters* was the first ballet in which she had a chance to play a role of length and distinction, and in it she won her first major success. When Fanny Elssler came to the United States in the following year, she promptly engaged Julia Turnbull as soloist in her company. During the first New York performances of Balfe's *The Bohemian Girl,* in 1844, Miss Turnbull and Jules Martin, brother of Madame LeComte, were the principal dancers. The ballet was lavishly staged and prominently featured during the long run of this popular opera, and the engagement further enhanced Miss Turnbull's growing reputation as a ballerina. Her first spectacular success, however, came in the spring of 1847, when *The Naiad Queen* was produced for her. Mary Ann Lee was to retire in this same spring, and thenceforth Julia Turnbull had no serious competitor among the American ballerinas. She danced the principal roles in *Nathalie, La Bayadère, Esmeralda, La Muette de Portici,* and even *Giselle.* In 1857

she retired, and lived quietly in Brooklyn until her death thirty years later.

In 1839, however, Julia Turnbull was just seventeen, Mary Ann Lee a year younger, and their rivalry added considerable spice to the summer season at the Bowery. On July 8 the President of the United States, Martin Van Buren, attended the performance, and Mary Ann Lee danced the cachucha for him. This particular cachucha had been arranged by her Philadelphia teacher, the accomplished Hazard; later Mary Ann was to learn the famous cachucha danced by Fanny Elssler.

During this same summer Paul Taglioni, brother of the great Marie Taglioni, was dancing at the Park Theatre with his wife Amelie. Mary Ann Lee, eager to absorb all she could learn about the classic ballet, must have studied their performances closely. It is even possible that she may have studied with Paul Taglioni, for although we have no record of it, she was hardly likely to miss such a marvelous opportunity.

After another winter spent as a member of a repertory company in Philadelphia, and varied by brief excursions to near-by cities such as Pittsburgh and Baltimore, Mary Ann Lee returned to New York in June, 1840. The great P. T. Barnum recognized her talent, and engaged her to appear at his popular place of amusement, the Vauxhall Gardens.

Fanny Elssler had just made her American debut, and was dancing at the near-by Park Theatre. Miss Lee seized this opportunity to study with Elssler's partner, James Sylvain, who taught her all of Elssler's famous character dances: the cracovienne, the bolero, El Jaleo de Jeres, La Smolenska, and the famous cachucha. Mary Ann Lee actually dared to challenge the great Elssler by dancing the cachucha at Vauxhall while Fanny was performing it at the Park. Miss Lee won the victory in the eyes of at least one observer, for the *New York Herald* for July 1, 1840, contained the following note: "Miss Lee, the charming dancer, was received with shouts of

Lithograph of a contemporary production of *La Bayadère*, showing Madame Augusta, with whom Mary Ann Lee danced, in the leading role. Ca. 1839.

applause, on Monday night. In the cachucha dance, she can hardly be excelled." However, most critics agreed that while Mary Ann was very beautiful, and danced with much spirit, she could not seriously be compared with Elssler or the other really great ballerinas of the period.

At her benefit performance at Vauxhall on July 13 (a program quaintly announced as "a splendid bill, at this splendid place, for the benefit of this splendid girl"), Miss Lee proved her versatility by contrasting a classic variation from *La Sylphide* with a hornpipe!

Thenceforth Mary Ann Lee made extensive tours throughout the United States, going as

far south as New Orleans and Mobile. She was a particular favorite in Boston, where she danced frequently. The Cambridge students were among her most enthusiastic admirers. During an engagement in Boston in the spring of 1842, she gathered together some local dancers, coached them herself, and put on a production of *La Sylphide*. In addition to Elssler's dances, she performed the Tyrolienne, which Taglioni had made famous, and something called The Opium Dance, which she had arranged herself for a play called *Life in China*. Next she appeared in a broad burlesque of *La Bayadère*, called *Buy It Dear, T'is Made of Cashmere*. Her role was called

La Smolenska as danced by Miss Mary Ann Lee. Published by William H. Oakes, Boston, 1842. B. W. Thayer & Co.'s Lithog'y, Boston.

The face does not flatter this lovely artist but the lithograph is an excellent and striking study; in black and white, yet full of contrasts and "color." From "American Music Prints of the Romantic Ballet" by George Chaffee.

"Soloe"; her principal effort, the Grand Broom Dance. A few days later she was acting the part of Lisette, in *The Swiss Cottage*, with two interpolated songs, "The Banks of the Blue Moselle," and "Liberty for Me."

From one of her letters of this period, which is now preserved in the Harvard Theatre Collection, we learn that in return for all these varied efforts Miss Lee received the princely sum of $25 a week, plus whatever she might reap at a benefit performance, sometime during the season. How she managed to save anything at all is difficult to understand, but she must have done so.

Mary Ann Lee still considered Philadelphia her home, and she continued to appear there regularly every season. She had several interesting engagements in New York. In September, 1842, she danced in support of Madame LeComte in the first American performances of the ballet from *Robert le Diable*. This ballet, with its unearthly scenes of dead nuns dancing in a deserted cemetery, had been one of the favorite vehicles of Marie Taglioni. The complete opera was not given in this country until 1845, when Julia Turnbull and Jules Martin were the leading dancers. On September 15, 1843, at the Bowery Theatre, Miss Lee undertook one of the most difficult roles in ballet repertoire, that of Julietta in Auber's opera *La Muette de Portici*, which was translated into English for the occasion, and retitled *The Dumb Girl of Genoa*.

In spite of the fact that she was now an established favorite, with a loyal public which affectionately called her "Our Mary Ann," Miss Lee was still dissatisfied with her technical equipment. She had begun to dance professionally when she was fourteen, and since then her training and practice had been constantly interrupted by long and arduous tours. At last, in 1844, she decided that the time had come to take a year's vacation and devote it to study in Paris.

Taking her mother with her, she sailed from New York in November. In Paris she obtained admittance to the ballet school of the Paris Opéra, where she enjoyed daily lessons from the great Jean Coralli, choreographer of *Giselle*, *Le Diable Boiteux*, and *La Péri*. During her absence she was not forgotten at home. *The Spirit of the Times* for May 31, 1845, carried a delightful account of her progress:

"Our Mary Ann," better known as Miss Lee, is demonstrating to a perfect mathematical nicety that Native American legs are on an equal footing with the imported article even in its native state. . . . In addition to letters from foreign correspondents we have authority for saying, that she bids fair to rival the most accomplished in her profession. She is a pupil of the celebrated M. Coralli, director of the *danse* at the Grand Opéra in Paris. She is in no way connected with the *Ballet* at the Opéra, although she enjoys all the advantages of receiving her lessons in the Opéra building and of a seat in the director's private box on each Ballet night.

The following extract from a letter of hers to a friend at home, will undoubtedly be appreciated by her American friends: "Notwithstanding the charms and pleasures which are to be met with in Paris, I much prefer my own dear country. One can hardly appreciate the worth of home, until after having been in a foreign land. Here all around you have a smile in readiness, which is but a prelude to something farther, which the French call politeness—and so far as words and language go, they are exceedingly polite (or rather *gallant*, which I think the better word)— but give me the politeness of my own countrymen, who have sincerity in their words and will accompany them with polite actions."

Perhaps this quaint little letter explains one reason why Mary Ann Lee, unlike the more daring Augusta Maywood, chose to return to the United States instead of remaining in Europe! When she arrived in New York in September, 1845, she brought with her not only a vastly improved technique, but a thorough knowledge of the authentic versions of *Giselle*, Taglioni's ballet *La Fille du Danube*, and Carlotta Grisi's *La Jolie Fille de Gand*. Although these classics of the ballet had been

George Washington Smith, first American *premier danseur*.

well known in Europe for a number of years, not one of them had yet been seen in New York.

Hurrying back to Philadelphia, she spent the next two months in careful preparation for a second debut. For this momentous occasion she chose *La Jolie Fille de Gand*, an elaborate three-act ballet by the French choreographer Ferdinand Albert, with music by Adolphe Adam. It had been created by Carlotta Grisi at the Paris Opéra three years earlier, and Lee must have seen Grisi dance it often, during her stay in Paris. The story is

long drawn out, and the pantomimic action heavy and complicated. It must have been an expensive and difficult ballet to mount, for it required seven changes of scenery, a large cast, and lavish costumes. The Philadelphia manager staged it in all its original length and grandeur.

The first performance took place at the Arch Street Theatre on November 24, 1845. Mr. Wood mimed the role of the Marquis of San Lucar, Mr. Burke was Zephiros, a dancing master, and Mary Ann Lee was Beatrix. Other members of the cast were Madame Dunn and the well-known dancer George Washington Smith, who was soon to join Miss Lee on a long tour of the United States.

La Jolie Fille de Gand contains one famous classic variation, the *Pas de Diane*, which gave Miss Lee ample opportunity to exhibit her newly acquired technique. Her old Philadelphia friends gave her a royal welcome, the theater was crowded every night, and the papers were full of accounts of her remarkable progress. It must have been at this time that Davignon painted and lithographed his lovely portrait of her as Beatrix.

La Jolie Fille de Gand was given every night until December 1, when Miss Lee presented the second of the ballets she had studied in Paris. This was *La Fille du Danube*, to which she gave the new title of *Fleur des Champs*, after the name of the heroine. This ballet, choreographed by Filippo Taglioni, had been created by his daughter Marie at the Paris Opéra, nine years earlier. It was a favorite of the great ballerina, who had danced it in Russia during her first visit, in 1837. Before Miss Lee's production it had been seen in the United States only at the French Opera in New Orleans, and not in New York or any Northern city.

La Fille du Danube has a simple and charming little plot, concerning a girl and her lover who commit suicide by throwing themselves into the river, where they are reunited in a beautiful submarine grotto, surrounded by lovely water nymphs. The score was composed by Adolphe Adam, who also wrote *Giselle* and *La Jolie Fille de Gand*. Mary Ann Lee seems to have had a decided weakness for his music!

The principal male role, Rudolph, was danced by George W. Smith, who had a unique position among American male dancers of the nineteenth century. He seems to have been our only native *premier danseur noble*. Like Miss Lee, he was a Philadelphian, and he probably received his training under Hazard. He served his apprenticeship at the Chestnut Street Theatre, and when Fanny Elssler danced there shortly after her arrival in this country, she invited Smith to join her company on tour. He remained with Elssler during her two years in America, and studied under her partner, James Sylvain. When Fanny sailed for France, she presented Smith with an engraved gold pencil as a souvenir of their professional association.

During his long career Smith danced with almost every ballerina of importance who visited this country. Among his partners were Julia Turnbull, Giovanna Ciocca, Anna Bulan, Louise Ducy-Barre, Pepita Soto, and Louise Lamoureux. For two years he toured the United States as the partner of glamorous Lola Montez, whom he considered a clever showman, but no dancer. He danced in the Monplaisir Ballet and the Ravel troupe, and for a time he appeared in Italian pantomime with the Carlo family. Among his associates he particularly admired Leon Espinosa, a brilliant technician who visited this country in the fifties. Espinosa's son is teaching in London today. Like most dancers of the period, Smith was an actor as well, and he appeared in support of such stars as Edwin Booth and Charlotte Cushman.

As a choreographer, Smith's achievements were numerous and varied. He staged the original Philadelphia productions of *The Black Crook*, *The White Fawn*, and *The Naiad Queen*. Many years after the retirement of

Mary Ann Lee, Smith staged performances of *Giselle* and *La Fille du Danube* which must have been based on the choreographic versions she taught him on her return from France. He was actively engaged in choreography and teaching until just before his death in 1899, at the age of seventy-seven.

At the close of her engagement in Philadelphia, Mary Ann Lee gathered about her a small company consisting of Smith and six trained danseuses. With this group she toured the principal cities of the United States. Using her dancers as a nucleus for the more important roles, she would train local talent for the ensembles, and so was able to present ballets calling for large casts. Their first engagement was in Boston, where Mary Ann's loyal followers gave her a warm welcome even before she appeared, as we can judge by the following paragraph from the *Boston Transcript*:

The first appearance of our popular danseuse, Miss Mary Ann Lee, since her return from Paris, is likely to draw out this evening one of the most brilliant assemblies ever witnessed in Boston. She comes before us once more, after a long absence, perfected in her seductive art by all the advantages afforded by the most fashionable school of elegance and grace in Europe, and crowned with the laurels of foreign approbation. When she commenced her career on the boards of our theatres, all were captivated by the winning sweetness of her beautiful face, and the natural poetry of her bewitching figure; now we are to have the opportunity of beholding the same face and the same figure, adorned with all the embellishments of artistical refinement, and heightened by all the fascinations of cultivated taste. Among the youthful, the susceptible, the imaginative of our population, it is impossible but that her return will create a general furore, and her performances give rise to an enthusiasm that shall cause even the splendid triumphs of Elssler to wax dim. Again will our quiet streets resound, late at night, with the noise of returning Cambridge omnibuses, and again shall we hear La Cachucha and the airs of *La Bayadère*, the ballet for this evening, breathed from the sighing accordion and whistled through lips Ethiopian. Vive la danse!

It was during this engagement at the Howard Atheneum that Mary Ann Lee first danced *Giselle*, on January 1, 1846. This was the first American production of this long-lived ballet.[3] Madame Augusta, the same French dancer with whom Lee had occasionally danced at the beginning of her career, danced *Giselle* at the Park Theatre in New York on February 2, 1846, thus preceding Lee in that city by some two months; Mlle. Blangy, another popular French ballerina, also appeared in this famous role later in the same year. The Boston performance is, however, the first of which we have record; so to Mary Ann Lee must go the credit for the first American production of this great classic.

On this historic occasion the role of Albrecht was danced by George W. Smith; Myrtha, the Queen of the Wilis (erroneously called Berthe in the program) by Mrs. Hunt, and the two principal Wilis, Zulme and Mayna, by Miss Smith and Mrs. Jones. The Prince de Courlande was Mr. Howard, the Princess Bathilde, Mrs. Howard, Wilfred, Mr. Resor, and Hilarion, Mr. Russell.

We have no adequate account of this first performance of *Giselle*. Three months later, however, Miss Lee and Mr. Smith danced it at the Park Theatre in New York, on the occasion of Mary Ann's benefit performance. Next day (April 14, 1846) the *New York Herald* commented on the huge audience which had turned out for Miss Lee, "the accomplished, modest, and beautiful American danseuse. . . . It is a pleasure to every well-organized mind," continued this anonymous and benevolent critic, "to see talent and art obtain, at least in some degree, that which is the object of its painful toil and labors. . . . Miss Lee enacted Giselle with a beauty, charm, elegance, and grace that cannot be described, and we will not attempt it. . . ."

Later in April a return engagement in Boston provided the opportunity for further comment on *Giselle*. The *Boston Courier* for April 22, 1846, contained the following criticism: "The graceful and pretty danseuse, Miss Mary Ann Lee, is now fulfilling a successful engagement at this popular establishment [the National Theatre]. The production of *Giselle* attracted on Monday evening a full and fashionable audience, who testified their delight by loud and continued plaudits at the grace and agility of the beautiful heroine, who, independent of her salient qualifications, evinced a truthfulness of action that conveyed as plainly almost as in language, the feelings and passions of the character. She was ably supported by Mr. Smith, and the numerous members of the *corps de ballet*. The piece has been placed upon the stage without regard to expense, and with a tact, taste and ingenuity that reflects the highest honor upon the management of the theater. We think that we are not exceeding the boundary of truth when we aver that no ballet of action has ever been produced in Boston that could bear comparison with *Giselle*. . . ."

From one of Mary Ann Lee's own letters we know of her particular fondness for this ballet. In a note dated at Philadelphia on September 21, 1846, and addressed to the famous Southern managers Ludlow and Smith, she writes concerning an engagement for the following winter:

"I trust that you may be able to do *Giselle* for me as this is such a lovely ballet. I know you would like it, and I am quite sure it would draw in New Orleans and Mobile. If you should think of doing it I can send you the plot. I open in *Giselle* in Charleston."

Mary Ann Lee and her little company toured extensively in the season of 1846-47. The repertoire included *Fleur des Champs, La Bayadère,* and *Giselle,* as well as such *divertissements* as the bolero, the mazurka, and a *grand pas russe. La Jolie Fille de Gand* was too elaborate a production to take on tour,

Facsimile letter by Mary Ann Lee concerning *Giselle*. 1846.

but Miss Lee frequently danced its best-known variation, the *Pas de Diane,* as well as the *grand pas de deux,* in which she shared the honors with Smith. Another popular novelty was the polka, which she had brought from Paris along with her more pretentious importations.

During this tour, however, Mary Ann Lee's health began to fail. In New Orleans, where she danced from December 7 to 17, she be-

came ill and was obliged to cancel several performances. Recovering, she continued bravely on her tour. In the spring it became evident that she could no longer stand the strain of constant practice, public appearances, and touring. Reluctantly she announced her coming retirement.

In May, 1847, Mary Ann Lee gave a series of farewell performances in her native Philadelphia. The *pièce de résistance* was the in-

Mary Ann Lee, age 13, as Fatima in *The Maid of Cashmere*. 1836.

evitable *Bayadère.* Her last appearance took place at the Arch Street Theatre on June 18. The generous program consisted of a comedy, *Uncle John,* a farce, *The Loan of a Lover,* and a drama, *The Deserter.* Miss Lee's contributions were the Trial Dance from *La Bayadère,* and a *pas espagnol.* Although her retirement in 1847 was a final one insofar as any nationwide career was concerned, Mary Ann Lee did dance again, on several different occasions. At the Chestnut Street Theatre, Philadelphia, on May 27, 1852, a complimentary benefit was tendered to "Mrs. Van Hook, late Mary Ann Lee," who appeared in the Grand Trial Dance from *La Bayadère* (always a favorite of hers) and acted Lisette in *The Swiss Cottage.* In August of the same year she danced with Smith at the Walnut, as we shall remark in due time. Other appearances included one at a single benefit performance for J. Ingles Matthias, treasurer of the Arch Street Theatre, May 30, 1853, and a two-week engagement at the Chestnut, Sept. 6-20, 1853, when she again danced her favorite *Bayadère* as well as a new *divertissement,* the *Pas des Quatre Nations.* At this time she added a major role to her repertoire: Fenella in Auber's opera-ballet *Masaniello,* which she enacted with the Seguin Opera troupe. After the single performance of 1852 she seems to have dropped the "Mrs. Van Hook" and returned to her own name, Mary Ann Lee. A whole story of drama and tragedy may lie behind these few small details of her attempts to return to the stage.

It is difficult to give a fair and accurate estimate of Mary Ann Lee's status as an artist. She deserves great credit, of course, for her ambitious pioneer work in bringing to this country such ballet classics as *Giselle* and *La Fille du Danube.* Most contemporary critics seem to agree that while she was (with the exception of Augusta Maywood, who was dancing only in Europe), the best American ballerina of the period, she could not be compared with Elssler, the Taglionis, or the other foreign stars who visited this country. The *New York Herald* for April 16, 1846, devoted an entire article to a discussion of the ballerina: "As a danseuse, Miss Lee has much merit; she is hardly the equal, indeed, in many points to Augusta; her form is not so good, nor has she her muscular power, but she has great skill, much grace of movement, a pleasing countenance, a prepossessing manner, and is, we may say, superior to any other danseuse at present among us, except perhaps Mlle. Augusta. . . . What difference time will make (and to judge by her great improvement during her stay abroad, it may make a great deal) we will not undertake to decide. She possesses both taste and skill, united with graceful power. . . ."

If she had been able to continue her career without interruption, Mary Ann Lee might have become a really great ballerina, for she seems to have had all the necessary attributes. She was only twenty-four in 1847 when she retired, and the critics were still noting her steady improvement. She must have been an extraordinarily beautiful woman, for almost every notice mentions her lovely face and graceful figure. Audiences seem to have liked her instinctively; it is probable that her personality was stronger than her technique.

Entered according to Act of Congress in the Year 1838 by H R Robinson, in the Clerks Office of the Dist.t Court of the U.S. of the South.n Dist.t of N.Y.

LA PETITE AUGUSTA.

Aged 12 Years

In the Character of ZOLOE, in the Bayadere.

Printed & Publ.d by H.R. Robinson, 52 Courtl.dt st. N.Y.

AUGUSTA MAYWOOD

BY MARIAN HANNAH WINTER

In 1825 Mr. and Mrs. H. A. Williams became the parents of a girl child, christened Augusta, who was destined to become our first—and to date our only—great internationally famous prima ballerina. An expatriate whose private life was an enigma, whose reputation in Europe was comparable to Loie Fuller's and Isadora's, and whose professional integrity and superb artistry were constant factors, she was compared only to the greatest—Elssler, Taglioni, and Cerrito. Although Cyril Beaumont has sedulously ignored even her name, any history of ballet in nineteenth-century Italy is incomplete without her record. She was most particularly associated with the last glorious years of classic romantic ballet, and the great star of its final transitional period. About her raged the most excoriating polemics of the American press, in a period of fluent invective. Her most vindictive calumniators unanimously considered her a great dancer.

In 1828 Martha Williams, with two small daughters, Mary Elizabeth and Augusta, was legally disembarrassed of H. A. Williams after they had finished an extensive acting tour in the Southern theaters. She then met and married Robert Campbell Maywood, at that time one of the better-known actors and an enterprising, energetic theatrical manager as well. He had been instrumental in negotiating the American debut of Mlle. Augusta, the French ballerina with the London follow-ing. He became manager and chief lessee of Philadelphia's Chestnut Street Theatre. From all contemporary accounts he expended considerable care and money in training his step-daughters, both of whom assumed his name. Mary Elizabeth, the elder, was extremely beautiful and an undistinguished actress, whose career holds no interest.

Augusta Maywood was a ballerina. Her early training was competently directed by Monsieur and Madame Paul H. Hazard. Monsieur had done a stint at the Paris Opéra in minor capacities, Madame had been engaged at the *Théâtre de la Monnaie*, Brussels, and the couple had toured a variety of German theaters. Their repertoire included Porte Saint Martin swashbucklers such as *La Délivrance des Grecs* and *Wild Girl of the Ardennes* (ballet-drama). The Hazards, incidentally, established themselves in Philadelphia and trained other local ballet luminaries, including the famous Wells sisters, Louise and Amelia.

Philadelphia journals announced the first appearance on any stage of the little Augusta (shortly a Gallic *la petite*) as a feature of her mother's benefit on Dec. 30, 1837, noting that she was a "Pupil of Mons. P. H. Hazard," in *Le Dieu et la Bayadère* (*The Maid of Cashmere*). This was the ballet-opera based on Goethe's ballad with a book by Scribe and music by D. F. E. Auber. First presented in 1830 at the Paris Opéra, with choreography by Filippo Taglioni designed to display the abilities of Marie, its American première was given by Mlle. Augusta for her debut in 1836. It obtained an overwhelming success and remained in American repertoire beyond the middle of the century.

Francis Wemyss relates in his memoirs: "Zelica in the 'Maid of Cashmere' by a native American dancer is an era in the history of the stage worthy of the same page which sounds the praise of Edwin Forrest. Possessed of every requisite to acquire future fame; very ambitious; passionately fond of her art, Augusta Maywood won a triumph which her father should have improved to better advantage." (Wemyss meant to the parents' advantage.)

Augusta was an incontrovertible sensation, but engendered one of those seemingly indispensable ballet feuds, recorded thus by Wemyss: "There was another candidate for fame on this same 30th December, Miss Mary Ann Lee, who, in the trial dance, won for herself a reputation in public favor. The manager, justly proud of the success of his little daughter-in-law, was guilty of an injustice to the poor dependent girl, who aided her success. After Augusta's benefit had taken place, on the 5th of January, the citizens, anxious to afford Miss Lee some mark of their favor, applied to the manager to appoint a night for her benefit. This Mr. Maywood at first indignantly refused, as an insult to his dear child; and afterwards as foolishly granted. The excitement thus raised enabled Miss Lee to boast of a triumph over her more gifted competitor; wreaths were showered on the stage every night during the trial of skill, by the friends of both parties. They deserved these attentions from the audience; their success was but a just tribute to merit; and, if La Petite Augusta felt any jealous pang to mar her triumph, the injudicious conduct of her own parents toward 'our Mary Ann' as Miss Lee was now familiarly termed, was the sole cause. As a foil to her own excellence,

Miss Lee would have been the most valuable auxiliary she could have found; in claiming to be her equal, for a time she lost ground: yet her career has been a profitable one, if not so brilliant as Augusta's. What a pity two such young creatures should have been separated with rancor in their hearts, when, united, they would have proved a source of mutual profit. The public felt proud of them, as children whose talent should be encouraged. As the companion and schoolfellow of my own children, I felt an interest in the success of Augusta Maywood, which induced me to peril my own interest, by loaning to the managers Mr. Russell Smith, to paint the scenery of *La Sylphide* which was the next part attempted by the juvenile dancer."

New York was shortly apprised of the child wonder by the *Mirror*, which on Feb. 3, 1838, reprinted this notice from the Philadelphia *Inquirer*, shortly before her Park Theatre debut on February 12: "The favorable impression made by this young creature on the night of her debut, has been fully confirmed by her subsequent performances. She is, indeed, a most extraordinary child, and destined, we doubt not, to produce no ordinary sensation in the theatrical world. She is extremely youthful, being not more than eleven or twelve years of age; but her form is one of the most symmetrical that we ever looked upon, and her every movement is grace. This may seem extravagant praise, but we believe we shall be fully borne out in it, by the thousands who have already witnessed her delightful acting and wonderful dancing. Her success on Friday night was perfect and complete. She surpassed herself, and proved to any who could have entertained a doubt before, that she is indeed a prodigy in her way, and fully entitled to the praise that has been so liberally lavished upon her. The best evidence of her merit, however, is the fact that she personated the character of Zelica six or eight times during the last fortnight, and never to any but a brilliant, fashionable, and admiring audience. That a child of her age should have succeeded so thoroughly in a character which Celeste considered one of the most difficult in the whole range of dramatic opera, is surprising indeed, and a proper idea may be formed of her attraction, when we state that Saturday last, we heard an enterprising professional gentleman of this city, offer fifteen thousand dollars for her services, for a single year. We do not desire to be extravagant in a matter of this sort; but, as we perceive a disposition in other cities, to secure the services of Augusta for a brief engagement, we have thought this much due by way of explanation, as to the real character of her merits and success."

La petite Augusta was a major sensation in New York. As the *Mirror* noted on February 24, "Philadelphia has covered herself with glory in borrowing this native-born sprite of New York for a season, and returning her so rich in attractions to the home of her childhood. . . . Her bright, pretty elfish face and ariel-like figure, the mingled grace and precision of her movements, and above all the wonderful muscular powers she displays for a child of twelve, can hardly be overrated in their attractions; while as a mere actress, her versatility of expression, both of feature and gesture, and her winning archness and finished byplay, impart to her performance a charm infinitely beyond her years."

During entr'actes Augusta recited *The Seven Ages of Woman* to ecstatic applause.

In addition to ephemeral plaudits, Augusta received the accolade of portraiture. Henry Inman, noted American artist who later painted Fanny Elssler in her loge, did a full-length portrait of *la petite*. The New York *Mirror* on March 31, 1838, reported: "One of the happiest things Inman ever did is his full-length portrait of this dancing fairy. He has caught the very elvish look of the eye that gives such piquancy to the turn of her head and each movement of the buoyant and elastick figure. So life-like and natural is it,

that it seems almost as if it would bound from the canvas. We hope to see it engraved in a style commensurate with its extraordinary merit." Unfortunately no print was made that is on record (the Robinson print seems an unlikely candidate) and the picture disappears from sight in 1846, when it was in the collection of one W. T. Porter.

The popular print market offered H. R. Robinson's *La Petite Augusta*, a becurled pretty child, without the gaucherie usual to her age. In *Bayadère* or as Dewdrop in *The Mountain Sylph* (a ballad-opera thematically inspired by *La Sylphide*, occasionally billed under that title) she was acclaimed as a young divinity. Thus it was almost with a sense of bereavement that the *Knickerbocker Magazine* in March, 1838, announced her departure for Paris, where her professional education was to be completed.

Maywood's colleague Wemyss exclaimed: "How Manager Maywood, with his usual shrewdness, could have committed such a mistake as to suffer Augusta to proceed to Paris, until he had first gathered the dollars, which in America actually invited him to accept them, has surprised all his friends. A most brilliant future opened before the young lady, which a tour throughout the United States would have improved into fortune and independence; while one year so spent, would not have marred her prospects in France: for in Paris, the young American, La Petite Sauvage, would have been at any time regarded as a prodigy; petted, applauded and spoilt. As a novelty, sending dancers from North America to Paris, was carrying the war into Africa with a vengeance."

Paris had already heard of *la petite Augusta*. The *Revue et Gazette Musicale de Paris*, in its news column for June 24, 1838, reported that "despite religious austerity prevalent in the United States, New York splendidly acclaims pretty and svelte ballerinas. Madame Lecomte has recently excited transports of enthusiasm in the Dance of the Nuns from the third act of *Robert-le-diable*. People also speak of two young misses—Augusta Maywood and Miss Wells, as sharing American favor with Madame Lecomte." The paragraph, not too accurate, notes that Miss Wells is expected shortly in Paris; this was later corrected, and by the following July (1839), there was considerable talk of the *"jeune personnage de quatorze ans"* who was shortly to make her debut.

Wemyss conceded that the child was very ambitious, passionately fond of her art, and that "at the academy at Paris, she practiced with unremitting diligence." The flurry started around Augusta before her arrival was augmented by rumors of her astonishing classwork under Mazillier and Corally. Charles de Boigne, in his *Petites Mémoires de l'Opéra* (Paris, 1857), said that "she danced, or rather gamboled, with a petulance and passion to divert and electrify the most measured pupils of Mazillier's class."

By November 11, 1839, scarcely fifteen years old, she was ready for the supreme test of any ballerina during that century—a Paris Opéra debut. The Opéra prestige was unassailable; even an engagement in a minor capacity, entitling an artist to add "of the Paris Opéra" to his billing, was a tangible asset. An engagement as *première danseuse* was tantamount to a guarantee of a career. The Parisian audience, *Parisiens de Paris*, was the most brilliant intellectually, artistically, and sartorially in the entire world. During this period, at a top-flight salon such as Nodier's, one might see Chopin, Musset, Nerval, Tony Johannot, Hugo, Balzac, Beyle, Dumas père, Vigny, Nanteuil, and Devéria. A first-night audience invariably included such knowledgeable people as *les frères* Cogniard, librettists and guiding geniuses of the Porte Saint Martin, Roger de Beauvoir, the critic and aesthetic arbiter Jules Janin, the protean Henri Monnier, Musard, and Eugène Sue.

To this audience exoticism was almost a religion, whether of time as represented by a medieval lute, or space, by the Oriental guzla. An extraordinary costume, a strange and bizarre background, were in themselves *à la mode*. These years saw the loveliest of Gavarni's *travestissements*—Oriental, Greek, Spanish. In her own fashion Augusta Maywood was an exotic, a *personnage bizarre*, by the mere fact of being there. Yet this receptive audience was discriminating and articulate. Théophile Gautier, most astute of all theater critics, superlatively so of the dance, was able more than any other to catch the essential physical, technical, and spiritual capacities of a performer. His review of Augusta's debut on November 11 (one of the few, and the only major ballet criticism Mr. Beaumont has chosen to ignore in his translations from Gautier) was published on November 25, 1839.

The dance, for some time neglected at the Opéra, and which Mlle. Fanny Elssler alone has sustained on the points of her little feet, seems to have resumed a place of honor; fortunate debuts succeed one another; after Mlle. Lucile Grahn who comes to us from Denmark, behold now Mlle. Augusta Maywood who comes to us from America. Every part of the world seems to send us dancers; if this continues our *corps de ballet* will soon be the most cosmopolitan body one could see; Danes, Germans, Americans, English, are all found there; it is a veritable Babel with seventy-two idioms. Happily the language of the dance may be understood everywhere, and feet have no accent. [*Les pieds n'ont pas d'accent.*] Mlle. Augusta Maywood has a completely clear-cut type of talent; it is not the melancholy grace, dreamy abandon and nonchalant lightness of Mlle. Grahn, who reflects in her eyes the clear and cold blue of the Norwegian sky, and who seems a walkyrie dancing on the snow; it is yet less the inimitable perfection, shining constancy, allure of a classic Diana, and sculptural purity of Mlle. Fanny Elssler; it is something abrupt, unexpected, bizarre, which sets her completely apart. Daughter of a New York or Philadelphia theater manager, we aren't too certain which, she created a furor in America, danced the most

AUGUSTA MAYWOOD

Impareggiabile Danzatrice.

in Ancona nella Primavera del 53

Augusta Maywood. 1853.

complicated ballets, sang, played tragedy, in short was an infant prodigy;—she came in search of Parisian sanction, for the opinion of Paris agitates even United States barbarians in their world of railroads and steamboats.—For a prodigy, Mlle. Maywood is truly quite something.

She is of medium size, very well built, very young, eighteen years according to calumniators, with black eyes and a wide-awake and savage little face which gambles strongly on being pretty; add to this sinews of steel, joints of a jaguar, and an agility approaching that of clowns; for the rest, it would be impossible to be less intimidated by so formidable a test; there she came, under fire of footlights and lorgnettes, which strike fear in the most intrepid, as tranquil as an established dancer; you would have thought that it was simply a matter of her parterre of Yankees; in two or three bounds she cleared this great theatre from backdrop to prompter's box, making those almost horizontal *vols penchés* which made the fame of Perrot the aerien; and then she began to gambol, to pirouette *dans l'air sur elle-même*, to do back turns with a suppleness and force worthy of Lawrence or Redisha; [1] you would have said a rubber ball bouncing on a racquet; she has much elevation and spring; her little legs of a wild doe make steps as long as those of Mlle. Taglioni.

The costume she wore the day of her first debut in *le diable boiteux* was in rather American taste. Picture to yourself a pink waist, pink skirt without white petticoats underneath, and pink tights, the whole embellished with varicolored passementerie and sequins. A toilette to enchant a rope dancer (this is not a term of scorn; we adore rope dancers)! The second appearance in *Tarentule* she was gowned *en paysanne*, with that eternal black bodice and no less inevitable petticoat so lavished on ballets with sylvan pretensions; if the other costume was too savage, this one was much too civilized.

Mlle. Augusta Maywood will be a good acquisition for the Opera; she has a style of her own, a very remarkable cachet of originality; connoisseurs who attended the coronation festivities at Milan claim that Mlle. Maywood approaches very much the style of Mlle. Cerrito.

Charles Merruau, in the *Revue et Gazette Musicale*, also discussed this debut at length.

After grumbling that all good artists who came from foreign parts to train and make their debuts in Paris eventually went back to their native lands to garner rich rewards, he admitted that of course there was nothing else for them to do, since the Parisian audience was the *only* one in the world qualified to give the accolade. Reportedly *la petite Augusta* was to return to America, and undoubtedly her success would pass all expectations. "However that may be," he wrote, "the young dancer made her debut Monday in a *pas* which was introduced for her in the first act of *Diable Boiteux*. A petite creature, gracious and alive, with light movements, vigorous leg, well-defined gesture, piquant smile, mischievous eye, a pretty face and scarcely fifteen years—and there you have Mademoiselle Augusta. Imagine a madcap and frenetic dance, prodigious leaps, leaps which covered the stage in three bounds, *entrechats* combined with pirouettes such as would do honor to Perrot, *battements horizonteaux* such as Paul did once upon a time, extreme verve, incredible swing, miraculous composure, and you will have an idea of the surprise mixed with pleasure which the apparition of this strange child must have caused on the stage where a few days before one had applauded the poetic dance, the genteel grace of Mademoiselle Grahn, and where one had applauded the elegant and voluptuous Catchucha of Mademoiselle Elssler. Mademoiselle Augusta Maywood was vigorously applauded, as one might easily guess. A part of this success is due to M. Corally, her teacher, whose lessons developed the extraordinary talents of the young dancer and who, if he will temper a trifle this inordinate fervor, will make of his pupil the most original and piquant dancer one could possibly imagine."

There could have been no more auspicious debut; the physical equipment, which made comparison to the greatest male dancers and acrobats a feature of both reviews, the *diable au corps,* and completely individual style set her immediately in a unique category. Augusta took her place in the regular company, and appeared in a very special benefit arranged for Elssler in February, 1840. Curiously, in future years, wherever Augusta appeared Fanny had been there shortly before; there is somehow a feeling, for Elssler was notably generous and helpful, that Fanny was instrumental in advancing the little Maywood during those early years.

In any event, the Maywoods, settling down in Paris, were shortly unsettled by their vivacious daughters. Mary Elizabeth eloped with a Mr. Sidney Wilkins, trombone player at the Paris Opéra; she later returned to the parental fold. (Occasionally there is an er-roneous reference to Mr. Wilkins as Augusta's husband.) The great blow to their anticipated golden future faded with Augusta's startling marriage.

Theatrical annuals of 1840, which list all major performances, reappearances, and debuts of 1839, have an entry under Paris Opéra for January 4—"Debut of M. Charles Mabille (*la muette de Portici*)." This same annual lists Maywood, in company with the Elsslers, Noblet, Leroux, Grahn, and the Dumilâtres, as *première ballerine.* About Charles Mabille there is mystery and confusion. An Auguste Mabille, son of the famous Bal Mabille *patron,* had been a partner of Elssler's shortly before in London; he had an excellent career and was one of the last

Gustavo Carey and Fanny Elssler in *Faust.* Vienna, ca. 1850.

great *danseurs nobles* at the Opéra. Charles, who was probably his younger brother, is a shadowy figure; it would seem, despite the 1839 debut notice, that they might be the same person, save for the fact that when Charles was in Lisbon during 1844-45, *the* Mabille is appearing in Paris. In 1840 Charles Mabille is listed in the Opéra company, and no mention of Auguste. The strange lacunae in the histories of Charles and Auguste have led several interested ballet detectives to the conclusion that they were identical—a happy explanation save for documentary evidence that two separate bodies were in two separate places at the same time. If it had been the great Mabille, moreover, the Maywoods might not have been as upset as they were on losing their gold mine to Mabille *cadet*.

The marriage was a sensation of the Parisian boulevards and London green rooms (Robert Campbell Maywood was not a negligible theatrical figure). On November 4, 1840, a note in the *Revue et Gazette Musicale* says: "Everyone speaks of the disappearance of Mademoiselle Maywood of the Opéra. The wings are busy with this scandal." The fugitives had appeared in a performance of *Le Diable Amoureux* and disappeared immediately thereafter. On November 15 the *Revue* further reports that the fugitives were held at Boulogne, thanks to a telegraph order, were returned to Paris and had arrived that day; unless an amiable agreement and a *désistement conseillé par la raison* did not give pause, the parquet would be able to follow the complaint of abduction of a minor, which charge had already been registered in the law journal, and on which Mabille was held. Whatever potent arguments were produced in favor of the marriage are not recorded, but consent was finally given and the suit dropped. The New York *Spirit of the Times* received an account in a London theatrical gossip dispatch and relayed the elopement to her American public, which straightway began to disapprove the headstrong Augusta, although it was clearly stated that the couple expected to go home to the States.

Robert Maywood packed up the rest of the family and returned to America; the Opéra was in doldrums prior to Grisi's engagement, and during 1842 there is no record of Augusta's dancing; she was probably having that baby she allegedly abandoned later, and may well have used that as an excuse not to return immediately. Mary Elizabeth, for technical financial reasons, had become lessee of the Chestnut Street Theatre, and announced the return of her sister "formerly la Petite Augusta." Maywood himself, in a letter to J. S. Jones, manager of the Tremont Theatre, Boston, dated Sept. 7, 1842, wrote: "With regard to the possibilities of the present season I may say we expect J. Wallack, Mr. Balls, Augusta Maywood and her husband from Paris. . . . Wallack was to leave on the 4th of this month and Balls about the end— I expect to hear from Mrs. Stirling by the 19th or the 1st of October at latest—Augusta Maywood and her good man will be later." On Sept. 28 he wrote: ". . . with regard to Augusta, as soon as I know the exact period of her arrival—I'll let you know—and depend upon my taking care of you in the arrangement—and take my word for it she will be the best star of the season, and she has what others want, youth and beauty—with very superior talent and is besides a New Yorker by birth. . . ."

Unfortunately for the family exchequer Augusta never returned. Fundamentally she was above all else a ballerina, who loved dancing to such a degree that she preferred to risk competition and unremitting hard work in order to remain at its creative center. She undoubtedly knew that an assured fortune awaited her in America; her future in Europe at that point had only an auspicious Paris debut and her own conviction as assets. Perhaps she preferred to remain where she felt temperamentally at home, and decided to let her family fend for themselves.

She did not see her future in terms of the Paris Opéra. Charles de Boigne, to whom an engagement in Paris seemed the ultimate good of this world, blamed her marriage, and bitterly exclaimed: "This poor little Augusta Maywood! she couldn't let herself be re-engaged by the Opéra; she had too much life, too much future; she thought herself obliged to marry a myrmidon of a dancer, counterfeit and churlish, who peddled her about from city to city. O dancers! will you then always marry dancers?"

In any event, Mabille's marital *colportage* was now dignified by a major engagement. A Sr. A. Porto had assumed management of the Teatro de S. Carlos of Lisbon, and was determined that Lisbon audiences should no longer be known as the world's most patient amateurs. To ensure a good ballet company he engaged the amazing Gustavo Carey, one

Domenico Ronzani. Ca. 1847.

Teresa Gambardella. Ca. 1840.

great-grandchildren of the notable and eccentric British composer Henry Carey. His activities covered, among other engagements, the considerable period of 1827 to 1854 as guest choreographer and male premier at the Vienna Hofburgoperntheater. For the Lisbon season of 1843-1844 (which started Sept. 1) Carey is listed as choreographer, *los conjuges* Mabille as *primi ballerini*, *los conjuges* Montani as principal mimes, seconded by Luigi and Giuseppa Romolo, Francesco Pintauro, six mimes and thirty-six coryphees.

Augusta's debut, in *Giselle*, reported at length in the *Revista Universal Lisbonese* (Tomo III, p. 144) triumphed over a cabal organized by one of the discharged dancers, José Stephene, to demonstrate against the new company. Billed as Senhora Mabille, her Lisbon debut exceeded even the Paris ovation. Silva Leal wrote ecstatic notices of the "poetic ballerina" in *Giselle*, of her force, agility, and grace in Spanish dances, of her voluptuous appeal, of how she rescued one of Carey's less fortunate ballets, *Rolando e Morgana*, and how incomparable she was in a cracovienne. Mabille is never once mentioned; it is clear that his eighteen-year-old wife was the attraction.

Like Elssler, Augusta was never afraid of competition and always generous to newcomers; one such incident should be recorded. Judith Rugalli, twelve-year-old daughter of a Lisbon actress, danced at her mother's benefit a cracovienne in imitation of Madame Mabille, who gave her blessing and ensured an audience of all local balletophiles. After her triumph young Judith wrote a touching letter to the *Revista Universal*, telling how the art of Madame Mabille so enthused her that in childish dreams she formed the project of this dance; she concludes with a touching tribute to Augusta—"I took my inspiration from the graceful steps of the foreign Sylphide."

The only carping notice our American prodigy received during her entire stay was in her second season, when she introduced the

of the great male dancers of his generation, idol of St. Petersburg, who had even successfully braved the virtual ban against male dancers in Paris. Friend and partner of Elssler, his unusual vocation for an English patronymic indicates that he may have been, like Edmund Kean, one of the four fabulous polka on the Lisbon stage and was accused of substituting a polonnaise. In addition to *divertissements* Augusta danced *Giselle* (the only ballet staged by Mabille), Carey's *Rolando e Morgana*, *Mascaras de Venesa*, *Novo Azor*, *A aldeia polaca*, *O conscripto*, and his restagings of *Bayadère*, *Diable Amoureux* and *La Gypsy*. Her re-engagement for the season 1844-1845 was announced with joy in an *Alleluia Lyrica* on Nov. 28, 1844.

There was no mention of any rift in the *ménage Mabille* until February 6, 1845, when a cryptic paragraph, titled *Ma Bille* (a pun on the Portuguese word for document, pronouncement, or tax decree) says: "Everyone admired Madame Mabille's ethereal qualities in *Giselle*, her gracefulness in *la cracovienne*, and her exuberance in *Le Diable Amoureux*. She outdid herself—she did not fly, she veritably volatized herself with a verve and at the same time a grace that left the audience gasping. Madame Mabille, it was the unanimous verdict, was a lovely spirit. But the worst of it is, as the psychologists of opera put it, that spirits which depart do not return." On February 28, however, she is still dancing, in spite of the rumors, and the critic notes parenthetically that he did not propose "to enter into an examination of the stories current in this respect." Whatever occurred precipitated some sort of upheaval, which in turn sired a scandal in the States.

The New York *Mirror*, July 12, 1845, prints the following communication: "The desertion of her husband by Augusta Maywood, or rather Madame Mabille, the danseuse, is mentioned by the Paris correspondent of the *Courrier des Etats-Unis*—it took place February last at Lisbon, while they were playing an engagement at the St. Charles Theatre. She left the house in the evening, leaving a letter for her husband in which she says:

" 'At this moment I find myself in a position, which will not permit me to remain any longer in your house—our characters are unsuited, and my affections for a long time have been placed upon another, and I doubt not that our mutual happiness will be increased by my departure.

" 'I accuse you of nothing—since we have been married you have always been a devoted and good husband, but unhappily our relative situations do not accord, and with another woman less *exalted* than me I doubt not you will find more happiness.

" 'Pardon me if I have caused you discomfort, I know how much you love our little one, I need not commend it to your care, I only ask that it may never know the guilt of its mother.'

"Monsieur Mabille is an actor and the son of a celebrated professor of dancing, and the lover is also an actor attached to the Lisbon theatre."

The fact that the Mabilles were dancing together at Masoni's benefit toward the end of May in itself gives the lie to this flight, abetted by the obviously phony style of the alleged document, which leaves the child curiously sexless, and is written with the literary distinction of a third-class melodrama. More tangible evidence that they were together is offered in program files of the Vienna Hofburgoperntheater at Harvard. During the season 1845-1846 Augusta Maywood and Mabille are dancing there together. Augusta resumed her maiden name; very likely their domestic difficulties had been rooted in Mabille's professional jealousy.

Gustavo Carey was committed to one of his usual engagements as *premier danseur* in Vienna for the autumn of 1845. Through him Augusta received the coveted post of *prima ballerina*, with the sanction of Elssler, who had just finished an engagement there. Mabille went along as solo-dancer. The excellent Anton Guerra was choreographer and ballet master that season. Maywood's debut, as *Giselle*, with Carey dancing *Albrecht*, took place in October, and this ballet was performed repeatedly through November. On December 8 Mabille makes his appearance with a *pas de deux* composed by himself and danced with Augusta, inserted in Guerra's ballet *Der Mädchenraub in Venedig* (music by Mathias Strebinger of the theater staff). Carey moved on to other engagements and his place as premier was taken by Pasquale Borri, then one of Italy's greatest dancers, later one of her greatest choreographers, and long one of Maywood's partners. Mabille continued to arrange special *pas*, while Augusta moves from one lead to another—*Es ist ein Scherz, Manfred*, and *Die Hochzeit des Bachus*. The final and concise record of the Maywood-Mabille parting was not in the Lisbon letter but in the Hofburgtheater records; "Abgegangen: Hr. Solotänzer Mabille. Neu engagirt: Mad. Maywood."

Henceforth Augusta guided her own destinies with God's help and hard work. In September, 1846, the season opened with a revival of Guerra's *"grosses fantastiches ballet" Manfred*. In November Victor Bartholomin was engaged as choreographer and ballet master; the company was augmented by Beau and one of the omnipresent Mérantes as *premier danseur*. For Maywood, Bartholomin created a number of ballets—*Die Zauberlampe, Elina oder die Rückkehr ins Dorf*, and *Ein Ländlisches Fest*. These last two (with music by Wilhelm Reuling) were in the Bartholomin-Monplaisir repertoire for their American tour the following season.

Pasquale Borri resumes his place in the company, augmented by a famous guest star. In January, 1847, Eraklito Nikitin, of the St. Petersburg Opera, first Russian male dancer to appear outside of his prescribed precincts, arrived in Vienna. He was a brilliant performer and created a sensation in his very brief European *tournée*. Customarily distinguished visiting artists at the Hofburgtheater received larger billing than resident stars. La Maywood demanded—and got—equal billing with Nikitin and Adelaide Mérante, also a guest performer. They must have given an extraordinary performance—Maywood as Giselle, Nikitin the Albrecht and Mérante as Myrrtha. As usual Augusta seems to have been on excellent terms with her fellow artists. Nikitin, with an engagement for La Scala already set, probably added his recommendation for her engagement there at the famous 1848 carnival. Although but twenty-two years old, with a heavy performance schedule, she found time to coach the young Pauline Santi, who appeared on February 26, 1847, in a *pas de deux* with Borri, programed in heavy letters as a *"Schülerin der Mad. Maywood."*

In May she was dancing the title role of Perrot's *Katharina oder die Töchter des Banditen*, staged by the new ballet master Domenico Ronzani, thenceforward one of her most important associates and later an outstanding factor in American dance history. Ronzani had an excellent reputation as a mime; several members of his family turn up in various Italian companies. Domenico had appeared intermittently at La Scala since 1831, working under such choreographers as Antonio Cortesi, Livio Morosini, Antonio Monticini, and Bernardo Vestris. He was for some time impresario at La Fenice of Venice. He gained a reputation staging ballets of the greatest choreographers when they were not available. For example, in 1846 he staged Perrot's *Esmeralda* for Elssler's guest appearance in Vienna. His association with Maywood as director, agent, and impresario gave him essential experience to undertake his American tour a decade later.

Through her growing Viennese *réclame* the directors of La Scala at Milan decided to engage her for *carnevale e quaresima*, 1848. That particular season was one of such brilliance that a nostalgic glance at its roster is in order. The choreographers were Perrot, Augusto Huss, and Andrea Palladini; *primi ballerini*—Fanny Elssler, Augusta Maywood, Carolina Vendt, Giulio Perrot, Eraklito Nikitin; *primi mimi*—Paolina Monti, Effisio Catte, Bagnoli-Quattri, Gaspare Pratesi, Domenico Viganó, etc.

The ballets included a restaging of Henry's *L'assedio di Calais* with Maywood and Nikitin reunited in principal roles, by Huss, Cortesi's *Silfide* (182?) restaged by Palladini, and the première of Perrot's great fantastic ballet *Faust*, the title role created by Elssler *and* Maywood; Fanny danced Marguerite the opening night, Augusta followed the second performance—a fact which Mr. Beaumont has carefully ignored in his notes on this ballet. According to the *Gazzetta Privileggiata di Milan* (March 8, 1848), Perrot was still working on the ballet after its première, "omitting, changing, substituting, and abbreviating." It was Maywood whom he directed in this perfection by performance process.

Actually it was on Maywood's young shoulders that the mantle of Fanny was adjusted, and for the next decade it is Maywood who is an outstanding interpreter of the great dramatic roles in romantic ballet. With Elssler she shared the most coveted title in Italy— *prima ballerina e prima mima assoluta.* In 1854 when Carolina Pochini attempted *Esmeralda* at Milan, the comparison was to Elssler and Maywood.

At this point, with engagements offered from all parts of Italy, Augusta decided on a course which was the pioneer effort of its type. Hitherto important soloists had filled engagements at various opera houses, taking a partner here, another there, depending on the local stage director to set productions in order. Augusta joined forces with the Lasiná brothers, Giovanni Battista, and Giuseppe, to organize a semi-permanent company which toured Italy; Giovanni was an indifferent choreographer, a good *metteur en scène,* a superlative business manager. The *premier* was Antonio Parlerini, of the renowned dancing family, Vicenzo Schiano was *primo mimo* and the excellent Teresa Gambardella *prima mima.* This was the period during which Italy produced some of its most superb male dancers; the situation was radically different from Paris, where the male dancer had be-

Augusta Maywood. 1851.

come an adjunct or mere prop, where mimes capable of interpreting the great dramatic ballets who were yet fine dancers had almost ceased to exist. Augusta danced with the greatest in Italy. Even a superficial reading of Italian theatrical annuals and criticism establishes the standing of her company; subsidiary roles likewise were entrusted to good performers; Lasiná even had scenery designed and transported to smaller houses, and only local *corps de ballet* had to be enlisted.

Parenthetically it might be amusing to see what Wemyss had to say about Augusta in his reminiscences (New York, 1847). "She . . . married; thus blasting all hopes of fortune to her parents. An undutiful child never made a good wife. She has deserted her husband, and the heartless letter in which she recommended her child to the care of its father, at the moment she was abandoning him for the arms of a paramour, proves that her heart is even lighter than her heels. The very brilliance of her opening in life has been her ruin; the stage again pointed at as impure and immoral; and Augusta Maywood, who should have been, and who would have been the pride of it, as an American artiste—who had gained the highest honors abroad—has become its shame: and thus I draw the veil upon her and her crimes forever, hoping that she may never attempt to appear upon the stage of her native country again; and if she does, that her countrywomen, whose character for purity she has disgraced, will drive her from it indignantly, as a warning to others not to follow her example." Augusta did not bother to deny the canard. She was far too busy to trouble her pretty head with Wemyssian fulminations.

Italian journals exceeded themselves in hyperbole. The adjectives "graceful," "light," "bold," "forceful," "harmonious," "audacious," "sentimental," "vivacious," "incomparable," and "unique"; the titles "queen of the air," "new Terpsichore," "gracious Sylphide"; the comparisons "contemporary to Taglioni, Elssler, and Cerrito, she shares with them the highest place in the kingdom of Terpsichore," "Maywood, as always incomparable both as mime and dancer," and repeated judgments on the "force, dexterity, litheness, grace, and elegance of this exquisite dancer, and her genius for miming" become clamorous. Souvenir books of poetry celebrate her appearances, memorial plaques are cast, and lithographs of her sold to that general public which was *fanatizzó* for la Maywood. If the Italians liked her the compliment was returned. Save for one excursion to the scene of her earlier triumphs in Vienna, Augusta devoted her career to the Italian theater.

In 1849 she makes a happy return to La Scala in Perrot's *Faust* staged by Ronzani, *Giselle*, and a rather mediocre Ronzani spectacular ballet *L'orfana della Suleide*. From 1850 to 1854 she tours Italy, working with Ronzani or the Lasiná brothers. Her repertoire included *Esmeralda, Caterina la Figlia*

del Bandito, Giselle, Faust, La Jolie Fille de Gand, La Zingara, La Vivandiera, Ronzani's *La sposa di Appenzello, Erta la Regina dell'-Elfride, Zelia o il velo magico* (sometimes credited to Livio Morosini, actually a version of Guerra's 1841 *Il velo incantato*), Lasiná's versions of *Faust*, titled *Mefistofele* and *Il sogno di un alchimista* respectively, and his original ballets (rated by Cambiarsi as *cattivo*) *Una festa da ballo* and *L'araba,* Morosini's *I Suliotti,* and *divertissements* in such operas as *Spagnuoli al Peru* and *Rigoletto*.

In 1853 she appears for the first time in a ballet by Giuseppe Rota (1822-1865), one of the foremost Italian choreographers of the second half century, famous for ensembles, good-naturedly known as "lover of the happy ending," whose ballets remained for generations in Italian repertoire. Cambiarsi rates *Un fallo*, first ballet of the autumn season in Milan in which they are associated, as *ottimo*, or superlative (it had fifty-four performances).

Even more interesting to us is the November 10 première—*I bianchi ed i negri,* from the popular novel *Il capenna di Zio Tom*— our *Uncle Tom's Cabin!* Fantastic as it may seem, scarcely two years after its first American appearance as a serial, and but one year after its first American dramatization, Milan was applauding a theme which is an ironic commentary on a certain Ethiopian campaign. The first Italian edition of *Uncle Tom* was published in 1853, so that Rota had lost no time in adapting it. The music was by Paolo Giorza and the social overtones of the libretto were termed "allegorical." This ballet was often revived, sometimes as *La Capenna di Tom* by Ferdinand Pratesi, and by Rota himself through 1863. The critic of *Il Pirata* (correspondent to Turin, October 23, 1853) reported: "The first and second acts are of absolute beauty, and the *ballabile* of the Negroes aroused pronounced enthusiasm. Catte and Razzanelli stood out prominently. La Maywood was as usual an exquisite dancer." Although no record of distribution is available here, Effisio Catte, the renowned mime, was undoubtedly Uncle Tom, Assunta Razzanelli, *prima mima assoluta,* Topsy, and presumably la Maywood was little Eva, an assignment which would have infuriated the American press.

At this point it might be well to mention the other great sin of which Augusta was accused by every journalist and theater historian in America—filial ingratitude. The American point of view is summed up in a dispatch dated December 10, 1852, and the commentary which accompanied its publication in the *Daily Evening Traveller* (Boston, January 15, 1853):

A correspondent of the Boston *Traveller*, says the furore of the Italians for Miss Maywood's dancing has been most astonishing. She is from Philadelphia, and is really a wonderful dancer, unsurpassed, perhaps, in her vein. If we can credit the newspaper critics here, she excels Cerito, Elssler, and even Taglioni herself. So accurate is her time that the music seems to emanate from her, and if her grace has been equalled or exceeded by others, her activity and endurance are unrivalled. She has engagements for three years in advance. All the while she was in Florence the excitement continued unabated. Prices doubled; there was no end to the applause and callings out, often four or more times successively; and on the occasion of her benefit it took three carriages to carry away the bouquets. To handle such as were cast at her feet required no slight muscular effort. They were, without exaggeration, as large as flour barrels. As accustomed to exertion as is Miss Maywood, she absolutely staggered under the weight. They were most beautifully done up with ribbons. The shower of flowers from the Duke of Talleyrand's box, nephew of the late Prince, was particularly heavy. . . .

We have a few words to say upon this subject. The above person is an adopted daughter of Robert Campbell Maywood, some years since distinguished as the Lessee and Manager of the Chestnut St. Theatre in this city. He expended thousands upon the child Augusta, who since her European residence has fallen from that position of respectability adorning virtue and integrity, and in their declining days left Mr. and Mrs. Maywood neglected and in abject poverty.

"How sharper than a serpent's tooth it is to have a thankless child."

Yet even at this time Robert Campbell Maywood was obtaining a haven with Augusta in Italy! Of the other discredits the first advanced is that Mr. Maywood spent huge sums on Augusta's education; one might also note that he exploited her talents and that part of his investment paid dividends in her early engagements. Her elopement, considered a direct affront to the parents, may have been precipitated by some intolerable family situation.

In any event, after failing to recoup his fortunes in America, Robert C. Maywood joined Augusta in Italy, where he lived with her several years in what even the prejudiced Phelps admits was "great affluence." In 1855, so the story proceeds in Ireland's history of the American stage, Robert Maywood returned to America, bearing a letter which Augusta purportedly had admonished him not to open until he was on the boat, which he expected contained a substantial sum of money. When this letter was opened it allegedly contained a most bitter denunciation, and no money. Mr. Maywood had a stroke and died in the Troy Infirmary a year later. Both her mother and sister died in reduced circumstances, while Augusta, according to Phelps (1880) "amassed a fortune and retired to a half-million-dollar villa at Lake Como," that cosmopolitan retreat for retired bankers and ballerinas.

There is no attempt here to whitewash Augusta. It isn't necessary. However, one is impelled to note a consistent attitude in the American journals. It was one of a certain resentment, not only that Augusta's private life was considered beyond the pale, but that she seemed to thrive so well. It would have been so much simpler to point to her in horror if after a period of time she had lost her popularity, was ridden by some such vice as drink which ruined her looks, was impoverished, and generally represented an accepted nineteenth-century American tableau of the wages of sin.

For a certainty Augusta had become identified with the Italian theater. There is scarcely a reference to her as a *celebre danzatrice americana;* she is invariably mentioned as one of the glories of Italian ballet. In 1852, when she dances in *Il sogno di un alchimista* at Firenze, the little Teatro Mecanico in the Anfiteatro Goldoni presents a marionette version of her production. To be immortalized by the *fantoccini* meant a firm foothold in the indigenous culture.

Bologna, Padua, Trieste, Brescia, Venice, Milan, Verona, Naples, Ancona, Ferrara, Ravenna, Forli, Firenze, Genoa, Vicenza, Viterbo, Turin, and Rome were in her itinerary. Her period was the last great epoch in Italian ballet. Her colleagues were of such stature that they demand at least a passing note.

The great dancers in Italy, as in every ballet center, were *di rango francese*, schooled in the French tradition; thus training exclusively in the Italian school, which accounted for superb mimes, still left la Gambardella, as *prima ballerina italiana*, in second place. Nevertheless certain phases of Italian training were unsurpassed, and many dancers *di rango francese*, although not formed by Blasis as he claimed, undoubtedly passed through his training *pour s'y perfectionner*, in the way that Pavlova and Nijinsky worked with Enrico Cecchetti long after their professional debuts. It is imperative to realize that Italy had male dancers of such brilliance that any estimate of la Maywood must take into account the necessity of measuring up to and surpassing them. In addition to almost acrobatic ease of technique they had a most rigorous training

to supplement what seems a natural aptitude for pantomime. A glance at Italian prints in the Chaffee Collection, which revolutionize any usual concept of the aesthetic of Italian nineteenth-century lithography, discovers a gallery of extraordinary people. There is in these portraits a curious mixture of extreme sensitiveness and extreme literalness, rarely elements of great personal beauty but always wonderfully compelling faces and eloquent bodies. It was the unhappy capitulation of Italian ballet to spectacular opera that foreshadowed the end of this superb *primo ballarino*.

Maywood danced with the greatest—Pasquale Borri, Antonio Pallerini, Giovanni Lepri, Ferdinando Croce, Davide Mochi, and Antonio Lorenzoni; the latter four had worked with Blasis. (Parenthetically, Lepri passed on certain Blasis traditions to his pupil Enrico Cecchetti, so that we maintain a derivative clear into the twentieth century.) By 1857, to the dismay of discerning critics, a new group of male premiers strong on technique but with complete lack of taste develops with the new type of ballet; one finds the word "vulgar" applied to the exertions of Carlo Foriani, one of Maywood's last partners.

This debacle was due to increasing concessions made by choreographers to opera. The two most encouraging figures were Giuseppe Rota, then developing brilliantly after a brief while as a mime, and Pasquale Borri, turning more and more to choreography after a proud career as *premier danseur*. Neither was able, or probably desired, to change the course of Italian choreography, to which both gave its final distinction.

In the spring of 1854 Augusta returned to Vienna with Borri, under the direction of Ronzani, in *Esmeralda* and the impresario's own new fantastic ballet *Das Goldene Pferd*, later a great success of his American tour (as *The Golden Horse*). In addition to all his other duties the remarkable Ronzani was yet taking an active part in performances, main-

Maywood as Rita Gauthier. 1856.

taining his reputation as an accomplished mime. On the playbill it is apparent that Paris was still arbiter of ballet, for Maywood's billing reminds her public that she was "first dancer of the Académie impériale in Paris."

By June she is back in Padua on the first lap of a new tour which terminated in December, 1854-January, 1855, with an engagement for the Trieste carnival. Of the three choreographers originally scheduled for that season, Monticini had just died, Cortesi was immobilized by a stroke, and Galzerani not yet recovered from a serious illness; thus Augusta, who had always been able to carry even so slight a work as Ronzani's *Sposa di Appenzello,* consented to dance in *Evellina di Lesormes,* a ballet composed by her long-time associate Vicenzo Schiano. An excellent mime, he was unable to cope with choreography, and inevitably tackled an involved libretto; the music was by one Scaramelli, a local theater musician. Even a well-disposed press and the dancing of Maywood and Lepri failed to save this unhappy work. Maywood terminated her contract because of illness (Trieste gossip had it that this illness was caused by the chilly reception of *Evellina di Lesormes*), the only time she ever interrupted her scheduled tour.

For the remainder of 1855 she resumed her classic roles, save for an appearance in Rota's *Il trionfo dell' innocenza,* based on the story of il Fornaretto, the young noble falsely accused of murder. As a Rome dispatch to *Il Pirata* of Turin notes, since il Fornaretto had died once, to what purpose have him die again? Thus an elaborate libretto maneuvered a happy ending. Maywood's reception in this ballet was excellent, with Ferdinando Croce acclaimed as *il Fornaretto.* But, and this is a most unfortunate but for the history of Italian ballet, the critics wanted even more mime.

Augusta was famously equipped to satisfy this public clamor, and in her last years as a dancer she took as choreographer Filippo Termanini, who represented the unfortunate,

ultimate, and logical degeneration of Viganó's principals. He provided her with what became a "vehicle" just as *La Dame aux Camélias* was a vehicle for Bernhardt; co-incidentally, these vehicles had the same theme. In 1857 la Maywood appeared in Termanini's *Rita Gauthier,* and until her retirement some five years later, found it her most powerful drawing card, associated with her name, demanded by her public. It is somehow in character that she was able to close her career with a financially profitable work, completely typical of its period, which nonetheless demanded extraordinary artistic resources in execution.

The critic of *L'Opinione* (Turin) astutely sensed the lack of aesthetic justification, but laid it to "choreographers who avidly extend claws on some theme which presents itself before them and transform it, adjusting it to their talents and almost making a parody of it to introduce into it the eternal *pas de deux* and the final curtain of joy with analagous *ballabile.*" To remember just how powerful a realistic drama *Camille* was in its period, and that our critic considered it "more than anything else an analysis of human emotions, an anatomy of the human heart," is difficult today. Our anonymous critic felt bitterly about the whole affair.

The Teatro Carignano, which for two consecutive years was the temple in which one celebrated the apotheosis of the Lady of the Camellias, has now become the instrument of her profanation; to the laments of Violetta succeed the cabrioles of Rita Gauthier, in place of the impassioned melodies of the swan of Bussetto, are played for us the potpourris assembled by who knows what master; in a few words, instead of the sublime concepts of Verdi and Dumas we have had the sublime *pasticci* of Signor Termanini. . . . And it is very true that Signor Termanini was constrained to create a new Lady of the Camellias, to falsify the concept which informs the book by Dumas, and to change even the facts which serve as foundation to the actions. For the pathetic death of Marguerite Gauthier the choreographer has substituted a dream, after which the protagonist awakens repentant, chastened, happy and contented, and wife of the object of her affections. This is, as anyone can see, a new version of *Victorine*, of *La Jolie Fille de Gand*, of the *Rose of Florence*, and what can be born from such an agglomeration of old and disparate ideas is better left to the imagination of the reader. . . . A more unhappy thought was to have this mimic action accompanied by the music of *La Traviata*, which was found to be in continuous discrepancy with the stage action, and sometimes has a tinge of the ridiculous, as for example, towards the denouement, where the motive *Parigi o cara noi lasceremo* is reworked awkwardly to express malapropos the joy of Rita Gauthier who is reunited to her lover.

If the argument of the ballet was selected with little discernment, if the music of Traviata became in this case a contradiction, it is necessary to confess however that Signor Termanini gave proof of choreographic genius in disposing the *ballabile*, which, although they recall others already noted by the Turin public, succeed to a great enough degree nevertheless, and place in a beautiful setting the advances that have been made by the pupils of the Royal School of Ballet. And here to this is added the presence of la signora Maywood, the dancer who, especially in *pas* that require force and dramatic impulse, has no rivals, and it is no wonder that the public closed its eyes to all the absurdities of libretto and music, and absolved Termanini from all his sins.

Of course what our critic is upset about is desecration of opera, whereas it should have been desecration of ballet that needed worry. For here we have destruction of the ballet as dance, by opera, which eventually vitiated all other art forms in Italy. Even in the twentieth century when a new art form—the motion picture—appeared, it, too, was subjugated to opera, as one can see in the film *Cabiria*. Thus opera music, suitable or not, was grafted on

to ballet; five-act opera librettos were made into three-act choreodramas, with interminable vocal choruses changed to interminable *ballabile*, lengthy recitative transformed into mime, and intermittent ballet tours de force replacing the arias.

Termanini created another ballet for Augusta, *Elena Douglas*, which was a great favorite. Nothing, however, approached the demand for *Rita Gauthier*. Through 1862, shortly after which she retired, she was acclaimed in this hybrid. Yet, play her Ritas and Elenas though she did, we have her measure as an artist. For until the last, consistently, she danced her two great and favorite ballets —Perrot's *Esmeralda* and *Faust*, the two supreme examples of romantic ballet which maintained the fine balance between dance and mime.

For the rest, after her retirement Augusta taught briefly in Vienna, then retired again to Italy, this time as Madame Gardini. Of her second husband no information is presently available, nor have we to date discovered her obituary. Her monument remains in the prose and pictures of the Italian *Risorgimento*. The iconography * in the back of this book is doubtless but a fraction of Maywood prints.

All her portraits show the enigmatic Mona Lisa smile, striking eyes, determined chin, and well-turned little body. Although her private life was both public and unexplained, the only life which really counted was her existence as an artist. No good history of Italian ballet omits Augusta Maywood. Perhaps it would be wisest to emulate the Italian press of her period, which scrupulously passed no judgment on her, save as a dancer. For us she is, to date, our first and only American *prima ballerina e prima mima assoluta*.

* See Notes and Bibliographical Data, p. 265.

George Washington Smith.

GEORGE WASHINGTON SMITH

BY LILLIAN MOORE

THROUGHOUT THE NINETEENTH CENTURY, the classic ballet in America remained an exotic and transplanted art, living only through repeated transfusions of new blood from the great academies of Europe. Nevertheless, a century ago America did produce a few first-rate native classic dancers. The career of Mary Ann Lee has already been discussed, as has that of Augusta Maywood, an American ballerina who passed most of her artistic life in Europe. Romantic ballet in America even managed to produce one lone example of that rare phenomenon, a great classic male dancer. George Washington Smith, a Philadelphia boy, held his own against the finest guest stars in this country, and was certainly America's first native *premier danseur*.

The sheer length and variety of Smith's career are awe inspiring. He first danced in public about 1838; he was active as an actor and ballet producer as late as 1883. At his death in 1899, he was still a teacher of dancing. In the course of these sixty years, Smith danced in everything from grand ballet and opera to the circus; he worked for P. T. Barnum and Edwin Booth; he entertained between the acts of *Hamlet*; he put on the grease-paint mask of the clown; he partnered almost every great ballerina who visited this country, from Elssler on; he staged almost every one of the well-known romantic ballets, and choreographed many of his own; he taught social dancing, Spanish dancing, and academic ballet; he trained several pupils

who became famous; he spanked Lola Montez; he was the cause of a riot at the Bowery; he even found time to marry a beautiful convent-bred heiress and produce ten children! It was almost as though he alone, through the sheer force of superhuman effort and accomplishment, were attempting to compensate for the scarcity of American dance artists.

The beginnings of Smith's career are obscure and, as a matter of fact, unimportant. He was born in Philadelphia, during the second decade of the nineteenth century, and appeared at the Chestnut, the Walnut, and the minor theaters of that city in the early 1830's. In an interview many years later, Smith himself said that he made his debut in 1832 "as a clog, hornpipe, and flatfoot dancer."[1] Charles Durang, who makes no mention of Smith's early appearances in his detailed *History of the Philadelphia Stage*, does cite a "Master Smith" who sang "Is There A Heart That Never Loved?" at a benefit performance at the Walnut in the summer of 1830. To make matters more confusing, another George Smith was appearing in Philadelphia at this time. This man, much older than George Washington Smith, played character roles at the Chestnut for several years, and then suddenly left the stage to become a dentist! During the late eighteenth and early nineteenth centuries there were at least two George Smiths appearing regularly in the theaters of London, but they were actors, and insofar as we have been able to discover, they were not related to the American dancer.

Before he became a dancer, George W. Smith was a stonecutter by trade. Possibly he combined the two professions for a short time, while he was becoming established in the theater. The Philadelphia directory for 1840 lists a "George Smith, stone mason," at "6th above Poplar," while that for 1841 lists "George Smith, stone mason," at "2nd and Mud Lane." Both of these entries may possibly refer to George Washington Smith, who was just beginning his theatrical career.

Smith probably had little early training, if any, before his professional debut. The "clog and flatfoot" dancing which were his original stock in trade were most likely picked up through observation and imitation, rather than formal instruction. Several members of the Durang family, famous exponents of the hornpipe, and other dances in what was then called the "English style" (to distinguish it from the French academic ballet) were active in the Philadelphia theaters while young George Smith was growing up there. But if Charles, or any other Durang, had been the first teacher of George W. Smith, there is every reason to believe that the fact would have been mentioned in the *History*. As a matter of fact, Charles Durang speaks of Smith so seldom and so casually, when one considers the extent of his distinguished career, that it almost seems to constitute an intentional snub. Was it professional jealousy which caused Durang to ignore his younger competitor?

Another possible teacher of Smith was P. H. Hazard, a former member of the *corps de ballet* of the Paris Opéra, who was in Philadelphia at this time. Hazard taught Augusta Maywood and Mary Ann Lee, and quite probably Smith worked with him too. But the influence of Hazard would be pale compared with that of the great artist who actually shaped his destiny.

This was Fanny Elssler. When she died in 1884, a Philadelphia reporter remembered Smith's association with her forty years before, and questioned him about her. " 'Do I remember Fanny Elssler?' said the veteran ballet master, . . . 'Do I remember her?— Friend—' and a far-off look came into the eyes of the old man—'No one who ever knew Fanny Elssler could forget her. She was the queen—the matchless queen—of the ballet. The world is full of imitations, but there never was but one Elssler. . . . I shall never forget the wonderful form and superb carriage of that woman. . . . She was the embodiment of all that was graceful, beautiful, ravishing. . . .' "

In the same interview, Smith told of the beginning of his apprenticeship in Elssler's company. " 'Fresh from her triumphs in Paris she had come with the Chevalier Wykoff (her manager) to kick her way into the American heart. A two-weeks engagement in New York, at the old Park Theatre, at a salary of $500 a night, prepared her for a tremendous ovation in Philadelphia. And she got it, too. She opened at the old Chestnut Street Theatre, on Chestnut, above 6th, the site where Rockhill and Wilson's clothing house stood for so many years. It was my second season at the Chestnut. Between the acts I used to entertain the audience with exhibitions of jig and fancy dancing.

" 'Elssler immediately engaged me for her company. She had previously contracted with the French Vallee sisters, who had been living in Philadelphia, and these charming dancers, with myself and [James] Sylvain, the ballet master, who, by the way, was a brother of Barry Sullivan, and Mme. Jardienne (Pauline Desjardins) who came over with her from Paris, formed the company which afterwards stormed the country.' "

Elssler's two-year visit to the United States has been the subject of a number of studies, and there is still enough fascinating and untouched material available to make a small volume about her triumphant progress from city to city. Elssler was the inspiration—or the victim—of an enthusiasm amounting to hysteria, which has been equaled only by the Jenny Lind mania which swept the country a decade later, and perhaps in our own day by the "swooning" of the teen-age admirers of Frank Sinatra. Here, however, Elssler concerns us only in the decisive influence which she exerted on George Smith.

From the interview quoted above, one would infer that Smith joined Elssler's company during her very first visit to Philadelphia, which began on June 13, 1840. In the same article Smith mentions "the autumn of 1839" as the date of his engagement; this is obviously a slip of memory, since Elssler did not arrive in this country until May of the following year. At first he was not a featured member of the company. His name does not appear on any of the early Fanny Elssler programs. He probably danced in the ensemble, and certainly a great deal of his time was occupied in studying and rehearsing with James Sylvain, the Irish dancer whom Elssler had brought from Europe as her partner and ballet master. Years later, Smith told his son Joseph that Sylvain was responsible for the development of his ballet technique, and that he had also taught him the classical attitudes of the English pantomime character Harlequin, as they had been developed years earlier by James Byrne. Since Harlequin had no place on Elssler's ballet programs, we may assume that Smith ambitiously seized the opportunity for private study with Sylvain in order to enlarge his own repertoire. Certainly, his thorough knowledge of the standardized Harlequin role was to serve him well in later years, between ballet engagements!

As Elssler's ballet master, Sylvain had the thankless task of assembling an ensemble from the available native talent in each city which they visited. He was obliged to whip this raw material into presentable shape in a few days; sometimes in a few hours. His hopeless struggle with the dark-skinned cory-phees in Havana makes an amusing episode in the story of Elssler's travels, and many a time he must have saved the day for the star through his cleverness at improvisation and his ability to make the best of the most difficult situation. The young Irishman had an acute sense of his own worth; his contract, signed in Europe, had stipulated a straight salary of $150 a week plus benefits at stated intervals; later on, when he saw how valuable his services were to Elssler, he demanded—and received—as much as $700!

Sylvain was a brother of the actor Barry Sullivan, and had changed his name at a time when it was fashionable for dancers to be French. His career, as one of the earliest British dancers to become internationally famous, deserves a study in itself. Before coming to the United States he had danced at the Paris Opéra and at most of the principal theaters of London, in association with some of the most distinguished artists of the day. He had danced with Pauline Duvernay and Pauline Leroux; later he was to become a favorite partner of Marie Taglioni and Carlotta Grisi. Undoubtedly Sylvain was a well-schooled technician, and the dance education of young George Smith was in good hands.

After Elssler's original engagements in New York and Philadelphia, her first tour took her to Baltimore and Washington, back to New York for a few days in August, 1840, and then to Boston in September. Here Sylvain evidently had difficulties. Catherine Prinster, Elssler's cousin, who accompanied her on the entire American odyssey, wrote from Boston at the time:

"I must admit that we had considerable anxiety, because the ballet master found no real ballet school here. Fanny has her own, well-rehearsed ballet group which she takes with her everywhere, but the theater manager in Boston thought so much of the strength of his own resident company, that he was not inclined to bring the dancers from New York. Fortunately things are going better than we feared. The public has eyes only for Fanny and grants her associates hardly any attention at all. . . ." [2]

Was Smith among the dancers left behind? Possibly. Returning to New York, Fanny once more turned toward the South. She revisited Philadelphia, where she waited for four days for her trunks of costumes, delayed by a blizzard, to catch up with her. Then she continued by way of Washington, Fredericksburg, and Richmond to Wilmington, North Carolina, where she took a steamer for Charleston. She sailed—literally sailed, in an old-fashioned clipper ship—from that port for Havana, on January 12, 1841. The next month was spent in Cuba. By the middle of March she had arrived in New Orleans, where she danced until May. Then she took a Mississippi River steamer to Cincinnati, and came overland by stage and railroad to Baltimore and Philadelphia, where she arrived on the second of June, 1841.

We have given this itinerary in detail, because it is still an open question whether or not Smith accompanied Elssler on this particular tour. The programs which we have been able to check bear no sign of his name. One thing is certain: he did go to Havana with Elssler. But Elssler went to Cuba again in the following year. In a late interview, Smith said that he had "traveled once to the West Indies." The inevitable conclusion is that Smith joined Elssler not on the occasion of her first visit to Philadelphia, but when she returned there in the summer of 1841, or when she danced there in September of that year. It should be noted that the Philadelphia playbills of September, 1841, contain exactly the names which Smith himself later mentioned as his associates in Elssler's company: Sylvain, Pauline Desjardins, the Vallee sisters, and Charles T. Parsloe.

The first program on which we have located Smith's name is a Boston playbill for *La Sylphide*, on October 18, 1841, where it appears simply in a group: "Peasants: Messrs.

Curtis, Parker, Ring, Thomas, Dunn, Smith, etc." At this performance Sylvain danced Reuben, Desjardins danced Jessie, and smaller solo roles were taken by Miss Boquet, Mr. Parsloe, and the Boston ballerina Fanny Jones.

Elssler's winter tour of 1841-42 included comparatively few cities. Following the Boston engagement, she spent most of November in Philadelphia and then returned to New York for another month of appearances at the Park Theatre. According to Joseph C. Smith, his father replaced Sylvain as Elssler's partner when the Irish dancer returned to Europe. We have been unable to discover just when or why Sylvain departed, although depart he certainly did, for his name is not to be found on the bills for Elssler's farewell American performances—but neither, for that matter, is Smith's! According to Joseph C. Smith, there is in the Théâtre du Grand-Guignol, in Paris, a picture of Fanny Elssler dancing with his father. Smith must, therefore, have been her actual partner at some time in this winter of 1841-42.

When Elssler closed her New York engagement, on January 3, 1842, Sylvain was still in the company. It is highly probable that he returned at once to Europe, possibly because of further disputes about his salary. On January 15 Elssler set out again for Havana, where she remained until the end of May. On this voyage she was accompanied by Jules Martin, a French dancer, brother of the renowned ballerina Madame Lecomte, and his wife. The pair was well known in America, for they had appeared with Jean and Marius Petipa in their ill-fated New York venture of 1839, and had toured extensively. At any rate, Smith also went with Elssler to Havana this time, and it is our surmise that in Havana he danced as her partner.

Catherine Prinster, preoccupied with the success of her glamorous cousin, seldom mentions her professional associates in the course of her lengthy letters. Even the references to Sylvain are tantalizingly few. She barely recognizes the existence of the Martins, and nowhere does she mention Smith. Nevertheless, as the only other male member of the Havana group, Smith probably had a number of opportunities to substitute for Martin and also to dance roles of equal importance in ballets where two leading male characters were called for.

After her return from Havana, Elssler appeared briefly in New York. A program of her final American appearance, at the Park Theatre, New York, on June 27, 1842, is preserved in the Harvard Theatre Collection. She danced two ballets; *La Tarentule*, with Jules Martin, Madame Martin, and Mr. Fisher (in the pantomime role of Dr. Omeoquaco), and *La Sonnambula*, with the Martins, Pauline Desjardins, the Vallee sisters, and Messrs. Andrews, King, and Povey. Mysteriously enough, Smith's name is missing again. Nevertheless, we have irrefutable evidence that he and Elssler parted good friends. He treasured one of her ballet slippers for years, and bequeathed it to his son Joseph. In recent years, unfortunately, it has disappeared. Smith even journeyed to Boston to bid Elssler farewell when she sailed to Europe, on board the *Caledonia*, on July 16, 1842. Speaking of this event years later, in an interview, Smith mentioned the exact date of Elssler's departure.

" 'You remember the dates well,' said the reporter.

" 'Yes,' replied the old dancing master, 'I have cause to. The date was engraved on a gold pencil she gave me as she said farewell. I stood on the pier watching the ship as it sailed away. I never saw her again. It was her last and only visit to America.' "

In 1858, Smith paid tribute to the great ballerina by naming one of his daughters after her, Fanny Elssler Smith.

During her American sojourn Elssler danced a number of *divertissements*, but only eight grand ballets: *La Tarentule, La Sylphide, La Fée et le Chevalier, La Rose Animée, La Bayadère, Nathalie ou la Laitière Suisse, La Sonnambula,* and *La Gypsy.* Strangely enough, in a list of twenty-six ballets which Smith staged or in which he danced leading roles, in the course of the next thirty years, we find only one which was in Elssler's repertoire: *Nathalie,* which he danced with Julia Turnbull in 1847. Turnbull also had appeared with Elssler, during her first summer in America, and had even danced the role of Kelty to Elssler's *Nathalie* in this ballet.

It is hard to explain Smith's avoidance—one might say his deliberate avoidance—of the ballets associated with Elssler, unless he had been so deeply impressed by her incomparable interpretations that he did not care to see anyone else in her particular roles. Nevertheless, Elssler left a definite mark on Smith's style. Her predilection for the Spanish dance, shown in her most famous solo, the Cachucha, and in other *divertissements* such as the Bolero, the Zapateado, and El Jaleo de Jeres, is reflected in Smith's work. He became an expert in the Spanish technique, so that he was quite capable of partnering native Iberian dancers like the renowned Pepita Soto, and meeting them on their own ground.

To the influence of Elssler we must credit George Smith's high standards of artistry, standards which he refused to lower even in the depressing days at the end of the century when the glamorous era of the romantic ballet had long been a thing of the past. Even then, in the darkest days of the dance art, he was able to inspire his young son with a genuine love and understanding for the pure classic ballet, epitomized in his memories of the divine Fanny.

II

With Elssler gone, Smith went back to Philadelphia. He may have continued his studies under Hazard or Jules Martin, both of whom still taught there. Certainly he must have devoted a great deal of time and energy

Smith's choreographic notations. Montage by Joseph Cornell.

to careful practice, for he became an accomplished classical technician, and it is difficult to understand how he could have achieved this in his short period under Sylvain. At most, he could have studied with him from the summer of 1840 until January, 1842 (when Sylvain returned to Europe); probably, if Smith joined Elssler in the summer of 1841, the association was even more abbreviated. Nevertheless, it was to Sylvain that Smith himself gave the credit for his training in academic ballet and in the traditions of the English pantomime.

His knowledge of the harlequinade soon proved useful. At the Walnut Street Theatre, on December 13, 1842, Smith appeared for the first time in an elaborate pantomime called *Mazulme, or The Black Raven of the Tombs.* This piece, sometimes called *The Night Owl,* was a stand-by in the repertoire of the famous French Ravel family of panto-mimists and rope dancers, and it had been adapted by numerous local American companies until it was a standard favorite. The story concerns an evil lord, Signor Montano, who, abetted by his valet (a combination reminiscent of Mozart's Don Giovanni and Leporello) plots all sorts of evil schemes to prevent the union of two peasant lovers, Emile and Marie. In the "transformation scene" so typical of the old pantomimes, Emile and Marie miraculously become Harlequin and Columbine. Smith was to become something of a specialist in *Mazulme;* he appeared in revivals of the spectacle as late as 1855, and at one time or another acted almost every role in the cast.

At this first performance, Smith appeared in the small comedy part of "Sawbones, a surgeon"; Marie-Columbine was danced by one of the Vallee sisters. The manager of the Walnut this season was the distinguished American actress, Charlotte Cushman, who, although she was known as a tragedienne, did not scorn to produce pantomime. *Mazulme*

was one of the greatest successes of the season. It ran steadily from December 13 to January 4, 1843, a total of twenty-three nights. On February 25 it was revived, with "new scenes, machinery, tricks, change of dresses, etc.," and a new Signor Montano, Mr. E. L. Davenport, who later became one of the most celebrated actors on the American stage, and a new Marie-Columbine, Anna Walters.

Miss Walters, one of Philadelphia's favorite ballerinas, had made her debut at the Walnut a few days earlier, in a solo called *Il Pirule Vetteramo,* "never danced in this city before"—and never again, insofar as we have been able to discover! According to Charles Durang, "Miss Walters . . . really displayed infinite grace and immense agility. Her style was the French operatic (i.e., the classical ballet). She had great natural powers for the art but we should judge had never been regularly taught and trained in that graceful school. Her performances were crude at times and quite unfinished, showing that her acquirements were through aptness and tact for imitation. Miss Walters, however, pleased, and that nowadays is quite enough." Smith danced with Anna Walters many times during the next two years.[3]

In July, 1843, the Walnut opened for a special summer season of pantomime and ballet. George W. Smith was prominently featured in the company, which was advertised as "a combination of the greatest pantomimic talent ever offered in this city. It included Mr. Barnes, as choreographer and mime, Charles T. Parsloe, a British dancer, contortionist, and actor who had appeared with Elssler, Anna Walters, and the three Vallee sisters. *Mazulme* had an important place in the repertoire, and by this time Smith had been promoted to the role of Flodoardo, the valet. One of the ballets which Barnes produced was *The Three Lovers, or Mad as a March Hare.* Smith had the comedy role of Fan-Fan la Julipe. An unusual feature of the casting was the appearance of Anna Walters

145

as Colin, the hero. This is one of the earliest examples of *travesti* which has come to our attention, and it is hard to understand why it was necessary to resort to this artificial expedient when there was a male dancer like Smith in the company. Perhaps the Philadelphians just wanted a glimpse of Anna Walters in tights!

The dances incidental to the ballet of *The Three Lovers* included an *allemande comique*, a gavotte, a *pas de galope*, a *pas grotesque*, and a Tyrolienne, while the *divertissements* listed on the same program were a hornpipe by Mr. Barnes and Miss Walters, and a morris dance by the three Misses Vallee, with Barnes, Parsloe, and Smith. The *allemande* and the gavotte were decidedly old-fashioned ballet fare for 1842, and the morris dance and hornpipe must have been quite a letdown for Smith after Elssler's glamorous character dances. It would appear that Barnes, as a choreographer, was quite untouched by the recent developments in the romantic ballet, and was content to stick to old simple forms. Among his other productions that summer were two "comic pantomimes," *Vol au Vent*, in which Smith danced the role of François, and *Harlequin and the Ocean Imp*, with Smith as Leonardo. The young dancer was gathering valuable experience in a varied repertoire.

During the next year, Smith appeared in all of Philadelphia's leading theaters. In February, 1844, the Walnut again revived *Mazulme*, with Smith, Barnes, and Miss Walters. The same group appeared on March 12 in the "new musical pantomimic romance," *The Imp of the Elements*, and on the 30th of the same month, Charles T. Parsloe took a benefit with the "new comic ballet," *The Ladder of Love*, in which George W. Smith danced Jemmy. It would be interesting to know just how these ephemeral pieces compared with the romantic ballets of which we have more definite knowledge, such as those which Elssler had danced here. These Phila-

delphia productions were probably more popular in style, with a greater emphasis on comedy and trick "effects" (such as the sudden entrances and exits of Harlequin via trap door and springboard) and greater simplicity in the actual dancing. But this is only a deduction.

In May, Smith made his first appearance in grand opera, dancing a Bolero with Anna Walters in the masquerade scene of Auber's *Gustave III*, at the Chestnut Street Theatre. This production ran for several weeks, and then was cut short by the indisposition of the leading tenor, a Mr. Shrival. In July the Walnut announced another summer ballet season with one novelty, *A Night's Adventures*, which featured a *pas de deux* by Smith and Anna Walters, as well as a *comic pas* and a *comic allemande* by Smith and Mr. Barnes. *The Three Lovers* was revived, and so, of course, was the inevitable *Mazulme*. By this time Smith was dancing Harlequin, the leading role.

Years later Joseph C. Smith, in an article in *The Saturday Evening Post*, described how his father had studied the traditional pantomime and dance of Harlequin with James Byrne.

In the late eighteenth century, the traditional Harlequin had only five fixed "attitudes," or poses, representing admiration, flirtation, thought, defiance, and determination. He carried a stick tipped with the wings of a bat, which supposedly had magic powers. Byrne, at Drury Lane, London, abolished the fixed "attitudes" and replaced them with varied ballet steps and combinations, woven into a real dance, and mingled with more natural and amusing bits of pantomime. Byrne substituted a plain wand, still called a "bat," for the wing-tipped one. He retained the mask and skullcap, which were supposed to denote invisibility, but instead of the loose-fitting Watteau-type costume (still worn by Canio in the opera *I Pagliacci*) Byrne designed all-over tights, covered with diamond-shaped patches in colors which represented the "seven passions":

Black: Death
White: Purity
Blue: Truth
Green: Envy
Yellow: Jealousy
Red: Love or Passion

Harlequin conveyed his feelings by a sort of a primitive sign language, in which touching a certain color was supposed to indicate that he felt the corresponding emotion.

Later, after Smith's marriage, he would put on his tights and stand while his wife sewed on the diamond patches by hand—a task which demanded hours of patient labor.

Harlequin's Dance, as George W. Smith learned it from Sylvain, included *entrechats-six*, double *tours en l'air*, and pirouettes *à la seconde*. Joseph Smith was able to execute an *entrechat-huit*, a triple *tour en l'air*, and 120 successive pirouettes *à la seconde*. He learned them from his father, who presumably had attained the same standard of technical excellence.

Shortly after Smith's first appearance as Harlequin, in *Mazulme*, he transferred to the Arch Street Theatre, where he made his debut on July 28, 1844, as Hassan in the pantomime of *The Arabian Nights' Entertainment*. In September he was called upon to dance the polka (in 1844, a brand new sensation) between the acts of *Hamlet!* Our grandfathers certainly demanded varied entertainment on a single evening, and no one cried sacrilege!

III

At this point, we come upon an interesting hiatus in Smith's career. From the autumn of 1844 until the autumn of 1845, we have unearthed no evidence that he danced anywhere in the United States. This is just exactly the period which Mary Ann Lee, a Philadel-

Fanny Elssler Smith.

phia girl who became our first American interpreter of Giselle, spent in studying under Jean Coralli at the Paris Opéra.

There is no mention of Smith in the newspaper items which chronicled her departure, the progress of her studies, and her return to this country. Nevertheless, when she came back to America her first engagement was at the Arch Street Theatre, Philadelphia, and Smith was her partner. Miss Carrie Smith, the daughter of the dancer, has assured us that her father both studied and danced in Europe, and this would certainly seem to be a logical time for such a venture.

However, if Smith did join Mary Ann Lee in studying under Coralli, it is strange that he never spoke of it in later interviews. He gave the credit for his early training to Sylvain, an accomplished artist, but certainly a less distinguished teacher than Coralli, who had taught most of the great ballerinas of the day. Smith's name is not to be found in such European records as we have been able to

147

Giovanna Ciocca.

Lee for her first appearance after her return from Paris, at the Arch Street Theatre on November 24, 1845. *La Fille du Danube*, retitled *Fleur du Champs*, after the name of the heroine, was given one week later. Toward the middle of December, Lee and Smith, with six trained coryphees, set out on a tour of the country. Their first engagement was in Boston, where, on January 1, 1846, they produced the first American performance of *Giselle*, the only ballet of the romantic era which remains in the active repertoire today, more or less in its original form.

Of Smith's interpretation of the role of Albrecht we have no adequate description. Nineteenth-century critics were notoriously shy about praising male dancers, no matter how well they performed. All the critical attention was devoted to the ballerina, who was usually featured far more prominently than her partner. With this regrettable custom in mind, it is gratifying to note that Smith, throughout the rest of his career, invariably got "billing" equal to that of the ballerina with whom he was dancing, and that on at least one occasion during this Boston visit he actually got a criticism, and a good one. *The Boston Evening Transcript*, on December 29, 1845, said: "Mary Ann Lee appears again this evening in . . . *The Daughter of the Danube*. This piece includes many of her most fascinating dances, and was received two evenings last week with rapturous applause. Mr. Smith also appears in it with her, and alone, executing in the course of it several tours de force, in a manner which entitles him to the first rank as a professor of the *gai science. . . .*"

examine, since war conditions made a really thorough investigation impossible. Meanwhile, it is interesting to speculate on the possibility that he may have accompanied Mary Ann Lee, and shared with her the advantage of learning *Giselle, La Fille du Danube,* and *La Jolie Fille de Gand*, at the Paris Opéra, where they had been created.

The two-year period which George W. Smith spent in dancing with Mary Ann Lee has already been covered in the article on that ballerina. We shall only synopsize it here. The ballets which Lee brought back from Paris were typical examples of the French romantic school, quite different from the harlequinades and simple pantomimes in which Smith had been appearing since Elssler's departure. Smith now danced three of the greatest roles in the contemporary ballet repertoire: Albrecht in *Giselle*, Rudolph in *La Fille du Danube*, and Benedict in *La Jolie Fille de Gand*.

The last ballet was chosen by Mary Ann

The repertoire of the two dancers included a number of interesting *divertissements*, such as a bolero, a mazurka, and a *grand pas russe*. The *grand pas de deux* from *La Jolie Fille de Gand* and that from *Giselle* were also lifted from their respective frames and presented as *divertissements* when circumstances prevented the production of a complete ballet. Smith

Fanny Elssler in *La Tarentule*. Collection of George Chaffee.

George Washington Smith.

contributed two solos to these programs: a *pas de sabot* and a *pas de matelot*. The latter may have been inherited from James Sylvain, who frequently danced a *pas de matelot* on Elssler's programs. Much later Smith was to stage a complicated pantomimic sailor's dance for Lola Montez; this may have derived from his own solo or have been an entirely new creation. As for the *pas de sabot*, knowing Smith's early successes as a clog and "step" dancer, it can only be assumed that this was another early ancestor of our American tap dance.

During this Boston engagement Smith, for the only time in his life, resorted to the expedient of elaborating his plain American name into an affected "Smythe." Was this a souvenir of recent months in Paris, or was it a small concession to the American weakness for foreign rather than native dancers? What-

ever the cause of this change, it fooled nobody, and did not remain in effect for very long. Even before they left Boston, Smith was once again plain Smith.

Engagements in New York City, and a return to Boston, filled out the season, and in the following winter, 1846-47, the two dancers toured the South. Their stay in New Orleans was marked by a series of joint appearances with another American dancer, Julia Turnbull. The manager of the St. Charles Theatre, with two star ballerinas of equal magnitude at his disposal, decided to promote a rivalry between them in order to stimulate public interest. The most effective *divertissements* of each were cleverly juxtaposed on the same programs, so that the New Orleans connoisseurs could compare the technical virtuosity and interpretive abilities of the two dancers. Lee, of course, had a decided advantage in the assistance of George W. Smith, because while Turnbull was limited to solo variations, the partners were able to vary their offerings with several well-chosen classic *pas de deux*.

A short illness unfortunately marred this engagement for Mary Ann Lee, and took her out of the contest for several days. She soon made a triumphant reappearance, but this brief indisposition must have presaged a more serious malady, because just five months later she retired from the stage, because of ill health.

This New Orleans engagement was probably Smith's first contact with Julia Turnbull, with whom he was to dance during most of the following season. Turnbull had danced with Elssler during the Austrian ballerina's first season in America, but this was probably before Smith joined the company.

Meanwhile, Lee and Smith continued their tour through the South, although the health of the ballerina was failing rapidly, and it soon became apparent that she could no longer endure the strain of constant travel. Smith returned to Philadelphia for her farewell appearances in May, and danced the *pas l'espagnole* with her on her final program, June 18, 1847.

These two years had been invaluable experience for Smith. He was now completely capable, not only of dancing in, but of staging, some of the most famous and typical ballets of his day. Stage them he did—not once, but many, many times, throughout his entire career. *Giselle* remained one of his lifelong favorites, and *La Fille du Danube,* as we shall see, had a way of popping up under various disguises in his later work as a choreographer. The *divertissements* he danced with Lee served for many other ballerinas.

Equally important is the fact that, in his very dancing of *Albrecht,* we have a sort of yardstick with which to measure his technical and artistic achievements at this early stage of his career. *Giselle* is still the standard test of a ballerina, and so is *Albrecht,* for the male dancer. Even without the evidence of full contemporary descriptions of his interpretation, we may feel certain that, as the creator of the role of Albrecht in this country, George W. Smith had earned the right to the laurels of America's first *premier danseur.*

In the autumn of 1847 Smith obtained an engagement as first dancer and ballet master at the Bowery Theatre, New York, under the management of Mr. Jackson. Although Julia Turnbull had been at the Bowery for several years, she had just made her first outstanding success there, during the spring of 1847, in *The Naiad Queen.* A pupil of Jules Martin and Madame Lecomte, she undoubtedly knew a good dancer when she saw one, and it is quite possible that her influence may have had something to do with Smith's engagement. At any rate, they were to enjoy a happy and successful partnership, before its abrupt and disastrous ending the following summer.

The first piece produced under Smith's supervision was *The Naiad Queen,* which opened on November 29. Since this popular extravaganza, with its songs and marches and underwater Amazons, had been in the Bowery

repertoire for nearly a year, it is safe to say that Smith, in his new capacity as ballet master, simply had the task of seeing that it was properly rehearsed. During the first half of the nineteenth century, managers were extremely lax about crediting choreographers on the playbills. Unless it is a question of a famous foreign "name," imported at such great expense that he simply had to be advertised in order to recover the original investment, the task of assigning proper credit for original choreography or for the restaging of a ballet is usually a matter of guesswork.

Nevertheless, Smith supervised the Bowery production of *Giselle,* which opened December 6. James Gordon Bennett, reviewing the performance in the New York *Morning Herald* next day, said: "The gorgeous manner in which it was brought out by the manager, in regard to cast of character and scenic effect, will ensure its success for some time. Miss Turnbull, as Giselle, excelled every other character which we have seen her in— the simple and beautiful peasant girl—the accomplished danseuse—and subsequently, the fascinating Willie, bounding from tree to tree, and by order of her queen, trying to seduce her lover in the fatal dance, were elegantly represented by this favorite danseuse. Prince Albert, by Mr. Smith, was well sustained. The *Sur la Pointe, d'Aeriel,* and *Pas de Tambourine,* given by Miss Turnbull and Mr. Smith, were executed with great dexterity and grace, and elicited repeated cheers from the audience."

This *Pas de Tambourine* may be puzzling the present-day connoisseurs of *Giselle.* No trace of it survives in current productions of this ballet classic. However, in a contemporary woodcut found in *Beauties of the Opera and Ballet,* there is shown a scene in which Giselle, as queen of the vintage festival, watches the villagers dancing with large tambourines. A Bowery program for December 11, 1847, indicates that in the New York production, at least, the *Pas de Tambourine* was a *pas de deux* by Giselle and Albrecht, although of course they may have been assisted by the entire ensemble. *Beauties of the Opera and Ballet* was a London edition of a French work, *Les Beautés de l'Opéra*, issued in Paris in 1844-45.[4] Presumably it is an accurate record of the Paris production of *Giselle*. Is this tambourine dance an original detail which has been lost during the century in which *Giselle* has held the stage?

The Bowery program also explains the *Sur la Pointe* mentioned in the criticism quoted above. This was simply the Grand Waltz, danced by Miss Turnbull *sur la pointe*. Evidently *pointe* work was still enough of a novelty, in New York in 1847, for particular attention to be drawn to it. *D'Aeriel* was the fancy name for the *grand pas de deux*.

The Bowery programs usually included a number of attractions, such as farces, operettas, vaudevilles, ballets, and even, upon occasion, educated animals. On December 14, *Giselle*, which had run for a week, shared attention with the waltzing horse "Tammany," who created something of a sensation with his expert execution of the polka!

On December 15 Smith produced *Nathalie, la Laitière Suisse*, which had been in the repertoire of Fanny Elssler. Filippo Taglioni had originally staged this ballet for Elssler in Vienna, and had later produced it at the Paris Opéra with his daughter, Marie Taglioni, in the title role. The music was by Gyrowitz and Caraffa. Of the Bowery production, James Gordon Bennett wrote merely that: "The *Pas de Deux* by Miss Turnbull and Mr. Smith was beautifully performed, and had to be repeated." The waltzing horse, who appeared on the same bill, got much more space in the reviews!

Nathalie, Giselle, and *The Naiad Queen* now alternated on the bills, with Smith dancing his *pas de matelot* as a *divertissement* on the nights of *The Naiad Queen*, in which he did not appear. On December 21 he took a benefit performance, with a bill consisting of the play *Oliver Twist*, a farce, *The Married Rake*, the second act of *Giselle*, and a burlesque of the same ballet, called *La Chiselle*. The New York *Morning Herald* commented next day: "Although the weather was excessively cold, the house was well attended, though not as crowded as we have seen it. The receipts must have amounted to a handsome sum for Mr. Smith, for whose benefit they were set apart. . . ." Actually, the receipts totaled just $197, as we learn from the Bowery Receipt Book, now preserved in the Harvard Theatre Collection. From the same source we learn that Miss Turnbull's benefit, on December 1, had drawn $488—but the Bowery "b-hoys" were notoriously partial to ballerinas.

At the close of this engagement Turnbull and Smith left on a brief tour which took them to Baltimore and then to Washington, where they danced for Henry Clay. In April they were back at the Bowery, where a new manager, Thomas H. Hamblin, advertised a gala season of opera and ballet. The musical half of the entertainment was provided by the Seguin Opera Troupe, which had an excellent reputation in this country. There was a large orchestra directed by Mr. A. Tyte, who had no less than three assistant conductors. During this season Turnbull and Smith were in far more distinguished company than when they had appeared in competition with the farces, the burlesques, and the waltzing horse. The two dancers were featured more prominently than any individual singers of the opera company—and rightly, it seems, for their contributions were extravagantly praised, while the operas often received mediocre criticisms, or worse.

The season opened on April 13, 1848, with *The Bohemian Girl* and *Nathalie*. In the review which Bennett wrote for the *Morning Herald* of the 15th, the opera fared very badly, but, he declared: "The ballet which followed . . . was eminently brilliant, rich, and seductive. Miss Julia Turnbull is an ar-

Louise Ducy-Barre. Harvard Theatre Collection.

George Washington Smith.

mimed the role of Zoloe in Auber's *La Baya-dère*, and danced the Fairy Queen in *Cinderella*. The drama—not the ballet—of *Esmeralda* was in the repertoire, with Turnbull (who later became a very popular actress) in the title role. In addition, there were two *divertissements*, both danced by Smith and Turnbull: *El Bolero de Cadiz* (probably a heritage from Elssler, and certainly no novelty, as Smith had already danced it with Lee) and *La Zingarella*. The last deserves a more detailed note.

In the autumn of 1847 a large ballet company headed by Victor Bartholomin, former ballet master of the Théâtre de la Monnaie in Brussels, and Hippolyte and Adèle Monplaisir, both very distinguished artists, had arrived in New York and opened at the Park Theatre. *L'Almée*, one of the ballets in their repertoire, included a highly original *pas de deux* called *La Zingarella*, which became extremely popular. During the next decade it appeared on the programs of most of the well-known dancers. There exists a charming music-cover lithograph, published by Sarony and Major, of the Monplaisirs in this dance. Later George W. Smith used a woodcut of this pose of La Zingarella to advertise the Southern tour which he made with Louise Ducy-Barre.

Julia Turnbull and George W. Smith were to appear together at the Bowery in one more gala season, but before discussing this engagement, it is necessary to turn aside to remark a ballerina who had arrived from Italy in the previous year.

Giovanna Ciocca was a pupil of Carlo Blasis, one of the very first of his pupils to appear in America. In the later half of the nineteenth century his famous school at La Scala, Milan, was turning out expert dancers almost in mass production, and ballerinas were inevitably Italian, just as in the days of Diaghilev they had to be Russian. But in 1847 Blasis's school was not yet so world famous, nor had it begun to export dancers

tiste of first rate ability, which is conjoined with a youthful person, a fine figure, and . . . a handsome face. With the excellent *corps de ballet*, uniting their fascinating powers and lovely charms with those of such a charming and distinguished leader as Miss Turnbull, no wonder *Nathalie* is successful, and this vast theater so crowded."

During this season Smith produced *Giselle* again, as well as *Fleur des Champs* (*La Fille du Danube*) which he had previously danced with Lee. Of Julia Turnbull's characterization, the *Morning Herald* said, on May 4: "The grand ballet entitled *La Fleur des Champs* succeeded, Miss Turnbull taking the principal character. She was warmly greeted on making her appearance, and went through the part in a manner highly creditable. The new ballet went off well." Turnbull also on such a large scale. Blasis himself seems to have been rather proud of Ciocca; he mentions her several times in his *Notes upon Dancing*, and even speaks of her triumphs in America.

Ciocca made her first appearance in this country in Philadelphia, on January 23, 1847, in the ballet *Diana and Endymion*. She was advertised as the "premiere danseuse of the Teatro La Scala, at Milan and Naples, etc." Another Italian dancer, Gaetano Morra, "from Florence, Naples, etc.," made his American debut in the role of Endymion. Charles Durang wrote of this performance: "The attitudes, poses, and groupings were very classical. . . . Ciocca . . . had great force and agility . . . with infinite grace of the animated Italian school. In that meretricious expression of passion she greatly resembled the celebrated Cubas. . . . She had not the excessive voluptuousness which marks the Spanish style . . . but Ciocca had all the graceful merits of the operatic Italian and French schools."

After her New York debut, on February 1, the *Spirit of the Times* said of Ciocca: "The prima ballerina is beautiful, graceful, and as agile as a faun. Her pantomime is speakingly eloquent, and her poses the extreme development of statuesque grace; while in the pirouette, and indeed in all the varied attractions of the ballet, she is certainly unexcelled by any one since Fanny Elssler, among us."

Since her debut Ciocca, assisted by Morra, Mlle. Fanny Mantin, and a small ballet ensemble, had been touring the country, with occasional appearances in New York. In August, 1848, Thomas H. Hamblin, manager of the Bowery, engaged Ciocca, Julia Turnbull, and George W. Smith as leading dancers for a short season of ballet. Turnbull had been a featured star at the Bowery for a number of seasons, and was an established favorite with its audiences. Now she suddenly found herself forced to play second fiddle to the Italian ballerina. The advertisements of the opening of the season carried the names of Ciocca and Smith in large type; there was no mention of Julia Turnbull. "This week," wrote Bennett in the *Herald*, "we expect the house to be more crowded than ever, as in addition to the present attractions, the beautiful danseuse, Signora Ciocca, will appear." Turnbull was quietly ignored. On August 14, the day of the opening, the *Herald* was more explicit (perhaps because the American dancer had already registered a complaint), but Ciocca still came off with the lion's share of the attention: "Bowery Theatre:—Opera and ballet are to be the chief amusements at this house, this evening; and Signora Ciocca, Miss Turnbull, and Miss Taylor will all appear, as also Mrs. Phillips and Mr. G. W. Smith. Signora Ciocca is well known as a most elegant and beautiful danseuse, who, since her arrival in this country, has been an immense favorite whenever she has performed. Mr. Hamblin has done well and liberally to engage her at this time, and thus afford his patrons most elegant amusements. Tonight Signora Ciocca will appear in the grand ballet of *The Magic Flute*, as Lisa, a part she fills to perfection. Miss Turnbull also will appear in the course of the evening, in the *Polka Nationale*, which she will dance with Mr. G. W. Smith, and thus, will afford an opportunity to the admirers of both of these beautiful danseuses to compare their different styles of dancing. Both are excellent, both are beautiful, and both have troops of admirers, consequently, an exciting time may be anticipated. . . ."

An exciting time was certainly enjoyed. For some reason Smith, who was dancing the role of Lubin to Ciocca's Lisa, suddenly decided that he did not wish to appear with Miss Turnbull in the *Polka Nationale*. The reason for his decision is not clear. Perhaps Turnbull had made her jealousy of the Italian ballerina all too obvious, and he was attempting to lend moral support to the young foreigner. Perhaps—as we suspect—Ciocca was a better technician and a more finished artist than the

American girl, whose balletic training had been sporadic at best. Perhaps there were personal reasons for the decision. Ciocca had quite a reputation for seductive beauty! Whatever his reasons, Smith refused to dance the Polka.

Julia Turnbull, a young woman of spirit, promptly walked out on the stage and addressed the audience, telling them that she had been insulted by her partner. The Bowery "b-hoys," eager to champion such a lovely young woman, resolved to prevent Smith from appearing at all. When he tried to dance, he was pelted with overripe fruit (Julia's supporters must have been warned to expect trouble in advance, for they seem to have been appropriately armed with vegetables!) and driven from the stage, while the audience proceeded to tear up the benches and wreck the place. The police had to be called in and the theater emptied, for it was in danger of complete destruction!

The *Spirit of the Times* for August 19 carried a colorful account of this eventful evening: "The Bowery, on Monday last, was the scene of a petty riot which threw the gods of the gallery and the demigods of the pit into a high state of nervous excitement. It appears that in consequence of some disagreement between Miss Turnbull and a Mr. Smith, with regard to the execution of *La Polka Nationale,* that young lady claimed the protection of the audience, enlisted in her behalf, and they forthwith demanded the exhibition put down in the bills. Whether Mr. Smith refused to be the executioner of the Polka or whether that ill-used dance refused to be done by any individual possessing such an Anglo-Saxon cognomen, does not appear, but the audience vented their displeasure by a strong employment of their lungs and a manifest destruction of sole leather. After an interlude performed by the whole company, both on and off the stage, the tumult subsided beneath the benignant smile of the stage manager, the Polka was represented by the lady and the identical

Smith, the American flag waved over their heads, and everybody returned to their homes after a slight destruction of the benches and glass of the establishment."

On the morning after the riot, the *Herald* carried an advertisement, which must have been inserted on the previous day, of *The Magic Flute,* plus the *Polka Nationale* by *Ciocca* and Smith—proving that his prejudice was directed against Miss Turnbull, and not against the Polka. At the evening's performance, it seems that Smith had to pay for his highhanded conduct by dancing the Polka not once but *four* times, twice with Turnbull, twice with Ciocca. The *Herald* for the 16th carried the following note: "After the opera, *Cinderella,* . . . Mr. Stevens appeared in front of the curtain and announced that the difficulty of the night previous, between Miss Turnbull and Mr. Smith, had been amicably adjusted, and they would, with the permission of the audience, dance the *Polka Nationale.* Mr. Smith, after mature deliberation, acknowledged that he had acted ungenerously and unmanly; but he was now willing to dance with Miss Turnbull during her engagement at this theatre. This announcement was received with the greatest applause, and many voices exclaimed, 'That's all we want!' Mr. Stevens then led Mr. Smith and Miss Turnbull before the audience, when the house resounded with applause. The curtain then rose, and Mr. Smith and Miss Turnbull appeared in the Polka, which was received with deafening applause; and so great was the enthusiasm, that they were obliged to repeat it; after which, three tremendous cheers were given for Miss Turnbull. Mr. Smith and Signora Ciocca then appeared in the Polka, and a disposition to hiss was manifested, which was immediately put down by the applause of the audience. They were encored, and loudly applauded. The grand ballet of *The Magic Flute* wound up the performance, in which Signora Ciocca appeared as Lisa, and Mr. Smith as Lubin. The piece was re-

Lola Montez in *Un Jour de Carnaval à Seville*. Collection of George Chaffee.

ceived with great applause, and properly, for Ciocca is an accomplished danseuse. She was called out after the falling of the curtain, so great was the enthusiasm. The whole performance passed off most quietly, plainly showing the tact and management of Mr. Hamblin, whose aim is always for the public's amusement, and will not allow disorder to exist around him. The Bowery is still the place to go to."

The immediate result of all the excitement was the production of several of Turnbull's favorite vehicles, such as *Fleur des Champs* and *La Bayadère*, with the American dancer once more starred. The critics, evidently divided between loyalty to the native favorite and admiration for the foreign ballerina, did their utmost to give an equal and impartial amount of praise to each. After a performance of *Bayadère*, Bennett wrote: "Miss Turnbull acquitted herself admirably; from the moment she came bounding on the stage before the old Caliph, up to the last scene of her union with the unknown, she was much applauded. Miss Turnbull's dancing is remarkable for its freedom and grace, and the perfect self-possession she retains in the midst of the most intricate *pas*."

But on the very next day, he said: "After the drama, Signora Ciocca and Mr. George W. Smith appeared and danced a Swiss *pas de deux*. Signora Ciocca is a most beautiful dancer and lovely woman, and the applause elicited by her performance was tremendous. Mr. Smith is also a fine dancer. His style harmonizes well with that of Signora Ciocca. . . ." And in another review, "Ciocca is a most superb danseuse, and few can equal her, either in symmetry of form or elegance of dancing."

One person who definitely benefited from the battle of the ballerinas was Thomas Hamblin, for interest was stimulated and business boomed. "The ballet has been quite a card for the Bowery during the past week, as every evening the house has been completely filled," noted the *Herald*. "The rivalry which of course must exist when two favorite danseuses appear on the same evening, has put both the ladies on their mettle, and the consequence has been that both have danced most excellently."

Discussion of the Bowery riot and its aftermath has caused us to neglect a point of more serious interest, the production of *The Magic Flute*. This ballet may have been created by George W. Smith, although the available records do not mention any choreographer. If Smith arranged it this was his first major original work. The other ballets which he had staged were the creations of European choreographers, but *The Magic Flute* must have been an original production. The only clues we have are the names of the two leading characters, Lisa and Lubin. These bear not the slightest resemblance to the characters of Mozart's opera, *The Magic Flute*, and so we may deduce that this was not the source of the ballet, although choreographic works were frequently derived from successful operas during the nineteenth century, as they still are occasionally today (for instance, the Rimsky-Korsakov-Fokine *Coq d'Or*). *The Magic Flute* had not previously been in the repertoire of Turnbull or Smith, nor was it among the ballets which Ciocca's teacher, Carlo Blasis, had choreographed prior to 1847.[5] We have not found it in the earlier repertoire of Ciocca, either, although an announcement of Bennett's which we quoted above ("Signora Ciocca will appear in the grand ballet of *The Magic Flute*, as Lisa, a part she fills to perfection") sounds as though Bennett had seen her dance the role before. Perhaps, of course, he had witnessed rehearsals.

The only ballet of this title noted by Cyril W. Beaumont in *The Complete Book of Ballets* is one choreographed by Lev Ivanov for the pupils of the Imperial Ballet School in St. Petersburg, in 1891. By a strange coincidence the heroine's name is again Lise (a role later danced frequently by Anna Pavlova, who included *The Magic Flute* in the repertoire of her company for several tours); the hero is Luc, instead of Lubin—a not dissimilar name, to be sure. Could Smith and Ivanov have had reference to the same story?

At any rate, if this ballet was really Smith's it was his first major work, and it is too bad that all the details—even to the composer of the music—have been buried in the sea of words which appeared about the personal contest between the leading ballerina and her American rival. We only know that Bennett considered it a "beautiful ballet."

On August 31 *Diana and Endymion*, the ballet in which Ciocca had made her American debut, was added to the repertoire with Smith replacing Morra, her former partner, in the principal male role. "The truly elegant Ciocca and Mr. G. W. Smith appeared to much advantage in it," commented the *Herald* of this ballet.

Julia Turnbull retaliated by appearing as Esmeralda on September 2, the last night of the season, and her benefit. This production is a confusing one. Neither Ciocca nor Smith was in the cast, and the other characters were taken by members of the Bowery's *acting* company (Miss Lockyer, Mrs. Jordan, Mr. N. B. Clarke, etc.). Nevertheless a review next day called the piece a ballet. "The ballet of *Esmeralda* followed," the *Morning Herald* declared quite plainly. "Miss Turnbull, as the dancing girl, was much admired. It is a most thrilling story, and Victor Hugo never wrote a more interesting one than the work on which it is founded."

In the face of this flat statement the Monplaisirs, just a few weeks later, announced the "first production in America" of "the grand ballet of *Esmeralda*." We believe that Turnbull's piece was a play in which one important role was principally a dancing one, just as in another favorite of that time, *La Bayadère*, the title role was mimed by ballerina and the rest of the work was sung.

Pepita Soto. Harvard Theatre Collection.

With the production of *Esmeralda* this eventful season at the Bowery came to a close, but it had several lasting effects. Although outwardly peace had been restored, and Smith, the bone of contention, danced impartially with both ballerinas, there evidently remained more than a trace of bad feeling. Turnbull did not appear at Ciocca's benefit, as would have normally been the case, nor did Ciocca dance at Turnbull's. The American dancer never again appeared at a theater managed by Thomas Hamblin, nor, during their long and parallel careers, did she ever again dance with George W. Smith.

159

In the meantime, another Italian dancer, Gaetano Neri, had arrived from Italy. He was a technical virtuoso, excelling in pirouettes, and an old friend of Ciocca, with whom he had worked in the classes of Carlo Blasis at La Scala. Hamblin had just announced the important autumn opening of the newly decorated Park Theatre, which was also under the management. For this gala season he now engaged Ciocca and, as her partner, not Smith, but Neri. It would seem that Smith had fallen between two stools, for he was left for a few weeks without any job at all, while Ciocca and Neri enjoyed a triumphant success at the Park, where they danced *divertissements* (as Smith had done a few years earlier in Philadelphia) between the acts of *Hamlet*.

On the eighteenth of September, the Monplaisir Ballet commenced an engagement at the Park, while Ciocca and Neri moved back to the Bowery. There, a week later, Smith joined them. On the 25th a new ballet, *The Abduction of Nina*, was produced. During his association with Ciocca, Neri seems to have done most of the choreography (he complained loudly, in the press, when Smith was given credit for one of his ballets, later on) and he was probably responsible for *Nina*. This was not the famous old ballet by Louis Milon, *Nina ou la Folle par Amour*, first given in 1813. It was evidently another original production. The cast was distributed as follows: Edward, Gaetano Neri; Nina, Giovanna Ciocca; Adèle, Mrs. Dunn; Bibone, Mr. E. Warden; Roland, Mr. G. W. Smith. The première followed (as usual!) a performance of *Hamlet*, and was reviewed by Bennett the following morning: "The grand ballet of *The Abduction of Nina* concluded the performances, and in it Signora Ciocca, Signor Neri, and Mr. G. W. Smith, three of the best dancers in the country, had the opportunity of showing off their graceful and elegant dancing to the best advantage. The ballet is splendidly got up, and the various dances and tableaux were executed with the greatest taste. Talk of theatricals declining! Let anyone visit the Bowery and then talk about declining!"

A few days later the indisposition of Ciocca necessitated the cancellation of the ballet, but it was restored to the bills on September 28, and given nightly for another week. On October 1 the *Morning Herald* said: "Signora Ciocca has become an immense favorite with the public, and her appearance is nightly the signal for great applause, supported as she is by Signor Neri and Mr. G. W. Smith, two of the most graceful dancers on the stage. . . .'"

At the end of October the dancers left the Bowery, to return in less than a month. Although during this engagement Ciocca and Neri were the only dancers mentioned in the advertisements, Smith invariably received an equal amount of attention in the reviews. "Signora Ciocca, Signor Neri, and Mr. Smith are now performing nightly at the Bowery," the *Herald* noted on November 30, "and their graceful dancing and well-arranged ballet *divertissements* are much admired." And again, on December 8, "The beautiful dancing of Signora Ciocca, Signor Neri, and Mr. G. W. Smith elicited the most enthusiastic applause. The artists are immense favorites, and during this, their present engagement, have delighted thousands."

At the Bowery the trio rounded out the year 1848, dancing *The Abduction of Nina* on Christmas Day. They returned to the same theater under interesting circumstances, on March 12, 1849. Ciocca and Neri were dancing their usual classical *divertissements*, but the versatile Smith was appearing as Micos in an equestrian drama called *Eagle Eye*, which starred J. H. Hall and his Arabian steed, Arbaces. For this production the ballet master—in this instance, probably Smith—arranged a series of American Indian war dances! *Eagle Eye* ran for a fortnight.

On April 11, Smith danced a leading role in the new ballet *Les Jardinières*, which Neri had produced. "It is a most elegant ballet," declared the *Herald* of the 13th, "and as the

charming Ciocca and the favorite Neri and Mr. George W. Smith himself sustain the principal parts, it is danced in the most graceful and beautiful style. . . .'" This same review wrongly credited Smith with the choreography, a mistake which was corrected on the following day: "In noticing *Les Jardinières* yesterday, we were in error in stating that it was composed by Mr. G. W. Smith; it is the production of Signor Neri, who by this and his many other successful productions has proved that he is as excellent a composer as he is universally acknowledged to be a dancer." *Les Jardinières* ran until April 21, and was reviewed again and again, always in superlatives, almost every morning.

On April 26 the dancers enlarged their repertoire with a new *divertissement*, from Rossini's opera *William Tell*, given after a performance of Shakespeare's *Richard III*. Evidently Shakespeare, without a little dancing to lighten the evening, was not to be considered! The famous Tyrolienne in *William Tell* is traditionally danced as a *pas de trois* between two women and one man (it had been composed especially for Marie Taglioni and Madame Montessu) but here Neri, as choreographer, reversed the procedure, using two men and one woman. After this performance Ciocca and Neri left the Bowery to fulfill other contracts, but Smith remained for a few weeks as ballet master and first dancer, appearing in his favorite solo, Sylvain's *pas de matelot*, and staging an effective tarantella in which he was assisted by Mrs. Dunn and the *corps de ballet*. For his dancing in this number, he won a rare tribute—he was praised in the *Herald*, while the presence of his partner, Mrs. Dunn, was completely ignored—an unheard-of triumph in the days of the romantic ballet, when the ballerina was queen and the male dancer barely tolerated! Smith's last appearance took place on May 8, just before the famous Macready-Forrest riots, in which many persons were killed and wounded, at the Astor Place Opera House. Smith may quite easily have witnessed this tragic event, which fortunately is unique in the annals of the American theater.

IV

Smith now returned to Philadelphia for a season of pantomime, at a theater which was variously called the "National Amphitheatre" and the "National Circus." It has been noted that Smith was extremely catholic in his tastes; he appeared at the most fashionable opera houses, but he did not scorn Barnum's Roman Hippodrome. For this interlude of 1849-50 the pantomimes were produced by William Wood, whose two sons also appeared in them. George W. Smith was widely advertised for "his first appearance in this, his native city, for four years"—a claim which was almost, if not literally, true. Since his appearances there with Mary Ann Lee in the autumn of 1845, he had danced only once or twice in Philadelphia, at her farewell performances in the spring of 1847.

Now he made what constituted a second debut, on December 3, 1849, as Robin Red Breast (afterward Harlequin), in the pantomime of *Mother Bunch and her Magic Rooster*. Pretty Jenny Wren (afterward Columbine) was danced by the beautiful Fanny Mowbray; Heavy Heels (afterward Clown) was William Wood, the director, and Farmer Grizzle and Gripe (afterward Pantaloon) was Mr. Whittaker. Various small members of the Wood family were in the cast, too. The pantomime ran for about a month, and was followed by another called *Il Don Giovanni, or The Libertine of Madrid*, with Smith in the title role. For this spectacle Wood used all the old tricks of the harlequinade, with opening trap doors, spouting the flames of hell, and other startling devices. Toward the end of February, 1850, at the same theater, J. H. Amherst staged a pantomime called *The Sleeping Beauty, or The Knights of the Golden Crest*, but it is not clear whether or not Smith took part in it.

For a brief period in the autumn of 1850 Smith was ballet master at the Arch Street Theatre, Philadelphia, where he produced an elaborate set of schottische quadrilles, starring a Miss Carline as *première danseuse*. Early in December, however, Smith returned to New York to begin rehearsals for an engagement as ballet master and first dancer at Brougham's Lyceum, a brand-new theater which was just opening its first season. The *première danseuse*, imported especially for the occasion, was Mlle. Louise Ducy-Barre, who had appeared as a minor soloist at the Paris Opéra.[6] For her American debut she chose a *grand pas de deux* and a *pas de caractère, La Sicilienne*, both of which she danced with Mr. Smith. The *Herald* review next morning said of her: "Mlle. Ducy-Barre . . . is graceful and buoyant . . . and 'was received with a burst of applause which must have convinced her that Americans can welcome a stranger who, by ability, proves deserving of their hospitality. She was well supported by Mr. Smith, the ballet master of the theater. . . .'"

Smith and Ducy-Barre remained at Brougham's Lyceum until the middle of the following summer, dancing a long list of *divertissements* which included the *pas de deux* from *Giselle, La Zingarella*, a *pas styrienne*, a new polka, *La Taquenette*, and a new Spanish dance, *La Manola*. Smith's notebook contains descriptions of both the Manola and the Taquenette Polka. When Ducy-Barre was incapacitated by illness for a few days, Smith saved the situation by resurrecting his ever useful solo, the *pas de matelot*.

The season of 1850-51 was an active one for ballet in New York City. When Smith and Ducy-Barre opened at the Lyceum, the extraordinary dancer Leon Espinosa was appearing with Celestine Franck at the Broadway, while Smith's early Philadelphia partner,

Anna Walters, was dancing with M. Frederic at Burton's Theatre. The French ballerina Mlle. Albertine, who had been a soloist at the Paris Opéra and at the Italian Opera in London, also appeared in New York during this winter season. Smith must have been a favorite with his colleagues, for when he took a special benefit on July 5, 1851, the guest stars who volunteered their services for the occasion were Espinosa and Mlle. Albertine. The ballet *The Jolly Millers* was staged just for this performance, with Espinosa as Nicais, Mlle. Albertine as Collette, and George W.

Smith as Colin. The incidental dances included an *allemande comique*, by Espinosa, Albertine, and Smith, and solos by each dancer.

Many years later Smith, in an interview, spoke of his association with Espinosa as one of the high lights of his career. This amazing little man was just four feet ten inches tall, and his height—or lack of it—prevented him from becoming one of the finest classical dancers of the day. He was able to execute twelve pirouettes from a single preparation, and an *entrechat-douze*. The former feat is

Scene from *The Seven Sisters*. Theatre Collection, New York Public Library.

163

The Fairy Grotto. Collection of George Chaffee.

equaled today by André Eglevsky, and perhaps by others, but we have seen only one dancer (Jean Guelis) execute a clean *entrechat-dix,* and know of no one who is capable of twelve crossings. Espinosa had studied under Coulon, Coralli, Filippo Taglioni, Perrot, and Lucien Petipa. When he came to America and danced with Smith, he was only twenty-five years old. Later he became a sensation at the Théâtre de la Porte St. Martin, in Paris. Theodore de Banville described him as "A nose with a little man on the end of it and a dancer never equaled." After several seasons at La Scala, Milan, he went to Russia, where Marius Petipa gave him a contract for seven years at the Imperial Theatre. After producing ballets at Covent Garden, he returned to Paris to dance at the International Exhibition, in 1878, when he was fifty-three years old.[7] It is a high tribute to George W. Smith that international artists of this caliber were eager to honor him by appearing at his benefit.

V

During the following season Smith enjoyed—or suffered—a unique experience. He had the dubious pleasure of directing the ballets in which the notorious Lola Montez made her bow to the American public.

The spectacular politico-amorous career of Lola Montez, Countess of Landsfeld, has been the subject of a number of weighty volumes, and there is no need to discuss it here. We are concerned with her only as a dancer. Montez's first ballet engagement, at one of the opera houses of London some years earlier, had lasted exactly one night. She was hissed off the stage by the balletomanes of the Omnibus Box, who were used to artists like Taglioni, Elssler, and Cerrito. Since this unfortunate debut, however, Montez's box-office value had been considerably increased by her association with King Ludwig of Bavaria and her various attempts—which, to do her justice, seem to have been sincere enough—to use her powerful influence to introduce a democratic liberalism into the government of that retrogressive country. She had been literally driven out of Bavaria in 1848, and three years later, finding herself again in London and almost penniless, she welcomed an offer from the theatrical agent Edward P. Willis, for a series of appearances in America.

When Lola Montez reached New York, on December 5, 1851, she was one of the most notorious women in the world. Her arrival would undoubtedly have created more of a sensation, had it not been for the presence on the same boat (the *Humboldt*) of the Hungarian patriot Louis Kossuth. The landing of the great statesman completely overshadowed the itinerant adventuress, who had to wait for her theatrical debut several weeks later before she received the amount of publicity to which she had become accustomed.

Lola Montez was certainly no ballerina. Smith, faced with the problem of arranging a ballet which would present her satisfactorily, did not have an easy task. It was necessary to give full play to her undeniably magnetic personality, without revealing her glaring technical weaknesses. He seems to have been completely successful in the first requirement, for every contemporary criticism speaks of her extraordinary charm, but all his choreographic skill could not disguise her inadequacy as a dancer.

For Lola Montez, Smith arranged three full-length ballets and several *divertissements*. She made her debut at the Broadway Theatre on December 29, 1851, in *Betly, the Tyrolean*. The story (and probably the music) of this ballet were drawn from an *opéra comique*, *Le Chalet*, by Adolphe Adam, which had first been given at the Paris Opéra in 1834. Smith had allotted himself the character role of Max Starner, while Daniel, the hero, was danced by Gaetano Neri, the former partner of Ciocca. At this performance the dancing of Neri and the choreography of Smith seem to have had a much greater artistic success than the efforts of the featured performer.

"She did not excel as an artist, or accomplish much with her heels and toes," wrote James Gordon Bennett in the *Herald* next morning, "but was regarded rather as a graceful, girlish, pretty, piquant, ladylike woman, moving with great natural ease and presenting some beautiful attitudes."

The curiosity seekers all expected Lola's performance to be slightly shocking, if not absolutely lascivious, and they were first surprised and then charmed by the simple and lovely dances which Smith had arranged for her. "Contrary to all expectations, though not a great artist, she is the most modest danseuse that ever appeared on the stage," wrote one reviewer in amazement.

The anonymous dramatic critic of the *Morning Herald* has left us a fairly good description of the ballet itself:

When the curtain was raised a very fine tableau of the whole *corps de ballet* presented itself, amidst loud cheers, and many eyes searched around for Lola Montez, but could not find her. In a few minutes she made her appearance on the staircase representing a winding path down the mountain, when she was greeted with tremendous applause. . . . She then descended gracefully, and on reaching the stage was received with another burst of applause, which she acknowledged with a ladylike bow. She was neatly dressed as a Tyrolean. . . . Her first dance was a Tyrolienne, and was well received. Her next dance was a *pas de deux* in which Neri as Daniel and Lola Montez danced together. On

Giuseppina Morlacchi. Collection of Lillian Moore.

entering the stage this time she did not receive any applause, and Neri, at the close, was applauded far more enthusiastically by the audience, doubtless because he was a better dancer. She made a false step in this dance which brought a slight hiss from the audience.

The Mountaineer Dance, by the *corps de ballet*, followed, and after its conclusion there was considerable delay in her returning to the stage, when an idea seemed to prevail that she would not come back. There was some hissing in consequence. At length she appeared in a new costume, which accounted for the delay. She looked well and was loudly applauded. Her dress consisted of a very pretty Hungarian satin skirt, striped with white and red, with a military black velvet jacket faced with gold, and a pretty red hat with a feather. In this dance she was more successful than in the other two. It was a sort of war dance in which she exhibited the martial bearing and military tread remarkably well. She led a company of soldiers off the stage in a sort of dancing step, and was enthusiastically applauded. . . .

Her dances were short and simple, and she performed nothing that could be called a feat. None of these performances were her peculiar Spanish dances, in which she excels. As a danseuse, she is decidedly inferior to Cerrito, to Augusta, and others, but there is a nameless grace about her person and movements which, with her history, gives her an attraction which a better artist could not command, but which, however, is not destined to be very lasting. . . .

From George W. Smith's own notebook we know that *Betly* also included a "Polka for 12 ladies," "La Normandare, for 12 ladies," and another untitled dance for ten ladies, two of whom had semisolo parts in the center. His choreographic notes for this ballet include tiny sketches of charming and unusual figurations and poses.

On January 5, 1852, Montez appeared in a second ballet, *Un Jour de Carnaval à Seville*, which Smith had arranged for her. She danced the role of Donna Inez (the name of the character was later changed to Mariquita, if we are to accept the evidence of later reviews and of the charming lithograph by N. Currier showing her in this ballet) while Smith appeared as Marco. Gaetano Neri was not advertised, and seems to have left the company, being replaced by a Mr. Schmidt. One would suspect that Montez was jealous of the applause Neri had received for his far superior dancing, and had gotten rid of him. (She might have fired Smith for the same reason, of course, but there she was helpless because she was completely dependent upon him as ballet master and choreographer.) However, there was a more tragic reason for Neri's departure. He was seriously ill. Charles Durang tells us that he died in Philadelphia in the same year, 1852, after a long and painful illness. In his last days the dancer—still a very young man— was cared for by a kindhearted merchant named William Heaton, who lived at No. 110 Chestnut Street.

Durang has left us a brief description of *Un Jour de Carnaval à Seville*. "A new grand Spanish ballet was produced, . . . a mere dancing *divertissement* without a plot—a simple display of steps and figures. . . . Many of the characteristic dances of the day were introduced. . . . These Germanic character *pas*, with the sprightly melodies of the polka and the mazurka blended with the Spanish, are certainly not only pleasing to the ear, but the novel, vivid steps and *allemande* figures are pleasing to the eye. . . ."

By this time the irrepressible Montez found herself involved in no less than two lawsuits, one with a Paris firm of theatrical agents, who claimed that in coming to America she had broken a contract to appear in France, and one with her business agent, Edward P. Willis, whom she had promptly discarded upon her safe arrival (and financial, if not artistic, success), in the United States.

These small distractions did not prevent her from appearing in a third ballet, *Diana and her Nymphs*, which Smith had created. This was something more in the style they had expected from Montez, and one critic wrote: "When a certain piece first presented a partly unclothed woman to the gaze of a crowded auditory, she was met with a gasp of astonishment at the effrontery which dared so much. Men actually grew pale at the boldness of the thing; young girls hung their heads; a deathlike silence fell over the house. But it passed; and, in view of the fact that these women were French ballet dancers, they were tolerated." [8]

In addition to these full-length ballets, Smith taught Montez a *pas de matelot*, which may have been the same one he had danced for years, or a new one specially devised for her. It was most dramatically advertised in the playbills: "A grand *pas de matelot*, in which Lola Montez will portray the vicissitudes of a sailor's life, exhibiting while engaged in the merry dance the sudden rising of a terrific storm, the rush to the rescue of those in peril, and the safe return to land with the ship's flag of liberty."

The Spider Dance, in which Montez usually had a certain modicum of success, was an adaption of the Tarantella. She had used it as a solo before, and was to do so again; for these appearances, Smith arranged it as a *pas de deux* and danced it with her.

Besides Montez's shortcomings in balletic technique, Smith had to put up with her complete lack of the slightest sense of rhythm, and since he was a sensitive musician this must have been particularly painful. Matters actually came to the point where the manager had to give special orders to the conductor of the orchestra: "When you play to the Countess, follow her precisely. When she stops, you also stop, no matter whether or not the music is finished." [9]

On the last night of this New York engagement Montez, who was certainly energetic enough, danced all three ballets of her new repertoire: *Betly*, *Un Jour de Carnaval*, and *Diana*. With Smith she then appeared in Philadelphia, where a group of disabled firemen for whose benefit she danced presented her with a medallion likeness of George Washington, in token of her "liberal republican sentiments," and in Washington, where at least one puritanical paper, *The National Intelligencer*, accepted her advertisements but otherwise completely ignored her existence.

Lola was a temperamental creature, and when irritated it was by no means unusual for her to administer a few well-directed lashes with a horsewhip which she carried with her constantly. When, in Philadelphia, she flew into one of her tantrums, Smith amazed the trembling company by turning her over his knee and administering a sound spanking! The gay and gallant lady was too astonished to do anything but submit to her punishment like a spoiled child.

In Boston, where she danced in March, her "refinement," her "ladylike charm," and her "chaste and queenly movements" delighted the critics until she overstepped the bounds of New England propriety by daring to pay an official visit, squired by Frederick Emerson of the Board of Education, to three of the city's public schools. Although she seems to have behaved in an exemplary fashion, addressing the pupils of the Latin School in Latin and those of the English High School in French, this audacity caused the Boston papers to rise in arms against her for "contaminating the young by her evil influence," and poor Emerson was nearly ruined. The resultant publicity was enough to warrant a re-engagement in Boston, but Smith and his well-trained *corps de ballet* walked away with the better part of the critical attention, as usual.

Returning to New York for one single appearance, on May 1, she was welcomed by an enormous audience, which reserved its approval for Smith and her lesser assistants rather than for the star. "So far, Lola was perfectly triumphant over the machinations of her indefatigable persecutors, the army of Jesuits," commented the *Morning Herald* of

May 2. "But [last night] she had a stronger opposition to contend with, for the meed of applause, in the successful rivalry of an excellent *corps of ballet* dancers, the best perhaps that ever graced the stage in this city. The contest for superiority was spirited, but Lola was not so triumphant on this occasion. . . . If she did not suffer a defeat, she was at all events sorely crestfallen. The piece represented was the grand Spanish *divertissement* of *A Day of Carnival at Seville*, which was excellently produced by the enterprising manager, the scenes, dresses, masks, and all the other accessories having been got up with much taste, liberality, and effect. Lola in the character of Mariquita danced the Andalusian, the festival dance, in company with Mr. George W. Smith, the Neapolitan, and the sailor's dance passing well, and with pretty good attention to time. (!) She dressed well, looked well, but was by no means satisfied at the tameness of the applause she received. . . . The several dances of the troupe were well and prettily executed. Two young ladies of the *corps de ballet,* Miss Price and Miss Josephine, danced a *grand pas de deux* with much taste and artistic skill, vying with Lola, as well in the talent displayed, as in the applause with which they were greeted. Some beautiful bouquets were thrown to these beautiful girls, from one of the private boxes. The success of these promising young artistes must have been somewhat nettling to the Countess. . . ."

This performance must have clearly shown Montez the futility of continuing to attempt to win approval as a ballerina, for although she retained her company for a few more appearances (including one in Buffalo, May 10, when the Eagle Street Theatre burned to the ground just after she and Smith had finished dancing there) she soon gave up the idea of presenting ballets, and dissolved the group. Although she toured through the South during the following winter, 1852-53, she appeared only in plays, and solo *divertissements*

such as the Spider Dance and the *Pas de Matelot.* As a final note on these appearances of Smith with Montez, we may remark that for the closing performances he created a new dance for the *corps de ballet,* satirizing a fad of the day—the Bloomer Polka! In 1852, nearly a century before the advent of the modern hit, *Bloomer Girl,* Smith was already turning that odd costume to his own theatrical advantage!

VI

Smith now turned from the exotic Montez to a less glamorous but more capable partner, his former associate, Miss Mary Ann Lee. In the spring of 1847 Lee had retired from the stage, because of failing health, and later had married. Who knows what vicissitudes now caused her to return to the ballet, after an absence of five years? At any rate, on May 27, 1852, at the Chestnut Street Theatre, Philadelphia, a complimentary benefit was suddenly tendered to "Mrs. Van Hook, late Mary Ann Lee." [Had sudden widowhood and the necessity of earning a living forced her back on the stage? It is impossible to say. In 1852 there was no Van Hook, so spelled, listed in the Philadelphia directory; a Mr. Edmund Vanhook, clerk, is listed, but if this was Lee's husband he certainly did not leave her a widow in 1852, since he was still in the directory fifteen years later.]

Whatever the reason for Mary Ann Lee's return to the stage, her new career did not last long nor carry her far from home. She appeared sporadically at the three Philadelphia theaters (Chestnut, Walnut, and Arch) during the next two years, disappearing again after a gala benefit in which Joseph Jefferson appeared, on September 20, 1853. However, we are now concerned only with her renewed partnership with George W. Smith. This took place at the Walnut Street Theatre, where during a brief engagement (August 30-September 4, 1852) she appeared with him between the acts of plays, in a *Pas Styrien* (souvenir of Elssler!) and the Spanish dance, *La Manola*.

As a matter of fact, Spanish *divertissements* were to make up the greater part of Smith's repertoire during the next few years, for he now formed a partnership with a celebrated Spanish dancer, Pepita Soto.

Señorita Soto, as she was usually billed, had come to this country as a member of a troupe of French and Spanish dancers engaged in Paris by the actor-manager, James H. Hackett, then acting as agent for Niblo's Garden. In addition to Soto, as *première danseuse,* the company included Mlles. Leontine Pougaud and Octavie de Melisse, both of whom had appeared at the Paris Opéra, and M. Mege, as first male dancer. The ballet company made its debut at Niblo's on June 14, 1852, and enjoyed a certain amount of success both in New York and on tour. "Soto was by birth a Spanish woman, and in several of her dances evinced the natural vigor characteristic of Spain," wrote W. W. Clapp. "Pougaud ranked first in popular favor on the score of personal beauty, but Melisse was far the best danseuse of the troupe, possessing a muscular strength which enabled her to execute tours de force with astonishing power; but unfortunately she lacked beauty of facial feature." [10]

During a Boston engagement in February, 1853, receipts fell so low that it was necessary for the management to discharge several dancers, in order to make both ends meet. As a result the company broke up and most of its members made their way back to Europe. Soto remained in this country, and formed a partnership with George W. Smith which became brilliantly successful.

For Soto, Smith arranged several new ballets and restaged an old one, *Un Jour de Carnaval à Seville,* which he had created for Lola Montez. Soto must have danced it much better. "Of admirable physique and of enchanting symmetry, she was no doubt fasci-

nating to the young, but the tendency was to pervert the innocent mind," wrote Charles Durang, shocked by the Spanish fire and passionate vigor of Soto's dancing. *Un Jour de Carnaval* was, as we have seen, a series of *divertissements*. The program of a performance which Soto and Smith gave in Charleston, South Carolina, April 13, 1854, lists the dances as follows:

A new and grand divertissement

entitled the

CARNIVAL DE SEVILLE

Lo Jota Aragonesa, by	Senorita Soto & Mr. G. W. Smith
Quadrille, by	Corps de Ballet
Pas Brillant	Senorita Soto
Pas de Matelot	G. W. Smith
La Cachucha and El Zapateado	Senorita Soto

Grand Finale

La Maja de Seville was a new production, which had its premier in Philadelphia on May 11, 1853, during the early days of the partnership. A ballet of this same title had been given at Niblo's Garden by the Rousset sisters, in January of the same year. At this late date it is difficult to trace the relationship between the two productions. However, from a few notes, which Smith evidently jotted down in haste in his "Copy Book," we can get an idea of the action of this little ballet as he staged it:

La Maja de Seville

Waltz

Ballet discovered seated at table. Basileo comes on L. Business after lover comes on L. Business & dispute with rival, draws knife & then La Maja comes on between them & reconciles them they dance a pas de deux & exit. La Maja's lover asks the ballet to dance. They dance the Aragonesa & all out, lover last.

La Maja de Seville became one of Smith's favorite ballets; he produced it again and again, with different ballerinas, in theaters all over the country. It suited Soto especially well, according to a brief review which appeared in the *Philadelphia Public Ledger* on the morning after the first performance: "Senorita Soto, in the new ballet of *La Maja de Seville,* displays new and pleasing evidences of her artistic skill, and the elegance and grace which distinguish her movements. In the course of the ballet, she dances a new cachucha, zapateado, and a grand finale." As has been noted, these three dances later appeared among the *divertissements* of the *Carnaval à Seville;* so we assume that occasionally Smith varied his ballets by interchanging separate numbers of similar styles.

La Belle de l'Andalusia, which Smith first produced at the Chestnut Street Theatre, May 19, 1853, was an old favorite in a new guise. The cast list (taken from a Mobile, Alabama, program of December 13, 1853) reveals its derivation at once. It was simply *La Fille du Danube,* transplanted from Germany to Spain, with appropriate changes in the incidental variations. Smith probably even used Adolphe Adam's music; he could easily have obtained the orchestra parts from Mary Ann Lee, with whom he had danced *La Fille du Danube* so often.

The program in its entirety is worth quoting:

Mobile Theatre: — Dec. 13, 1853

2nd time in the South, the beautiful Spanish ballet called

La Belle de l'Andalusia,
or, The Daughter of the Tagus

The Spanish legend dramatic ballet, in 1 act, with dances, etc., arranged expressly for Senorita Soto by Mr. G. W. Smith.

VIOLETTA (Fleur des champs) ... Senorita SOTO
Dame Gertrude (Violetta's
mother) .... Mrs. Waldauer
Uno (Spirit of Water) .... Miss Watkins

Carolina (Spirit of Water) ..... Miss Rederer
Rudolfo .... Miss Barret
King of the Tagus............ G. W. SMITH
Ulrico (intendant) .... Mr. Allen
Baron .... Mr. Veitch
Baron .... Mr. Wolfe
Herald of the Castle......... Mr. Schoolcraft
A Vampire................. Mr. Morrison

Officers, Pages, Ladies and Gentlemen, Soldiers, Valets, Vampires, Devils, Spirits of the Water, etc.

In the Course of the Ballet the following dances:
Pas Seul.................... Sen. SOTO
New Spanish Galop.......... Sen. SOTO and
                                    G. W. SMITH
Mazourka .... Corps de Ballet

Grand Pas des Quatre Nations

1. English Dance
2. Bolero—Spanish Dance
3. Original French Dance
4. La Napolitaine—Italian Dance

This same *Pas des Quatre Nations* was also danced by Mary Ann Lee at her second series of farewell performances, September, 1853. Smith had probably taught it to her.

In the early autumn of 1854 Smith and Soto, after a profitable tour through the South which had occupied all of the previous season, obtained a New York engagement at Wallack's Theatre, on Broadway near Broome Street. Between the acts of plays, they danced all their familiar *pas de deux*. This pleasant engagement had lasted some seven weeks when they were suddenly called upon to provide the incidental dances for a series of opera performances starring Grisi and Mario.

Giulia Grisi and Giovanni Mario, Conte di Candia, were among the most brilliant opera singers of the nineteenth century. When they came to this country they had been before the public for about twenty-five years, appearing with equal success in Paris and London. Grisi (a first cousin of the ballerina Carlotta Grisi, creator of the role of Giselle) was famous for her interpretation of Bellini's

171

Norma; Mario, a versatile and well-rounded artist, was idolized as one of the great tenors of his day. The pair had been brought to this country several months earlier by the impresario Hackett, who had also been the original manager of Señorita Soto; so when the opera repertoire called for the introduction of a ballet, he naturally thought of her.

Smith and Soto made their opera debut at the Academy of Music, on Fourteenth Street, then a brand-new theater, on October 30, 1854, in a *grand pas de deux* in the first act of Rossini's opera *Semiramide*. After only a week with the singers, they returned to Wallack's Theatre to resume their interrupted engagement.

Two months later, however, in January and February of 1855, they obtained an excellent contract with Grisi and Mario, in Boston. Here they were joined by the Italian ballerina Giovanna Ciocca, who had caused the Bowery riot of 1848. The three dancers were billed equally with the two renowned opera stars. Grisi and Mario sang only three times a week; so in addition to appearing in the opera ballets, the dancers provided more elaborate *divertissements*, which were featured on the "off nights." Luigi Arditi, composer of a waltz which is still popular to the point of triteness, was the conductor for both the opera and ballet performances. In the opera *La Favorita*, Smith and Ciocca executed a classic *pas de deux*, while Soto appeared alone in a Spanish dance, *La Madrilena*. Soto and Smith danced the famous Minuet in Mozart's *Don Giovanni*. Among the *divertissements*, the only novelties were a *Pas de Tambourine* and a *Polka Capricieuse*, both solos by Ciocca, a duet, *La Savoyard*, danced by the two ballerinas, and a *Pas de Trois, L'Ecos del Tyrol*, which echoes strongly of the Tyrolienne from *William Tell*.

Smith's production of *The Black Crook*. Theatre Collection, New York Public Library.

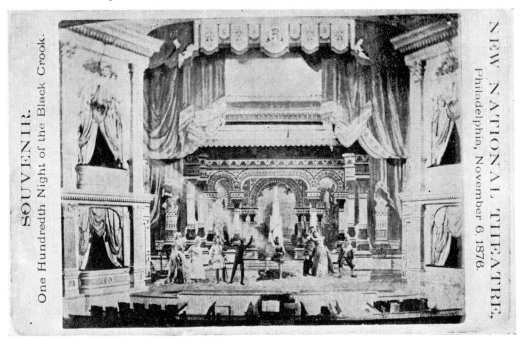

SOUVENIR.
One Hundredth Night of the Black Crook.

NEW NATIONAL THEATRE,
Philadelphia, November 6, 1876.

This association with Grisi and Mario must have been highly gratifying to Smith, who was passionately fond of music throughout his life. "Take the children to the opera," he would tell his wife, later on, when he left for a tour. "Keep them at the opera! They must learn to understand and love music!" When Mrs. Smith, who was a quiet and domestic woman, educated in a convent, would protest that she had no time to spend at the theater (and since she raised ten children, she must certainly have been busy enough!) he would insist that the musical education of his children was one of her most important responsibilities. Smith himself seems to have been a talented musician. He frequently prepared the orchestrations for his ballets, copying out the parts himself, and later he even composed the music for some of his productions. Much of this manuscript music, which had been carefully preserved by his son, was lost with the disappearance of a theatrical trunk, in recent years. Smith had been married, in 1854, to Miss Mary Coffee, the daughter of Joseph Coffee, a shipbuilder, who operated the first night line from New York to Albany. Mr. Coffee was a wealthy man, with estates in Philadelphia, in Keyport, New Jersey, and in New York City, where he owned extensive property at what is now the corner of Lexington Avenue and Thirty-ninth Street. He disapproved of his daughter's marriage to a dancer, and disinherited her. Later, when he learned to know and appreciate Smith's qualities, he announced his intention of changing his will, but he died before carrying out his promise; so Mrs. Smith was left one dollar.

James Hackett was now lessee of the Metropolitan Theatre, New York. In May of 1855, while he himself was acting Shakespeare there, he decided to feature a first-class ballet company on the alternate nights. For this purpose he engaged George W. Smith, Pepita Soto, Louise Ducy-Barre, a number of lesser soloists, and a large ensemble. The orchestra was conducted by Mr. Fenelon. The season opened May 15 with *La Maja de Seville* and several familiar *divertissements*. A week later there was an event of major importance—the first performance in America of *La Péri*. One of the most celebrated ballets of the romantic era, *La Péri* had been created at the Paris Opéra on February 22, 1843, as a vehicle for Carlotta Grisi. The music was by Burgmuller, and the choreography by Jean Coralli, who, in collaboration with Théophile Gautier, had also supplied the plot. The story concerns the love of a Péri, or Oriental fairy, for a mortal; the choreography was notable for the introduction of a sensational acrobatic leap, in which Grisi fell from a considerable height into the arms of her waiting partner.

The program of the American première, preserved in the Harvard Theatre Collection, correctly credits Coralli and Gautier with the authorship of the ballet, but it names no choreographer at all. Since Smith had been acting as ballet master, it can be assumed that he staged the ballet. But did he follow the original choreography of Coralli? Since he (Smith) claimed no program credit for a production of such unusual importance, the wording of the program leads us to imagine that he did follow Coralli, whose name he was so careful to mention. *La Péri* had remained in the repertoire of the Paris Opéra until 1853; so Smith could have learned it there at any time during the preceding decade. The Paris production was in two acts, the American in one; the latter may have been an abbreviated version, or it may have been staged in its entirety and simply programed differently (one act can contain any number of changes of scene). The names of the characters on the American program are identical with those of Paris, save that Nourmahal (perhaps by a misprint) has become Mourmahal; the slave dealer, anonymous in Paris, has acquired the name of Onmeyl, and the principal Odalisque, whom Paris called Avesha, is nameless in New York.

The complete program was as follows:

LA PERI

Grand Ballet, in one act, by Coralli and Gautier

Mourmahal	Senorita Soto
La Peri	Mlle. Ducy-Barre
Achmet, the Sultan	M. Carrese
Roucem, Chief of the Eunuchs	G. W. Smith
Onmeyl, dealer in slaves	Mr. Flannery
Odalisk	Mlle. Adeline
Shawl Dance	Mlle. Adeline and the Odalisks
Spanish Dance	Senorita Soto
Grand Pas de Fascination	Mlle. Ducy-Barre, M. Carrese, and the Peris
Mazourka	Mlle. Adeline and the Corps de Ballet
Finale, Grand Pas de Deux	Mlle. Ducy-Barre and M. Carrese

Although *La Péri* was given several times, we have been unable to locate a single criticism of it; the advertisements of the second performance declared, however, that it had been "received with enthusiastic applause."

The second novelty of the season was less successful. This was *Masaniello*, a ballet version of Auber's opera *La Muette de Portici*. The cast included Ducy-Barre, Smith, and Carrese, with Soto in the leading role, Fenella. Let the scathing criticism, which appeared in *The New York Times* for May 30, 1855, speak for itself: "Metropolitan Theatre:—A grand operatic and melodramatic ballet in three acts, called *Masaniello*, was produced here last evening. The old story and portions (the worst) of the old drama are retained, and the balance supplied by dances, procession, etc. Some expense has been incurred in the production of this spectacle, but there is still a lack of liberality. A ballet depends, more than any other entertainment, on the nicety with which it is placed on the stage. Appealing almost exclusively to the imagination, it must be elegant, or it is inevitably coarse and vulgar. The superb dancing of SOTO in the part of the dumb heroine, Fenella, alone saved the piece. The scenery, music, etc., are beneath mediocrity. Mr. Hackett must depend on something more than the reputation

of a few names if he would achieve success in his new enterprise. . . ."

Whether by plan, or because of the losses attendant upon the failure of *Masaniello*, Hackett's promising ballet season came to an end on June 9, after running for less than a month.

For a short time during the summer of 1855, Smith returned to his old favorite, the "grand, gorgeous, and expensive pantomime" (as the bills announced it), *Mazulme*. At the National Theatre, New York, he was engaged to play the villain, Chevalier Bariano, in a cast which included M. Wiethoff as Maclon (Clown), M. Schmidt as Emile (Harlequin) and Mlle. Thérèse as Julie (Columbine). These cast names are slightly different from those used in Philadelphia twelve years earlier, when the Chevalier was Montano and Columbine was called Marie. Probably *Mazulme* itself had undergone changes, as was often the custom with the standard pantomimes.

After a few weeks Smith left this company to play Harlequin, a role more to his taste, in another production of the same pantomime, at the Bowery Theatre. The synopsis of *Mazulme* on the Bowery program mentions a scene where "Harlequin leaps from the floor of the hall THROUGH A PICTURE," an incident which reminds us of Petrouchka's breaking of the picture of the Magician (although, to be sure, he does not leap through it) in Fokine's ballet. Perhaps Smith's Harlequin leap was closer to the one at the close of *Le Spectre de la Rose*, where the dancer disappears through the open window.

At the Bowery on September 7, Smith and Wiethoff (who had also transferred to that theater) took a joint benefit, with Smith's ballet *La Perla de Andaluza* (presumably the same as *La Belle de l'Andalusia*, which has already been discussed). On the following day, with a production of the comic ballet *The Eccentric Lover* (in which he had first appeared during his early days in Philadelphia) Smith closed his engagement at the Bowery.

In the spring ballet season at Hackett's Metropolitan, Smith had renewed his earlier association with the French dancer Louise Ducy-Barre. They now undertook an extensive Southern tour together, dancing all their favorite *divertissements*. The partnership was continued during the season of 1856-57, when the two dancers obtained, at Burton's New Theatre, an engagement which kept them busy in New York City from September until June. Charles T. Parsloe, the English contortionist and mime who had been associated with Smith intermittently ever since the days with Elssler, was a member of the stock company of actors. The ballet master was Mr. Fredericks (probably the same M. Frederic who had danced for several years with Mme. Augusta), but Smith seems to have done a good deal of choreography in the course of the season. In his notebook there is a description of *Les Lanciers Quadrille*, with a notation next to the title, "First time in America introduced by G. W. Smith, Nov. 10, 1856." His ballet *La Maja de Seville* was in the repertoire, and so were most of the *divertissements* which he had danced on tour with Ducy-Barre. A novelty was a new *pas de deux*, *La Fille de l'Air*. There was also a new ballet, first given on November 6, 1856, called *La Nymphe des Bois*. This may have been related to the *Diana and her Nymphs* which Smith had staged for Lola Montez, or it may have been *The Nymph of the Chase*, a ballet which is outlined in his notebook—or it may have been an entirely different creation by Fredericks. The lack of concise data on programs is particularly confusing and infuriating.

In a play called *The Slave Actress*, the scene of which was laid in feudal Russia, Smith and Ducy-Barre danced an interpolated Mazurka-Cracovienne. They also had a *pas de deux* in a "legendary drama," called *The Bottle Imp*, the theme of which has a number of points in common with Elssler's famous vehicle, *Le Diable Boiteux*. However, the two plots are quite different. On November 26, Smith appeared as Ivan, a peasant, in a comic extravaganza called *Bluebelle*. This was the Mazilier-Adolphe Adam ballet, *Le Diable à Quatre*, which had been rearranged to include a number of songs and spoken lines. Smith's role demanded both singing and acting as well as dancing. Although he often appeared as an actor, especially in his later years, there are very few mentions of Smith as a singer. During the season at Burton's, Smith was closely associated with the great actor Edwin Booth, and often danced between the acts of the plays (*The Apostate*, *The Stranger*, *The Taming of the Shrew*, etc.) in which Booth was appearing.

In June, Smith turned once more to choreography, arranging the dances for a "new Dramatic, Spectacular, Extravagant, Pantomimic Ballet, written, arranged, adapted and produced by Johnston, Chanfrau, Smith & Co., called MOSE'S DREAM," as the program described it. This was produced on June 15 at the Bowery, where F. S. Chanfrau had won a tremendous following with his characterization of "Mose, a New York fire boy." Mose, a stock character, had already been the hero of innumerable sketches and farces. Using him in a ballet was something new, and Smith evidently allowed his imagination full play, for the program goes on to say that "Mose goes up in a balloon, and comes down in China." Smith did not appear in the cast himself; he was negotiating with Thomas McKeon, manager of the National Theatre in Philadelphia, for a contract for himself and Mlle. Ducy-Barre. Whether or not this engagement came through it has been impossible to discover; we rather doubt it. After August 18, 1857, when he danced a *Pas de Bouquet* with Mlle. Celestine Franck (a new partner, but one who reappears later) at a single benefit performance in New York City, Smith makes one of his periodic disappearances from the American scene, and is not heard of again until May of the following year. Miss Carrie Smith is certain that her father was in Europe when her sister, Fanny Elssler Smith, namesake of the great ballerina, was born, early in 1858. This would explain the hiatus. During this same absence Mrs. Smith, in Philadelphia, supervised the building of a new home at 1858 Camac Street, which was finished and ready for her husband when he returned. During all of Smith's tours, his wife and the growing family of little Smiths remained at home in Philadelphia.

Smith's reappearance was made quite modestly, May 4, 1858, at the New Yorker Stadt-Theater, a German institution located at No. 37-39, the Bowery. Here he danced a one-act version of *Giselle*, with Celestine Franck in the title role and the Hungarian dancer, M. Szollosy, as Hilarion. Evidently it was only the first act which was given; the program makes no mention of Myrtha or the other Wilis who appear in the second scene. The ballet was repeated four days later, with the same cast.

VII

Here we must take temporary leave of George W. Smith, to consider the work of another artist who was to exert a major influence on his later career. This was Domenico Ronzani, the great Italian mime, choreographer, and impresario. Born in Italy in 1800, Ronzani had been engaged as first mime at La Scala at the age of 26. In 1829, under the imposing title of Primo Ballerino Mimico Assoluto, he appeared in Vigano's ballet *La Vestale*, restaged by Giuseppe Villa. He remained at La Scala over a period of thirty years, sometimes departing for a season or two to make guest appearances at other theaters on the peninsula. At La Scala he was associated with the most noted Italian artists of the dance, including, of course, the great teacher Carlo Blasis. In 1845, as choreog-

rapher in Bologna, he staged several ballets especially for Fanny Elssler, who appeared there as guest artist. When Perrot's *Faust*, created by Elssler at La Scala in 1848, was revived in the following year for the American ballerina Augusta Maywood, Ronzani, then the official ballet master, supervised the rehearsals. A number of his original ballets were produced at La Scala.

In the summer of 1856, Ronzani went to London to dance the role of Conrad in the first English production of Mazilier's elaborate three-act ballet, *Le Corsaire*. This was quite an undertaking for a man who had passed the half-century mark. *Le Corsaire* became a classic in the repertoire of the Imperial Theatres of Russia, where the role of Medora, created by Caroline Rosati in Paris, was danced by Marie Petipa and Adèle Grantsova, and later by Anna Pavlova and Tamara Karsavina. It was Carolina Rosati who appeared in the London production with Ronzani. Later the Italian ballet master was to bring *Le Corsaire* to the United States, where the role of Conrad was danced by no other than George W. Smith!

In the meantime, Ronzani spent a season as ballet master at the Teatro Regio of Turin, where he produced *Le Corsaire* with Louise Lamoureux as Medora. Returning to London, he spent another summer season as ballet master at Her Majesty's Theatre. There he signed the contract for an extensive—and, as things turned out, a most disastrous—tour of the United States.

The Philadelphia Academy of Music, which is still in use today (the Philadelphia Orchestra, the Metropolitan Opera, and the ballet companies appear there regularly) has on its façade a large, clearly legible date—1857. When it was built, it was one of the finest and most luxurious theaters in America. The first manager, Mr. E. A. Marshall, sought all over the country for a suitable attraction with which to open the new opera house. When he found nothing sufficiently impressive for a spectacular opening, he asked the conductor and impresario, Max Maretzek, who was then in London, to look for something there. Maretzek engaged Ronzani and sent him back to Italy to collect a first-class ballet company.

Just how well he succeeded may be judged from the fact that Cesare and Pia Cecchetti were the leading mimes, and their seven-year-old son, Enrico Cecchetti himself, was in the company. Cecchetti's biography [11] contains a wealth of fascinating stories about the wanderings of the Italian dancers in the wilds of America. In addition to the Cecchetti family, Ronzani's troupe included the whole clan of Pratesi—six of them, no less, Mamma Pratesi, Papa Pratesi, two daughters, and two sons. The prima ballerina was Louise Lamoureux, the first male dancer, Filippo Baratti.

The Ronzani Ballet made its debut in the grand ballet of *Faust* (Perrot's version, of course, staged by Ronzani) on September 15, 1857, at the Philadelphia Academy of Music. From the very beginning everything went wrong. There were mechanical difficulties in the staging, which marred the beauty and effectiveness of the first performance. The critics, disappointed at first, later amended their harsh judgments, but the public still stayed away. There was good reason, for September 28 marked the beginning of a terrible financial panic which swept the country. Two weeks later the banks closed in New York, and then in Boston; thousands of little investors saw their small savings wiped out. It was hardly a propitious time for the launching of a new ballet company. If George W. Smith did choose this unfortunate year to dance in prosperous Europe, he was a clever or a lucky man.

There was another reason, worse for the balletomane to consider than financial panic, which contributed to the failure of the Ronzani Ballet. The high tide of the popularity of the romantic ballet in America, which had slowly increased through the thirties until it

Joseph C. Smith in his father's Harlequin dress.

reached its height with Elssler's triumphs, and the rich decade which followed, was now beginning to ebb. The ballet was to enjoy another flurry of favor, through *The Black Crook* and similar spectacles, before it faded into almost complete oblivion at the turn of the century. Charles Durang, writing many years later about a second-rate ballet company which had appeared in Philadelphia in 1839, when ballet was riding the crest of the wave, remarked sadly: "Such a *corps de ballet* as the Ronzani corps, that appeared . . . at our new opera house some years ago (but we

177

are sorry to say, to empty benches) would have secured a success at this time. . . ."

In the space of this article we can only briefly summarize the first American season of the Ronzani Ballet, since Smith was not in the company and it concerns him only indirectly. The company left Philadelphia after two weeks, opening in New York on October 5. In addition to *Faust*, the repertoire included two other ballets, *Il Cavallo d'Oro*, and *Il Biricchino di Parigi*, in which the title role was danced by Enrico Cecchetti, aged seven!

During the winter Ronzani went back to Milan, where he produced *Le Corsaire* and *Il Biricchino di Parigi* at La Scala. When he returned to America in the spring, he brought with him a new prima ballerina, Annetta Galletti. She was an extraordinary artist, who was later to dance with George W. Smith on innumerable occasions. Ronzani also brought two new ballets, *The Village Apothecary* and *Theresa, the Orphan of Geneva*. In the latter Ronzani startled his audiences with a sensational stunt, rolling backward down the full length of a flight of stairs, and landing on his head!

But all these new attractions could not save the ballet from disaster. Financial conditions all over the country were still too precarious; it was amazing that the company had been able to complete its winter tour. Most of the dancers, including the Cecchetti family, now returned to Europe, but Ronzani and Galletti remained to form the nucleus of a new company, composed almost entirely of American —or, at least, resident—artists, which opened the following year. It was in this new ballet troupe that Smith became associated with Ronzani.

Annetta Galletti had studied at La Scala under Blasis, Casati, and Hus. While still a pupil at the school, in 1855, she had made her debut on the stage of Milan's great theater. Two years later she was made prima ballerina. She remained at La Scala for only one more season, before coming to America. Gal-

letti had a strong Italian technique and a sparkling style. In her photographs, which are remarkably clear and distinctive, she seems to bear a striking resemblance to Anna Pavlova. Galletti had slender legs for a ballet dancer of the sixties, and a high, well-developed instep. Her dark, melancholy eyes were deeply expressive.

In May, 1859, Galletti undertook to dance the role of Zoloe in Auber's *La Bayadère*, presented at Niblo's Garden by the Lucy Escott English Opera Company. The work had not been seen in New York for about six years, although it had formerly been a great favorite. Galletti now danced it with a brilliance which brought new life to the entire piece.

Perhaps as the result of her success, Domenico Ronzani, who was then organizing a new ballet company, arranged to join forces with the Escott Opera troupe. He gave one tentative benefit performance in New York, on the first of June, of a two-act ballet called *La Vedova Scaltra*, which must have been a complete failure, since it never appeared in the repertoire again. The company was made up of fine dancers, however. It had Galletti as prima ballerina, G. W. Smith as first male dancer, Ben Yates as first comic and character dancer, Mlle. Henri as second soloist, and Ronzani himself for mimed roles. The pantomimist William A. Wood, Jr., Smith's friend of many years, was also on the roster. This young man, talented son of a talented father, died just a few years later, while still very young.

Ronzani now assumed direction of both the opera and ballet companies, and took the entire ensemble to Philadelphia, where, on June 23, he commenced a new season. The opening program included *La Bayadère*, with Galletti, and the familiar *Maja de Seville*, with Smith in a leading role. Although the weather was stiflingly hot, the audience received the new company enthusiastically, and the reception from the press was equally cordial. "The Ronzani opera and ballet troupe is thoroughly trained and the pantomimes are very interesting," commented the *North American and U. S. Gazette*. A few days later the same paper waxed even more complimentary: "The ballet corps is the best we have ever seen in our city, and Signorina Galletti eclipses all of her predecessors. . . . Her endurance and strength are remarkable, and as graceful as a fawn, she is light as a zephyr. Mlle. Henri is . . . a worthy companion of Galletti, and, indeed, a rival of the best danseuses of the world."

Judging from the presence of *La Maja de Seville*, Smith's ballet, on the program, it seems that Ronzani had engaged the American not only as first dancer but as a choreographer. While the more elaborate ballets in the extensive repertoire of this interesting company must be credited to Ronzani, there were several productions which surely were directed by Smith—for example, the *Comic Trick Pantomime, The Jolly Millers* (in which Smith had danced years before, with Espinosa). Smith's hand is evident, too, in the selection of some of the *divertissements*, such as *La Manola* and the *Pas de Matelot*.

On June 30, Ronzani presented Perrot's ballet *Esmeralda*, with music by Cesare Pugni. George W. Smith danced Gringoire, the role which Perrot himself had created at the première of the ballet in London. Galletti, of course, had the title role. Ronzani played Claude Frollo, and Ben Yates was the dwarf Quasimodo, the bell ringer of Notre Dame. *Esmeralda* was based on Victor Hugo's famous novel, *Notre Dame de Paris*. Created for Carlotta Grisi in 1844, the ballet had won a permanent place in the romantic repertoire. In Russia its popularity has continued unabated right down to the present day.

Ronzani had appeared in the Italian première of the ballet, staged by Perrot himself, in 1845, and had been charged with the supervision of a revival of the work at La Scala in 1854; so his version must have been an authoritative one. This important production called forth a very modest note in the *North American and U. S. Gazette:* "The very interesting ballet of *Esmeralda* has been given in admirable style." However, a paragraph a few days later declared Galletti to be "one of the most efficient and gifted dancers ever seen here—quite equal to Lamoureux in agility, and her superior in dramatic power."

Another novelty, *La Bouquetière*, was presented during the Philadelphia engagement. This may have been based on an opera of the same title, by Adolphe Adam, presented at the Paris Opéra in 1847, or upon a ballet which Elssler danced in London in that same year. It is difficult to say, for little information about this work is available, save that Galletti and Smith danced the leading roles (Marie and Pierre), and the incidental dances included a *pas de trois suisse* (perhaps the inevitable Tyrolienne), by Miss Cross, Miss James, and Mr. Yates, a *pas de deux valse*, by Mlle. Henri and Mr. Wood, and a *Pas de Bouquet* by Galletti and Smith.

Toward the middle of July the double company, still presenting both opera and ballet, moved to Boston, where they opened at the Boston Museum on July 18. On the first all-ballet evening, July 23, there was an addition to the repertoire, *The Fountain of Love*, with Galletti as Isea, a Nymph, Smith as Teseo, Henri as Flora, and Yates as a Satyr. "La Petite Angelina" was L'Amour, no doubt a sweet but modest cupid, costumed in the mid-Victorian style, in allover fleshings.

Jocko, a ballet-pantomime in which the chief role was that of an ape, served as an effective vehicle for William A. Wood. This piece had been popular since the first quarter of the century, when the title role had been played by the great French dancer and mime, Mazurier. In *Jocko*, G. W. Smith had the role of Fernandez.

On the first of August Ronzani played a trump card, with the production of *The Corsair*, "Grand Spectacular Ballet, in two acts and seven tableaux, composed and arranged

179

by Ronzani, and produced by him with un-paralleled success at the Theatre Royal Hay-market, Theatre Royal Turin, La Scala Milan, etc., etc. Music by Adam." We have already mentioned Ronzani's London appearances as Conrad. Here in America he ceded the role to George W. Smith, while Galletti followed in Rosati's delicate footsteps, as Medora. It is impossible, at this late date, to determine just how closely Ronzani's production followed Mazilier's choreography. Probably it re-mained fairly faithful to the original.

From George W. Smith's notebook, we learn that later he produced an abbreviated version of *The Corsair*. He called this little ballet *Medora*, after the heroine. His notes convey the impression that it was a plotless series of *divertissements*, but one cannot be quite cer-tain, as they were obviously jotted down hastily, and only meant to refresh his memory later on. Nevertheless the page is an interest-ing one, worth quoting:

Medora

opening—all discovered in group
3 lines balance to Conrad & back—cast off
Mazurka—Coryphees
Entre—principals
Waltz by corps de ballet (slide hop & turn, slide hop & turn 4 times Polka, balanze & throw over 4 times Polka square & turn—)
Variations—principals
Corps de ballet gallop to center & throw over & back
pas de basque around & gallop around
take your partners to places & coryphees down line gallop & high pas basque & 2 line gallop & cast off
Principals solo—all dance & turn & first group

While some of these directions are quite un-intelligible (What on earth was "throw over & back"?), other phrases give a fairly clear picture of the simple, repetitive patterns used for the ensemble dances.

To return to Boston and Ronzani, we find that one more major work was in prepara-tion. On August 8, *Nathalie* was presented, with Galletti in the title role and Smith as Ernest, a Duke. This production is a confusing one, for the Boston cast list bears not the slightest resemblance to that of the Paris per-formances of this thirty-year-old ballet. Not a single character, save that of Nathalie, bears the same or even a similar name. Smith had danced the original Nathalie with Elssler, and later on with Julia Turnbull. Perhaps now he danced an entirely different ballet, a new creation of Ronzani's. The Boston program is not very helpful, since it does not even name the composer of the music. As a matter of curiosity, we will give the entire cast, since someone may be able to trace the sources of this puzzling ballet:

NATHALIE

Nathalie	Annetta Galletti
Ernest, a Duke	G. W. Smith
Prince Artholf, brother to the Duke	M. L'Ecuyer
Alfred, brother to Nathalie	William A. Wood
Adam, father to Nathalie	Domenico Ron-zani
Chamberlain to the Duke	Ben Yates
Victorine, sister to the Duke	Miss Cross
Liza, sister to Nathalie	Mlle. Henri
Maria, sister to Nathalie	Miss Jackson

On August 18, the Boston season closed. Ronzani had poured all his resources into this company, presenting ballet and opera on a grand and lavish scale. Such productions had not been seen in this country for many years, but in spite of every effort, the company had the same bad luck which seems to have plagued every venture Ronzani attempted in America. Perhaps it was just the wrong season for such an undertaking, and the August heat led the Bostonians to seek the cool breezes of Cape Cod instead of the hot benches of an ill-ventilated theater. At any rate, the company disbanded.

This season with Ronzani had marked a high point of Smith's career as a dancer. He was now about forty years old, yet he must have been at the prime of his technical powers. Male dancers always mature more slowly than women; many years later Joseph Smith, his son, wrote: "Take a man who does my style of dancing, for example. Though he must begin almost as a baby, he is no good at it until after he is twenty years old, because he has not the balance, the precision, the physical control. Today, at forty, I am more finished in my dancing than I was at twenty-five."

Earlier in his career, George W. Smith had shown a marked preference for character parts and mimed roles. Now, in every ballet, he was the *premier danseur*, the first male classical dancer. He had proved himself capable of executing a role created by Jules Perrot, and had been chosen for it by a man who had closely studied Perrot's own interpretation. George W. Smith was the only American male dancer of his century who could lay claim to such an achievement.

Smith was to dance with distinction for many more years. He was to partner several ballerinas who were still practicing in the children's class at La Scala. Nevertheless, this season seems to be the pinnacle of his success as a dancer. In the future he turned more and more to choreography, though he continued to dance himself. Symbolically, his very next engagement was to bring unstinted praise for his gifts as a choreographer and stage director.

When the Ronzani Ballet disbanded, most of the members of the ill-fated troupe found their way back to Philadelphia. Here the prima ballerina, Galletti, was promptly engaged to dance a *divertissement* in a play called *The Black Agate*, at the Academy of Music. The choreographer was a rival ballerina, Signorina Pratesi, one of the famous family which had come to America with Ronzani. (The rest of the tribe had returned to Italy, where in 1859 they were dancing at Modena.) Whatever Signorina Pratesi may have been as a dancer (photographs of the sisters certainly do not look attractive!) as a

choreographer she was a complete failure, and a few days later Ronzani himself had to be called in to stage a new *divertissement* for Pratesi and Galletti.

In the meantime, a play called *Faust and Marguerite* (as produced at the Princess' Theatre, London)—probably a translation or adaption of Goethe—was in rehearsal at the Walnut Street Theatre. George W. Smith was engaged as ballet master, and most of his former associates of the Ronzani Ballet were in the group he selected to assist him. In the third act of the play there was a *Grand Pastoral Divertissement*, danced by Smith with Mlle. Henri, Miss Gross, Miss James, and Mr. Ben Yates. Smith's triumph, however, was the beautiful scene which he arranged for the close of the play. "The apotheosis of Marguerite is one of the finest scenic effects it has been our pleasure to witness," commented the *Philadelphia Evening Journal*. "Angelic forms floating in the air slowly ascend, bearing in their arms the lifeless body of the sinning but repentant woman, upon whose pale, exquisitely lovely and spiritual face, celestial light is streaming. . . ." The *North American and U. S. Gazette* was just as enthusiastic in its praise: "With Ary Scheffer's picture to guide the way, it was easy to make an effective picture, since it was only necessary to copy the original; but in the present instance, costly machinery is employed to accomplish the effect, so that the audience may perceive no ropes or platforms. So well is the whole affair managed as to rivet the gaze of the spectators on a scene of matchless beauty. . . . We were especially pleased to notice that every evening the audience remained seated all through it, without making a movement to leave until the fall of the curtain. . . ."

VIII

In investigating the career of an artist, whose life seems to have been quite typically removed from all things political, it would

181

be easy to forget that 1859, the year of Smith's finest achievements as a dancer, was also the year when John Brown and his band of anti-slavery fanatics invaded Virginia at Harper's Ferry. These were troublous times. The shadow of war hung like a dark and threatening cloud over the entire country. Smith had enjoyed many prosperous tours through the South; he knew New Orleans as well as Boston; the applause of Charleston and Savannah had echoed as sweetly in his ears as that of Philadelphia and New York. Miss Carrie Smith believes that her father took no part in the Civil War, and we have unearthed no contradictory evidence, but, on the contrary, have discovered that Smith danced at intervals throughout the years of the war.

On April 12, 1861, when Southern guns fired on Fort Sumter, Smith was in Philadelphia, quietly rehearsing for the first performance there of Verdi's opera, *Un Ballo in Maschera*. The ballerina was Annetta Galletti, just arrived from New York, where she had participated in another brief and unsuccessful attempt to revive the Ronzani Ballet. The company, with a M. Topoff as first dancer instead of Smith, had been appearing on the "off nights" during one of Edwin Forrest's engagements at Niblo's Garden. Unfortunately the people crowded to see the popular tragedian, and left the house empty on ballet nights. It was another of the increasing symptoms that the art of the dance was fading into obscurity. By October of the same year a remnant of the Ronzani Ballet, which had made its American debut so proudly, in the newest and finest theater in the land, had descended to appearances in a cheap beer hall, the New York Melodeon.

During the next few years the aging Ronzani, who had enjoyed such triumphs in his native land, had to content himself with odd jobs, directing ballets for occasional performances of Max Maretzek's opera companies, arranging the dances for one play at Niblo's Garden in 1863, and so forth. The faithful

Galletti danced for him whenever she could. Ronzani's one remaining chance came when, in the autumn of 1866, he had the opportunity to stage the ballets for a road company of the sensationally successful *Black Crook*. The playbills carried his name in enormous letters, announcing that "his great reputation both in Europe and America is a guarantee of the excellence of the department under his charge." The criticisms, alas, were not so flattering. One which appeared in the *New York Clipper* for January 26, 1867, declared: "The ballet, alone made attractive by the graceful dancing of Kate Pennoyer and Kitty Blanchard, is clad precisely the same as in New York, but the execution of the dances is lamentable. Marietta Ravel finds herself somewhat out of her element off the tight rope, and her dancing is gross rather than artistic, and as for the *corps de ballet* movements, they were absolutely painful to witness. The small number of Amazons participating in the march makes it anything but attractive, and the execution of it is badly arranged. . . ."

Poor Ronzani! After this fiasco, he retired and died in New York just a year later, February 13, 1868.

This excursion into the later history of Domenico Ronzani has led us considerably ahead of George W. Smith and *Un Ballo in Maschera*. The first Philadelphia performance of the Verdi opera took place on April 18, 1861, with Signor Muzio as conductor, and Smith in charge of the choreography. He had arranged a galop and a figure quadrille for the *corps de ballet*, and a mazurka for Galletti and himself. The *North American and U. S. Gazette* commented next day: "The story necessitates the composer to express the deepest passions and the lightest frivolity in the same strains, as in . . . the last scene (the masquerade) where the death plot is culminating and a merry dance is going on, the duet of the lovers and the *pas de deux* of the two leading dancers keeping time together. . . ." The Philadelphia opera season closed on April 20, the singers going on to Cincinnati, St. Louis, Chicago, and other cities. If Smith accompanied them he must have returned fairly soon, because during the summer he was acting as ballet master for Frank Rivers' Melodeon Company of Philadelphia.

This troupe included Kitty Blanchard (later a well-known actress), Millie Fowler, Susan Summerfield, and the character dancer Szollosy. The Civil War had closed the South to them, and the summer was spent in an informal tour of New England. As they arrived in each town, the actors and dancers formed a procession in carriages, and paraded through the streets, preceded by a brass band. These tactics smack strongly of the circus, but it should be remembered that in those days "advance publicity" was by no means the exact science that it is today.

In Boston the company appeared at the Howard Atheneum, under the management of Smith's old friend, the distinguished actor E. L. Davenport. One of the pieces in the repertoire was an extravaganza called *The Seven Sisters* (daughters of the devil) which Laura Keene had presented in New York for a long run, during the preceding winter. In Smith's version, the scenes included such provocative incidents as "The Grand Court of Satan. His Majesty entertained by the champion Clog-dancer" and "The Moonlight Flitting of the Fays, and magnificent FAIRY BATHING SCENE." Another item was the "Grand Zouave Drill, by the Female Fire Zouaves." All of this sounds pretty far removed from the misty romanticism of the ballet productions of the forties. Nevertheless, the final scene seems to have been a lovely and delicate one. Lacking an adequate account of Smith's staging, we quote the criticism of Laura Keene's production of *The Seven Sisters. Leslie's Illustrated Newspaper*, on December 22, 1860, described the final tableau, somewhat fancifully:—"In the dis-

tance are seen the sylph-like forms moving as it were through mid air, and surrounded by rosy clouds; nearer the waters of a fairy lake glisten in the fairy-like atmosphere, while over its surface floats the queen of the realm, radiant in glittering garments and crowned with choicest shells. Over all this hang the fairy ferns, their leaves quivering as at the touch of a whispering zephyr, and every fibre apparently instinct with life; and, as a crowning wonder, a huge water lily, floating down upon the bosom of the water, opens its pearly leaves and discloses a living child nestling amongst its petals."

During the war years Smith frequently disappears from the American theatrical scene, perhaps seeking refuge in peaceful Europe, perhaps going into temporary retirement. Conditions in this country were certainly disturbed enough! Late in 1862 he was again dancing in *Un Ballo in Maschera* in Philadelphia. In the columns of the *North American and U. S. Gazette* for December 20, there is an account of the bloody battle of Fredericksburg, side by side with a criticism of the opera, which occupies almost the same amount of space. Maurice Grau, later a manager of the Metropolitan Opera, was director of this company. Evidently his artistic conscience was none too strict, for he permitted the conductor, Signor Muzio, to interpolate a Grand Galop of his own composition in the middle of Verdi's tragic final scene.

IX

The Civil War had been over for two years before, in the season of 1867-68, we once more find Smith taking an active part in ballet production. Engaged as ballet master at the Theatre Comique, Boston, he produced a number of ballets in collaboration with two well-known pantomimists, James S. Maffit and W. H. Bartholomew. For a pantomime called *The Forty Thieves*, he staged a Grand Turkish Ballet and also a Grand Transformation scene, "The Grotto of the Fairies of the Silver Lake." Since he later presented this in New York, it was probably the source of inspiration for two Currier and Ives lithographs, published in 1867 and 1868, called The Fairy Grotto and The Fairies' Home.[12]

Here he also revived—perhaps for the last time, for the taste for this type of ballet was dying fast—Giselle, with Ida De Vere in the title role and himself (still dancing, at nearly fifty!) as Albrecht. Annie Chester danced Myrtha, and Mlle. Albertina (Albertina Flint, an American girl, not to be confused with the French Mlle. Albertine who had appeared with Smith earlier) was Bertha. This version of Giselle included a pas de quatre danced by Wilfred, Bathilde, Bertha, and Myrtha—a strange combination of characters, surely, and very hard to reconcile with the plot! Not a trace of such a pas de quatre is evident in present-day productions of Giselle, and it is impossible to imagine just when and where it would occur. Evidently this 1868 Giselle was an abbreviated, even a mutilated, version, with all the action condensed in one scene, in an effort to whet the public's weakened appetite for the ballet. It was high time for poor Giselle to return to her grave, to await a more auspicious era for resurrection.

For a short period in May, 1867, Smith transferred his allegiance to the Boston Theatre, where he renewed his many years' acquaintance with Edwin Booth, who was now making his first appearances on the stage since the tragic assassination of President Lincoln by the actor's brother, John Wilkes Booth. Edwin Booth was one of the lessees of the Boston Theatre, and another brother, J. B. Booth, was the stage manager. Here Smith revived an old favorite, Julia Turnbull's vehicle of twenty years earlier, The Naiad Queen. Its "Military Evolutions, Grand March of Female Warriors, in Full Armor" and so forth were always more suggestive of the latter half of the century, with its tasteless Amazonian parades, than of the period in which it was first conceived. The Naiad Queen had been a quarter of a century ahead of its time (no great credit to it, to be sure) and only now other productions began to catch up with it—or perhaps we should say, to descend to its level.

At Boston George W. Smith was briefly associated with a very great artist, Giuseppina Morlacchi. This lovely young ballerina, who had made her New York debut in an extravaganza, The Devil's Auction, in the preceding season, had been a pupil of Blasis at La Scala. With her exquisite artistry she illuminated a period of ballet history which was otherwise notoriously dull. She had a strange and fascinating career, culminating in her marriage to Texas Jack (John Omahundro) a plainsman from the West and the dearest friend of Buffalo Bill.

Morlacchi's flawless technique and artistic sensitivity made a profound impression on the renowned critic and Columbia University Professor, Brander Matthews, while the late Philip Hale of Boston, who saw her in his youth, declared her to be unsurpassed. Morlacchi's photographs are lovely and gracious; her body is fine lined and delicately modeled, the perfect instrument for the classical ballet, and her face, with its great dark eyes, unusually mobile.

Early in February, 1868, Morlacchi arrived at the Boston Theatre Comique with a touring company of The Devil's Auction. Although Charles Constantine, who had danced in it previously, remained in the company in an acting role, George W. Smith promptly took over all the dances. Elisa Blasini and Mlles. Ricci and Baretta were among the coryphees of this troupe. During the run of The Devil's Auction the ballet divertissements were varied from time to time, so that on various occasions Smith danced a pas de trois with Morlacchi and Blasini, a comic polka with Blasini, a grand pas de deux with Morlacchi, and other numbers.

As the run of The Devil's Auction drew to

a close, Maffit and Bartholomew prepared to take their "Boston Comique Ballet and Pantomime Troupe" to New York, where they opened on March 2. The *première danseuse* was Ermesilda Diani, another of the Milanese dancers who found their way to America in such large numbers, during the latter half of the nineteenth century. The ballets in the repertoire, all staged by Smith, included the inevitable *Maja de Seville*, with Smith as Don Vincentio, *The Fairy of the Forest,* and something called *La Doctor del Confusion*, in which Smith, as "Henri, in love with Millie" once more played the role of a young hero! There were also several pantomimes, such as *The Italian Brigands, Nicodemus,* and *Kim-Ka, or The Adventures of an Aeronaut.* Although it conflicted with Fanny Kemble's first appearance in several years, the ballet opening was well attended. "Three pantomimes made up the programme of the evening," commented the *New York Herald* next day. "In each of these there is an infusion of ballet that cannot fail to make the performances popular, while the pantomime itself is sufficient to attract appreciative audiences every night. Mlle. Diani, the *première danseuse,* drew forth rapturous applause in the Hungarian Polka and in the *pas de deux* which she danced with Mr. Smith. . . ."

Diani was one of the soloists in J. E. MacDonough's production of *The Black Crook* at the Walnut Street Theatre, Philadelphia, for which Smith staged all the ballets and marches, in August, 1868. The ranking ballerina was Mlle. Ermina Venturoli, who later, in middle age, disgraced her profession by getting herself arrested in New York as the keeper of a disorderly house. Smith was the featured male dancer in addition to his work as choreographer, and he had the assistance of five solo dancers besides Venturoli and Diani: Mlles. Lea, Lina Wendel, Baretta, Albertine and Alexandria.

In his later years Smith supervised many productions of *The Black Crook.* A Philadel-

phia photograph of 1876, which we reproduce, shows a Harlequin who bears a striking resemblance to George W. Smith, although the picture looks like a man of thirty-five or forty, and not far past fifty, as Smith must undoubtedly have been at that time! Yet it is quite possible that this is Smith. Giuseppina Morlacchi was the star of that particular *Black Crook* revival.

In New York, in 1882, Smith staged another production of the *Crook*, which called the following comment from the *Herald* of November 14: "Every seat was occupied in Haverly's Theatre, and 'standing room only' was announced before the curtain went up on *The Black Crook* last evening. The famous old spectacle has lost none of its attractiveness, and . . . still has the power to draw large paying audiences whenever it is revived. The management . . . presented the pieces as regards scenery, costumes, etc., in a manner worthy of the reputation of the theatre, and there was not a single hitch in the performance from beginning to the end. In order to obtain the necessary room to do the principal marches and ballets the stage was enlarged. . . . Bright new costumes, new marches, ventriloquism, Tyrolean warblings, etc., contributed to the popularity which the present revival is destined to achieve. . . ." The ballerina was Mlle. Josephine De Rosa, a dancer from the Teatro San Carlo, Naples. She had worked under Smith's direction as early as 1869, when she was his *première danseuse* at Fox's American Theatre, Philadelphia, shortly after her arrival in this country.

Smith had been teaching, whenever his professional engagements permitted it, throughout his career. In 1881 he opened a regular studio at Broad and Columbia Avenues, Philadelphia. Here each morning he gave a professional ballet class, while in the afternoon he instructed the wealthy socialites of the city in the ballroom dances of the day. His daughter, Fanny Elssler Smith, assisted him. At that time it was impossible to buy good ballet shoes in this country; most of the dancers were obliged to import them from Italy. Smith, eager for his pupils to have every advantage, often used to make their shoes himself. He had his own last, and patiently stitched the delicate slippers by hand.

Smith was extremely bitter about the degeneration of the classic ballet, in his later years. In an interview at the time of Fanny Elssler's death, in 1884, he said: "Bah, there is no dancing nowadays, it is only antics. Like myself, it has died out and is no more." Nevertheless, he often returned to the theater to assist in the staging of some great spectacle. *The Little Tycoon* and *1492* were two extravaganzas which benefited from his lengthy experience. For a time he was ballet master at Fox's American, a variety theater in Philadelphia, where Marie Bonfanti, Josephine De Rosa, and other fine dancers appeared under his direction.

In the seventies Smith toured for a time with Barnum's Roman Hippodrome, staging the circus ballets and marches, and the Hungarian dancer Arnold Kiralfy, who had a virtual corner on pantomime production in the last quarter of the century, learned much from Smith.

X

Much of the energy and enthusiasm of the aging man was devoted to the teaching of his talented little son Joseph, born in 1875. Mrs. Smith strongly disapproved of the theater, and made each of her ten children promise not to seek a theatrical career. Nevertheless, at home they were constantly surrounded by an atmosphere of music and dance, and could not help but absorb much of it. Joseph Smith spent a great deal of time at the studio and theater with his father, who gave him a thorough and well-rounded theatrical education. Joseph has described some of his father's methods: "When I was only a little boy, he wanted to teach me to be a harlequin, but I did not want to be one—doing all those quick

movements of head and body and having everybody laughing at me. . . .

"My father would listen to my protestations and then, just to throw me off my guard, would say: 'Oh, well, I must rest a while now.'

"Then he would sit down and yawn and stretch his body, and do all the funny little movements of the harlequin. That was his way of amusing me, of engaging my interest, of making me like a thing I did not like—in brief, of teaching me to be a harlequin without knowing it." [13]

At another time, Joseph was having difficulty in learning to do turns in the air. He fell so often that finally he told his father that he thought it could not be done.

" 'Can't, eh?' said he. 'Come to the show with me tonight!'

"When we got there he pointed out an Italian who was doing a $1\frac{3}{4}$ turn.

" 'What one man can do, another man can do,' he said.

"I was only a boy at the time, but I went to the theater next morning, practiced a bit, and actually did a triple turn before my father got there. And I can do a triple turn today, although I am forty years old."

Smith taught his son how to use the quarterstaff and single stick, and to handle every kind of sword known. He also saw that his son learned to ride well. Young Joseph became quite proficient in the riding tricks of the circus. "In my day," he wrote, "the child had to stand on the horse's back without any support, and every time he fell off he got cut with a long whip which sometimes drew blood. Many a time I have fallen off a horse's back and hung onto his tail, his hind legs kicking me, and then struggled up onto his back again, rather than touch the ground and get a cut from the awful whip. . . ."

Joseph learned such physical control that much later, when a suspension wire broke, hurling him to the stage forty feet below, he was able to land so that he was unhurt except for a few bruises, and was able to dance again two days later.

The basis of Joseph Smith's education was, however, a firm knowledge of the traditional, academic ballet technique. On this classical foundation he developed a personal and original style which made him an outstanding theater performer.

George W. Smith, who did not live to see his son's successes on the stage, died in Philadelphia on February 18, 1899. He had continued to teach until just a few days before.

Because of his mother's disapproval, Joseph Smith did not begin an active theatrical career until after her death. He soon became one of the most versatile and sought-after performers on the stage. His achievements ranged from appearances in classical ballet at La Scala, Milan, to the invention of the turkey trot. He created this dance after watching Negroes on the banks of the Mississippi, slouching under their sacks of cotton, half gliding and half loping along. The gobbler glide and the bunny hug, ballroom sensations around 1912, were adaptations of this dance.

Joseph Smith claimed to have been first to dance the tango in this country. He learned it in Spain, and when he introduced it at the old Winter Garden everyone laughed. They thought it exaggerated, ludicrous. Later it caught the public fancy and swept the country.

In a dimly lit, smoky Paris *boîte*, Smith watched the underworld characters whirling through their own rough and sadistic dances. These crude barbarities were translated into a strange and sensuous grace, and with Louise Alexander, in the Ziegfeld Follies of 1907, Smith introduced the apache dance. For years, no vaudeville program was complete without one.

Joseph Smith was the first man to dance in public in a dress suit. Arriving at the theater too late to change, one night in London, he dashed out on the stage in his formal evening clothes. The effect was so surprisingly good that the manager asked him to continue to wear the new costume.

He also indirectly caused the popularity of the still-familiar song, "Every Little Move-

ment Has a Meaning of Its Own." The song was written for the Broadway show, *Madame Sherry*, but the producer didn't like it. Smith, who was directing the dances, suggested a method of staging the number by combining it with a dance scene, and the result was the hit of the show. Smith married Frances Demarest, the charming star who sang it.

At the Shubert Theatre, New York, in 1914, Joseph Smith danced for the last time the original Harlequin routine, heritage of Sylvain and Byrne, which his father had taught him. The dance was interpolated in a fantasy by Percy MacKaye, called *A Thousand and One Nights*.

Joseph Smith staged New York's first restaurant "floor show" at Maxine's Café Madrid, in 1910. He directed the dances for numerous Broadway shows, the last being *The Vagabond King*, in 1925. He was killed by a truck, while crossing Madison Avenue at Thirty-fourth Street, in December, 1932, and at the time of his death had been planning to produce a revival of *Madame Sherry*.

XI

George W. Smith's notebook, a small, fascinating, fragmentary record of his work as a choreographer, has been referred to frequently in these pages. This invaluable souvenir of an extraordinary career contains a number of interesting things, worthy of analysis, and several that are fairly puzzling. The earliest entries, evidently made shortly after Smith acquired the little book (it is dated 1848) are the most detailed. The later ones are brief and hurried notes, many of them in another handwriting (that of his wife, according to Miss Carrie Smith).

The first entries consisted of a series of ensemble dances, carefully described and often illustrated with tiny figures and indications of figurations.

#1. Pas des Fleurs (illustrated with many group formations reminiscent of the old lithographs of the Viennese Children in their Flower Dance).

#2. Pas de Amoret (danced with tambourines, and showing several unusual and charming figurations, in addition to the inevitable diagonals, stars and semi-circles).

#3. Pas de Rococo.

#4. Pas de Berger.

#5. Gallop des Drapeaux (there was a dance of this title in the repertoire of the Viennese Children, who were in this country in 1848).

#6. Polka Passane (Paysane?).

#7. Mazurka.

#8. Redowa Quadrilles No. 1—Contredanse.

#9. Another set of Redowa Quadrilles.

#10. Redowenska from La Vivandiere.
There is no #13—Was Smith superstitious?

#14. Ballet L'Illusion.

#15. Polka Pas de Deux.

#16. La Sicilienne.

#17. Taquenette Polka.

#18. 12 ladies Polka in the Ballet of Betly.
12 ladies—La Normandarc in Betly.
10 ladies in Betly.

This list brings us up to 1851, when Smith staged *Betly* for Lola Montez. Some of the dances seem to have been used as incidental numbers in plays, some are pure *divertissements*. Most of the steps described are simple, and the same step is repeated many times. Smith's favorites seem to have been balancé (which he spelled with a z, balanzé) and *pas de basque*. Of course, these dances were planned for the inadequately trained ensemble dancers of that time. Nowhere in the notebook is there any indication of the actual steps executed by the solo dancers in the ballets.

No. 14, *Ballet L'Illusion*, is the complete outline of a ballet, Perrot's *Le Délire d'un Peintre*. Created for Elssler in London, in 1843, this ballet was first danced in America (under the title *L'Illusion d'un Peintre*) by Herminie Blangy, four years later. We have not discovered when or where Smith produced it, if, indeed, he ever did.

Among the early notes there are listed a serious family polka, a Maypole dance for the play *Watt Tyler*, a morris dance in Toodles (!) and three incidental dances for Shakespeare's play, *A Winter's Tale*: a rustic dance, a satyr dance, and an amazon or pyrrhic dance. There are dances (including a polka) for *The Bohemian Girl* and the opera *Maritana*. Under the heading *La Bayadère*, Smith (or his wife) has copied all the words of a speaking part—a complete role, evidently.

In the later entries are found evidences that Smith was not averse to inserting bits of one ballet into another—a time-honored if regrettable custom which is still in use! Under "Ballet—Pas de Scharp" (Pas d'Echarpe?), another hand has written "(1) Commence with Andante from Danube" (Adam's *La Fille du Danube*, of course) "all discovered in group. (2) Groups of birds," and so on.

A curious note concerns a ballet called *Metamorphus*. The entire action is carefully described, and it includes an incident where a supernatural visitor sits in a chair, is covered with a cloak to hide her from the jealous fiancée of the hero, and then vanishes without a trace, which is lifted bodily from Taglioni's *La Sylphide*. Smith danced Sylphide with Elssler, of course. But *Paul* Taglioni produced a ballet called *Les Metamorphoses* in London, in 1850. Smith's plot bears little resemblance to Paul Taglioni's, so he must have borrowed only the title from this work.

Another ballet outlined quite completely (one of the latest entries) is *The Misfortunes of an Irishman*, which concerns the adventures of Pit Pat, an Irishman, Monsieur Poinson, a rich farmer, and the farmer's two pretty daughters. After pages of the complicated plot, the whole ends up with a jolly Irish jig, danced by all concerned!

188

AMERICAN INNOVATORS

Isadora Duncan. Photo by Arnold Genthe. New York.

ISADORA DUNCAN*

BY WILLIAM BOLITHO

WE SHOULD NOW take up again the difficult case of the woman adventurer; and indeed would long ago have done so, if examples that are not merely trivial were not also extremely rare. The matter has even a practical interest. Our own times seem half to cajole, half to bully women to search for a life of their own, and not quite to be satisfied, in many cases, when they have only found a career. The one case yet handled, Lola Montez, appeared to lead to a disappointing conclusion, or rather, suspicion. But was not the shadow of general law, half perceived, possibly only the special case of a time, place, and personality? In such a doubt, the life of Isadora Duncan, of all the select groups of extraordinary lives of our time, has the most illustrative content and value. She herself thought the story of her life was "fitted for the pen of a Cervantes, or Casanova." I consider that mistaken, for almost too many reasons. It is not for the picaresque, or incidental of her life (to tell the truth, often very meager, however padded with fine and medium-fine names of the times) that she figures here. Nor, in the least because I agree with her followers, imitators, and copyists that her contribution to art was much more than a misdirection. Many actresses of the French stage, for example, may have had lives richer in the whimsical, unexpected turns of fortune, lovers of finer quality, adventures and vicissitudes more fantastic and interesting. Nor is Isadora Duncan here because of

the underlying dignity of her life, which certainly was there, and which we certainly ought not to fail to observe in its extremely precious tragic unity. We are vowed to objectivity. She has the right to stand beside all the extraordinary and sometimes illustrious people here, because she, above all women of our time, in scale, in courage, in the spirit, made the purest attempt at the life of adventure. So we can say, if you like, that she questioned the Sphinx closest on the mysteries that here interest us. And obtained a strange set of replies. The details of her early life she herself evidently considered entrancingly strange. But virtually the same family, and its way of life, appear so often in the lives of those who afterward have earned their living by the arts, that they may well seem banal almost to orthodoxy. These Duncans of San Francisco, as she describes them, were shabby, thriftless, and intelligent. They scrambled along in a sort of gypsy opportunism, borrowing as a right, spending as a duty, and of course the mother gave private lessons on the piano. I had the closest personal experience of such people in my own youth, and out of my mixed reaction of dislike and admiration I remember I made a theory: that in reality such people were what I called "behaving a private income." That is, and it may be, as good an explanation of all their conduct as I know now, that

* From *Twelve Against the Gods*, copyright, 1929, by Simon & Schuster, Inc.

such people are at bottom doing nothing more wild and free than living like a good class of newly rich bourgeois, rather wasteful, a little pretentious, with a charming surface culture. Only they have not any money. In one decisive particular alone, it is easy to see where the real affinities of their mode of life and sentiment are, and are not: their inflexible, perfectly middle-class morality. No, here are no rag and bobtail strollers, but a fragment of the rock of respectable society, economically displaced.

We must now go a little deeper into the formative influences so at work upon her young character than the somewhat tawdry romantic view she puts forward herself. The "Constant Nymphism," the "Beloved Vagabondism," or whatever you like to call the color of such a childhood, can stay by itself. I feel there two significantly important other features. The lesser of these is the taste for books, and all the other cultural feeling and direction clustered around this, that she acquired. Such families almost by definition read a great deal, a special quality of book, and in a special way. They read, as the neighbors say, "out of their station," and the children especially are only drawn toward books whose titles seem to promise them a higher, stranger, above all, unusual, world to tour. That is, for example, they are extremely seldom attracted by Shakespeare, Shelley * (not to mention accessible novels)—such names seem too common, and their magnificence is for quite a different class of child. The Brontës in their scrupulously clean old vicarage, much poorer, much more isolated than ever the ragged, somewhat cheeky little Duncans were, were haunted by the very names of Prospero, Hamlet, Lear and his Fool. Scarcely our San Franciscans, who stopped at the bookshop windows before large copies of *The Sayings of Marcus Aurelius*, books with foreign, mysterious names, especially Greek. But please notice that it never occurred to them to learn Greek.

It is useless to conceal that in such circumstances, besides the leaning to pretentiousness, natural and not completely a bad thing, there is in such ways inevitably a great danger of smattering, of messing with half-read books, cover fluttering, and all the other indignities to which great books and subjects that must needs ask a moderate degree of attention are subjected by dilettante autodidacts.

Somewhere in her memoirs Isadora naïvely illustrates this. In the wings of a provincial theater while waiting her call, she would "be deep in Marcus Aurelius." But no one noticed it, and she always felt a little peeved. Also, I would risk something that she never finished, not quite finished, the volume.

And so it may easily be likely that of all this miscellaneous reading, and general jackdaw culture, very little more than a collection of charming miscomprehensions, untargeted enthusiasms, and a general habit of skimming, remained. Perhaps also, when her ruling prejudices formed, a jealous dislike, actually, of sound knowledge and hard study, and all that can be founded upon them.

Then, in the second place in this amusing upbringing, we must observe the effect of her mother's failure in marriage. It is Isadora's resolute rejection of the ordinary hope and destiny of women, the legal support of a man, indeed, that spiritually entitles her life to be considered as an adventure. For by a short cut through what might be a very long reasoning, let us mark out the institution of marriage as the most plausible visible reason (and quite sufficient too), why women are so rarely in any strict sense adventurers.†

The adventurer, by minimum definition, is an individualist. The life of adventure is an unsocial game; therefore in direct contrast with the married, supported life which is nuclear society itself. It may well be, or so I

---

* The mother, by the way, read Shakespeare and Shelley to the Duncans, according to Isadora's account.

† The feminine form has too special a meaning.

think, that the mere idea of marriage, as a strong possibility, if not always nowadays a reasonable likelihood, existing to weaken the will by distracting its straight aim in the life of practically every young girl, is the simple secret of their confessed inferiority in men's pursuits and professions today. If instead of looking for some obviously nonexistent feminine inferiority of brain power, educationalists would cast a look at the effect, during the training and learning years of such an underthought: "but, after all, I may get married," at the fiercely desperate corners where a man student or beginner passes in a spirit of life or death, they might count that in. And, in consequence, when drawing up their comparative tables, set their statistics of women's work, not against the mass of thus unhandicapped men, but against some restricted group, of those only who have some weakening third responsibility before their eyes in a crisis than straight success, or failure; such, for example, as rich men's sons, who cannot be absolutely in earnest. The vast mass of men, then, have to depend on themselves alone; the vast mass of women hope or expect to get their life given to them. It is the first condition of a woman adventurer to do as Isadora did and bar from the beginning any such dependent.

Her mother was so affected by the failure of her own marriage, which ended in a divorce, that she not only ever afterward taught the children that their father was a devil and a monster, but changed her religion. From Catholic she became in a jump Ingersollist, and an equally pious one in that arid form of Puritanism, for orthodox atheism certainly is one. But just for that reason, we are not allowed to search for Isadora's resolution against marriage in her mother's teaching, or anywhere but in her own audacious, confident soul. A young girl, a beauty, with all the added fascination of the education we have criticized, but not forgotten, is more graceful and easily won than a more serious one at her age; that she could have firmly, unreluc-

tantly decided to win her life for herself, to play her own hand against the gods is as remarkably daring as anything in this book. But it is curious, and necessary to notice, that this spiritual gesture was not complete. In place of the husbandage she scornfully renounced, as I diagnose it, sprang up in her naturally and inevitably a social theory, recognizable underneath its innocent sentimentality, its vagueness, and everything else, as the genuine unmistakable embryo of the socialism which is immanent in our times and will quite probably be dominant in the next. She wanted no husband to look after her, support her, feed her. She was quite convinced that someone should. That someone, when she learned the vocabulary, was the state. But at first it was the landlord, rich people, the public; not relatives, not parents—she never even thought of turning to them. Let us say, just Society. Beautiful examples of this occur in profusion in her own confession. After a concert in New York, where she had performed, been applauded, paid, and praised, she does not hesitate to go back to the giver, a rich woman, and ask her for money. "This rich woman, with sixty millions, went to her desk, after I had explained our need and wrote a cheque." Only fifty dollars. Think of it. The significant incident in variations was often repeated. When she was quite small, when there was nothing to eat in the house, "I was always the volunteer sent to the butcher, and who cleverly got the cutlets out of him without paying. . . . I was the one sent to get credit out of the baker. . . ." If, even at this age, she had discerned the least indignity in such acts, be sure she would have refused them with indignation. It was a matter of simple justice to her; those that have must give.

And in this, this essentially social, if not socialistic, anti-Nietzschean conception of the rights of the poor, an indefinite number of men might not concur. How many women do so in their hearts, I do not know. The concordance, in fact, between the form into which the modern state is undeviatingly proceeding everywhere, and the womanly, as distinct from the masculine social ideal, cannot be quite accidental. Somewhere at the end of it, is the State, the great provider, husband for every woman and father to every child; an interesting research for daydreamers. And, if it is so, or approximately, the adventurous, unsocial, masculine life is destined to take on even more rigorously the character of a revolt.

However that may be, the form of Isadora's life from its start includes a social dependence and sentiment, sincere, unquestionable, probably compensatory. It is, therefore, difficult to conceive of any other direction for it than the stage. And on that road with that beautiful floating inevitability with which large portions of her life were embellished, she began to go almost as soon as she could walk.

She has given us a very candid account of her invention of what was afterward ineptly known as "classical" dancing. On any analogy with the use of that illustrious adjective in other arts, this abandonment to individual mood and individual taste should surely be "romantic" rather than "classic": which name probably has been taken in allusion to some fanciful imitation of—better, borrowing from —the decorated attitudes of ancient Greek potters. If anything is certain in the obscure subject, it is that Greek dancing of the heyday had no more resemblance to Isadora's than the poems of, let us say, Theocritus, to the poetical works of Gertrude Stein. At six years already she had begun to jump and caper about to her mother's playing, and other children admiring this, which must have had some unusual vigor and grace, procured pennies from their parents to pay her to give them lessons. Giving lessons was the first consequence of ideas in the Duncans' practical philosophy.

Later, her mother seems to have thought there might be some fertility in this play, and sent her daughter to learn the elements in a regular school of ballet. The master was "one of the most famous in San Francisco" which, given the low mondial ebb of the art, at the time, must mean rather queerly bad. He was such a nincompoop anyway that when the little girl confidently told him she did not like the steps he taught "because they were ugly and against nature," he appears to have been unable to answer her. This happened at the third lesson, and she never went back. Instead, henceforward she began to invent the art of dancing for herself.

Here, therefore, is an absolutely spontaneous outcrop of that feeling, theory, practice of the arts (and by no means dancing alone), whose sudden fortune in the first decade of this century has lasted, though it may be waning, right into our own days. Since it was the instrument, chart, or sword, at your choice, of her adventure, we must once more halt, to examine it attentively. From a purely academic point of view, this "free-art" theory may be ticketed as some far-off descendant of the inspirationism of the romantics, nominally, let us say, the English lyrical school; and even perhaps, still more impressively, of such wild oracles as Dionysius or Isaiah. I feel an absurd dislike for venturing, even in play, on comparisons between the dancers we are strictly occupied with and their poet-painter friends, and such magnificences as the works of, for example, William Blake. I prefer the risk and trouble of attacking the matter at its butt end. Isadora's idea, then, was, as far as I can make out, and if I am right, identical with those exploited at the same time in all the other arts, that the artist should "return to nature" and especially to himself. No more rules, no more tradition; for which things she, and they, usually have ready the word "artificial," in which they sum up all that is opposite to this "nature," and all that is trivial, false, and bad. Now I consider that all this theory is a clear by-product of that Puritanism she was in other affairs of life never tired of damning. The same two sentiments, one open, one hidden, are present in both theories. One, the open fear and hatred of the "artificial," the humanizing embellishment which is the very essence of civilization. She anathematizes, for example, tiptoe dancing—that exquisite and ingenious invention by which a dancer can seem to have achieved humanity's universal flying dream, and cast off the shackles of weight; exactly as a deacon condemns the lipstick, a Tolstoian brocade, or a Quaker church vestments and stained glass.

But this Nature, this dear, beautiful mother to which all these people invite us, wants none of us. Nature is the night, the iceberg, the uninhabitable crags of mountains, the black gulfs of the ocean, in whose unveiled presence we are dumb-struck and tremble. This giant brooding power, which will not even look straight at us, like a captive tigress, when we dare to put ourselves in her presence protected by ships, ropes, convoys, is not imitable! The suburban landscapes, the neatly growing trees, the gently curving rivers, with, naturally, a dear little cottage in the foreground, is not Nature, but artifice, the work of man. Even here, though we have painted a friendly smile on her mask, beneath the artifice (and it is thin), there is the same implacability. The nightingales, dear naturalists, do not sing for us or you. The flowers are proud, and those trees your own grandfather planted in sweat have no feelings of gratitude toward men. All animals except the parasitical dog and cat which we have debauched hate us; a sparrow that will not move aside for an elephant will hide itself before the most angelic child on earth can come within reach. One night, at the height of summer, walk in the most humanly artificial park, and clearing your brain from all the kindly cant of the lesser poets (for Shakespeare never misled you), perceive first in delight the huge rustling flood of life that is playing—in the hope you would not come; and then notice bitterly how at the first sound of your step everything living and dead closes,

hushes, disappears. The trees themselves, it might seem, turn their backs to you, you the wet blanket, the human, the unwanted, the horror. A strange experiment, that one of carnivorous anthropoids, killer monkeys; the whole of Nature hopefully awaits the day we shall be extinct. It is wise and necessary to leave her awful symmetries to themselves; to build for ourselves a beauty and a world out of her ken.

Her standards of beauty, here is the crisis, are not ours. In an ancient abominable scorn, she judges us, perhaps, as we find a negroid beauty, with plates in her lips. A naked woman, even Isadora at seventeen, in a forest —the commonest deer passes, and if you have not much unimaginative complacency, you may suspect the scorn of Nature for this bleached, forked, curved thing.

And now let the fondest mother remember her sweetest baby, remember the secrets of the nursery, and dare not to feel embarrassed if she hears Saint Francis *dared* to preach to unrevengeful, undestructive, quiet minds. Let us, as that old railer Johnson said, talk cant if we will, but prudently beware of believing it. Nature's standards of beauty, physical, moral, are outside our reach. By nature we are ugly. Abandoned in a jungle we would grow only into the most loathsome crawler, with this fault in addition, that we were horribly dangerous.

If what this little girl of San Francisco in a calm temerity set out to teach us were all our hope, it is a poor outlook. What is Caliban to do except live lonely and dig a deep hole? I think and hope she was mistaken. Man can look Nature in the face and return scorn with contempt, set standards against standards with a loftiness that might put that great stupid goddess out of countenance, if she had any intelligence. The noise of the open sea is not the equal of a dying speech in Shakespeare. The mere height of Mont Blanc is less than that of a Beethoven sonata. A woman, any woman, beside a fawn, says Schopenhauer, is grotesque. But let Michelangelo dress her, put her in silk, put shoes on those feet, and the fawn may come and lick her hand. By artifice, which is the accumulated inspiration of artists, women, men, and cities are as far above the natural as the clear light of the stars above the crawling life of a lagoon. The child, for all his stepmother Nature gives him, may be a horrible animal; human poetry treats him as, and will one day make him into, a god. This is the function of art: to make a supernatural world; not to imitate the natural.

In the same way that I reject her juvenile dictum about Nature, whose relative position to herself she misunderstood, so must be put out of the question the corollary that the artist, without learning, refusing the help of all the genius of the past, must only express his poor self, and be certain that that more, that that only, is worth while. To put Nature in her place is not the work of any single genius; such as appear amongst us, not every year, but in certain epochs, rarely. In practice it is in a high degree unlikely that John, or Jean, Blank out of his own untaught nature can produce a poem, a sonata, a dance worth the meditation of an earthworm. Why should it be otherwise? Where, except in some exalted religious optimism, does this confidence in the intrinsic value of all self-expression base itself?

So much, too much, for the fundamental theory, the instrument of Isadora in her adventure. After all, she was a great personage and though she never admitted it, nor probably ever knew it, she tricked with it. To eke out her nature, she borrowed and adopted the attitudes of Greek vases. She, the pure inspirationist, gradually constructed an intricate technique of her own, surpassing in certain few ways the old, which by *parti pris*, until it was too late, she never knew thoroughly. She taught Diaghilev's ballet many things; she could never dance in a ballet herself.

But that is in anticipation. When she set out for the conquest of the world, to a greater fame and influence than any other American woman has ever achieved, do not forget, with her family in her knapsack, the great idea is still childish, rudimentary, like a wooden sword. Powerful in a very different degree, her untheoretically real possessions, blossoming youth, a round beauty, magnificent health, simplicity and energy in a unique alloy. Not to shuffle round it, it was her bare legs more than her translation of recondite music into jumps and sways that opened her success.

That success was amazingly quick; so pure was her self-faith that it seemed to her intolerably long. Everyone on even tangential contact with her was entranced with this naïve little American girl, with her stock of impassioned abstract nouns, her unconscious and so charming pretensions, and her thoroughly novel turn. With a yard or two of Liberty muslin, a tragic expression that "everyone wondered at" she gave them Mendelssohn's *Spring Song* and afterward her sister read verses of Andrew Lang's translation of Theocritus. Then one of her brothers would lecture the audience on "Dancing, and its Probable Future Effects on Humanity."

The English did not like the lecturing and the recitation so much as the bright-eyed Isadora. The coldness, the polite coolness, like an unconvinced admiration, of the various strata or reaches of London society she explored rather damped her. In London, if only because of the language, the Duncans seem soon to have dropped the verbal part of the performance. Her personal success there, however, must have been wonderful. But afterward there seems to have been a period when the rent bilking, and park-bench mediations, stereotyped through her youth, recommenced. In the written biographies of most artists of the stage there is something disconcerting in these sudden descents into obscurity and poverty, after blazing success. In the intervals, the family visited museums, one of them "invented sandals," and Isadora herself dallied with Platonic young poets.

Then, of course, Paris. There was a deep

difference between the receptions and the applause of the two cities, which she felt and noted, but, misled by the easy nationalist formulas which formed part of her stock of ideas all her life, she did not quite correctly calculate it. It was not because "the English are cold and unemotional," whereas the French, that lively and artistic nation, are "much warmer in their response," that the difference was one between a blind alley and a high road. The specific differences of national characters, so unexpected and inexplicable if true—for the thousand or so years involved is a short time for such deep evolutions to sport in—belong to the same lovely region where imagination beckons science and is snubbed, that telepathy, water dowsing, and the theory of the Lost Ten Tribes inhabit. The realm of the unnecessary hypothesis. The English character may or may not be undemonstrative; but the English civilization certainly dislikes the new. The English, by education and the neurosis produced by it, want in art something above all to worship, to pray to in their hats as they do in church; and the first essential of the sacred is age. If today, or still safer some decade hence, Isadora could revisit London, old, lame, but an institution, she would waver in her theory of English coldness. But in France, the natural obverse of modern civilization, novelty is the essential, and the *déjà vu* inexorably hissable. They found Isadore not only new, but in the fashion. For to that same mode of the "natural," the inspirational, to which the great American Puritanism in its irresistible ebb had carried her, the French obsession of originality had begun to carry all the arts. Everyone spoke like Isadora; everyone like her had begun to find the great secret by refusing to learn rudiments. The feast of self-expression was in the oven; Isadora came in with the hors d'œuvres. Such, as I see them, were the environmental conditions that tempered and favored the public career of the brave little dancer. Every year, every month almost, at the beginning, her fame increased. Quite

early she had the enlightenment to refuse a well-paid, undignified engagement for a Berlin music hall. But there was in her the ordinary paradox of all true adventurers, that queer foresight among this people consecrated to risk, which is the moral translation of their directed will. Isadora at this speed was going somewhere; the naming of her direction haunted her thoughts. At one time it was, as she answered the German impresario, "that she was come to Europe to bring about a renaissance of religion by means of dancing." For longer stretches of time, she tried to work out a connection between her artistic ideal and the indecisive humanitarianism, the vague socialism we have noted in her before. Vegetarianism floats in and out of her scheme, the state support of poor children is mixed up with (of all things) "back to Sparta." She makes violent efforts to fix what she means. She stands hours "in an ecstasy which alarmed Mother, to find out how to achieve the divine expression of the human spirit in the body" and summed up in a misty formula what she found; in her frantic efforts to prophetize there is a queer resemblance to the fabrication of the old Suras that we watched in the life of Mahomet. Leaving the cryptic results reverently to her disciples, we need only notice that, at whatever degree of intention, here was a perfectly intelligible effort to lift her art out of dependence on the attraction of her youthful body, the working of a foreboding that to be an art at all, her dancing must be something that a middle-aged woman can practice as well as a beauty of nineteen. An old ballerina may still please, at least as well as a debutante; could she not make classical dancing something more than the charming spectacle of lightly clad nymphs, intolerable and insufferable with any fading or thickening of these charms?

That, it is not my business, or competence, to decide. I mark the depth of the problem, her concentrated attention to it, now, and to the end of her life. Meanwhile the success curves up in a steady crescendo, drawn through every capital of Europe. The city that pleased her most was St. Petersburg, where to his own great and declared profit she met the maker of the unofficial Russian Ballet, Diaghilev, also Pavlova and Nijinsky.

Now as to the progress of that other life, of her private adventure, let us call it, I can have no intention of sketching chronologically what she has given the world in detail in her autobiography. To make any love affairs interesting to others is perhaps the most difficult feat in literature; as in her admirable common sense she never hesitated to confess, she was not a good (though she was an honest) writer. The affairs themselves seem of impenetrable banality, except for the generosity which she put in them, which is very likely as rare as its confession. The men who figure, robed in girlish adjectives, are almost embarrassingly awkward. They seem in their relations with this utterly disinterested girl, asking nothing (of anyone but the state), to be reduced to the woebegone role of the male among the insects and spiders.

The result of all this incommunicable poetry was, the world knows, two exquisite children. It knows also, with aghast sympathy, their fate. They were drowned with their governess in a taxicab that fell into the Seine. The frightful simplicity, and the stupid malevolence of this accident; that, also, is Nature and Fate. The natural cause of the destruction of Lisbon, San Francisco, Messina, the *General Slocum*, the *Titanic*, and the fire at the Charity Bazaar in the Avenue de la Seine. This, too, is at the heart of things-as-they-are, and all optimisms must make some account of it, if they are to be more than narcotics. Nor, unfortunately, will the appeal to a future life, with compensatory rewards for such brutality, even if they comprised a million years of bliss and forgetfulness, absolve the agency, or put us, the onlookers, at ease in the universe where children are drowned and then given some bag of celestial candles to make them forget those

suffocating instants. However generous the surplus of pleasure over pain on the entire operation, its horror except to those—and after all they are probably the vast majority—whose ethics are resolutely commercial, remains, staining the whole fabric, like a blood-red dye. Danger, and its emotional accessory terror, is an integral element of the universe. Every life is therefore a desperate adventure; and, on as calm a view as anyone who is doomed willy-nilly to share in it, can achieve, it is more dangerous, more adventurous, to be born than to die. The adventurer goes out to meet the monster in the open; we that stay indoors, with the social mass, run no less risks.

Any life, the coarsest and sternest, is necessarily broken in two by such a stroke; it is far outside the limit of human elasticity. Only in a metaphysical sense can there be even continuity of personality. But this clean snap may present a different appearance, in a variety that includes even disguise. The most obvious and least beautiful response is to die, or to go mad. Then there is suicide, and there is a form of suicide known to those who have been tortured beyond the sill of endurance, which is to count oneself dead. "I died there," said Isadora to a person whom I believe. Only the formality of bleeding was unfulfilled. In such cases, to the surprise of the simple or dull, there may be a deceiving appearance of continuity. It looks like the same person and the same life, going on in the same direction and the same plan, with a smoothness that onlookers can admire, or secretly condemn as callousness, according to their degree of spiritual taste.

Such a deception we will not fall into. And therefore Isadora Duncan, the one we knew, light and cloudy, a little absurd as all delightful people must be, the generous girl who misled nearly the whole of European culture for a decade, has now ended. It is another of the same name who now uses up to its frightful and strange conclusion, like an unfinished lease taken up, the adventure of the dead girl. It is not of the same quality; there is a sensible thickening, banalization of the thread of the story and of all its details, which I fancy I notice. The dazzling little portent slips by steps into the prima donna; every year she becomes serious instead of enthusiastic about the marvelous discovery. Nothing new is added to her dance; but the technique, the gymnastic, becomes more labored and fuller.

The naïve sparrowishness of her claims on humanity, in step, changes into a more and more definite socialism. No doubt her adherence to Leninism was never very intellectual; still the flag waving, the red-tunicism, this was disagreeably nearer, by whatever the distance, the hysterical earnest of a woman with a cause, than to the exciting daydreaming of the other Isadora. I find the account of her visit to Russia, her marriage to Essenine, her disastrous return to America, that two of her friends have very properly and capably, as a historical duty, given us, more distressing than interesting. She moved there among people for the most part pretentious nonentities, the first crop of thistles of the greatest plowing up of the century. Lunacharskys, Mariengoffs, Imagists, belated Futurists, all the band. And she does not always, as the other Isadora would have, make them into a grotesque supporting background against which to pick out her own magnificent dance of life. Incident after incident, as set down by her dearest friends, makes us uneasy. She accepts the use of a flat belonging to an artist, a dancer (ballet, it is true), exiled from Moscow, and criticizes the furniture gleefully and without amenity. She goes to select a fur coat from the vast store of those commandeered from middle-class women, and is snubbed by the very official when she chooses one, thinking it was free of charge. The Communist conductor leads his orchestra out disdainfully when she reminds him she has sacrificed a great deal to come to "help the children of Russia."

The chief of all these disappointing happenings is her marriage with young Sergei Alexandrevitch Essenine. He was one of those literary discoveries of the new Russia, whose merit does not survive a translation. All sincere partisans of the new regime, they may be suspected of thinking of talent and genius as strictly analogous to riches and property, things which stouthearted lads with feelings of class solidarity could take by force from their former possessors. Genius was confiscated by the proletariat of the arts. They drank more than they wrote or knew, and were intoxicated perhaps out of proportion to the quantity of liquor. Everything in their lives was on the group system. They lived, fought, and even loved in common, and arranged the criticism and judgments on what they did strictly co-operatively. But though the general tone and choice of subjects may have been their own, or at any rate authentically national, incidents in the lives of tramps, bullies, strumpets, and so on, most of their technique and theories seemed to have a genealogy. Most of what they did seemed to proceed from the Latin Quarter: the Latin Quarter of ten or twelve years before.

And so, coincidentally, these young self-expressionists, who, "led by Essenine and Koussikoff with his omnipresent balalaika, burst into the room, the calm, Isadoran temple," had some third degree of the spiritual blood of the old, young Isadora, who had tried to think out an entirely new art of dancing for herself a generation back. With that in mind, make what you please of the rest of the account of Isadora's first meeting with her young husband.

"She arose then from her divan and asked the pianist to play a Chopin waltz that she felt would appeal to the lyric soul of the golden-haired poet. And with what rapturous joy and seductive grace she moved through the rhythms of the dance! When the music ended, she came forward with her ingenuous smile, her eyes radiant, her hands outstretched towards Essenine, who was now talking loudly to his companions, and she asked him how he liked her dance. The interpreter translated. Essenine said something coarse and brutal that brought howls of coarse and brutal laughter from his drunken friends. The friend who was acting as interpreter said with evident hesitation to Isadora: 'He says it was—awful . . . and that he can do better than that himself.'

"And even before the whole speech was translated to the crestfallen and humiliated Isadora, the poet was on his feet dancing about the studio like a crazy man."

So ended, for the developments of her marriage to this person virtually fill the rest of her life, the adventure of Isadora. To me it is on the whole the most tragic of all the bad ends we have related; but marriage has an interior as well as an exterior aspect. This young man, whom Isadora married "because she wanted to take him out of Russia to show him all that Europe had of beauty and all that America had of wonder," in short, to give him a good time; and which plan he instantly accepted, was a blond fellow, with the face of a spoiled child, and yellow hair, dressed advantageously over his forehead, in the fashion once common among English private soldiers —the "fascinator." As a typical false adventurer, he requires our attention for a while. He was an indeterminate number of decades younger than she, but already in chronic ill health owing to his habits. Little conversation was possible between them, for he knew only Russian. In his general attitude toward life, besides his poetical pretensions, he claimed to be an adventurer himself, and naturally, the bravest, most disinterested, airiest of them all. He lived from hand to mouth, wasted anything he could not consume at the moment, never repaid a loan, broke anything fragile he could reach, disdained all except the members of his gang, without whom he never stirred, and yet in whose company he never ended an evening without a loud quarrel and

a woundless fight. In short, just as he wrote according to his idea of an improved Rimbaudism, he lived according to his idea of a gallant figure.

But this bulky package of self-expression with which Isadora now encumbered herself in a tour of half the world, turned out when unwrapped to contain an ordinary nucleus of instincts of possession and self-preservation. Certainly he accepted the proposition of being supported, aeroplanes, rides, suites in great hotels, a place of honor at Isadora's parties where there was usually very good company; all this with the most complete contempt for bourgeois scruples. In many things on the lamentable trip he outdid all the traits of his former life: thus "coming into the hotel room at the Adlon, and finding Isadora weeping over an album containing portraits of her unforgettable Deirdre and Patrick (the children) he ruthlessly tore it out of her hands, and throwing it into the fire cried in drunken rage, as he held her back from saving her precious memorial: 'You spend too much time thinking about those —— children.' " In fact, he carefully carried out the doctrine he summed up for his school in a letter, "Let us be Asiatics. Let us smell evilly. Let us shamelessly scratch our backsides in front of everyone." He got her turned out of her hotel in Paris by an orgy of drunken smashing and shouting, and performed many other sacrifices to his peculiar gods. But with a subtle, yet significant nuance, his hectoring always ceased as soon as the police appeared. "Bon Polizei," he would murmur, meek as a lamb, when those testy, quick-tempered fellows, the Paris police, led him off.

At the end of it all, the smashing, the spending, the bullying, drinking, the spoiled furniture in Berlin, the wrecked suite in Paris, the gala in the Carnegie Hall, the scarf waving in Boston, when they were back in Russia Isadora and her friends found that he had stolen all her underclothing to give to his poor family. He was as fond and generous to his sister and mother as the most stolid Paris grocer boy; everything he took he neatly folded. In his trunks, opened by force, was "a veritable arsenal for a traveling salesman in barbershop supplies; boxes and loose cakes of expensive soaps, large and small bottles of assorted perfumes, bottles of bay rum, lotions, brilliantines, tubes of tooth paste and shaving soap, and packages of safety-razor blades."

In the middle of the search, in comes rushing the young husband. "My trunks. Who's been meddling with my trunks? Don't you dare to touch my trunks. I'll kill the person who touches my trunks."

Her road therefore led to a sort of marsh. The reason for the deflection of a flight that started gaily and gallantly is our business only so far as it might or might not be an invariable of the adventures of all women. Moral praise or blame is out of our imposed range. Yet it is easy to see that a certain falseness of taste, "the adoption of a lie" and not a reasonless law of fate, is at work; in one small point, the character of Essenine is almost exactly the expression of an ideal she had preached all her life; she was saved from being one herself by an illogical decency, at war with her principles that kept breaking through. A true contempt for possessions and comfort, and not merely the possessions and comfort of others, is perfectly possible; but it expresses and must express itself in a life of an ascetic, a hermit. Those who love spending, breaking, wasting, the best hotels, lashings of drink, good company and the delights of the flesh must settle themselves to earn money to pay for it themselves, or be damned as parasites—with an ugly protective coloration. Nor make Bohemians your ideal, or one day you may have to go round the world with one.

But this marriage was only one feature of the sad landscape she had journeyed to, the smell of the stagnant water. Every other brittle error she had built into her universe was a weakness, that transformed itself sooner or later into a collapse. Her dancing, even,

and her idolization of the uncultured, the poor, betrayed her rather horribly in Russia, which was her dream come true. A man can build on a well-constructed fiction. We saw Charles, who had swallowed a boys' book, go a long way into Russia. But a mistake, honestly believed in, if big enough, will rot the strongest life, the most soaring adventure, like a gangrene. And so if she ever consciously admitted it, the failure of the art she had invented just for them, to interest the victorious proletariat of Russia, the long and frightful trail over an immense part of their country in the steps of and just behind a ballerina of the old school, who was having an ecstatic success, while Isadora had to pretend hard even to find politeness—would have hurt worse, even, than Essenine. With the help of staging, masks, young and slim bodies, all the artifices of lighting and music, her dancing, or adaptations, more or less acknowledged, or mere plagiarisms, still draw audiences all over Europe, and will in obscurely traceable derivatives perhaps become an addition to the repertory of the art, which she neither killed, as she hoped, nor superseded forever.

But, then, to end, the tragic deflection of Isadora's life, unique in spite of everything in our day of woman's ambition, in size and fame and originality, was brought about by factors special to herself. And (which is less reassuring only to the superstitious), to that horrible, extraneous intervention of the unplumbable evil. You perhaps remember that in Lola's life, too, we played with the idea that the gods are goddesses in their cruelty to the woman adventurer.

All her life, those who have followed me so far do not need to be told, Isadora affected a loose, flowing style of dress. Flou, as the French seamstress slang calls it. So it was a trailing shawl caught in a wheel of a fast car, as if pulled suddenly in a fit of irritated spite, that killed her instantly, one night, on the Promenade des Anglais at Nice, in the middle of many new plans.

201

Film strip of Fuller's *Fire Dance*. Cover montage by Joseph Cornell.

LOIE FULLER

THE FAIRY OF LIGHT

BY CLARE DE MORINNI

PREFATORY NOTE

The fame of Loie Fuller, dancer, actress, and dabbler in the sciences, can rest on the fact that she was the first to utilize, if not to invent, many features of modern stage lighting. Indirect crossbeams and variations of direct electrical illumination were characteristic features of her earliest performances. She anticipated one of the most spectacular of modern inventions—luminescence, the use of cold light by luminous salts. The chief practical uses of her innovations have been found outside the theater: outlining the entrance of air-raid shelters and the staged lighting of Nazi party meetings. As dancer, she inaugurated, before other more widely remembered artists, a dramatization of emotion through natural or at least simple body movements, to the background of important music. Yet all of this is almost forgotten today. However, even a cursory glance at the transformation of a precocious temperance lecturer and "bit" actress to a leader in the theatrical world shows us she was not so simple as some have pictured, nor may she be ignored.

In her field, Fuller made concrete contributions as important as the influential theories of Gordon Craig and Adolph Appia. These
men were chiefly preoccupied with the architectural *scale* of theater decoration, restoring to the stage a kind of dynamics, or heroic stylization which the static naturalism of the late nineteenth century had obliterated. Naïve, largely unconscious of the implications of her discoveries, Fuller was interested neither in paint nor in architecture, but in light. Yet Max Reinhardt's glass floor for *The Miracle*, and his fingers of light picking out solo actors in mass spectacles at the Grosses Schauspielhaus during the early days of the Weimar Republic, connects Loie with the post-Wagnerian decor of a Nuremberg Congress, when, transfixed on the grid of searchlights, the new Siegfried howls.

Manifestations from her immediate person were visible as late as 1925 when she appeared on the broad stairs of the Grand Palais at the exposition of Decorative Arts in Paris, to dance *The Sea*. Here she was seen by a young painter and stage designer, recently out of Russia via Berlin, and about to collaborate with the Diaghilev Ballet. Pavel Tchelitchew in his *Ode* (1928), *Errante* (1933), *St. Francis* (1938) and *Balustrade* (1941), has continually manipulated the translucent, the luminous, the actual presence of light projected on shifting stuffs. André Levinson first noticed the closeness of *Errante* to Loie Fuller's ideas. Recently, in decor for Giraudoux' *Ondine*, produced by Louis Jouvet, which has toured South America, Tchelitchew used the developed gamut of electrical and plastic possibilities which Fuller had previsioned. Only now, substantial marble, under the influence of his wonderful lights turned to water, stone became fire, and the very stage floor itself, impermanent air.

WHAT A LONG JOURNEY it would be from the Fullersburg, Illinois, tavern where Marie Louise Fuller was born. It was an unusually cold winter, and as her parents lived on an isolated farm, they went into town and requisitioned the only room possessing a stove capable of throwing out heat, which happened to be the barroom. This, according to Loie herself, was in 1870. The Dictionary of American Biography unchivalrously gives her 1862. In either case, she maintained she came into the world with a cold she never got rid of.

The initial chapters of her career are typical of any American minor actress of the epoch. At six weeks she appeared in a dance hall in a minor sleeping role. Her father was in demand as a fiddler; there was a surprise party in town and no one with whom to leave Baby, so Loie was brought along. When but two and a half, this child, whose early idols were such feminists as Louisa M. Alcott, Frances Willard, and Carrie Nation, was carried to the Chicago Progressive Lyceum. Quite on her own she decided to "speak a piece," and before her mother could stop her, she was on the platform reciting "Mary Had a Little Lamb." She contrived an effective exit by sliding down the steps, her copper-nailed shoes stuck straight out in front. At four she made her debut in a Chicago stock company, playing Little Reginald in "Was She Right?" Hereafter, her acting career often called for the impersonation of a boy, which may have commenced from accident but long continued through choice. This had an important effect on her psychological development.

The year following, 1875, finds her a temperance lecturer. She practiced the horrible-example method. Having hunted up the town drunkard and placed him on the platform, she delivered her sermon with this constant reminder as her text. She next toured as a Shakespearian "reader," only to return to New York to join the Felix Vincent company. In 1878, H. T. Hinds put on a new production of Dion Boucicault's popular favorite, *The Shaughraun*, and Loie took a small part. The early eighties saw her in Frank May's stock company, then with Dave Henderson's Imperial Burlesque. She produced *Larks*, a play which she wrote herself, and in 1883 toured the circuit with Buffalo Bill. Although she later spoke enthusiastically about her experience with the circus, she may not have felt the same about it at the time; for abruptly in 1884, she retired, as she said, "to study music," and a year later she appeared in Chicago at Hooley's Opera House in *Faust*, singing as well in the Chicago Music Festival.

She returned to the stage for *Our Irish Visitors*, *Turned Up*, and *Humbug*, in 1886, in all of which she had boys' roles. She was in Nat Goodwin's *Little Jack Sheppard* at the Bijou in New York, receiving $75 a week. In 1887, Goodwin produced three plays in which she appeared, *The Big Pony*, *Aladdin* (in which Loie took the lead), and Rider Haggard's *She*. It is said that she was assigned the role of Ustane, the slave girl, not because of any unusual histrionic capacity, but simply because she was willing to roll down the steps of a property pyramid farther and harder for the ten dollars per performance than anyone else. The following year found her back in vaudeville.

Although such experiences would scarcely lead one to believe that Loie Fuller was on the verge of rivaling Sarah Bernhardt, she had gained enough experience as a trouper to play *Camille* once, almost by chance, on just four hours' notice. Then there was a sudden change. She had met a Colonel William Hays, nephew of Rutherford B. Hayes, during the run of *Little Jack Sheppard*. He had been kind to her, lending her money to meet expenses on her Florida farm, and again to take her troupe to the West Indies. This, she was accustomed later to refer to as her "South American Tour." She did, however, play Havana. As a result of these enterprises she owed Hays $9,200.00, and in May of 1889 they signed the following contract: "I, William B. Hays, in

Jules Cheret poster.
1893.

Loie Fuller in early stock.

career as dancer and experimenter in light began.

Rehearsing one of the scenes for *Quack, M.D.* at the Harlem Opera House, she desired an effect of mysterious, hypnotic attraction. Hunting through her wardrobe for a suitable costume, she came on a small box, containing a present from an Indian army officer. On opening it, she found a filmy, voluminous silk skirt. The officer had told her it was once ordered for the D'Oyly Carte Gilbert and Sullivan company, though never used. She drew it out, put it on, and "gently, almost religiously" waved about her its translucent folds. She was standing before a mirror, the sunlight falling through the yellow blinds of the window behind her, illuminating the gauzy material, and as the silk billowed, it seemed like light itself. She describes the first performance of *Quack, M.D.*:

My robe was so long that I was continually stepping upon it, and mechanically I held it up with both hands and raised my arms aloft, all the while that I continued to flit around the stage like a winged spirit.

There was a sudden exclamation from the house:

"It's a butterfly! A Butterfly!"

I turned on my steps, running from one end of the stage to the other, and a second exclamation followed:

"It's an orchid!"

This, she tells us, was the origin of her Skirt Dance. But the New York *Town Tattle* of June 3, 1893, supplies quite another tale. It claims that in 1891, appearing in Holyoke, Massachusetts, she was scheduled for a number of skin-tights. But finding her audience so tiny, she scarcely bothered to take off her ordinary street skirt, and performed in it, flouncing about the stage, so inventing her Serpentine. In any case, Loie Fuller's Skirt Dance was by no means the first of its genre. It had been long popularly developed in English music halls from a compromise of a classic ballet

the presence of God, do take Loie Fuller for my lawful wife."

Despite the fact that there was never a church ceremony, and it was shown in the subsequent trial that they never lived together, Hays does not seem to have lost interest in his peculiar bride; he followed her to London where he admitted to being her husband, and engaged to pay all her expenses. This first stay in 1889 was a short one, for although she enjoyed a personal success, her vehicle *Caprice* did not, and she soon returned to New York for Hoyt's *Trip to Chinatown* and *Quack, M.D.* It was, then, almost accidentally that her variation and the Lancashire Clog, or "step dance." Its leading exponent was Kate Vaughan, who first appeared as a skirt-dancer in a *Ballet of the Furies* at the Holborn Theatre in 1873. The original skirt dance degenerated into a romp because Kate Vaughan's imitators were not so precisely trained in the academic ballet as she. Fuller's early "Widow Dance" in which she wore a black skirt and white powdered wig may well have been an echo, however far removed, from Vaughan's original role as the Spirit of Darkness, for which her costume was a black skirt profusely trimmed with gold.

That play *Quack, M.D.* was a failure, too, never coming any closer to Broadway than Brooklyn. But Loie's dance seen in it was such a great success that she decided forthwith to abandon her career of actress for that of a dancer. This was not so easily done. She was an actress in the minds of all the New York managers she knew, and they refused to consider her as anything else. She suffered a long struggle before the director of the Casino Theatre finally gave her a grudging audition. For him she danced on an empty stage lit by one long gas jet, without music. But when she reached its climax and fell, a heap of rippling silk at his feet, he decided she had something. He told her to repeat the number, this time accompanying her himself on the piano with a popular piece of the day, Gillet's *Loin du Bal*. When she had finished, it was he who christened her creation, "The Serpentine Dance."

She was engaged to appear as a feature act in still another play, a kind of extravaganza labeled *Uncle Célestin,* and began at once to develop her dances, for which she had classified "twelve characteristic motions." She gave no name to these dances, only numbers: Dance One was to be given under a blue light, Dance Two under red, Three under yellow, and so on. She had always intended to use lanterns of colored glass, but now she became preoccupied with their proper placing relative to her dance movements, arranging rays of light

The original Serpentine. 1891.

that projected across a darkened stage, falling upon her swirling silks in a novel and effective way. When *Uncle Célestin* was produced at the Casino, her act was the hit of the evening, but her name had been omitted from the program. Her manager paid her little since he anticipated that if she were a success she must certainly leave him; so he had trained a chorus girl to take her place, thus avoiding building up any expensive personal publicity. Nevertheless, a good friend of hers, Marshall Wilder, the humorist, was in the audience, and noticing the omission, climbed onto his seat, shouting her name to the applauding public. This was more effective than any printed announcement in a program, for with the give-the-little-girl-a-hand spirit of our audiences, she received an ovation—and also the flattery

Miss Loïe Fuller
Souvenir des Folies Bergère.

Paris, 1892.

of immediate imitation. The Serpentine spread like wildfire and its American originator sometimes had difficulty in convincing managers that she was not an imitation of herself. But she held one important element the other dancers lacked, no matter how proficient their capers might be, and that was her lighting effects. In this she definitely launched a novelty. As a matter of fact, except for a brief infantile episode, she had fewer than half a dozen dancing lessons in her whole life. In order to minimize the danger of having her effects stolen, which they continually were, she tried to maintain a band of loyal electricians, with her brother Burt as their chief.

By this time not only ambition, but restlessness too, was working in the active brain behind Loie's somewhat pudgy little face. That, plus a recent painful experience, combined to turn her thoughts away from America, and to try her luck in Europe. For, while appearing

in *Uncle Célestin* in Philadelphia in 1892, Loie Fuller filed suit against her husband, Hays, accusing him of bigamy; she had discovered that his previous wife, Amelia, was by no means divorced from him. Loie won despite Hays' allegation that her document of proof was a forgery, and her suit blackmail. The case was settled out of court for $10,000, but a second charge of perjury landed Hays in Sing Sing.

How humiliating all this had been may be guessed by an account printed in the *Spirit of the Times*, in 1892, which commented on Loie's "double success": her dancing at the Casino, and the publication of an apology and statement by Hays:

Loie Fuller is free from all taint of immorality. I never had any indecent or nude picture of Loie Fuller, nor have I seen one, nor do I believe that any such picture has ever been taken.

Loie Fuller, right. Prince Troubetzkoy's Garden. Paris, 1909.

The newspaper added, of its own accord, "This certificate ought to be framed in gold and worn as a brooch."

The reaction drove her to Europe and something better than a brooch. She desired Paris, but chance offered Berlin. She took a second-class boat to Hamburg, dancing on board. Her German engagement was successful, but an unscrupulous manager let her down badly. However, it was a step toward her goal. Eventually she reached France, even though obliged to dance her way there in a traveling circus, appearing between an elephant act and a team of jugglers. An old trouper could take that in her stride.

Once in Paris, she tried for the top, addressing herself directly to the Opéra, but its management was unimpressed. She turned on her heel, and sought the Folies Bergère, either indifferent to, or unconscious of the fact that it was practically taboo in respectable artistic society. At the Folies she found an imitator already performing, but somehow persuaded the director to take her on, and to everyone's surprise, made a tremendous hit.

One recalls Baudelaire's, *"J'ai vu parfois, au fond, d'un théâtre banal un être qui n'était que lumière, or et gaze."*

Everybody has seen Loie Fuller and knows the novelty she has introduced upon the stage. Instead of the traditional dancer in tights and short muslin skirt, instead of the familiar but ever entertaining acrobatics, bounds, pirouettes, etc., in the even steady glare of the footlights, there appeared one evening at the back of the darkened stage, the indistinct form of a woman clothed in a confused mass of drapery. Suddenly a stream of light issued apparently from the woman herself, while around her the folds of gauze rose and fell in phosphorescent waves, which seemed to have assumed, one knew not how, a subtle materiality, taking the form of a golden drinking cup, a magnificent lily, or a huge glistening moth, wandering in obscurity.[1]

The next few months were unquestionably the most important in her career. "La Belle

Américaine" became a popular idol of Paris, to such an extent that the hitherto questionable Folies Bergère was transformed into an artistic shrine, even women and children flocking to see her in the wake of writers, artists, and sculptors. The enthusiasm of her audiences at over three hundred consecutive performances was expressed with characteristic Parisian exuberance. One evening the entire house was bought up by students, and literally bushels of violets were thrown onto the stage. It took fully five minutes to pick them up. She was not even denied the traditional "carriage drawn by admirers" so dear to ranking prima donnas.

Her spectacular success caused no relaxation in her efforts. She worked night and day inventing new dances and experimenting with novel lighting effects. No longer numbered, these dances were now called *Danse Blanche*, *Danse Fleur*, and *Bon Soir*. She was frequently so exhausted at the end of an evening, for her own part of the program was forty minutes of continuous dancing, that she had to be carried from the stage to her tiny apartment back of the theater, where she was living with her mother, a chronic invalid to whom she had always been exaggeratedly devoted. As frequently as possible, she wore her original D'Oyly Carte dress, for which she had a sentimental and almost superstitious feeling. Whenever she put it on, the pleats between her fingers "seemed alive" to her. One of her new dances, a "Fire Dance," was particularly popular, because of the effects of flame and smoke produced by dancing on a pane of glass lighted from beneath. This innovation, a pioneer realization of indirect lighting, was acclaimed as an effect "greater than Bayreuth," and was the direct inspiration for the Toulouse-Lautrec lithograph.

This is the moment when simple Loie Fuller emerged as "La Loie." Mantelet painted her, Jules Cheret drew a poster of her, and more flattering still was Lautrec's lithograph. This was limited to fifty copies, and although drawn off in black and white only, was hand-colored by the artist, who used a wad of cotton to apply the color, afterward powdering the damp plate with gold dust. This lithograph (Delteil cat. no. 39), is reproduced in color as cover of the monograph "Henri de Toulouse Lautrec. 1864-1901," by Maurice Joyant (Paris, 1926). The few lines of his crayon indicating her full-blown face—a mask of the epoch, so close to Oscar Wilde's as almost to be his sister—is one more glimpse of Lautrec's mastery in characterization. The plate is rose and gray, ashes of roses adored in Whistler's "Arrangements and Nocturnes," and Charles Conder's fans. Lautrec painted a *Ballet de Papa Chrysanthème* in 1892 (Museum of Albi. no. 26). We recall the sunflower and the chrysanthemum were par excellence the blossoms of the *fin de siècle*. Pierre Louy's great popular success was *Mme. Chrysanthème*, and there was the Belasco-Puccini *Madama Butterfly* and Mascagni's *Iris* as well. Joyant describes this ballet as a *Fantaisie japonaise et nautique*, given at the Nouveau Cirque in 1892. In the middle on a lotus leaf, the Étoile dances in veils, imitating *la Loie Fuller*. In a very free sketch of the same year, *Au Music Hall*, formerly in the collection of Yves Busser, "*La Loie* is standing, profile towards the left; yellow hair, surrounded by veils; in the background, at the right and above, the balcony of the hall."

But through it all, Loie Fuller was living quietly, "chastely," in her little Paris flat, with occasional trips to London. For, by a peculiar trick of fate, she, the "fairy of light," was earning only bare living expenses. All the surplus of her reputedly fabulous salary was going to pay off a broken Russian contract for which she had been sued. Her mother had been ill, and Loie turned back at the border.

At this time Loie had already surrounded herself with a group of young girls who also appeared with her, and to whom she was attached with extraordinary affection. Actually living in the house with her was a girl known as Gab who always dressed as a man, who stayed with her for eight years, and who was at least ten years younger. Loie's eccentric manner of life caused almost as much comment as her dancing. A somewhat ingenious tribute was the inclusion of a course entitled *foie gras de l'oie: Loie Fuller*, at a dinner given by Paul Sescau, a photographer friend of Lautrec's.

In her experimentation with lights, color became more and more her preoccupation. Starting with a lamp on either side of the stage, the two throwing upon her a single color, she began to use more lamps, changing the colors. Then, through a happy accident, she discovered the value of blended lights. One night, a drunken electrician, instead of throwing upon her one color at a time, mixed them at random. She was furious, but the favorable reaction of her audience showed her there were possibilities of developing further spectacular effects. She began to arrange colors as if they fell on her through a prism. These new arrangements were effective, as the following account in the London *Sketch* (1900) bears witness:

The orgie of color was so wonderful as to leave objection mute. Light came from every side. La Loie danced upon glass, from which the vivid splendor of the headlights was reflected, while from the wings, stage and orchestra, wonderful luminous streams seemed to flow toward her. With the rhythm of the music the colors changed, and where white ruled before, there was a kaleidoscopic vision. Violet, orange, purple and mauve movements succeeded in rapid succession until a rich deep red dominated the dancer, and she became, for one brief moment, a living rose, with palpitating heart and flying leaves. Then the hues of the rainbow came from all sides, and ranged themselves upon the ever moving draperies. Every fold had its tint and scheme of color intensified by the surrounding darkness until the eye could scarcely bear to look. Just as the strain was becoming almost intolerable, the colors disappeared, there was a white flash of appalling

brilliancy, and La Loie faded under diaphanous drapery.

If the effect on Fuller's spectators was almost intolerable, the strain on Loie was terrific. There were fourteen electricians to be directed for her *Fire Dance* alone. This she did with gestures, taps of her heel, and other signals worked out between them. She wrote of a first rehearsal:

A skilled electrician has to go ahead to cut the floor properly and to lay the wires. When this is done I can go to work. Sometimes I use ten lamps, sometimes sixteen, again twenty, and I have used as many as thirty-four, and it requires a skilled electrician to run each of them. . . .

So it is not surprising that even her boundless energy began to flag. There were reports that she was ill, going blind, that her arms and legs were paralyzed. However, she managed to return to New York in triumph before a breakdown which, despite a consultation of doctors, resulting in an order for complete rest, was apparently of short duration, for she was soon dancing again.

Loie Fuller was completely an artist of her epoch. It is important to place her not only with creators in her own field, the theater, but among her peers in the other visual arts, in order to realize her independent, perhaps unconscious, but nevertheless parallel attitude. From the haphazard, instinctive broken color impressionism of the series of Claude Monet's haystacks, springing from Delacroix's researches, emerged the "scientific" postimpressionism of Georges Seurat. This great artist's preoccupation with formal plastic composition was no less precise or impressive than his innovations in color. But in spatial composition he was a classic extension of Piero and Poussin and, like Lautrec, an admirer of Hokusai and Utamaro, while in the disposition of color he was certainly a radical inventor. With the painters Paul Signac and Henri-Edmond Cross, he investigated the actual physics of light vibration. He studied Chevreul,[2] Helmholtz, Humbert de Superville, as well as the American professors Henry of Princeton and Rood of Columbia. As Alfred Barr wrote in his catalogue to the First Loan Exhibition of The Museum of Modern Art (1929):

A few years earlier the Impressionists had taken hints from the theory of complementary reflexes, had painted purple shadows and broken up their surfaces into little dabs of more or less pure color. Seurat, the logician, found this method too inexact. He asserted that color in painting should consist only of "red and its complementary green, orange and blue, yellow and violet." He then proceeded to apply these six primary colors systemically in little round dots of equal size, thereby eliminating, theoretically at least, all trace of the personal "touch."

Seurat had, as far as we can find, no direct connection with Loie Fuller. Yet his *Parade* (1887-88), and particularly his *Chahut* (1889-90), give us perfectly the atmosphere of the Parisian music halls in which Loie appeared, and his puffy ravishing *Poudreuse* (1886) might almost be her portrait. In different fields, their interests were close. Seurat consciously, Fuller instinctively (in spite of her lip service to science) were using the results of their century's research. Not since the Italian Renaissance anatomists and masters of aerial perspective had the exact sciences so importantly contributed to the visual arts.

Her brief appearance at Koster and Bial's Music Hall in New York in 1896, after four years' absence in Paris, was nothing short of sensational. Her salary was the largest ever paid in vaudeville up to then; sixty-seven dollars more per week than the chanteuse Yvette Guilbert, and double that of opulent Lillian Russell. Something of the transformation of the audience which had taken place in the Folies Bergère now occurred in New York, where the newspapers suggested Saturday matinees for ladies, an unheard-of innovation, in order that the feminine portion of New York society might watch Loie in her four dances, *La Nuit, Le Feu, Le Firmament, Le Lys du Nile*, without the "protection" of male escorts.

She did not stay long in New York, and, in fact, most of her subsequent trips were more or less flying visits; highly paid vaudeville engagements, in addition to a somewhat gaudy appearance at the St. Nicholas Rink, until she returned in 1909, not as vaudeville performer, but as an artist making a bid for the same artistic and social recognition she received in Paris.

Her acquaintance with influential Frenchmen of her time was more than a friendship. It was a collaboration. She must have inspired the creators of *l'art nouveau*. Emile Gallé, France's best-known artisan in glass, the predecessor of Lalique, sought her new colors; and she indirectly influenced furniture and architecture as well. Henri Sauvage's beautiful small theater [3] for her at the Paris Universal Exposition of 1900 is an example. In its exquisite *salle* she danced and presented authentic Japanese actors and dancers of the Hanako company, headed by Sada Yacco; and here young Ruth St. Denis was deeply moved by her. The extraordinary energy of this pug-nosed Chicagoan was nowhere more evident than in the building of her theater, which was accomplished in one-third the time expected. Loie was much affected by the Japanese, and in the spiritual company of Whistler and Degas, composed works imitating them.

L'Art Nouveau came as a reaction against the foul taste of the July Monarchy, the bastard pastiche of decorative fragments from the epoch of Henri Trois, Louis Quinze, or the rococo bibelots prized by the brothers de Goncourt. Already Whistler in London had painted his Peacock Room. The iridescent plumage of the peacock's tail was a badge for the movement which worshiped the accidental iridescence of a film of oil freely spread over water, the running glazes of Chinese jars,

Les serpentins.

La corbeille.

L'Espagnole.

Au repos.

L'hélice.

Au repos.

Les serpentins.

Les papillons.

LA DANSE SERPENTINE. — Mlle Loïe Fuller et ses transformations.

glass vases studded with insect wings, the tie-and-dye scarves offered by the house of Liberty, Fortuny dresses with all their thousand pleatings, Tiffany gold-shot lamps and stained bubble glass, Lalique snakes, "natural" flowered forms, and arts-and-craft jewelry.

Around 1894, the Belgian architect van de Velde was the apostle of the new ideas, which were partly motivated by flamboyant Gothic ornament, Japanese stylization and observation of vegetative forms. In his small house in a Brussels suburb, he commanded an informal guild of artisans to execute his own designs. Specialists in tapestries, faïence, metalwork, murals, and cabinetmaking evolved a "natural" style. And turquoise and opal, the glowing browns and ash blues smoldering with light, the fiery chiffons burning with lush chromatics were to be caught in yet another medium by Claude Debussy, to whose music Loie also later danced. *L'Art Nouveau* had as dominant principals fluidity, impressionable elasticity, mercurial light with intense but ephemeral accents. The sweep of Loie's scarves, caught in the wild race of iridescent lights playing madly on her filmy tempestuous folds, was a living monument to his new decorative style. Suitably enough, in one of her last public appearances at the Exposition of Decorative Arts held in Paris in 1925 she evoked "the Sea." Her whole approach to the stage, in fact, was always essentially decorative. She had little personality of her own, or physical attractiveness, or indeed, much emotion to project. Her body became grosser than Isadora's, far earlier in life. Her vaunted interest in religion seems superficial compared to Ruth St. Denis'. Her essential talent was for stage decoration, and this she realized through electricity and dancing.

One of her most interesting friendships was with Marie and Pierre Curie, the Nobel prize winners. Her acquaintance with the Curies commenced when she wrote them shortly after their discovery of radium. The reported fact that radium gave off a pale magical light fascinated her. Could she not use it for some new and sensational dance effect? Eve Curie tells of Loie's first naïve letters requesting information; she wanted "butterfly wings of radium." The Curies gently explained that this was not very practical, if only for the great expense involved. In reply she wrote: "I have only one means of thanking you for having answered me. Let me dance one evening at your house. . . ."

The Curies accepted her offer, but were more than a little astonished at the large troupe of electricians which arrived at their modest little house one morning, laden with theatrical projectors, festooned with strings of electric lights. Loie herself followed, and spent the entire afternoon arranging her effects. At night she returned, and before the Curies, a few friends, and their enchanted children, appeared in the narrow dining room as "The Fairy of Light," surrounded by all the flowers and flames of the Folies Bergère. The Curie children never forgot that evening. And Eve Curie finishes her account of the dance by commenting "Loie had a delicate soul."

Other scientists became her intimates. Camille Flammarion, the celebrated astronomer, arranged for her admission to the French Astronomical Society, explained to her his theories of color as a physiological and psychological determinant on plants and humans, and became a warm admirer, calling her "the little star from the West."

Although the butterfly wings of radium were not practical, as a result of the friendship of the Curies Loie began to experiment in a laboratory of her own with "fluorescent salts" extracted from the residue of pitchblende. These salts were supposed to derive their fluorescence from the influence of radium, but evidently were the result of "invisible light" playing on a sensitive mineral substance. Loie wrote later:

I suppose I am the only person who is known as a dancer but who has a personal preference for Science. It is the great scheme of my life. In Paris I have a laboratory where I employ six men. Every penny I earn goes to that. I do not save for my old age. I do not care what happens then. Everything goes to my Laboratory.

I have had some success, for I have invented a process for treating cloth with phosphorescent salts. Scientists in Paris worked with me, but it was reserved for me to discover that by striping a fabric with the stiff salts, I could produce a strong and beautiful glow at an expense of about $600 a pound. Part of my hair was blown off in an explosion while I was experimenting in my laboratory, and it made a great sensation in the neighborhood. The people called me a witch, a *sorcière*. My hair will not all grow again, but I do not care.

This led to what she called her "Radium Dance," the first of luminous phosphorescent effects, with patterns on the costumes and scenery glowing from a blackened stage. Its importance was commented upon by such outstanding personalities as Jules Claretie, director of the Comédie Francaise, who wrote:

It is certain that new capacities are developing in theatrical art, and that Miss Loie Fuller will have been responsible for an important contribution. I should not venture to say how she has created her light effects, but she has actually been turned out by her landlord because of an explosion in her apparatus.

Auguste Rodin avowed "Loie Fuller is to my mind a woman of genius. She has re-created effects of light and background of great initial value."

Besides her special interest in lighting, her art was progressing along more and more aesthetic lines. The days of such vulgar accompaniment as *Loin du Bal* were over. Now was she dancing to the music of Gluck, Beethoven, Schumann, Delibes, Schubert's *Ave Maria*, Chopin's *Marche Funèbre*, and the *Peer Gynt* suite. She was the first to use the perennial *Spring Song* of Mendelssohn as a background later worn threadbare by Isa-

dora Duncan, Maud Allan, Gertrude Hoffman, and Ruth St. Denis. She also planned three biblical numbers, and in addition to her solo dancing was busy training her band of youthful "muses" to surround her in a "Ballet of Light." Isadora Duncan tells of having traveled with them for a time in 1902, only leaving when her roommate, one affectionately known as Nursie, attempted to strangle her. Loie kept a strict maternal watch over her girls, many of whom came from society families. Three of the most famous were Sacchetto, an Italian ballerina from La Scala, Orchidée, "a child of nature," and Gertrude von Axen, "The perfect Grecian danseuse whose very motion was *raisonée*." A tabloid once reported an imaginary dialogue between Gertrude and Loie. Von Axen was bemoaning the fact that her hair, blown in the wind, was scarcely Greek. Said sensible Loie: "Listen, Dearie, even the Greeks washed their hair once in a while."

Later, when Fuller returned to America in February of 1910, Orchidée and von Axen temporarily deserted her, attempting to give a performance on their own. Loie, not exactly a simpleton in legal matters, brought out an injunction against them.

It was this ballet that she brought to New York and later to Boston in 1909, no longer into vaudeville houses, but into the more dignified atmosphere of the opera. She played on double bills with such short operas as *Pagliacci* and *Cavaliera*. This proved to be an agitated visit marked by deputy sheriffs trying to collect bills from her at the Hoffman House, a verdict won against her in a suit brought by Maiden Lane Jewels, indignant letters from her to the *Times* complaining she'd been slandered, enormous difficulties with her fifty imported French electricians, to say nothing of her temperamental "muses." But her performances aroused excited comment and Loie was more in the public prints than ever before. The press was greatly struck by her absence of tights and

Entrance to
Loie Fuller's Theatre

the presence of bare feet. The New York *Dramatic Mirror* inquired: "Is it necessary for Art's sake to make young girls appear without fleshings and in bare feet, with nought to shield their forms save a few folds of filmy gauze?" Loie replied: "It is an American monopoly to combine stage dancing with self-respect." She seized the occasion also to express abhorrence of the "hideous man-made lines of the corset."

When the reporters came to her hotel for an interview, they found her wandering about in a long gray dress, her blue eyes and white teeth flashing in her heavy face, by no means the aesthetic creature they had expected. "I was born to be a mother," she told them, somewhat to their surprise, "and to spend most of my days in the kitchen. But some strange perversity of fate led me to the motherhood of natural dancing. People have the idea that I am such an occult, mystical, ethereal sort of creature. Instead I am the personification of the practical."

Then she went on to tell them what had become almost a patter line about the three primary colors, the seven prismatic shapes, the four thousand color motifs of the Gobelin tapestries, all of which appeared in her dances. These interviews bristled with statistics: some of her costumes contained as much as five hundred yards of material, some were one hundred yards around the skirt, which was thrown up in swirls twenty feet high; she claimed that she could carry six thousand stage settings in a small handbag since the backgrounds could be infinitely varied by the use of light; and in one effect she used 1,000 amperes of electricity, enough to light a town of thirty thousand souls.

Loie's 1909 visit to America came immediately after the sensational appearance of the Diaghilev Russian Ballet in Paris. She was quick to realize that one of the chief reasons for their phenomenal success was their music. She had followed Duncan's example in using music by Handel, Johann Strauss, Rossini, Liszt, Mozart, and Rubinstein. Now Fuller turned to Debussy (*Nocturnes; Faune*), Purcell, Stravinsky (*Feu d'Artifice*), Scriabine (*Prometée*), Fauré, Moussourgsky, Wagner (*Ride of the Valkyrs*). She retained an early discovery, Gabriel Pierné, in her repertoire, and he later conducted for her.

When she returned to Paris after the American season, Loie entered upon what might be called her social aesthetic period, in which she frequently appeared in public and privately for fashionable charities. Hitherto she had been a special pet of artists: Riviere, Houssin, Roche, Dumas *fils*; now she was taken up by the *haute monde*. She had prominent social leaders as pupils, and also performed their amateur compositions. Among these polite composers were Armande, the Princesse de Polignac's niece, and the Countess de Chabannes-La Palice. She danced in the magnificent gardens of the Comte de Cahen-d'Anvers, just north of Paris. The grounds of his château de Champs were a miniature Versailles. Countless lights were hung in the long *allées* of clipped trees, the fountains leaped in the same fantasy of color that fell upon Loie as she whirled on the shallow stone terrace.

She danced also for the Comtesse de Galiffet, in the garden of her town house, and was the great attraction of fashionable fetes at Trouville and those of the Marquise de Pomerou at Deauville. Her "muses" enchanted in a veil *danse de Diane*, and by the time it was finished they had done with their veils. It was impossible to be more *en vue*. Her most curious association was with Prince and Princess Troubetskoy. He was the cousin of Pierre Troubetskoy, the sculptor. The princess was one of her pupils, but the prince had in mind even more interesting collaborations. The family had a fine estate at Fontainebleau, where he indulged his humane fantasies with Slavic earnestness. He had a pack of wolves, of the best Siberian breed, and wanted to train them to dance to the sound of a shepherds pipe. Loie, who never lacked courage, was willing to share the experiment, and apparently got along famously with the wolves. Then he proposed an even more difficult problem; the prince tried to convert his wolves to his own ardent cult of vegetarianism. He explained, while slipping between the teeth of a wolf a bread ball flavored with something that resembled meat juice, that to eat beef is a sin against love. "You kill a cow, but a bull loves a cow. . . . Why, if I ate beef, I could not look the princess in the face."

It was during this period, before the First World War, that Loie met the Princess Royale of Rumania, later to become Queen Marie. It was not strange that a friendship should develop between them. They both loved veils about the brow, floating scarves, color, mysticism, young protégés, and publicity. When Loie first danced in Bucharest in 1901, the princess sent her children to see her, and the eldest, who strongly resembled her grandmother, Queen Victoria, could be heard in the royal box expressing her enthusiasm and contradicting her sister, who said that Loie was a butterfly, by insisting that no, she was an angel.

When the Queen came to America in 1926, partly for the sake of Rumanian charities and partly for the sake of *The Saturday Evening Post,* this long friendship came to its spectacular end. The story of her trip to America in 1926 is more fantastic than choreographic. She and the Queen and a Mrs. C. C. Calhoun were involved in plans for a "Mothers Memorial Foundation," which they induced Mayor Walker, a Harriman and a Vanderbilt, as well as other prominent society ladies, to sponsor, to the extent of some sixty thousand dollars. Their avowed purpose, among others, was to create an Acropolis to Womanhood. To accomplish this modest end Loie presented the Queen's ballet *Le Lys de la Vie,* already filmed in Paris (with René Clair in a bit part) in 1920. (Loie had made two or three remarkable pioneer films for Pathé in 1905, with slow motion, shadows, negative printing, etc.) However, this ballet enjoyed no success either in New York or at the Philadelphia Sesquicentennial, at which performance the Queen was ensconced in a box that did not even face the stage. The New York proceeds were attached for $3,000, while Loie got her own cut of $8,500.00, half of what they were alleged to be. There were, needless to say, innumerable scandalous rumors concerning the Queen and the dancer. Innocently or not, the two were involved in one of the more genteel rackets of the decade. It also had little to do with personal publicity or prestige, as such. It was a simple device for obtaining easy money. Meanwhile, Loie was shadowed by the Rumanian Consul, Djuvara, in charge of the Queen's progress through our States, who feared the influence of the American over the Rumanian Crown. Loie boarded the royal train in Spokane, but finally left it in Denver. The exact cause of her final abrupt departure was never disclosed; but the rumor was allowed to circulate that the Queen was displeased with Loie's attempt to bring about a reconciliation between herself and her son Carol.

The first great war had found Loie in Neuilly, surrounded by her muses, her Oriental jars, shaded lights, crinkly glass, and iridescent scarves. Her unbounded energy threw her at once into war work, for which she received military decorations not only from France, but also from Belgium and Rumania. She was back and forth between France and America, campaigning for war charities, organizing entertainments for the soldiers. In 1915 she was in San Francisco, where for a time she had her own theater, and was interested in founding a Rodin museum. This project eventually grew into the Palace of the Legion of Honor in San Francisco, erected by Mrs. Adolph Spreckels in memory of the California soldiers killed in the last war.

Loie was frequently at the front in connection with her Army entertaining. In 1919 a reporter on the Detroit *News,* writing of his own war experiences, says of her—"At one stage she drew us all in close around the table while she confided to us in a voice that could not be heard more than twenty feet away (her usual speaking voice fills the room) that the Germans have only to cover their Zeppelins with black velvet to make them quite invincible."

Following the war, her own professional appearances were more and more infrequent, though wherever she appeared she was sponsored by the cream of Parisian society. She continued to direct her school, produced a "Hell Fire" scene for the Opéra performances of Berlioz' *Damnation of Faust,* and presented the *Tragedy of Salome* to music of Florent Schmitt. It was in 1893 she had first danced *Salome.* She also organized tours for her pupils.

The development of moving pictures drew her back to her laboratory and to experimental science, and before long she had worked out new silhouette and shadow effects based on cinema technique, particularly the *cinema en relief.* In this, lights were arranged in such a way that the shadows of the invisible dancers seemed to lean forward stereoscopically into the audience. Her last professional appearance was in this *Shadow Ballet* in London in 1927.

The ethical or religious note, acquired from her early days as a temperance lecturer, was present throughout her life, and Anatole France was to comment upon it. But more fortunate than many actor-preachers, who can express themselves only by preaching, she could function in the rightful air of her theater. In a long stage career, one of her most remarkable traits was a complete lack of professional jealousy. She helped Maud Allan, a struggling young pianist who wished to become a dancer, to the extent of substituting her on a Swiss tour already arranged for herself. Even more striking was her launching, in 1902, of Isadora Duncan in Berlin and Vienna.

It was Mme. Nevada, a singer, who had brought the two dancers together in 1900. To Isadora she said with some naïveté: "Sarah Bernhardt is such a great woman; what a pity, my dear, that she is not a good one. Now there is Loie Fuller, she is not only a great artist, but she is such a pure woman. Her name has never been connected with any scandal. . . ." Nevada took Isadora to see Loie dance and asked her for aid. Loie, as was her custom, responded with utmost generosity. She suggested that Isadora follow her to Berlin, then to Leipzig and Vienna. She put herself out tirelessly to make her known, introducing her to ambassadors, even to the fabled Princesse Metternich, and to others. She arranged auditions for the press, and for an audience of sculptors and painters. With really human kindness she pushed the cause of a rival in every way. On the other hand, Isadora was obviously impressed by her theatrical innovations. She writes in *My Life*, after seeing Loie dance: "Before our very eyes she turned to many-colored shining orchids, to a wavering flowing sea-flower and at length to a spiral-like lily, all magic of Merlin, the sorcery of light, color, flowing form. What an extraordinary genius. . . . She was one of the first original inspirations of light and changing color—she became light."

But it was perhaps inevitable that, as Isadora swept on her expansive exuberant way, she should leave Loie Fuller quite behind. This, at any rate, was Loie's impression, and she came to believe that Isadora even said, in answer to a question, "Loie Fuller? I've never met her." Whether this be true or not, it should be remembered that Loie, as well as helping Isadora, actually antedated her in the use of classic music for dance accompaniment, in her theory of spontaneous bodily movement to express emotion, and in her training and educating groups of young dancers to demonstrate her personal theories. It is true that when Isadora first saw these groups surrounding Loie she appears to have been a little alarmed by them and wondered what she was doing among these "beautiful but demented ladies."

It was only two years after her last appearance in London and her trip to America with Marie of Rumania that Loie Fuller died of pneumonia, January 1, 1928, having been ill two days. Her dancing memory has stayed brighter in Europe than here; for ten years after her death there was still a troupe of Loie Fuller girls to be seen, not only in provincial towns, but from time to time in the capitals.

It is understandable that her style of dancing, fertile as it may have been, should have become *démodé*, but her contributions in lighting have spread and been developed. They were recognized in her lifetime as her outstanding achievement, and they were even more important than she or her commentators realized. Her detractors said she was no dancer, that she relied for her effects entirely on light. But this was her own contention, for she referred to her dancers as "instruments of light."

Her fluorescent "salts," mixed with paint,

that glowed on her whirling skirts were of the same family as the powder, mixed with paint, that is excited by ultraviolet light. Her employment of the excitant and the fluorescent material in the same container with the resulting "cold" light is the first radical departure in lighting since the discoveries of Edison half a century ago, and now, among other uses, indicates the entrances of air-raid shelters.

In Cocteau's *Portrait: Souvenirs* there is a frightful little drawing of her, a symbol of her last days. Swathed in veils, her visage emerges, a bulldog with a black mustache. She wears tortoise-shell spectacles. And her memory will be inextricably connected with the music hall, where vulgarity is somehow alchemized into *le vrai chic*. She is of the immortal gallery of Jane Avril and La Goulue, and of Barbette, the amazing Texan. They all had chic; the essence of their epoch inhabited their bodies. Their acts created style for their time.

MAUD ALLEN

BY CARL VAN VECHTEN

January 21, 1910

MISS MAUD ALLAN, an American girl, who has won no inconsiderable amount of fame in Europe and in England with her dances, made her initial appearance before a New York audience yesterday afternoon in Carnegie Hall. A large and very fashionable gathering greeted the dancer. In fact it has been a long time since so many automobiles have been lined up in front of this staid concert hall. Apparently all of the seats were filled and many were standing at the back. It was an enthusiastic audience, too, and Miss Allan was forced to repeat several of the dances which particularly caught the public fancy.

Most of Miss Allan's European reputation rests on a dance which she has called *A Vision of Salome*, which introduces light and scenic effects, and which was one of the earliest symptoms of the later Salome craze which swept rapidly down from Germany across the Atlantic to New York, where it is just beginning to be brushed away.

It was not in this dance, however, that Miss Allan chose to make her first American appearance. Instead she elected to appear in another sort of dance with which New York is at present very familiar, thanks to Miss Isadora Duncan, the group of dancers which Miss Loie Fuller brought over, and finally to the ballet in Gluck's *Orfeo* as it is danced at present on the Metropolitan Opera House stage.

These dances, accomplished to music written by the great composers—it will be remembered that Miss Duncan even went so far as to use Beethoven's Seventh Symphony—exploit the dancer in poses presumably inspired by a study of Greek vases. Bare-limbed and scantily draped in filmy gauzes, diaphanous in texture and unvivid in color, she floats from one pose to the next, emphasizing the plastic transitions with waving arms and raised legs and sundry poses of the head.

Miss Allan in spirit and in the nature of her dances resembles her predecessors. However, she is more beautiful in face and figure than some of them, and she has a grace, a picturesque personal quality, which is all her own. Yesterday the stage of Carnegie Hall was hung in green draperies and the lights but dimly indicated pale colors. The orchestra was the Russian Symphony Society, under the direction of Modest Altschuler.

It has sometimes been complained of in these columns that dancers take great liberties in dancing to music which was never intended for that purpose. However, Miss Allan in her program yesterday scarcely transcended the bounds of good taste in this direction. She danced to Rubinstein's *Melody in F*, Mendelssohn's *Spring Song*, two mazurkas and a valse of Chopin, Grieg's *Peer Gynt* suite, the *Funeral*

Maud Allan as Salome. New York, 1910.

March from Chopin's B flat minor sonata, and Rubinstein's *Valse Caprice*.

January 30, 1910

MISS MAUD ALLAN, having launched herself at a previous New York matinee as a classical dancer, yesterday afternoon at Carnegie Hall presented herself in *The Vision of Salome*, the dance which made her name well known in London. This dance was devised by Miss Allan at the period when Oscar Wilde's play, Richard Strauss's music drama, and Franz von Stuck's pictures were creating the stir in Germany that they shortly afterward created in America. There is no record of Miss Allan's having received any suitable recognition of her talents at that time, however. A little later,

to be exact, in May, 1907, she crossed the border line and appeared in Paris.

The Théâtre des Variétés was celebrating its one hundredth anniversary with a revue, much more splendid than those which are given in the ordinary Parisian music halls. This revue was nearing its seventieth performance, when the first rendering of Strauss's music drama *Salome*, in Paris, was announced at the Théâtre du Châtelet for May 8. Manager Samuel of the Variétés saw his chance. He brought out Miss Allan in the *Vision de Salome* on the 7th. Her appearance at this theater caused some discussion, but no sensation. That was reserved for her London appearance, which occurred some months later at the Palace Theatre. Since her debut at this London music hall, Miss Allan's name has steadily grown in fame. For over a year, in fact, she continued to do her nightly characterization of Salome in London.

Yesterday's representation differed in no marked respect from that of three years ago, and the stage setting was the same she had used in London. It is true that in Paris she had caressed the severed head of John the Baptist. Yesterday the head itself was left to the imagination, but none of the caressing was. However, New York has seen so many dances of this sort by now that there were no exclamations of shocked surprise, no one fainted, and at the end there was no very definite applause.

Miss Allan's version of Salome presents a young girl who, having danced before Herod and asked for the head of John at the command of her mother, goes through the scene again in a dream. The stage is set to represent a garden of the palace, and in this garden Miss Allan yesterday executed steps and curved her body in contortions which are now conventionally supposed to suggest Salome.

Earlier in the afternoon Miss Allan danced to the *Peer Gynt* suite, a sarabande and gavotte of Bach's; Mendelssohn's *Spring Song*, and Strauss's *Blue Danube*. All of these dances were accomplished in the prevalent classical manner and evoked much applause. The quality which Miss Allan possesses to a greater degree than her predecessors is a rhythmical sense.

The Russian Symphony Orchestra, under the direction of Modest Altschuler, played the accompaniments, and several other numbers. It should be appended for the sake of record that *The Vision of Salome* was not accomplished to the dance music from Strauss's music drama, but to an "arrangement" possibly of Eastern airs, by Marcel Remey.

Maud Allan. 1909.

Ruth St. Denis and Ted Shawn in *Egypta*. 1915. Photo by Hoppe. London.

THE DENISHAWN ERA

(1914-1931)

BY BAIRD HASTINGS

THE GREAT CONTRIBUTION of the Denishawn dancers in their generous absorption of the arts of our time was the establishment of the American dance as an independent art form. Although the pioneer Diaghilev tours of 1916-1917 in the United States powerfully affected our decorative arts, and Duncan had already stated the dance as a supreme personal expression, the thirteen Denishawn tours in seventeen years created a basic audience for the art among middle-class theatergoers. It is due to Denishawn more than to Pavlova, the Ballet Russe, or any other single factor, that theatrical dancing today does a two-million-dollar business.

While Denishawn brought the world's exotic dances to our legitimate theaters, its leaders were also aware of their native scene. St. Denis' "Oriental" numbers and "music visualizations" were revelations to ordinary and critical audiences. Shawn led in the creation of works based on indigenous material. Later, as choreographer and teacher, he developed styles of movement attractive to the male dancer. Their common avidity for anything that could be adapted to theatrical use gave them a variety of program assimilable to a public used heretofore mainly to vaudeville, and it gave scope to their teaching. Their eclecticism was the necessary approach for

their era. Dance as such, apart from variety or *divertissement* in opera or extravaganza, had never taken deep root in North America as it had in nineteenth-century Europe, although the fragmentary brilliance of its movement had always been genuinely appreciated. It took more than a little Yankee shrewdness for Denishawn to sell dancing to the American people.

The stylistic catholicism apparent in the Denishawn repertory found itself in all our arts of the epoch. The tower of Stanford White's Madison Square Garden appropriated Seville's Giralda, and Cass Gilbert's Woolworth Building reared itself in a late Gothic skin. St. Gaudens carved General Sherman conducted by a Renaissance angel, while the Vanderbilts dwelt in their Touraine château. At the same time there were strong native statements in the work of Louis Sullivan and Frank Lloyd Wright. Robert Henri (who was later to paint Miss Ruth in *Peacock*) became responsible, with Sloan and Bellows, for a rising nationalism to stand against the purely French taste of Glackens or Mary Cassatt. In music, Foote, H. S. Gilbert, and John Alden Carpenter were beginning to employ native melodic material with themes from our verse and folklore.

Ruth Dennis was born in Newark in 1878

of Irish-American parents, and while absorbing early instruction from Karl Marwig, a social dance teacher, a book on Delsarte, and Maria Bonfanti, the aging star of *The Black Crook*, she participated in an array of theatrical activity, high-kicking, skirt-dancing, acrobatics, as well as appearing on the "legitimate" stage. Although this training may seem fragmentary and accidental, nevertheless it included the main traditional currents of her day: Delsarte's codified gesture, the spectacles of the brothers Kiralfy, the local brand of classic ballet, the polite ballroom graces. Up to the moment she married Ted Shawn, her career had claimed her entire life.

In 1904, while playing "Mlle. LeGrand, a dancer from the Grand Opera," with Belasco's company in *Madame Dubarry* on tour, St. Denis noticed a cigarette window card for Egyptian Deities. Something in the stiff pose of the seated goddess aroused the young actress-dancer. Vaguely symbolizing a new attitude toward a lyric theater, it began to focus her still dreamy plans. St. Denis' fabulous career as "Oriental" dancer was launched at that instant, although it would take two years of preparation before it came to full realization.

Preoccupation with the Orient was scarcely a new fad, but with St. Denis it received a particular definition, in fact, its first consciously artistic presentation in an America which was still groping out of its insulated provincialism. It was a vision of the Near East, crystallized by Napoleon's Egyptian campaign and the researches of Champollion and Maspero, that inspired Americans of the late nineteenth century. The travels of the painters Decamps and Delacroix had given an iconography of harems, odalisques, Moroccan riflemen and Turkish corners, now chiefly seen in the luxurious lobbies of movie palaces built in the twenties. In literature, Kipling's Indian tales and novels like Edwin Arnold's *Light of Asia* or Lew Wallace's *Ben Hur* which received elaborate stage productions certainly reinforced the vision, while Elihu Vedder's illustrations for FitzGerald's *Rubaiyat*, along with the cat-tails, blue-china willow plate and peacock feathers, were decorative relics of Oscar Wilde's lecture tour to our Wild West in the early eighties.

And in the dance, one remembers Taglioni's role in *Le Dieu et la Bayadère* (1830), based on poems from Goethe's free adaptations of the *Divan of Hafiz*. This ballet was performed in many versions all over Europe and America for thirty years. The sylphide's nautch dress definitely recalls St. Denis in her famous *Rhada*, first performed at the Hudson Theatre (March 6, 1906), the music for which was taken from the *divertissement* in Delibes' *Lakmé*.

In 1862, Marius Petipa produced *La Fille de Pharaon* at St. Petersburg, and *Aïda* was commissioned by the Khedive from Verdi in 1871 to celebrate the completion of the Suez Canal. Its brassy triumphal scene and *divertissement* must have inspired the Manzotti spectacles in Milan, which in turn reached America via the "Oriental" pageants of the Kiralfy brothers. One of these, *Egypt through the Centuries*, little Ruthie Dennis tells us she saw with rapture in 1893, the same year "Little Egypt" was doing her stuff at the Chicago Columbian Exposition. Her own orientalism was perhaps unconsciously compounded of these several sources, direct or indirect. She also read the Indian tales of F. W. Bain, and the French orientalists Gustave Flaubert, Loti, Louys, and Anatole France.

From 1909 to 1912 Ruth St. Denis toured in concert and vaudeville with numbers from her first New York program, "Oriental" dances created in Europe and parts of *Egypta*. It was on the 1911 tour that twenty-year-old Edwin Myers Shawn first saw her dance.

Shawn had long been interested in the stage, since most of his mother's family were show people. During a period of inactivity following an attack of diphtheria, he managed with the "help" of a skeptical Christian Scientist, to think himself out of the Methodist ministry into the rituals of the dance. (He was later to create an entire church service in dance form, and the religious impulse has never been far away from any of his activity.) Still another factor in this secular "conversion" was the departure for New York of Dr. Christian Reisner, the expansive barnstorming sky pilot who was to electrify Broadway with illuminated signs and schemes for a colossal temple.

Shawn says he never actually decided to dance, but once he began to take ballet lessons (from Hazel Wallack, who had had some training at the Italianate ballet school kept by the Metropolitan Opera in New York), he was irresistibly swept toward it. At the University of Denver he learned how to use a library systematically and how to organize source materials. The reading room with its *Arabian Nights* illustrated as a pastiche of Persian miniatures by Edmond Dulac, its files of the *National Geographic Magazine* (the 1912 volume of which provided sources for the entire Denishawn repertory), more than contact with the Russian Ballet or any direct influence from abroad, molded his eclectic taste.

Moving to Los Angeles, Shawn had a variety of business experience, including working for the city water department, and he partnered a well-known teacher, Norma Gould. For the early Edison Company he created a film, *Dance of the Ages*,[1] which began with the Neanderthal man, contained Greek, Roman, Oriental, medieval, eighteenth-century, Spanish dances, concluding with the latest ballroom steps. Then came a transcontinental tour with these same dances to the vacation centers provided for employees of the Santa Fe railroad. In the spring of 1914 he walked into Ruth St. Denis' Eighty-ninth Street studio where he stayed talking to her for eight hours.

The great volume of their work together, thus starting from a profound emotional il-

St. Denis. 1900.

lumination, would, if detailed, fill many books. For present purposes four typical productions of the Denishawn company, and one earlier creation of St. Denis which embody their seminal ideas will be discussed.

O-Mika, the early St. Denis dance drama, certainly stemmed from a performance of Sadi Yacco and the Hanako troupe in Loie Fuller's tiny theater, at the Paris Exposition of 1900. These Japanese actor-dancers in the great Noh tradition were perhaps the first concrete human examples of Oriental art the West had seen, although for long Japanese paper and pottery were idolized. Degas, Whistler, and Toulouse-Lautrec had fallen in love with Nipponese prints, supposedly first circularized in the West as tea wrappings. The work of Denman Ross and Ernest Fenellosa

227

at Harvard and the foundation of the great Oriental collection in the Boston Museum of Fine Arts dignified the vogue of kimonos and ivory with a substructure of scholarship. Today one may forget that America was wildly pro-Japanese in the Russo-Japanese War of 1905, and heroic tales of the Samurai soldiers were indirect support for Belasco's and Puccini's *Madame Butterfly*.

The crystallization of St. Denis' desire to present a Noh drama came in 1912 when, tired out from her vaudeville tour undertaken to recoup the loss from *Egypta* for H. B. Harris, her manager, she arrived in San Francisco where she saw a Japanese play in the native quarter, and at the same time came under the influence of Clarence Ramiel McGehee, a young American journalist. He had taught at the University of Tokio and had been the English tutor of the Emperor Motu Hito.

After studying the Noh drama—which is far more rigidly stylized and compact than the Chinese drama—she found a Lafcadio Hearn story which exactly fitted her impulse.[2] "The Legend of Fugen Bosatsu" was included in his *Stray Leaves from Strange Literature*. It tells of a priest searching for the perfect soul. Entering a house of ill fame, he is chosen by the courtesan O-Mika to be her companion for the night, but when she looks into his eyes, she is transformed into Kwannon, Goddess of Mercy. He finds peace at last. This element of Nirvana, peace, absolution, and ecstasy assumed its important part as the ultimate theme Miss Ruth always loved to portray.

The music of *O-Mika* was by R. H. Bowers. It was first presented March 13, 1913, despite scant hope of financial success. The drowning of H. B. Harris on the *Titanic* was a sad blow to plans for proper publicity, and the loss of $7,000 was disastrous. However, it was an artistic triumph.[3] Its lighting was remarkable, and St. Denis secured new intensities by lowering and raising the lamp in the graded gelatin tower. Her brother Buzz successfully assumed the role of a Samurai soldier. From this three-act work came Miss Ruth's *Flower Arrangement, Peacock* (Roth) inspired by Whistler's Peacock Room, *Chrysanthemum, Thirteenth Century Poetess, White Jade* (Vaughn), and *Kwannon* (Satie). Also from *O-Mika* evolved Shawn's *Oriental Group, Momiji Gari, Spear Dance*, and *Japanese Lion*. Martha Graham, Charles Weidman, and Doris Humphrey all took parts in some of these rearrangements. Today, thirty years afterward, St. Denis still wants to relate the stylized fusion of art and religion in terms of human values to America, perhaps through the motion picture. St. Denis' dancing has never been "authentic," it has always made theater use of movements employed in different styles. She has studied the form and created her own conception and then danced with extraordinary grace and a minimum of technical brilliance. On the other hand, Shawn always copied as exactly as possible the motions of the dancer he was studying rather than attempting re-creation of the mood in a more personal manner.

Between *O-Mika* and preparations for the Hearst pageant, Denishawn, the first serious school of the dance with a considered curriculum and standard of achievement in America, was opened in Westlake Park in Los Angeles. Near by was their cottage, "Tedruth." Students dropped their tuition money in a cigar box as they passed through a doorway to an open-air studio where the classes were held. From these modest beginnings grew the greater Denishawn School and its branches throughout the nation under Kathrane Edson, the Braggiotti sisters, and Hazel Kranz. The California headquarters supplied dancers for films and gave instruction to the Gish sisters, Ina Claire, Ruth Chatterton, Myrna Loy, and many vaudeville headliners. In 1922 the New York school was established, and thereafter replaced Los Angeles as center of their activities, both theatrical and educational. Through its branches and teachers of

O-Mika. 1913.

Denishawn in smaller cities, it touched the layman as well as professionals. Winter and summer instruction was offered in "music visualization," "Oriental" dances, Delsarte, training in ensemble dances. Burton Holmes travel films,[4] and supplementary lectures were offered in the history of the dance, its religious aspects, the attitude of the dancer toward the human body, the handling of draperies, costume, photography, publicity, and stage make-up. As the years passed, new material from revolutionary foreign sources was added to the curriculum. In 1930 the first course in Mary Wigman's radical technique was authorized in America under Denishawn auspices by Margarete Wallmann, the Viennese ballet mistress. Of the two principals, Shawn was the more interested in the school, arranging schedules and teaching most of the classes. With admirable candor, Miss St. Denis writes:

I was never a good teacher. Obviously I am too deep an egotist to have that particularly unselfish attitude toward a student which is the basis of teaching genius. I confused rather than clarified, and someone's help was frequently needed to finish what I started. What I gave Denishawn, and what I shall give pupils as long as I am able, is an artistic stimulus to go and do something, anything, that is a release and a joy to a young artist.

The first important production of Denishawn came on July 29, 1916, the second summer of their school. Professor Armes of the University of California offered them

Los Angeles, 1915.

the open-air William Randolph Hearst Greek Theatre in Berkeley where Sarah Bernhardt and Maude Adams had already appeared. In each of the six scenes a broad walk at the front of the stage represented a great river, the Nile, Styx, or Ganges. The Egyptian scenes with music by Walter Myrowitz and sets by Robert Law, presented "The Life" and "The Afterlife: The Hall of Judgment." In the first was portrayed the rise of Egypt, beginning with the duet, "Tillers of the Soil" (see page 224), continuing with the shepherd kings, the growth of religion, the union with Ethiopia, and finally the overthrow and crumbling of Egyptian civilization. The second scene showed the soul of Egypt, Isis, wending her way to the Hall of Judgment to appear before the Judges of the Dead. Osiris accepts the Soul which

passes the test and arises to the realm of the Justified. Ceremonial dances of the rebirth begin.

It was in Europe that the original inspiration projected by the cigarette poster had grown up. When Harris felt she was ready, St. Denis, accompanied by her mother and brother, made her pilgrimage abroad, during which the *Nautch* and *Yogi* were added to her small repertory. At first unappreciated by the English, she later appeared before Edward VII, and G. B. Shaw, the painter Sargent, the poet Yeats, Max Beerbohm, and J. M. Barrie sponsored her. She experienced the usual difficulties in securing a theater in Paris, but once arranged by her new Russian manager Braff, she achieved a considerable success. However, she never understood the French, nor did she

230

very much try. Miss Ruth was terrified by Rodin's almost automatic impetuosity, and she turned to Germany, where she enjoyed an immediate and unqualified triumph. For once she felt she could discuss her art on an independent intellectual basis. After all, she considered herself something more than a French music-hall artist. She was quite happy in Germany until her devotees declared they must build her a theater of her own and keep her near Berlin for at least five years. Suddenly Miss Ruth at the height of her European success realized that she belonged to an America that had not yet really appreciated her. So she went flying home before she lost her roots.

In Germany St. Denis executed her "Oriental" arm ripples for a college of medical men, who decided she must be in some way deformed. True or not, this story gives us some idea of her originality. It also suggests that contemporary knowledge of human movement and its potential for dancing was rather slim. Here she saw Wedekind's *Loves Awakening*, Reinhardt's production of *Lysistrata*, and Wagner's *Tristan*. She met Count Kessler, the great art patron, and was painted by the younger von Kaulbach. With Hugo von Hofmannsthal she discussed the philosophy of the East, reinforcing her early theosophism fed by the novels of F. Marion Crawford and the writings of Madame Blavatski. She felt these talks with the librettist of *Elektra* were her most profound experience in Germany. St. Denis saw the Glypoteck with the Aegina marbles and the Barbarini Faun as well as the Secession in the Glas Palast with the school of Franz von Stuck. The Munich school had created a vivid, pornographic antiquity, replacing the frigidity of Ingres by a physicality derived from the romantic realism of Delacroix and Courbet. The German revivalists of the antique had a sensual immediacy outrivaling Alma Tadema or George Frederick Watts.

The first scene of the Greek episode of the Berkeley pageant, including a Fortuny veil

Shawn in *Xochitl.* 1920.

dance by Miss Ruth (from her Munich period), synthesized two contrasting aspects of Grecian life, the philosophical and the athletic. There was a Pyrrhic dance led by Shawn entirely for boys. Margaret Severn as Priestess of Bacchus was particularly praised. In the second scene Orpheus attempted to rescue Eurydice from Hades, and failed because he could not resist stealing a glance at his beloved before she emerged. Persephone's brief visit to the underworld brought only momentary relief. Louis Horst arranged the music from Massenet, Ada de Lachau, and others. St. Denis' inspiration may possibly be traced

231

Cowboy Tommy. 1922.

second scene with music by Arthur Nevins already had been performed as *Bakawali* at the Ravinia Festival, Chicago, in 1914. It may have been inspired by Lawrence Hope's *India Love Lyrics,* illustrated by the English watercolorist Byam Shaw. The reincarnation of the man and woman of the first scene displayed them again as yogi and sacred courtesan. A *divertissement* for *Nautch* girls, fortunetellers, jugglers, snake charmers, finally priests followed. The beauty tried to seduce the yogi, but failed. When he recognized in her his wife of a former existence, he commands her to discard all possessions, and at last she finds Nirvana.

Although a famous solo "Black and Gold Sari" derived from it, *Bakawali* never enjoyed the popularity of *Rhada.* Perhaps Nevins' score was not so distinguished as Delibes', or Miss Ruth was tired. More likely, the production was hurried and the element of processional spectacle introduced by Shawn was not controlled. Miss Ruth must then have realized that a large production was not an end in itself, and could never replace pure dancing.

Stimulated by the playing of George Copeland, and also by his ensemble of six girl dancers, in 1917 Ruth St. Denis first conceived of her "music visualization." Shawn, who always had a real facility, in a serious or light vein, for "Oriental" or American numbers alike, immediately arranged choreography for several Bach Preludes and Inventions. The idea was further developed by the program of the Ruth St. Denis concert dancers of 1920. Feeling that her touring in *Theodora,* a Byzantine dance drama (however necessary financially), was neither vital nor constructive, St. Denis attempted to surpass Duncan in her use of the entire body. She made no conscious use of the Dalcroze system of Eurythmics, which gave a comment in simple movement to every note in the musical structure, but the Dalcroze ideas had been in the air since the start of the century and had even

back to an early vision of Genevieve Stebbins, Delsarte's disciple. And always before her there had been Isadora; but St. Denis' Hellas was more concrete, less personal than Duncan's.

In the early *Rhada* Miss St. Denis had related, at least in her mind, the teachings of Mary Baker Eddy with the Gautama Buddha. The texts of both she read continuously. Now in *India* (the final section of the Berkeley pageant) she developed a more complete approach to these ideas. Here, a hunter and his companions depart, leaving his wife on the banks of the Ganges. When day is done, the wife performs his funeral rites, the hunter having given his life to save another. The affected Vaslav Nijinsky by 1913 (in his *Jeux*).

Inspired by her own almost accidental improvisation to Liszt's *Liebestraum*, she commenced with the first movement of Beethoven's *Sonata Pathétique*, working in close collaboration with the young students Doris Humphrey and Clair Niles, and particularly the pianists Louis Horst and Dane Rudyahr. She attempted to translate each phrase into pure movement. The emotional content of the action varied with the music, as did the vigor of the movements. In "visualization" there were plastic dynamics in harmony with the music. In the "synchoric orchestra," each dancer represented a specific instrument and his or her movements were absolutely regulated by the entrance or combination of brass, woodwind, or strings. Gradually compositions of Scarlatti, Mendelssohn, Godard, and Schubert (*The Unfinished Symphony*), were added to the repertoire. As the result of an article Martha Graham saw on Mary Wigman, Humphrey's *Tragica*, originally created to a MacDowell sonata, was at one time danced entirely without music. St. Denis' first audience of trained musicians to her experiments in the new form was equally unimpressed by the versions in bathing suits or in colored veils, but the public received them with enthusiasm, and for ten years they had a place on almost every program, usually as an overture. Recent works by Doris Humphrey, such as *Passacaglia* (1939), stem from the "music visualizations." As a matter of fact, much of the "abstract" or absolute interest in dance as dance, apart from historic style or literary sentiment, in the "modern" repertory of Graham, Humphrey, and Weidman may be traced back to this aspect of Denishawn.

On a less organized and ambitious scale than the Diaghilev ballet, though with more imagination than any other native group, Shawn and St. Denis had already pioneered in the use of music for dancing. They were among the first to base works on Griffes,

Fauré, Honegger, and Palmgren. After hearing George Copeland play *Gnossiennes* and *Gymnopedies*, Shawn bought every piece of Satie available. Shawn was acute musically, appreciating Debussy and Scriabin, but preferring for theatrical usage a Strauss waltz or a Drigo serenade. In other instances such as *Cuadro Flamenco* or *Spear Dance*, the music was arranged by Louis Horst. Originally a violinist in a theater orchestra, he has had a significant influence on the American scene as collaborator with Denishawn for ten years as well as fifteen years with "modern" dancers.

Some of Denishawn's most effective productions were performed to music commissioned from Robert S. Stoughton (*The Spirit of the Sea, Idylle,* and *Garden of Kama*), Harvey Worthington Loomis (*Incense*), Lily Strickland (*The Cosmic Dance of Shiva*), E. G. Stricklen, and Anis Fuleihan.

Opportunities were given to a few young painters, notably Robert Law, Carol Sax, and the English illustrator Maxwell Armfield, but the *décor* of Denishawn was never particularly distinguished. None of the decorators, for example, could be considered easel painters. Their sets were enlarged book illustrations, with the heavy outlines, flat surfaces, and broken color of a dilute impressionism. The Denishawn productions never found themselves far from vaudeville, due to the historic economic difficulties of sustaining an independent company, and constant traveling left less energy for teaching, though the schools issued catalogues for seventeen consecutive seasons.

Xochitl, a Toltec drama in two scenes, was Shawn's production on an Aztec theme, music by Homer Grunn, settings by the Mexican decorator, Francisco Cornejo. Performed by twelve dancers completely on the half toe, the movement of *Xochitl* was stylized in the direction of Aztec reliefs. The story told in pantomime how Xochitl's father brewed an intoxicating potion from the maguey. Xochitl of-

The Lamp. 1929.

fered it to the emperor, who, becoming drunk, tried to seduce her. The father would have killed the emperor, but the girl falls in love with him, and is crowned empress.

Shortly after coming out of the Army in 1919, Shawn had arranged *Xochitl*. At this time he also had five vaudeville units on tour. *Xochitl* was hurriedly done, but enjoyed a considerable success, remaining in the joint repertoire for five years. In it Shawn starred Robert Gorham, and later Charles Weidman and Martha Graham. He may have recognized in this maturing student some instinctive leaning toward the essential stuff of dancing, a feeling for stark movement which would emerge years later in *Primitive Mysteries* (1932) and *Penitente* (1938). The following year Shawn assumed the male lead, and for the English tour Miss St. Denis took over Martha's role, for which Miss Ruth herself said she was unsuited.

Contact with Havelock Ellis and Edward Carpenter in England in 1922, and their admiration for Emerson and Whitman had, if anything, only reinforced Shawn's determination to fight for a specifically American rep-

ertory, and on his return he arranged *Boston Fancy, Crapshooter* and *Cowboy Tommy* to the music of Eastwood Lane's American Sketches. He was the first to use the phrase "American Ballet," and his book with that title tells of his ideal, a very different one from that of Balanchine. Shawn believed in indigenous dances, Balanchine in American dancers. From the inspiration of paintings by Robert Henri and George Brush, the sculpture of A. P. Proctor and Cyrus Dallin, and the Indian suites of Cadman, C. S. Skilton, and John Philip Sousa, Shawn had already created *Invocation to the Thunderbird* (1918). He was to do *Osage-Pawnee* (1930), and *Zuñi Indian* (1931). Later his men's group danced *John Brown*, and *O Libertad*, deriving from *Leaves of Grass*, which was also Isadora's Bible, and brought to the theater the early American, Spanish, colonial, and contemporary stylistic movements that have become a major source of the American repertory. The stage Indian was now caught in the current which was to presage Ballet Caravan's *Billy the Kid*, choreographed by Eugene Loring.

Shawn's most ambitious North American

Indian work was *Feather of the Dawn*, with music by Charles Wakefield Cadman, and a practicable stage pueblo (so bulky as to have to be replaced by a backdrop for touring) designed by Earl Franke. The splendid clothes were made at Denishawn by Pearl Wheeler after authentic designs collected by Shawn on a visit to the Hopi reservation. First presented in 1923, its plot describes how an Indian youth at dawn watches a feather rise and float out of sight. This marks a propitious day, so he requests the hand of his beloved. There follows the wedding celebration, with a Corn-grinding song, Basket dance, a Dance of the Corn Maidens, an Eagle dance, the proposal ceremony, the blessing of the bride, the Wolf dance (entirely by boys), and the assemblage of the tall masked Katchinas (Hopi tribal Gods) for the wedding. Shawn, Louise Brooks, and Pauline Lawrence took the leading roles.

Shortly after this, Denishawn lost Louis Horst and Martha Graham. Miss Graham left first. She has always acknowledged that her training from Denishawn was irreplaceable, but she felt then she was obligated to attempt something on her own, and she accepted a call to the Eastman School, Rochester, N. Y. Horst followed, realizing that he did not wish to tour the Orient, only to return with rearrangements or restatements of the themes they had been continuously presenting for the past ten years. The departure of Horst involved much more than the replacement of a pianist; it marked the loss of a friend and collaborator.

On the return of the Denishawn company from the Orient in 1926, a tour with a Ziegfeld Follies company was arranged to help pay for Denishawn house. Looking at it later, Miss Ruth remarked: "Every brick, a one-night stand." The following year, Doris Humphrey and Charles Weidman left, after nearly a decade of work together. Miss Ruth and Shawn had wanted them to go out again in vaudeville to help pay for the school. While wishing to stay at Denishawn, Humphrey and Weidman felt their own position as creative

Ruth St. Denis. 1941.

artists was not considered. They themselves were beginning to sense a new attitude toward the dance, and they resented personal restrictions. Despite the continued brilliance of the Denishawn "salon" to which came Constance Smedley, Albert Herter, Coomaraswami, Kolbe, and many others, the cost of Denishawn house, and the loss of their best dancers, as well as difficult personal relationships, forcibly indicated the end of the era.

Shawn's later contributions included *Jurgen* [5] (1928), suggested by several episodes of James Branch Cabell's satire, with music by Deems Taylor, and in 1931 *Job*, a masque for dancing in eight scenes, inspired by William Blake's drawings, with music by Vaughan Williams. This same year Ninette de Valois choreographed the score for Sadler's Wells. *The Lamp* (1929) was Miss St. Denis' last large work. To music of Liszt's *Les*

Jacob's Pillow School of Dance. 1940.

Preludes, based on Blake drawings, she portrayed the metaphysical lamp of the perfect life. *Jurgen, The Lamp,* and *Job* had their first performances at the Lewisohn Stadium in New York City. The Stadium season was always a gala for the Denishawn dancers.

The story of Denishawn, detailed so far in Miss Ruth's *An Unfinished Life,* and eventually to appear in Shawn's *Thousand and One Night Stands* records their personal life together, their initial idyllic happiness, their inevitable separation. Shawn resented what he felt was her overweening ambition, her mother's possessiveness, and his ambiguous position in the theatrical advertising. Though less well known, he had enthusiasm and egotism as fierce as her own. In a sense probably neither understood the other. The basic reason for their split was the sincere desire of each

to develop independently his fullest creative powers. They were never divorced.

In 1933 Shawn set forth with the first all-male dance ensemble America had seen. The position of the male dancer had always been questionable. As long as he was a comedian or acrobat he was tolerated, particularly if he sang and acted. But a boy dancer as an independent artist seemed to have borrowed the odor of effeminacy from the male dancers of the late nineteenth century who were reduced to being mere supports by the canonization of the *prima ballerina assoluta.* Shawn's *Labor Symphony* and *Kinetic Molpai* were a manifesto of the right of men to dance. They were based on movements of workers in fields, forests, on the sea, and in factories. For these works Shawn chose men who had been scout masters or gym instructors. He provided them

with movement which was sufficiently collo-
quial to be assimilated by provincial audiences
with minimum resentment. He was an evan-
gelist for the male dancer. He lectured, he
gave demonstrations, he insisted, and he succeeded. His belief in the ideal of Whitman is
a heroic affirmation of our national artistic
tradition. The debt of male dancers to Ted
Shawn is tremendous.

There was also a period devoted to the
place of dance in education. Miss St. Denis
taught at Adelphi College on Long Island, and
created the church service *Mary Magdalene* as
a companion piece to *Rhada* and *Ishtar;* and
Shawn lectured at the College of Physical
Education, Springfield, Massachusetts. This
work symbolized what has been the real contribution of Ruth St. Denis and Ted Shawn:
the education of audiences, the education of
dancers. From their system, which was no
system, but rather a broad exposure to theatrical styles and stage experience, have
emerged a second generation of important
American artists: Martha Graham, Charles
Weidman, Doris Humphrey, and their peers.
Denishawn permitted them, even in their rup-
ture from it, the achievement of an independence, maturity, and a sequence of creation which the idiosyncratic followers of Loie
Fuller or Isadora Duncan never did.

Martha Graham. Photo by Cris Alexander.

THE RECENT THEATER

OF MARTHA GRAHAM

BY ROBERT HORAN

A DISCUSSION of the recent theater of Martha Graham, that is of works created within the last five years, provides the opportunity for comment upon those mature conflicts and issues of her art which have been in preparation for twenty years. A close examination of them makes evident the whole quality of her contribution to the contemporary dance, and allows us to see the final directions it is taking, without attempting a historical summary which, because of its scope, would be largely a calendar of names and dates. By now the earlier works have been quite fully chronicled, whereas the development of Graham's art into a split between the more literary or narrative and the abstract has been less so.

This distinction, between the narrative and the abstract, is the simplest possible one to be made between *Letter to the World* and *Dark Meadow*, for instance, although it refuses to cover the entire case. It does not suffice, of course, for the obvious reason that none of these works is interested in establishing purity or is seeking to set any precedent. Graham, like other figures of her stature, is not much concerned with the theoretical scaffolding from which works of art are presumed to hang by their teeth. To quote directly:

I am interested only in the subtle being, the subtle body that lies beneath the gross muscles. Every dance is, to some greater or lesser extent, a kind of fever chart, a graph of the heart. I do not compose ideologically and I have never considered my dances in any way intellectual. Whatever theory may be read into them proceeds from the material and not vice-versa.

This is a plain, honest statement, and of special importance because there is a tendency, both among dancers and the general audience, to think of Graham, indeed, of all "modern" dancers, as primarily exponents of a movement, with a primer of aims and ambitions, undeviating sets of principles and prejudices, and on the whole a rather intellectual approach to their art.

The fluctuation, then, between the narrative and the abstract in Graham's dances is without particular calculation, except in a work like *Letter to the World* which is openly committed to literary reference. The specific content of her most recent works is rarely set in motion by narrative, representational elements (again we have an exception, *Punch and the Judy*, which is intended as a satire), but she does, on occasion, borrow from a loose literary structure which seems a gesture of

239

dubious value at best. Because, within this framework of identified figures or "characters" (such as one like Jason in *Serpent Heart*) the real invention rises out of a purer and more immediate emotion than any supplied by text or program. So that, at these moments, one can have the feeling that Graham is straining to keep within the limits of an arbitrary subject, or is trying to give her title some definition.

A chronological examination of her recent works should make this more clear, illustrating at the same time the diversity as well as the repetition of her work, and that abundant, provocative imagination which makes her such a unique figure in the contemporary theater. Any attempt to suggest the power and poetry of her personal performance must remain merely a claim to be substantiated within the theater. The photographs reveal these qualities, even if fractionally, still better than verbal description.

PUNCH AND THE JUDY

Punch and the Judy is, at the same time, the earliest and the least interesting of the works considered here. It is a satire without irony, that is to say it remains a kind of farce, ribald and broad, without being really witty, as *Every Soul Is a Circus* is, and yet holding its head somewhat above the level of burlesque. Its noisy commentary upon rotary clubs, interpreted American history, domestic daydreams and quarrels, necessitates a narrative pattern filled with pantomimic gesture, and so it falls cleanly into the arena of pure theater. It is possible that since its first performances, some of the excessive vigor it now displays is the result of playing up comedy situations until the balance and proportion of the dance are endangered. It is a work performed with verve, and in Miss Graham's case with subtlety, but without that caution and respect that her more serious works receive. Her

company seems to feel increasingly at liberty to distort the original pattern, to the end that the work has become cluttered with innuendo and downstage grimacing. It shows, however, the great variety of accent of which Graham is capable. If its original intention was to be a more serious and pointed work, we can only regret the circumstance that deflected it. The bouncing and sometimes vulgar score by Robert McBride would be difficult to have set differently, but that should have been a matter of foresight rather than regret.

Graham has an extraordinary capacity for serious comedy, a shrewd and delicate irony, which could amuse and touch us at the same time. If she could find a subject of this sort with less narrative detail, crisper and more calculated than *Punch and the Judy*, she could undoubtedly make from it a work with the same choreographic sophistication, and play it with the same energy which she now reserves for more taxing works. *Punch and the Judy* has been, of course, a ballet of considerable popularity, particularly on the road. Its theatricality admits a more elaborate staging and a more individual treatment of her company, and it allows an audience, built up to a considerable tension in other works, to relax, laugh and free the attention. The other most marked occasion when Graham concedes her entire company this choreographic individuality is *Deaths and Entrances*.

DEATHS AND ENTRANCES

Deaths and Entrances stands in a critical relation to Graham's earlier theater pieces like *Letter to the World* and *Every Soul Is a Circus* and the later abstract theater of *Dark Meadow* and *Serpent Heart*. It still depends upon a defined physical setting, the gloomy cavernous house in which the three sisters enact their blind battle; it still partakes of a vague literary atmosphere, and uses stage properties which are too realistic to escape symbolic ref-

Letter to the World. Photo by Barbara Morgan.

Punch and the Judy. Photo by Eric Schaal.

erence, such as the goblet and the shell and the chess figures; its use of pre-Victorian costumes and the thin funereal veils all suggest the period and poetry of *Letter to the World*. And yet it is hanging on here only with one hand. Its most powerful and communicative moments are long stretches of irrational and abstract movement, very loosely associated with any theatrical drama we already know. Whereas in *Letter to the World*, the actual identification of the dancer with Emily Dickinson informs the dance with a special pathos and precision (for instance, *The Little Tippler* with its drunken, coy humor; the tender and lonely *Blue Seas* section; the scenes with the Ancestress and March, and the New England funeral), in *Deaths and Entrances*, it is exactly at those moments when the dance escapes into an upper air outside of its own pretensions and becomes a submerged but general drama, with its strange urgency and bewildered grief, that it is most touching. In *Letter to the World*, then, Graham created a ballet-theater with a libretto and characters and cumulative plot, although there is no exterior "action" as such;

and this is done with such unity and definition that it makes *Letter to the World* a masterpiece of its kind. In *Deaths and Entrances* we are simply following an emotion, deprived and turned in upon itself, that issues in madness. Perhaps it was this final "mad scene" that led Edwin Denby to remark in his review of the dance that "no more sincere actress than Miss Graham exists in the American theater." It was possible and justifiable to think of her performance in this double light of dance-acting. (This scene is incidentally of a peculiar, frightening power. I have noticed audiences shrinking back into their seats as it builds up its imagery of derangement.)

The elements in *Deaths and Entrances* that imply a shift into a purer medium occur frequently: the looped, birdlike solo of Graham's in the latter half of the piece; the dance for four men, with its aerial counterpoint and even a suggestion of individual conflict, which was, up to this point, the finest choreography for men that she had done. The ambiguity of meaning in a dance like *Deaths and En-*

trances arises partially from Graham's use of stage properties, like the goblet and chess pieces, which she clearly intends as spontaneous associations to further and enrich the action, like childhood's uncalculated memories, but which the audience worries into the foreground, trying to read into them some larger significance, usually of a Freudian nature. Graham would certainly prefer her audience to look at them in their particular use, and not damage the continuity of the dance by trying to divine them as obscure and calculated symbols. But to an audience already uneasy about meaning, this is a difficult discipline.

Deaths and Entrances has a very beautiful scheme of climactic movement, for which Hunter Johnson's score is theatrical if not musically very inventive. The movement builds, with less interruption than *Letter to the World,* to its peak, using thematic phrases to unify separate sections. One is never aware, for instance, of its extreme length as a ballet. The possessed performance that Graham gives of it, superbly controlled in technique (and it could have become a tour de force), makes it perpetually engrossing to watch. Its few weaknesses occur only upon reflection, and they are not of such a nature that on reseeing it we do not feel bound up again in its brilliance and its desperation.

SALEM SHORE

Salem Shore seems somewhat thin and false in its emotion, not as Graham dances it, but in its conception. Its tenuous, romantic subject has a blurred, hurried look, and the clear

Deaths and Entrances. Photo by Cris Alexander.

Salem Shore. Photo by Cris Alexander.

and sometimes radiant performance which it receives does not obscure its fundamental ineffectiveness. The plucking motions at the skirt as she dances in and out of the circled vine at the beginning are very strong, and the balladlike section, with its pathetic exuberance, is touching. These isolated moments make apparent what the dance might have been, but its essence is diluted and repeats technical facilities of the choreographer where inspiration has faltered. It indicates, however, a certain willful tenderness (which has also shown itself in *Letter to the World*), still far from defined, but a valuable addition to Graham's vocabulary, and deserving amplification in a stronger work.

The occasional use of spoken lines, like an extra instrument in the orchestra, is here very loose and distracting. They do not serve as a bridge between the dance and the audience in any continuous way, nor even as an ornament to the action, but are halting and apologetic. They do make clear the subject of the dance, but surely that should be the business of the dancer. The score by Paul Nordoff is one of the saddest with which Graham has yet been burdened. Its poverty of suggestion only underlines the smallness of feeling on the stage.

APPALACHIAN SPRING

Appalachian Spring is, perhaps, the most successful of Graham's lighter or tenderer dances. Not that it is less serious than other works, but what it reveals is simpler and more open, and has an emotional bias different from the works surrounding it.

The group of young girls in their nervous spirited cavorting remind one of children who, on a nod from their mother, are allowed to play a few more minutes before prayers. The variations on square-dance figures which they do, and the counterpoint they make in games around the preacher, have both charm and excitement.

Everyone has always seemed to dance *Appalachian Spring* with unusual love and precision, as if it were a ballet they knew everything about, and had very carefully rehearsed. The entire company is at ease and at home, unself-consciously American. Aaron Copland's score for this work is certainly one of the finest Graham has ever worked with. Its lyrical grace and rhythmic variety in the use of folk material pay the dance the compliment of independent imagination. The movement, it is true, is in a lower key and its invention less constant than in other works of this period, but this is a shortcoming only relative.

Appalachian Spring provides that variety to a program for which Graham seems often to have been searching, but without implying a dance of a wholly different caliber, as *Punch* and the Judy does, for example. The audience feels that it is still within the same theater, but looking at another landscape, this one more relaxed and blown over by those free winds and waters which the title suggests. It is particular, local, and subtle, just as *American Document* was general, pretentious, and vulgar (although it developed, incidentally, some marvelous group choreography and contains some of Graham's finest solos from this period).

Graham has a remarkable talent for invoking her heritage and environment almost as an unconscious gesture, except in those lapses of planned and patriotic effort of which her old and discarded solo *Columbiad* was a disarming example. The fact that she disdains the use of exotic materials in her dances may have gained impetus from that period in which she worked with Shawn and St. Denis in an emotional tour of the Orient. *Deep Song*, for example, a solo done during the critical period of the Spanish war, reflects that country and people in its patterns, cadences, beating heels, and arched back, but very indirectly, without ever attempting to imitate or reproduce Spanish movement.

What Graham has developed are more distant and deeper influences, archaic or primitive movements, some of them still surviving in the Mexico and Southwest which she has visited, and all manner of ritual styles, which she feels fundamental to our dance history. These ritual patterns actually provide an aspect of formalism in her dances, in somewhat the same way that the physical etiquette of court ceremony has influenced the ballet in its severe, upright elegance. Like the Greek dramatic structures, the Catholic mass, the rain prayers and witchcraft exorcisations, they are a continuous, formal history. Her use of them can be conscious and explicit, as in *Primitive Mysteries* and other dances of that period (perhaps it is the moment to reaffirm that *Primitive Mysteries* is a classic of this or any dance history), or it can be a structure

well beneath the surface as in *Dark Meadow*, or the archaic, oblique postures of *Herodiade*.

HERODIADE

Herodiade is a solo of astonishing power. This is said knowing, of course, that technically it is a duet, and not to minimize the quality or necessity of Miss O'Donnell's performance. But it is a solo in the sense in which the whole substance and conflict of the dance is focused upon Herodiade, and is worked out by her without any reference to the figure of the attendant, except as a habitual presence, a secular figure like the Greek chorus which points up the tragedy. The nurse is almost the spectator transferred to the stage (the conscience of the audience made active), handing Herodiade her brush or mantle or mirror, stepping back to comment or to warn, but unable to interrupt what is already inevitable in the opening measures.

This destiny that Graham has grappled with in several pieces is not to be interpreted as any simple variety of predestination in the ancient sense of Fate. It is more nearly the result of fixated and fired emotion which, when it has torn down all of its restraint and refused any offer of love or reconciliation, will rush headlong into self-destruction. It is possible to adduce this emotion from fear, as in *Deaths and Entrances*, or from inexorable pride and desire, as in *Serpent Heart*, a longing for freedom through the agency of destruction. Or it can be interpreted in the same way as the issue of that extreme zeal that wrapped Joan of Arc in a numbing cloak when she stepped into the flames, or which drove Emily Dickinson, in her virginal dress, deeper and deeper into her own house. A line from Dickinson which is used in *Letter to the World*, "there is a pain so utter it swallows being up," expresses it very succinctly.

In *Herodiade*, and in the "mad scene" at the end of *Deaths and Entrances*, Graham may

Appalachian Spring. Photo by Arnold Eagle.

be using this extremity of emotion almost to frighten her audience into some awareness of its danger and its power. She is not using it decoratively, with pathos and crooked grace, as it is used in *Giselle*, certainly; she is not using it eccentrically, or to delineate specific character. Its use is no more strained or symbolic than Kafka's cockroach in the *Metamorphoses* or the machine in *The Penal Colony*; a kind of privately deranged world in which some fragment of emotion has been allowed to become magnified until it crowds out every alternative.

Like a portrait of genius, these dances are intended to show us our own humanity illuminated in their intenser glass. Graham is not here concerned with morbidity or joy or heroism, but with "the graph of the heart." It has led her into constructing the visual complement of some fevers that have rarely been described outside of poetry, and she has done this, in a dance like *Herodiade*, with a unity of purpose, a beauty of design, and a compelling execution unique in our theater.

The cautious, romantic score Hindemith devised for *Herodiade* does not seem to me, for all its independent distinction, very provocative for a dance; much less so, for instance, than the theme and variations of his *Four Temperaments*, on which Balanchine has recently made a ballet. The *décor* for *Herodiade* is discussed in a later section.

Appalachian Spring. Photo by Arnold Eagle.

DARK MEADOW

Dark Meadow is perhaps the clearest and most unified dance that Graham has done in the last few years. Stark Young has described it as fascinating in its creation of a genuinely abstract theater. It is also an intensely poetic insight into the motive and history of gesture, almost a research on emotion. Its faults are due to undue haste and to a wooden, bloodless score that has about as much relation to Graham's intention as would *Gaieté Parisienne.* The long string quartet in the middle, which supports some superb choreography, is pedantically dissonant, with less rhythmic distinction than a vacuum cleaner. The opening "primitif" section and a few measures for winds supply the only musical relief. It is a surprise and a disappointment that someone who has written a score like *Antigone* should have chosen this occasion to clean house musically. Another fault is in the costumes which narrowly miss articulating the movement because of a certain fussiness of design and sloppy execution. The set is superb. Its curious blend of naïveté and sophistication is exactly suited to the nature of the work. Its small-scale monuments and fetiches establish remoteness more accurately than any period design. At his best, and this is it, Noguchi is one of the most poetic designers in America. Graham should not use such rare effects as his to the point of monotony because, like masks or archaic gestures, they lose some power in indiscriminate repetition.

Seeing *Dark Meadow* recaptures that remarkable fantasy that the theater holds for a child. Its enigmatic imagery, its unreal com-

247

Herodiade. Photo by Cris Alexander.

water, it reveals a variety of reverence among these couples for physicality; that springlike adoration of animals and lovers among their fires, branched, tender, and passionate, a force trembling and tired with desire, then quieted in suspense, as with an arched and hung wave before it breaks. It shows such a faultless and sensitive invention that it makes one regret the dry, busy stretches in some earlier works where the group seems introduced more out of charity than conviction. Graham has not always handled large group movements on the stage with the same ease as individual movement, and *Dark Meadow* is a fine exception to this insecurity.

There are direct and indirect images in *Dark Meadow* that suggest archaic memory. The brief moment where Graham bends forward from the waist touching her hands to the floor and runs rapidly forward, a scuttling, prehensile animal, then as suddenly erect; a compulsive effortless movement that flowers out of the preceding phrase and submerges into the oncoming one like an unexpected light. It might easily be missed so little is it stressed, and yet it becomes almost a key to this section.

Graham's whole company, entrusted with greater responsibility in this work, perform it with a physical devotion and intensity that is very moving, in much the same spirit that some of them have danced *Primitive Mysteries,* an instinctive tribute to its quality.

ment on our own reality, have the quality of a violent fairy tale. It suggests with amazing intuition a sense of history that swims slightly out of sight in us; a dim, primitive memory like that of a child trapped in a wilderness. That is why its frank sexuality seems so powerful and inoffensive. It is never tricky nor suggestive, but as honest as an animal surprised by a camera.

Graham's own solos are uneven, wavering slightly between earlier styles and genuine discovery, and not quite accurate in their rhythmic emphasis. The saraband for three couples is certainly one of the most brilliant pieces of group choreography in her repertoire. With its lifts like crucifixions, and its slow distortions as of figures moving through

SERPENT HEART

Serpent Heart, the most recently performed of Graham's dances, also develops a ritualistic pattern, at least internally. Its movement, like that of *Herodiade,* is at times very archaic, which suits its Medean subject. And its vindictive passion is very formally built, interrupted, as were the Greek dramas, by stanzas of choral comment, poetic odes which halted and explicated the meaning. As first given it was somewhat the victim of circumstances: an overcrowded, airless lecture hall instead of a theater, and a work rushed headlong into production a little too early. Both its title and many of its parts are now in revision, and if this adds clarity to its other virtues it should be one of Graham's finest works. Her own solos in the piece are very beautiful as they stand, although their theatrical focus seems a little awry. They are still experimental toward their audience, and give the impression of being more internally felt than they are projected.

The manipulation of four dancers commenting upon, or rather using as a foundation, the Medea legend, is a complicated undertaking. It is attempting to give great dimension in a work of almost chamber size. Perhaps if the issue is settled as to whether it is to be a legendary re-enactment of the Medea in contemporary dance terms, or a dance with slender threads that reach *as far back as* the Medea, the initial confusions will be overcome. As it stands, one remembers everything in it as separately forceful and striking, but discontinuous. One is not engaged in the flow of the work from beginning to end, but intermittently, as if one had closed one's eyes for a moment between each section and opened them somewhere further along, having missed an essential link. The relation between *One like Jason* and *One like Medea* was perhaps most seriously at fault, having begun at some undetermined point, as if the stream were without source and one started by throwing oneself in the middle. The role taken by Erick Hawkins suffered more fatally from this, in that he became, at the very outset, a foil for an emotional crisis already developed in the Medean figure, and could only aggravate her further into her crime.

The choral interludes have the compact poetry of odes, and May O'Donnell has managed to impart to them a lyrical, cunning strength that is appropriate and moving.

In her own role Graham develops disturbing, frightened flashes of unpredictable movement, a kind of crippled, hunted lurching of the body from one stage area to another; relentlessness, pride, avidity, arrogance, solitude. Her long solo with the snakelike strip of cloth is almost a variety of sympathetic magic, a self-intoxication giving impetus and courage toward the enactment of her crime. The tiny, fluttering beat of the body that begins it, and the incantations that ornament it, are extraordinary. The coppery cage which Graham pulls over herself at the end appears to emphasize an insectlike inhumanity, the mythological transformation of a woman who, by her crimes, has turned herself away from humanity, and stands frozen, immobile, a huge bronze structure like a grasshopper in a desert. Very provocative, too, is the handling of the burial cloth in which she drags in the princess behind her heels, finally enmeshing the figure of Jason in its folds.

One is conscious in this work, as in others of Graham's, of a static quality that occurs when she or another member of her company retires into inactivity in some nook of the stage, waiting to be spun back into the dance at a further point. They do not exist and enter onto the scene plainly enough, but often keep themselves in blank evidence, like silent figures in a play waiting for their cues. This damages the freshness of the image when they rejoin the action.

The use of various stage levels, accomplished on Noguchi's strange volcanic *décor*, was extremely interesting, and if all of these disparate elements are unified and given theatrical shape, the full, inhibited power of the dance should be released, in all of its now implied formal beauty.

Samuel Barber's score is brilliant, bitter, and full of amazing energy. The alternation of parts, like the swing of a pendulum, between relaxed lyrical flow and tense angularity make a wonderful scaffolding for the tragedy. Its very real beauties were muffled (and this is true of much of the more com-

Dark Meadow. Photo by Arnold Eagle.

plex music for Graham's dances), by an initial performance that lacked accuracy and spirit on the part of the orchestra.

THE STAGE OF ISAMU NOGUCHI

The quality of Noguchi's imagination, his great skill and tenderness in constructing stage images, are very sympathetic to Graham's intention. All of her most recent works have had his artistic collaboration. Certainly she is in a difficult position in relation to the choice of stage *décor*. We do not conceive of her dances in front of a drop by Chagall any more than we can imagine her dancers costumed by Berman's tireless Renaissance hand. This leaves her, often, with something less than a theater stage—a kind of studio im-

provisation, open, but intricate to look at, as in *Serpent Heart,* where the low-lying objects on the stage seem as much to be personal hazards to the dancer as they are formal decoration to the spectator.

Graham does not dance within a set, but on a stage which she can use, that has some nearer function than that of the eye. She prefers to climb over set pieces, move, carry, refocus the objects of her stage as an animal moves in his scenery, a kind of traffic with nature in which everything is, at some point, alive and capable of change. To this extent, then, stage paintings do not serve her purpose. Her stage and her costumes require, however, more mobility than they have yet had, more color and range of detail, or some sharper relation between subject and ornament. If there were more designers trained to adopt stage space as something living and flexible, rather than as a vacuum enlivened by a particularly large painting in front of which small people in fur or feathers parade their implausible humanity, then dancers like Graham would have a wider and more varied choice.

The Noguchi designs for *Appalachian Spring,* which is spare and formal without being empty, and *Dark Meadow,* which is more complex in its symbolism, more sophisticated in form and use, are those I like best. *Deaths and Entrances,* designed by Arch Lauterer, still seems inadequately staged, dull, stiff, and gray, without that accent on texture and shape which might help to direct its meaning. *Herodiade,* again of Noguchi, is somewhat of a museum piece. One would like to walk around the skeletal mirror as one would a piece of sculpture; as a stage construction it is too intimate and nervous. The audience must look from it to the dancer, and the simultaneity of the image is destroyed. The chair in this piece, however, is lovely furniture, and reveals that painstaking craftsmanship which makes the seeds of the apple in *Penitente* as delicate and precise as the

Dark Meadow. Photo by Arnold Eagle.

house in *Appalachian Spring*. Graham is fortunate to have found in Noguchi so sympathetic a collaborator, whose insight and imagination have added immeasurably to the beauty of her theater.

It is difficult to separate the quality of Graham's choreography from her personal performance for several reasons. Partially, because the burden of almost every work, particularly those most recent, falls upon her. She has constructed for herself the most luminous moments of its being, those epiphanies and periods of knotty intensity where the whole work can reveal itself as in a flash of light. She is the continual protagonist, the center of conflict; in its simplest theatrical sense, the heroine of her ballets. This is rendered more acute by the fact that there is really no hero. There is a parade of figures

that interrupt or influence her destiny, to a greater or lesser degree; there are combatants and lovers, and until recently these are almost identical in Graham's work; there are phantoms or conspirators. But there is never a figure outlined with the same *human scale*, and portraying anything like the complex range of psychological motive which she reserves for herself. This is not entirely surprising from so superb a dancer as Graham, and in this connection, we can afford to overlook her own sincere contention that she is a dancer primarily and not a choreographer, or that she thinks of herself as a dancer who has had to arrange her dances "because there was nobody else around who could do them." The whole point, of course, is that there was nobody else around who *could* do them, or anything like them, and there the problem

251

of creativity and invention determined her choice.

However, the burden of her programs for herself as a dancer is enormous; much too great for the good of her own performance. If she trusted her company to a greater participation in them, it would relax the fantastic demands that continuous dancing puts upon her, and might influence her choreography for her company in a more objective and rewarding direction. This has already happened to some extent. It would be interesting further to see Graham create works for her company alone, in which her whole effort was concentrated on making a ballet as expressive without her as it would be with her. Perhaps, then, her sophistication in pure movement, dissociated from her own physical manner of performance, would be thrown into relief. Works of this kind, moreover, would be much simpler to hand down to another generation of dancers than many of those which are so dependent upon her unique physical capacities as a dancer.

"Technique only services the body toward complete expressiveness."

It is not the business of an audience to be sophisticated in the matter of technique, but in the matter of meaning. One of the destructive emphases which ballet discipline has unwittingly encouraged in its audience is the recognition and worship of technique as such. Technique is professional; it is the artist's and, at most, the critic's concern. Knowledge about the intricacies of technical performance is a pathetic substitute for understanding of an art, as any studio full of dancers or musicians can well demonstrate. Graham depends less upon this professional insight from her audiences, and this throws them into some confusion. Too many among them have been accustomed to narrowing their eyes for the sign of too much preparation for a pirouette, possibly because there is so little beyond that to look for. We are burdened everywhere with a conception of technique that muffles instead of clarifying the human-

Model of Noguchi's set for *Errand into the Maze*. Photo by Rudolph Burckhardt.

ity and force of performance. Dancers work, and know it as their constant necessity, to perfect an instrument so that it may be free of restriction and capable of the widest and truest inflection in motion; free from dishonesty and uncertainty; alive, spontaneous, and exact.

But the dry dazzle, the fitful and deathly quality that victimizes much of the dancing in our time, is the inevitable result of this technical parade and competition between dancers, and between dancers and their audience. This can be achieved, of course, only where a standardized vocabulary, an endlessly repeated repertory, make recognition and comparison a dilettante's pleasure. This state is often referred to as classicism. Many performances of "classic" ballet that we see today cannot, with the utmost charity, be called anything more than a perpetuation of historical mistakes. They lack that stylized and formal accent, an action that takes place in bright, thin air, tight and full of grace, as dependent upon myth and tradition as a totem pole or a minuet. As it stands, they often succumb to the imitation of old photographs, or become vehicles for glassy competition in the realm of cold technique.

It is not pertinent that *Sylphides* or *Giselle* should look contemporary to their audience (this does not apply, of course, to *décor* and costume). They should, on the contrary, look old, as old as they are, the way Botticelli, Renaissance furniture, or Bellini arias look or sound old; the way even *Primitive Mysteries* looks old next to *Dark Meadow*. That is the way it should be, and it does not lessen their effect, or turn them into works of period peculiarity, to emphasize this quality. Rather it emphasizes their intimacy with time, a close, valid, temporal relation. Their genuine modernity is in question just as much at the moment of composition as at any time thereafter.

Of course, every performance is contemporaneous, and suffers or gains from the burden of our position in time, the patina of interpretation, whether toward clarity or indistinction, that time has set upon it. A constant revision of standard works is being made, in an attempt to lessen the distance between their time and our own, and is self-defeating. Whatever permanence or value they have as works of art is inviolable when they are given as they were made, with a precise, unapologetic honesty, and some conviction of that value. The physical restaging of works in each generation must take this into account. It is sufficient flattery to assume that we know how to execute an intention without presuming we can improve upon it. *Primitive Mysteries* and *Frontier* are landmarks in a particular dance expression, and they gain greatly, when they are restaged, from having been unmolested by revision.

Like all great dancers, Graham is not in competition with anyone but herself. As with Markova or Argentina or Nijinsky, one would not say that she danced better than someone else, but better than she herself did last week, or not so well as last season. These dancers became standards for judgment because they set them and were alone capable of maintaining them with any consistency.

There are qualities in her style of movement that belong to no one else, and are the unmistakable seal of her personality. Her body, moving on the stage, is built like a series of diamonds joined at their points, with the whole tension that releases movement knotted at the center, at the pelvis, and at the base of the spine. This source of energy that radiates outward, which we notice also in primitive dancers, the Oriental and the Spanish to a much greater degree than the Occidental, destroys terminal grace that flowers at the wrist and the ankle and in the tilt of the head, and replaces this loose ornamentation with gesture more deeply controlled and personally expressive. When the hand is not taut and assuming a definite pattern, it is relaxed from the shoulder blades without being limp, the fingers extended without tension, very seldom curved sharply inward like petals. The extension of the middle finger lengthens the hand as it moves through space, and does not swing the movement back in upon itself. The head rises out of the stem of the neck completely vertical when at rest. The remarkable articulation of the face is not merely a happy accident of nature, but comes from a fluidity of expression that is so constant and evanescent that it has the anonymity of a mask. This is quite another thing from the frozen expression of beatitude, or the drained mask of effort that is nonexpression. The very elongated torso, thinned at the waist and flat in the chest (Edwin Denby has pointed out, in his commentary on photographs of Nijinsky, the similarity between his [Nijinsky's] and Graham's posture in this respect), services the body toward greater speed, and knits together its parts so that it is not jointed, but moves in a wave through the body like the successive rippled movement of an animal. This simultaneity can be broken up by the particular angularity of movement that Graham uses, which is phrased and accented so differently from traditional balletic movement that it comprises almost a new vocabulary. But her fundamental training of the body is not romantic, and tries to avoid the distortion and personal expression of her own choreography.

There are really three problems in teaching technique in her own studio. The first must deal with that host of nondancers whose needs are for a more controlled or a more liberated expression; a sense of the body in any kind of motion; posture, speed, grace, flexibility, and honesty. The second must adapt itself to the needs of dancers, any dancers, that is, as a basic training in the sources of dance movement. The third element of technique is directed toward the particular needs of her company, to serve as a technical basis for some of the problems that arise in her choreography and in their own work. This is an enormous teaching problem, especially when circumstances demand that these separate approaches be combined in mixed classes.

Graham's teaching can be invaluable as a technique for controlled and varied expression. The fact that some dancers trained in her school have used it otherwise is unfortunate; their assumption that they must each choreograph for themselves; their constant repetition of technical and expressive devices which properly belong to Graham, suggest that there is yet no standard vocabulary or compositional approach for the contemporary dance, as there is for ballet or for music. If this is desirable, it seems to me it can be built only out of the same generations of accumulated effort which it has taken to establish these arts in their own traditions. One of the reasons this is not happening is because the "modern" dance cannot yet, at this point in its history, attract and hold enough dancers of the same proficiency as can the ballet, for reasons of its inferior finances, reputation, and glamour. It is only now, after generations of continuous effort, that the ballet has internationalized itself sufficiently to be able to make any kind of a company with purely local dancers. The modern dance has developed most particularly in this country. Outside of Mary Wigman (could one include the modernized ballet style of Kreutzberg?) there have been no major figures in European dancing of this kind. Perhaps Graham has greater sympathy and relation to the style of Antony Tudor than to many other, more "modern" dancers. (Her own technique consciously makes use of a great deal of fundamental ballet training.) But wherever young dancers in this art appear, they deserve, beyond the most professional and perceptive criticism, some further encouragement, rather than the nervous and jealous refusal that is often the reaction of those interested groups anxious to prove that this aspect of dancing is unlikely to outlive its first generation.

Graham has attempted, even if unconsciously, to break down the traditional limit of stage space in dancing. Western dancing in the last few centuries has made a vertical coffin of the stage, which is relieved only when elevation or lifts establish a dramatic stratosphere. The floor area is used in ballet when someone drops dead from a love potion, or kneels under the weight of a ballerina.

Historically, there is ample explanation for avoiding the floor as an expressive area in dancing. To begin with, the dance was social, upright, continuous with life as it was lived in seventeenth- and eighteenth-century Europe. The floors were not separate, enclosed stages, but often parquets of inlaid wood, intimately surrounded by an audience, hung over with chandeliers, like salons cleared of furniture.

Primitive Mysteries. Photo by Barbara Morgan.

The dance borrowed all manner of postures from social etiquette, from fencing; the nature of the costumes prevented any extreme freedom in use of the body; the entire theatrical convention stiffened and amputated expression. These motives no longer exist, except in a few minds and ballrooms, and should have brought about a comparable modification in dance technique. From the floor to the top of the head at the peak of a leap is all usable space for a dancer. He is surrounded by the entire framed air of the stage. We can expect

Appalachian Spring. Photo by Cris Alexander.

of him that he shall, at some time, fill that space within his physical reach with his presence or design. There are, of course, all of those formalized dances, like strict counterpoint in music, which accept an unnatural limit for purposes of particular expression. But this limit *refers* to sacrificed space, it does not *ignore* it.

If Graham has overemphasized the use of the floor, and at times it has become a manner with her, it might at least awaken other choreographers to its possibilities. It can be argued that the modern school has done this, and to excess. But these are the costs of imitation rather than of influence. Young dancers, crawling around from corner to corner with fierce determination, have done about as much to implement this technique as have ice skaters in using balletic figures. Doris Humphrey, who has used the lower stage areas in a very creative way upon occasion, is, of course, an exception to this criticism.

Recently, Graham has been using another and more difficult area of stage space, halfway between the floor and an upright position, about the level of a deep, second-position *plié* in ballet. This springlike posture is variable, and can be moved into and away from, more quickly than the floor. Another expressive element in Graham's vocabulary is the fall from varying positions in different speeds and accents, for widely separate purposes of expression. It is a powerful, contracting movement: the fall from the knees across the front of the stage in a repeated arc in first solo, *Deaths and Entrances;* the circular drop in the final solos in *Letter to the World.* All of these movements, because of their intensity and unfamiliarity, somehow suggest an extreme condition of feeling, and this is the way they are ordinarily used. The circular turns with leg extended in the "Blue Sea" section of *Letter to the World,* are a variation of that astonishing extension more evident in *Frontier* or *Every Soul Is a Circus.* Also typical of Graham's personal style is a beat of the body,

from contraction to release, like the clutching and releasing pattern of the heart. Very marked, too, is the archaic turn of the hips toward the front of the stage, parallel to the feet, like women carrying vases on a Greek statue, as it is used in *Herodiade.*

When one says of Graham that she has been remarkably courageous, it is not merely to indicate that she has had to face great adversity from her public or her critics, and the whole constellation of problems that surround and threaten innovation. These kinds of courage we expect of an artist, although not many artists exhibit them. (It is only the fantastic ingratitude of our society that it should resist and attempt to smother the artist whose work is their eventual heritage.) The kind of courage that is more rare in dancers is that toward strong, personal emotion in composition. Graham is not afraid of extreme emotional statement, and this gives her work a passion and humanity that are invaluable. She does not work with sentiment or the simulation of feeling, and the emotional states of being in her dances are not charted narratively, so that audiences must follow this journey on an unfamiliar ship. This is why I insist that Graham's dances are not intellectual or cold or autonomous or grotesque. They *are* unfamiliar, which seems hardly a criticism of a work of art. Part of their unfamiliarity is their honesty, which, at this timid and ornamental moment in the history of dancing, is a rare virtue. If her audiences are sometimes distraught at the imagery of *Dark Meadow,* it is because they are so ill prepared to face the psychological reality which is the basis of her art. It is rather like lighting an enormous bonfire in the middle of an icehouse in which everyone is comfortably frozen. To their distress, the subject of Graham's dances is not dancing.

There is a reaction in certain quarters against Graham's art that is of a piece with the animosity that has recently grown up

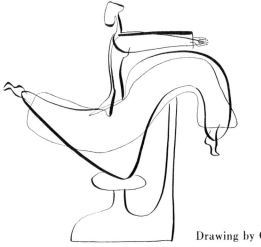

Drawing by Charlotte Trowbridge.

around figures as disparate as Joyce and Picasso. Leaving aside any deeper psychological implication in this battle against contemporaneity, it is at least typical of that nervous, vocal periphery which begins to want back what it imagines itself to have lost: grace and ease and charm, just a little shocking and off center perhaps, but not this frenzy of inelegant feeling; something cold and perfect as a glass of water or a slice of Mondrian, but no more of this disturbing poetry cloaked in violence. Most of these objections, however, come from professionals, other dancers or artists who feel the validity of their own choice threatened, since I can only presume that it takes an acrobatic intelligence to admire *Deaths and Entrances* and *Night Shadow* simultaneously. The secular audience has a more natural animosity as well as a more immediate vision, upon which an artist like Graham sooner or later comes to depend.

On the other hand, the danger, with a figure like Graham, is that she has attracted and perpetuated a legend, and her company and her school have not been the least to suffer from this sentimentality. The inroads that such a cult can make upon an artist's time, energy, and creative honesty are enormous. And, ad-

ditionally, they serve to alienate that potential part of Graham's audience which is irritated and antagonistic to such excessive, professional loyalty. This is as wasteful as it is unattractive, but it still functions at the intermissions of her concerts, and thickens the atmosphere of her studio. It can only burden her with distracting responsibilities, and surely she would be relieved, as anyone who has had to face it would be, if it were to die its unnatural death. This problem is, of course, shared by many artists of her reputation, and only intensified for those whose work depends upon personal performance.

There is certainly no effort more significant in the development of the American theater than that of Martha Graham. The history of an undertaking which has gone from *Primitive Mysteries* and *Lamentation* to *Letter to the World*, *Deaths and Entrances*, and *Dark Meadow* is more remarkable than our memory permits us to admit. For whatever brilliance and permanence these works have, or however short of any finality or perfection, their importance may be more extreme in another direction. Graham has anticipated and battled with a tremendous range of dance-theater problems in her generation. Her discoveries in this medium have influenced the dance with such remarkable thoroughness that she has been accused of imitating her imitators. At a further remove, this influence should have a more rewarding and subtle effect upon dancers. When the magnetism of her personal performance, and the battle for recognition are no longer the issue, it may be realized that the vocabulary of expressive movement owes more to her consistent courage and imagination than to any other dancer in our time.

Drawing by Charlotte Trowbridge.

NOTES AND
BIBLIOGRAPHICAL DATA

NOTES AND
BIBLIOGRAPHICAL DATA

THE DANCE IN SHAKER RITUAL

1. Rathbun, Valentine. Some brief hints of a religious scheme. Norwich, Connecticut, 1781.
2. Shaker communities were located in New York state at New Lebanon, Watervliet (Niskeyuna), and Groveland; in Massachusetts, at Hancock, Tyringham, Shirley, and Harvard; in Connecticut, at Enfield; in New Hampshire, at Canterbury and Enfield; in Maine, at New Gloucester (Sabbathday Lake) and Alfred; in Ohio, at Union Village, Whitewater, Watervliet, and North Union; in Kentucky, at Pleasant Hill and South Union; and in Indiana, at West Union (Busro). Except for the one at Groveland, formerly located at Sodus Bay, New York, all the New York and New England communities were organized by 1792. The societies in the Middle West were established within the first thirty years of the nineteenth century. There are small surviving colonies today at New Lebanon, Hancock, Canterbury, and Sabbathday Lake.
3. Andrews' *Western Star*. Stockbridge, Massachusetts, September 12, 1796.
4. Oesterley, W. O. E. The sacred dance: a study in comparative folklore. New York, The Macmillan Company, 1923. (Gives an elaborate background of Old Testament reference.)
5. Cf. the "proceedings" reported by the apostate Brown in 1812: "Some of them described circles on the floor, around which they would stamp, grin and perform all manner of grimace, and every act of disdain; they then jumped within the ring and stamped with utmost vehemence. . . . They considered the circle as representing sin in the world, and their actions round and in it marked their displeasure and abhorrence against sin; and

likewise their stamping in the ring with a noise was figurative of the destruction of sin and passing away of the old heavens, according to the scriptural expression, 'as with a great noise.' " (Brown, Thomas: An Account of the People called Shakers. Troy, 1812.)
6. Throughout its history, the United Society welcomed all nationalities. "Families" of Negroes were organized in the Kentucky communities; at one time there was a small Negro order in Philadelphia; and A. Imbert's lithograph of the Shakers dancing shows two Negroes among the brethren. In Ohio the Believers sent missions to the Shawnee Indians.
7. *Millennial Laws, or Gospel Statutes and Ordinances*. Recorded at New Lebanon, 1821. Revised, 1845. MS.
8. Lossing, Benson. The Shakers. *In* Harper's new monthly magazine, July, 1857.

REFERENCE MATERIAL:

Songs, dances and rituals of the American Shakers (published by J. J. Augustin, New York, 1940, under the title *The Gift to be Simple*) is to date the only book in the present field. Based largely on manuscript sources, this work gives the music of seventy-nine and the texts of over two hundred songs, several dance charts and illustrations of dances, rituals, and hand-written hymnals. See also *Shaker Songs, The Musical Quarterly*, New York, October, 1937. (Both by Edward D. Andrews.)
The Believers themselves have had little to say on the subject of their interesting religious arts. One document only has much to contribute to our knowledge of the development of ritualism: Isaac N. Youngs' unpublished *A Concise View of the Church of God and Of Christ, On Earth . . .*, completed at New

Lebanon in 1856. To this may be added the chapter, "Remarks on the Worship of God: the origin, practice and reasonableness of Dancing as an act of Divine Worship," in *A Summary View of the Millennial Church, or United Society of Believers* . . . , by Calvin Green and Seth Y. Wells (Albany, 1823). Other Shaker sources, in print and manuscript, are listed in the bibliography of *The Gift to be Simple*.

References to Shaker worship are scattered through the travel and historical literature of the eighteenth and nineteenth centuries. The following are selected as perhaps the most informative:

BENTZON, TH. (Mme. Theresa Blanc) Choses et gens d'Amerique. Paris, 1898.

BUCKINGHAM, J. S. America, historical, statistic, and descriptive. New York & London, Fischer, Son & Co., 1841.

CHANDLER, SETH. History of the Town of Shirley, Massachusetts. Shirley, The author, 1883. (Includes an account of Shaker worship taken from the *Berkshire American*, 1850.)

COKE, E. T. A subaltern's furlough. New York, J. & J. Harper, 1833.

Extract from an unpublished manuscript on Shaker history, giving an accurate description of their songs, dances, marches, visions, visits to the spirit land, etc. By an eyewitness. Boston, 1850.

GREELEY, HORACE. A Sabbath with the Shakers. *In* The Knickerbocker, or New York Monthly Magazine. New York, 1838.

HAMILTON, THOMAS. Men and manners in America. Philadelphia, Carey, Lea & Blanchard, 1833.

HASKETT, WILLIAM J. Shakerism unmasked, or the history of the Shakers. Pittsfield, The author, 1828.

HINDS, WILLIAM A. American communities. (Rev. ed.) Chicago, C. H. Kerr & Co., 1902.

LAMSON, DAVID R. Two years' experience among the Shakers. West Boylston, The author, 1848.

MAXWELL, COL. A. M. A run through the United States. London, H. Colburn, 1841.

MUNSELL, JOEL (ed.). Collections on the history of Albany. Albany, The author, 1867.

(Contains an account by the phrenologist George Combe of a visit to the Niskeyuna Shakers in 1839.)

NOYES, JOHN HUMPHREY. History of American socialisms. Philadelphia, J. B. Lippincott & Co., 1870. (Selections from the A. J. Macdonald MS.)

Original Shaker communities in New England, The. (The Plumer Papers, Frank Sanborn, ed.) *In* The New England Magazine, 1900.

TAYLOR, AMOS. A narrative of the strange principles, conduct, and character of the people known by the name of Shakers. Worcester, 1782.

TUDOR, HENRY. Narrative of a tour in North America. London, 1834.

JOHN DURANG

1. CHARLES DURANG. History of the Philadelphia stage, between the years of 1749 and 1853. (Partly compiled from the papers of his father, John Durang.) Published in the *Philadelphia Sunday Dispatch*, beginning with the issue of May 7, 1854.

2. CHARLES DURANG. The ball-room bijou, and art of dancing, containing the figures of the polkas, mazurkas, and other new dances; with rules for polite behaviour. Philadelphia, Fischer, 1855.

3. LINCOLN KIRSTEIN. The book of the dance. Garden City, New York, Garden City Publishing Co., 1942. p. 342.

4. Quoted by GEORGE C. D. ODELL. Annals of the New York Stage. New York, Columbia University Press, 1927. Vol. 1, p. 319.

5. Quoted by Odell: *op. cit.*, pp. 347-348.

6. O. G. SONNECK. Early opera in America. New York, G. Schirmer, 1915. p. 158. (Charles Durang is also the author of another book on dancing: The fashionable dancers casket, or, the ballroom instructor. Philadelphia, Fischer, 1856.)

THE BLACK CROOK AND
THE WHITE FAWN

The Black Crook is well documented. It was one of the great phenomena of the nineteenth-century American stage, and while not the first spectacle of its kind, it is the prototype of a genre of theatrical extravaganza which continued in popularity for over forty years and created the basis for the American music hall, variety theater, musical comedy, burlesque, and vaudeville.

The Black Crook was first produced at Niblo's Garden in New York on September 12, 1866, and ran continuously for sixteen months. Two years later it was revived. New York saw productions in 1869, 1871, 1873, 1879, 1881, 1884, 1889 and 1903—and on the road it ran almost continually until 1909, more than forty years after its opening.

New features and novelties were added in the new versions (one contained the first roller skating ever performed on an American stage) but the ballet was the feature of every production. Hardly a single great American dancer of the period failed to appear in *The Black Crook* at one time or another. "Legs," said one of the backers, "are a permanently salable commodity," but it seems from the reviews that the public was sincerely interested in the dance.

1. Choreography for the revival was by Agnes DeMille.

THE DODWORTH FAMILY AND BALLROOM DANCING IN NEW YORK

For references to social dancing in the United States consult:

MAGRIEL, PAUL. A bibliography of dancing. New York, H. W. Wilson Company, 1936. pp. 94-108.

WRIGHT, MABEL OSGOOD. My New York. New York, The Macmillan Company, 1926. pp. 165-174. (Personal reminiscences of a pupil of Mr. Dodworth.)

MARY ANN LEE—FIRST AMERICAN GISELLE

1. This Madame Augusta should not be confused with Maywood. The French ballerina enjoyed a long and distinguished career in this country,

while the American never appeared here after 1838. Before she attained stardom Mary Ann Lee was often to dance supporting roles in the company of Madame Augusta.

2. The *Philadelphia Saturday Courier*, August 25, 1838.

3. In his monumental *Annals of the New York Stage*, George C. D. Odell mentions a performance of a piece called *Giselle*, or *The Doomed Bride*, starring Mr. and Miss Wells, given at the Olympic Theatre, New York, on November 1, 1841. A thorough search through the files of the *New York Tribune* from September 15 to December 1, 1841, has revealed no mention of this production. Mr. and Miss Wells were indeed appearing at the Olympic, but on November 1 they danced "A new Comic Harlequinade, Old Dame Trot and her Comical Cat."

If on some other date they actually did give a version of *Giselle*, it probably had little to do with the original ballet, which had been produced at the Paris Opéra just four months earlier.

AUGUSTA MAYWOOD

1. Lawrence and Redisha were English clowns and contortionists then appearing at the Cirque-Olympique. See Gautier, *L'Art dramatique en France depuis vingt-cinq ans*. Vol. 1, Ch. XIII, pp. 154-155.

* ICONOGRAPHY

Portrait, full-length, dancing (in oils or watercolor?), painted by Henry Inman, New York, 1838; unrecorded since 1846.

Lithograph. La Petite Augusta—Aged Twelve Years—In the Character of Zoloe, in The Bayadère. Drawn on stone by E.W.C. (Clay)— Printed and published by H. R. Robinson, New York, 1838.

The Harvard College Theatre Collection and the George Chaffee Ballet Collection have each a water color of No. 2 above. These differ between them only in color details; both are unsigned. They may be by the original artist or one or both by Augustus Toedteberg, who executed such works for his superb extra-illustrated works on the American Theatre.

Lithograph. Ad Augusta Maywood (sic)—la Societa della Barcaccia nuova offriva nell' Autunno del 1851. G. Calza dis. dal vero. (To Augusta Maywood—A new Souvenir from the Barcaccia Society Drawn from life by G. Calza.)--Minardi lit.—Litografia Via Ponte di Ferro 1055.—(Vignette; 5¾ ins. wide x 7½ ins. high.) (Plate IV)

American Process Print of No. 4, published by A. Toedteberg, "Portraits of Actors, reproduced from rare originals," Brooklyn, N. Y., 1893. (5¼ x 6⅜ h.)

Lithograph. Ad Augusta Maywood—Imparegiabile Danzatrice (Incomparable Dancer)—In Ancona nella Primavera (Spring) del (18)53. Litog. Maggi. (Vignette; on India paper; 7 x 9 h.)

Lithograph. Ad Augusta Maywood—nella Primavera del 1856 in Ancona—Atto (Act) I nel Ballo "Rita Gauthier." Aug. Bedetti dis.— Ancona, Lit. Flli. Pieroni. (Oval, in oblong ornamental border in gold; 12¼ x 15½ h.) (Plate VI)

Mr. George Chaffee has also seen and noted, but not with precise specifications, another Italian print of Maywood, a half-length study of the dancer as Rita Gauthier.

In the Theatre Collection of the Castello Sforzesca, Milan, Italy, four further souvenirs of Maywood are preserved and recorded in its catalogue, "Ritratti di Musicisti ed Artisti di Teatro," etc., (Milan, 1934), which we note as follows.

Lithograph. Augusta Maywood—in Ferrara la Primavera del 1852. (Other details precisely as for No. 4 above, and same design; obviously a reissue. On India paper, 6¼ x 8 h. See "Ritratti," No. 2791.)

Lithograph. Ad Augusta Maywood—Ravenna Plaudente 1852. Miardi lit. (Bologna)—Lit. Angiolini.—(Three-quarter length, front, in costume, with facsimile signature. 5¾ x 7¼ h. "Ritratti," No. 2792.)

Lithograph. Ad Augusta Maywood—gli Anconitani nella Primavera del 1853. A Bedetti dis.— Ancona, Lit. Pieroni. (Three-quarter length, front, in costume; on India paper; 6 x 8¼ h. "Ritratti," No. 2793.)

Lithograph. Augusta Maywood—Daniele dis.— (Plate to) Galleria Teatrale, Torino, 1857.

(Full-length, front, dancing; 10 x 12½ h. "Ritratti," No. 2795.)

NOTE: It is entirely likely that both Portuguese and Austrian souvenir prints of Maywood exist; a Paris print may also have been issued. We have never seen any nor come across references to them, but we suspect that they are to be found.

GEORGE WASHINGTON SMITH

1. *Philadelphia Press.* n.d. (ca. 1884) *American Theatre Scrapbook*, Vol. IV; New York Public Library.
2. *Oesterreichische Rundschau.* Vol. III, 1905. Letter of September 10, 1840.
3. Another member of the company at the Walnut that season was Mr. G. Hubbard, who later danced with Mary Ann Lee in Boston, and is immortalized with her in a charming lithograph of their bolero.
4. CHAFFEE, GEORGE. Three or four graces. *In* Dance Index. pp. 141-143. New York, September-November, 1944.
5. BLASIS, CARLO. Notes upon dancing. London, 1847, pp. 141-142.
6. George W. Smith is said to have been instrumental in bringing a number of dancers from Europe to this country. Between his pantomime engagement in Philadelphia in February, 1850, and his reappearance at the Arch Street Theatre in October of that year, he had ample time for a trip to Paris. He may have gone abroad at the request of Brougham, then building the Lyceum, arranged a contract with Mlle. Ducy-Barre, and returned to the United States in early autumn to fill an engagement at the Arch before joining the ballerina in New York for the opening of the new theater.
7. For a fascinating account of the career of Leon Espinosa, written by his son, see the *London Dancing Times*, December, 1942, pp. 104-106.
8. Quoted by WYNDHAM, HORACE. The magnificent Montez. London, Hutchinson & Co., Ltd., 1935. p. 191.
9. GOLDBERG, ISAAC. The Queen of Hearts. New York, The John Day Company, 1936. p. 245.
10. CLAPP, W. W. Records of the Boston stage. Boston, J. Munroe & Co., 1853. p. 415.

11. RACSTER, OLGA. The master of the Russian ballet. New York, E. P. Dutton and Company, Inc., 1923. pp. 10-14.

12. CHAFFEE, GEORGE. American souvenir lithographs of the romantic ballet. *In* Dance Index. p. 27. New York, February, 1942.

13. SMITH, JOSEPH C. The story of a harlequin. *In* The Saturday Evening Post. New York, May 30, 1914.

LOIE FULLER

1. *The Architectural Record*, March, 1903.
2. *De la loi du contraste simultané des couleurs et de l'assortiment des objets coloriés.*
3. The manuscript documents concerning its building are in the Department of Theatre Arts, Museum of Modern Art.

Loie Fuller's autobiography was first published in France: Quinze ans de ma vie; préface d'Anatole France. Paris, F. Juven, 1908. Published also: Boston, Small, Maynard & Co., 1913; London, H. Jenkins, 1913.

Additional material on Loie Fuller can be found in the following: Green book album. Chicago, March, 1910, pp. 356-463; *L'artiste*. Paris, 1900, pp. 353-370.

MAUD ALLAN

My life and dancing. London, Everett, 1908. (The dancer's autobiography.)

For additional references to Maud Allan see:

CAFFIN, CAROLINE and CHARLES. Dancing and dancers today. New York, Dodd, Mead & Co., 1912. pp. 70-82.

MORGAN-POWELL, SAMUEL. Memories that live. Toronto, The Macmillan Company of Canada, 1929. pp. 231-239.

THE DENISHAWN ERA

1. Later Shawn appeared in Cecil B. De Mille's *Why Change Your Husband?* starring Gloria Swanson. For a total of four hours' work making a five-minute scene in which Miss Swanson was "shown love," he received $500.

2. In 1902, David Belasco had produced, together with J. L. Long, *The Darling of the Gods*, a five-act drama of Japan, starring Blanche Bates. There were six geisha girls listed on the program as well as native musicians playing authentic instruments.

3. The photographer, White of New York, has recorded Ruth St. Denis superbly and completely in this work. These are now in the files of the Department of Theatre Arts, Museum of Modern Art.

4. Constant touring led one Pittsburgh critic to remark: "In the life of every Denishawn dancer there is no place like Burton Holmes."

5. The program said: "All moves uncomprehendingly. All my life was a foiled quest of you, Queen Helen." Jurgen bidding farewell to that dream of beauty which he had the vision to see, but not the strength to follow.

MARTHA GRAHAM

RECENT WORKS BY MARTHA GRAHAM

Punch and the Judy—Music, Robert McBride; Artistic collaboration, Arch Lauterer; Costumes, for women, Edythe Gilfond; for men, Charlotte Trowbridge. First presented at Bennington College, August 25, 1941.

Deaths and Entrances—Music, Hunter Johnson; Set, Arch Lauterer; Costumes, Edythe Gilfond. First presented at Bennington College, July 18, 1943 (in practice clothes designed by Charlotte Trowbridge).

Salem Shore—Music, Paul Nordoff; Set, Arch Lauterer; Costumes, Edythe Gilfond; Reader, Georgia Sargent. First presented at the Forty-sixth Street Theatre, New York City, December 26, 1943.

Appalachian Spring—Music, Aaron Copland; Set, Isamu Noguchi; Costumes, Edythe Gilfond. Commissioned by the Elizabeth Sprague Coolidge Foundation. First presented at the Library of Congress, Washington, D. C., October 30, 1944.

Herodiade—Music, Paul Hindemith; Set, Isamu Noguchi; Costumes, Edythe Gilfond. Commissioned by the Elizabeth Sprague Coolidge

Foundation. First presented at the Library of Congress, Washington, D. C., October 30, 1944. (Originally titled *Mirror Before Me.*)

Imagined Wing—Music, Darius Milhaud; Set, Isamu Noguchi; Costumes, Edythe Gilfond. Commissioned by the Elizabeth Sprague Coolidge Foundation. First presented at the Library of Congress, Washington, D. C., October 30, 1944. (As this was the only performance, and the work has not remained in the repertory, Mr. Horan has not discussed it here.)

Dark Meadow—Music, Carlos Chavez; Set, Isamu Noguchi; Costumes, Edythe Gilfond. Commissioned by the Elizabeth Sprague Coolidge Foundation. First presented at the Plymouth Theatre, New York City, January 23, 1946.

Serpent Heart—Music, Samuel Barber; Set, Isamu Noguchi; Costumes, Edythe Gilfond. Commissioned by the Alice M. Ditson Fund of Columbia University. First presented at the McMillan Theatre, Columbia University, New York City, May 10, 1946. (Since its first performance *Serpent Heart* has been revised and retitled *Cave of the Heart.*)

Errand into the Maze—Music, Gian-Carlo Menotti; Set and costumes, Isamu Noguchi. Presented at the Ziegfeld Theatre, New York City, February 28, 1947.